PRINT AIN'T DEAD
A *MOUNTAIN GAZETTE* ANTHOLOGY

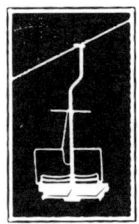

Copyright © 2025 by Double Chair Publications, LLC

ISBN: 979-8-9936760-0-5

Copyright and Licensing Statement

Every effort has been made to locate and properly license the works contained in this anthology, whether through the original authors or, when necessary, their next of kin. Each story, essay, and art work appears exactly as it was first published—unedited and true to its original form.

No part of this anthology may be reproduced, distributed, or transmitted in any form or by any means—electronic, mechanical, photocopying, recording, or otherwise—without the express written permission of Double Chair Publications, LLC, an imprint of *Mountain Gazette*.

Furthermore, no part of this book may be used in the creation, training, or development of artificial intelligence or large language models.

This work has soul. A.I. does not.

"Print Ain't Dead", "When in Doubt, Go Higher", and "Mountain Gazette" are registered trademarks of Verb Cabin, LLC.

Printed in the U.S.A. at Walsworth Printing.

Editor: Mike Rogge
Copy editor: Doug Schnitzspahn
Cover and interior book design: John Coleman
"Somewhere in the Wild" comic: Harry Bliss
Chapter artwork: Mike "The Dead Dirtbag" Handzlik
Front and back cover images: Josh Bishop
Original document scanning: Jon Buzdar

Dedicated to the readers of Mountain Gazette.
This isn't our magazine. It's yours.

Table of Contents

Print Ain't Dead
A *Mountain Gazette* Anthology

Hereyago .... *i.*
By Mike Rogge

Somewhere in the Wild .... *v.*
By Harry Bliss

Foreword .... *vii.*
By M. John Fayhee

1. Dirty Little Secrets *1*
By Tim Cahill

2. Where's Tonto *5*
By Edward Abbey
From *Mountain Gazette 28*

3. A Dream of White Horses *17*
By Royal Robbins
From *Mountain Gazette 28*

4. Mountain Towns *25*
By Ted Kerasote
From *Mountain Gazette 76*

5. The Ride *29*
By Katie Lee
From *Mountain Gazette 78*

6. The Guardian of Sleep *37*
By Jeremy Bernstein
From *Mountain Gazette 9*

7. Hallucinations *45*
By Barry Corbet
From *Mountain Gazette 33*

8. Hanging Around *61*
By David Roberts
From *Mountain Gazette 19*

9. Crooked Road to the Far North *71*
Written by Lito Tejada-Flores
From *Mountain Gazette 15*

10. Alaska: Journey by Land *93*
By Galen Rowell
From *Mountain Gazette 17*

11. Growing Up High *101*
By Randy LaChapelle
From *Mountain Gazette 40*

12. Fear *111*
By David Roberts
From *Mountain Gazette 25*

13. Flat Mountain *119*
By Charles Bowden
From *Mountain Gazette 79*

14. The Impsons, Ed & Ma'am *125*
By John Peters, M.D.
From *Mountain Gazette 79*

15. On the Frontier *133*
By Steve Wishart
From *Mountain Gazette 26*

16. Where the Trees Walk *149*
By Harvey Manning
From *Mountain Gazette 19*

17. Breaking Free from the
Human Potential Movement *155*
By Mike Moore
From *Mountain Gazette 38*

18. Wild Red Dharma
Pickup Truck *179*
By Lacey Story
From *Mountain Gazette 81*

19. There Was a River *187*
By Bruce Berger
From *Mountain Gazette 31*

20. For the Sport of It? *199*
By Gaylord Guenin
From *Mountain Gazette 11*

21. Confessions of a
Butterfly Chaser *213*
By Rob Pudim
From *Mountain Gazette 54*

22. The South Side of the
New England Soul *227*
By John Skow
From *Mountain Gazette 7*

23. Lobster Fishing in America *237*
By Geoffrey Childs
From *Mountain Gazette 45*

24. Confessions of a Sauna Junkie *251*
By Jack Aley
From *Mountain Gazette 70*

25. Gone Fishin' *263*
By John Nichols
From *Mountain Gazette 80*

26. Coyote Song *271*
By Dick Dorworth
From *Mountain Gazette 52*

27. Climbing the Walls in Berkeley *287*
By Karen Recknagel (Chamberlain)
From *Mountain Gazette 46*

28. The Wisdom of NEOWISE *295*
By Doug Schnitzspahn
From *Mountain Gazette 194*

29. Words in His Head: The Depth
of Henrik Harlaut *303*
By Henrik Harlaut, Intro by Gabby Dodd
From *Mountain Gazette 194*

30. New York is for the Birds *311*
By Sadie Stein
From *Mountain Gazette 194*

31. Drinking With a Dead Woman *319*
By M. John Fayhee
From *Mountain Gazette 194*

32. The Way the Wind Is Blowing *329*
By Amanda Monthei
From *Mountain Gazette 195*

33. Feel the Glide: How to
Make a Skier *341*
By Logan Imlach
From *Mountain Gazette 196*

34. It's All About The Bike *355*
By Joe Parkin
From *Mountain Gazette 197*

35. Into the Deep End *359*
By Megan Michelson
From *Mountain Gazette 198*

36. A Ramble in the City *369*
By Miles Howard
From *Mountain Gazette 199*

37. Palm Springs Shralpinism *379*
By Jeremy Jones
From *Mountain Gazette 200*

38. The Last Hike to King Lake *391*
By Jason Harmon
From *Mountain Gazette 200*

39. Kitzbuehel *407*
By Peter Kray
From *Mountain Gazette 182*

40. The Driving Lesson *411*
By Adam Howard
From *Mountain Gazette 200*

41. The Pathfinder *417*
By Rachel Sturtz
From *Mountain Gazette 201*

42. Learning to Dance *429*
By George Sibley
From *Mountain Gazette 202*

43. To Live is to Fly *435*
By Charlie Warzel
From *Mountain Gazette 203*

44. Raising Bull Riders *445*
By Ari Schneider
From *Mountain Gazette 199*

45. A Woman's Place Is at the Top *465*
By Ingrid Backstrom
From *Mountain Gazette 200*

46. Follow the Footprints *471*
By Kade Krichko
From *Mountain Gazette 200*

47. Good Work *477*
By Will Grant
From *Mountain Gazette 204*

48. What the Girls Know *481*
By Emily Leibert
From *Mountain Gazette 202*

49. Politics & The "F-word" *495*
By Hunter S. Thompson
From *Mountain Gazette 79*

Jaded Local: A Flower Grows Through The Pavement: The Resurrection of *Mountain Gazette* *499*
By Hans Ludwig

Photographed by Hank de Vré.

Hereyago
Written by Mike Rogge

As so many stories in *Mountain Gazette* over the decades begin, this one also takes place in a bar. The Norwegian Rat Saloon in Dutch Harbor, Alaska, is home to many fishermen and a captain or two who hasn't learned (or doesn't care) that drinking with the crew before a big outing is a terrible idea. The locals had to close the watering hole on Election Day one year, because—and this is true—nobody voted in the mayoral election. One evening in the late summer of 2019, my friend, the cinematographer Tyler Hamlet, and I saddled up to order wings and a beer after a long day.

We were shooting a short documentary for a commercial fishing apparel company. I had been contracted to direct. Tyler was the principal cinematographer. That tells you just about everything about where the state of freelance writing had brought me. The "pivot to video" had happened and, while I enjoyed short films, I missed writing.

We took up residence next to a crew member we'd met that morning. (I promised the angler in that bar he would forever remain anonymous so I'm keeping my word here.) Over hot wings and cold beer, he shared with us a story of how he'd accidentally killed a man with a brick during a break-in-gone-wrong.

The anonymous angler hadn't meant to kill the guy, he said. He simply intended to sell the TV he and a partner-in-crime were in the midst of stealing when the homeowner arrived in the middle of the attempted theft. It just sort of happened, he said, a crime out of fear gone tragically wrong. He was caught, tried, and sentenced. He spent 10 years in an Alaskan prison—no easy task he told us. Now, in Dutch Harbor, he hoped to rebuild his life fishing for king crab.

I've always been drawn to, not afraid of, these types of stories. My extended family's history in the Northeast was filled with tales of drunk driving, abuse in a variety of forms, arrests, jails, divorce, bankruptcy, near misses, survivals, and one cousin who thought it was a good idea to hire strippers for an underage birthday party and was later mocked across late night TV. The stories were many things, but, above all, they were comfortably outside the family unit of four of my mother, father, sister, and I occupied.

Trying to decipher between fact and fiction is a skill I obtained at a young age. I have a really good bullshit detector, but also trust strangers and generally believe people in the world, when properly cared for, are genuinely good. Being close to the story—but often not part of it—most likely led to a career in ski and later outdoor journalism. I was drawn to—but not afraid of—snow and mountains deeper and bigger than that of my upbringing. My 20-year boot pack to this current stage of life—as owner and editor of *Mountain Gazette*—is for another book, though.

Back at the bar, inexplicably, my phone rang. Who could be calling during the tail end of an accidental-murder-with-a-brick-turned-king-crab-fishing redemption story? I walked to the back porch, pissed that I would miss the end of the story, past an angler burning down a Marlboro menthol. I plugged my finger into one ear and lent the other to the iPhone to answer the call.

"*Mountain Gazette* is for sale," the person on the other line said. "At least, he's interested in hearing you out."

What happened over the next few months has become the stuff of legend in the outdoor community, part of that myth-making done by us at the magazine and our readers. The outdoor industry can be like a chatty high school and no secret is really too sacred to keep. It's true,

I bought the magazine in the morning at a bar in Denver, Colorado, with a personal check and a Coors Banquet. What's also true is the title's previous owner, Blake DeMaso, was willing to sell it to me for below fair price. I believe to this day Blake, like Mike Moore and John Fayhee before him, simply hoped the spirit of the title could live on. *Mountain Gazette* isn't so much of a magazine as it is a dirtbag baton. It was my time to grab it.

I've written and said the *Mountain Gazette* is not my magazine, but rather belongs to the readers. That is also true. There are no bankruptcies, shut downs, pivot-to-videos, or storage units that could keep it from changing hands in that bar that day. This says more about the resilient spirit of mountain culture than it does about the paper and ink of any era.

The people of the mountains are resilient, because they need to be, because that's what living in the mountains has always called for. I didn't know it at the time, but perhaps I—along with the help of too many to name here—revived this magazine because like the bar fellow in Alaska, I'd served my time (to be fair, as a dead-end, corporate, Top-10-listicle freelance writer and not in a prison) and wanted to rebuild my life as an editor and writer. Redemption comes in many forms.

The greatest joy since bringing back the *Gazette* has been meeting those who are deeply affected by the writing, art, and photography inside its pages. The readers are what make this whole thing possible Without them, a magazine today is nothing more than a trendy vanity project.

This is not a Best of *Mountain Gazette* book, because who really gets to make that call about what's "The Best?" Rather, it's an anthology of stories that affected the lives of our readers over six decades (nearly two decades without a new story published). That it resonates with an audience that was born when John Fayhee was leading the first revival says a great deal about its staying power. Above all, I believe the writers in our magazine today deserve a spot next to the great Edward Abbey and infamous Hunter S. Thompson, among the many literary giants to lend their work to the pages of *Mountain Gazette*. Their work is worthy, and what follows in these pages has been carefully curated to give the reader a good idea of "what we're all about" and "wow, this magazine is pretty weird." I like the weird. Let's lean-in together.

One day—it's for certain—I'll meet my fate as we all will. In my dreams, *Mountain Gazette* will carry on, revived and revered by generations to come, keeping those in power in check, those in mountain towns entertained, and forever being a home to those who see the outdoor landscape uniquely and creatively. This magazine has a spirit and it derives from and lives within you, dear reader. Keep us honest. Keep us wild.

When in Doubt, Go Higher,
Mike Rogge, Editor

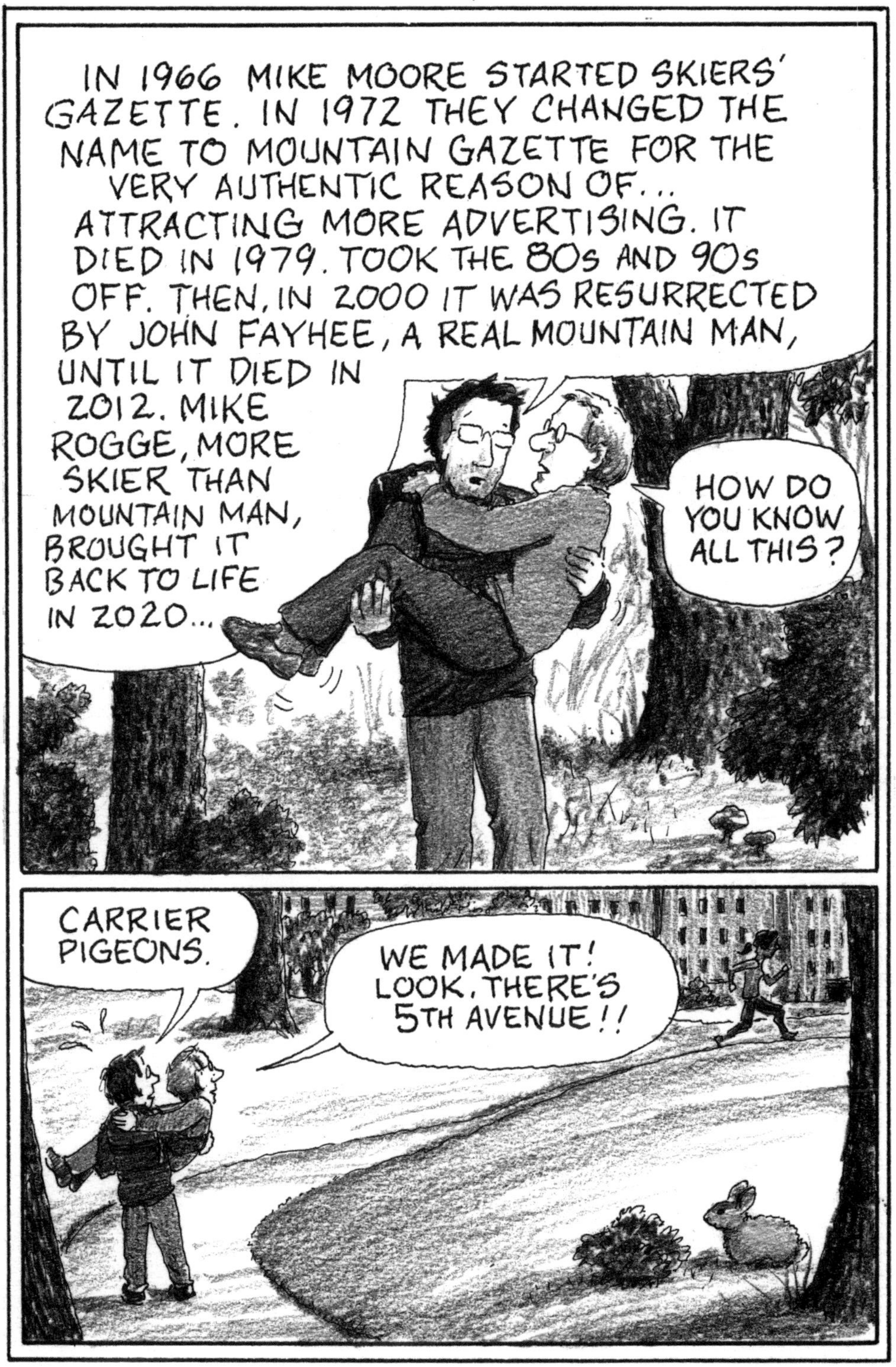

Foreword
Written by M. John Fayhee

The following is dedicated to the memory of Bob Chamberlain, whose photographs verily defined the Mountain Gazette *during its first two incarnations. Bob passed away in December 2024.*

"Everything is governed by the rule of one thing leads to another."
—Ani DiFranco, *"Hour Follows Hour"*

Not all transformative occurrences commence with a lightning strike. They need not land in your lap with a flash or a boom. Some arrive like a butterfly alighting upon a flower. Yet, despite their delicate nature, they can still shiver your psychic timbers and completely re-wire your DNA sequencing.

My 50-year relationship with the *Mountain Gazette* began with a subtle "swish" sound that pulled me from a deep slumber.

I had just completed my first serious backpacking trip into and out of the world-famous Gila Wilderness, having moved to southwest New Mexico only two weeks prior. After 41 miles of mostly disoriented bushwhacking, it is an understatement to say that my contused, bruised and battered newbie posterior was kicked. I had limped back to my college dormitory room and crashed face first onto a lumpy mattress that likely had been there since the days of Geronimo and Cochise, both of whom were born and raised in the immediate vicinity.

I was yanked back to wide-eyed consciousness when someone slid a large manila envelope under my door. By the time I arose, the hallway was empty. To this day, I have no idea who delivered what turned out to be a personal lightning strike. No single event has had more impact on my life.

The envelope contained a copy of a magazine I had never heard of. It had clearly seen heavy use. What pages were not torn were frayed and smudged, like maybe it had been stuffed into a side pocket of a Kelty Tioga pack and taken deep into the woods, where it was read by the flickering flames of a campfire. It smelled of smoke.

The cover was jet black, with what appeared to be a grainy telephoto shot of a distant star. (Turns out, it was titled, "Jupiter and Moons," by Bob Chamberlain.)

Only a few words appeared on the cover. In the lower right-hand corner were these:

DICK DORWORTH
ON NIGHT DRIVING

ED ABBEY
ON DESERT DRIVING

On the upper left-hand corner were these:
MOUNTAIN GAZETTE 30
FEBRUARY 1975/60 CENTS

"What in the world is *this*?" I wondered, as I stood there in my skivvies, bleary eyed, thumbing through the magazine's 40 newsprint pages, which were filled with funky hand-drawn ads for camping and climbing gear companies, many of which are now long gone and many of which are still with us. Jansport, Sierra Designs ("Send 50 cents for our latest catalogue"), the Great Pacific Ironworks (now Patagonia), Forrest Mountaineering, The North Face, Eastern Mountain Sports, Mountain Travel, Stephenson Equipment (featuring a delightfully naked young lady) and many others that now yank at my nostalgia heartstrings.

I ran my fingertips across those pages, which seemed tactile, almost like braille. The ink bled onto my digits and has not washed off to this day.

Despite my fatigue, I began reading through *Mountain Gazette 30*. I spent the rest of the weekend digesting every syllable.

Dorworth's "Night Driving" piece (I learned years later) came in at about 19,000 words. Within that novella-length narrative was found a meditative mélange of *On the Road*-esque meanderings that included drugs, alcohol, zigzags, backtracks, missteps and blacktop-based ruminations aplenty. There were diversions to various noteworthy points in the Mountain West, a sidetrack to Niagara Falls and, most noteworthy, a multi-month foray to South America.

Then there was Abbey's "Desert Driving," which centered around an ill-advised drive into the Big Bend backcountry undertaken in a completely inappropriate vehicle owned by a nubile lass who had no idea what she was getting herself into, either with Big Bend or with Cactus Ed.

As a 20-year-old who had just driven cross country to points unknown in a battered Opel Kadett station wagon that contained little more than a backpack and a trunk containing five pounds of homegrown weed, this shit was a revelation. It didn't just knock on the door of my psyche, it strode right on in, popped a beer and made itself right at home. I was amazed that adventures like those had been undertaken, survived and related in such a way that they could actually find their way into print. This was enlightening news for an aspiring wordsmith.

Over the course of the next few years, I got my hands on several additional issues, mainly via a scroungy cast of dirtbag reprobates I was proud to call my amigos, all of whom, like me, had become addicted to the *Gazette*.

I was then too young and stupid to fully understand the nature of that addiction.

It began with Mike Moore, the visionary behind the *Mountain Gazette*, who, I later learned, operated under the very reasonable assumption that those wielding red pens ought to adhere to the Hippocratic Oath of editing: First, do no harm. He let contributors be themselves, even if, occasionally, things went awry on the subject/verb-agreement front.

The *Mountain Gazette*, through Moore, gave writers—old, young, famous, unknown, soon-to-be famous—the opportunity to be their purest creative selves. They were not only allowed, but encouraged, to tell their stories the way they wanted.

A rarity indeed.

Then, just like that, it ended.

In 1979, the *Mountain Gazette*, after a seven-year run, ceased publication. Mike Moore had moved on to greener pastures three years prior. Gaylord Guenin had taken over the editorial reins and his tastes in content ran toward an esoteric extreme that, while being some of the best writing ever to appear in the *Gazette*, was often a bit stylistically "out there," and thus, did not translate well to advertisers, which, by then, were looking to spend their dollars with bright and shiny magazines—like *Backpacker* and *Outside*—which the *Gazette* assuredly was not. It had stuck to its funky newsprint roots, right up to the bitter end.

The one time I met Abbey—who was in town giving a presentation I helped organize—we ended up chatting on the front porch of a ramshackle abode a buddy of mine rented. Abbey had some manner of adult beverage in his hand (likely gin-based), while I was stoned and tripping on acid. I asked him about the recent demise of the *Gazette*, to which he had contributed literally dozens of stories over the years (to the point that the late writer Charles Bowden described it many years hence as "Ed's magazine").

"You know about the *Mountain Gazette*?" he asked in his baritone voice.

I proceeded to relate my personal *Mountain Gazette* origin story, by then three-plus years in the making.

He smiled, nodded his head in suitable sage-like fashion and said, "I am very sorry to see it go. But it was time."

It was also time for me to move, north, to Denver, where I spent several years eking out a meager living freelancing for the eminently forgettable likes of *Denver Business* magazine and the *Boulder County Business Report*, neither of which were open to 19,000-word screeds about doing drugs while driving around the country. More like 500-word mini-profiles of venture capitalists whose very existence made me puke on the page. The kind of people Abbey railed against.

Then, the first of a series of fortuitous *Mountain Gazette*-related serendipities transpired. I visited a used bookstore close to my urban hovel and, at the far end of a mildewed corner sat, of all pleasantly surprising things, a musty stack of *Gazettes*! $8 for the whole bunch. I could not buy them fast enough.

For the next several years, no matter what dilapidated piece-of-shit residence I called home, that stack of *Gazettes* lay next to my coffee table. I spent countless evenings perusing those issues.

(Here would be a good time to mention that five of those issues bore subscription labels for none other than Edward Abbey. They remain among my most-valued possessions.)

My time in Denver was defined by near starvation and severe disorientation, as I am not a city person. Fortunately, I was out-of-the-blue offered a salaried gig at a brand-new daily newspaper located way up high in the heart of the Rocky Mountains. My responsibilities included plenty of predictable assignments—such as covering town council and school board meetings that often went on till goddamned 1 o'clock in the morning—but, once such obligations were satisfactorily met, I was free to pen whatever stories I desired in whatever way tickled my fancy. First person, third person, a mix of the two combined with the liberal use of all 16 English-language verb tenses, as long as I did not get him sued, it did not matter to the man who signed my paycheck. If there was a spontaneous Jägermeister-drinking contest at a local dive bar three hours past legal closing time, I was free to cover it as though it were a formal sporting event. If I observed someone who did not know how to build a campfire, I could riff for 5,000 words on the subject of proper campfire construction, the sociological implications of campfires and how wonderful smoke smells.

I was trying with all the might my two-fingered typing could muster to emulate what I considered, and still consider, the definitive "*Gazette* style": Wide-ranging tales on often-obscure subjects that appeared stylistically helter-skelter but, in truth, were thoughtfully (and lovingly) constructed.

Eventually, I had attained enough seniority that I was able to essentially write my own job description. I launched an in-house publication called *Summit Outdoors* that was modeled—as far as fiscal and human resources would allow—on the *Mountain Gazette*. The design was almost cookie-cutter *Gazette*, clear down to the folio fonts. I published work by established writers, aspiring writers and people who did not know an adverb clause from a semi-colon but knew how to spin a good yarn. The publication became a local institution that inspired readers and writers alike.

Sadly, like the *Mountain Gazette* before it, *Summit Outdoors* did not inspire advertisers. Once the writing was on the wall, with the publication hanging on by its fingernails, I decided to do a story on the magazine that had been flowing through my circulatory system, by that point, for almost two decades. I hunted down Mike Moore, then living in Vermont, where he owned and operated a book-publishing company called Steerforth Press. Though cordial enough, he did not seem all that interested in talking about the *Gazette*. I had hoped he would jump at the chance to relate tales I had heard through the grapevine about frantic late-night paste-up sessions and scrambling for the funds to pay contributors at a rate of (and I am not making this up) a penny a word (which may explain why contributors submitted 19,000-word stories). I did manage to glean the line about the Hippocratic Oath of editing, but that was about it.

He had moved on.

It was also time for me to move on.

After 10 years, I was told by my immediate supervisor that, because of economic circumstances stemming from members of management not receiving as many end-of-the-year bonus dollars as they had hoped, I had to lay off one of my staff writers. After thinking about it for a few milliseconds, I proposed laying myself off. My immediate supervisor agreed, a bit too enthusiastically, I thought.

Thing is, I did not have anything resembling a backup plan, which did not make my wife happy. I decided to hike the Colorado Trail (which made my wife even less happy), figuring that somewhere in the middle of altitudinous nowhere, lightning would strike, that I would have visited upon me a vocational epiphany.

Shockingly, that's exactly what happened.

Somewhere between Fooses Creek and the Cochetopa Hills, I decided to look into the possibility of resurrecting the *Mountain Gazette*.

Thing is, I had no idea how to proceed.

I recollected that the man who had financed the *Gazette* back in the 1970s lived in Colorado's Roaring Fork Valley. I did not know his name, but I had a learned local connection.

Curtis Robinson and I had worked together several times. He was then employed by a paper near Aspen. And here I will paraphrase his side of the story.

Curtis—not by anyone's definition an outdoorsperson—was in the midst of his very first guided rafting trip, along the Green River. His wife had given him a copy of Abbey's *Down the River*. While lying on the very beach being described by Abbey in the very paragraph he was right then reading, Curtis came upon the fateful words: *Mountain Gazette*. Being entrepreneurially oriented, he decided, upon returning home, to investigate further. Unlike me, he knew who to ask: George Stranahan, the Gazette's sugar daddy during its short-lived but impactful run in the 1970s. Curtis got with George—who he knew through their mutual relationship with Hunter Thompson—and learned that he had been quietly searching for someone comfortable with the concept of literary resurrection.

Two counties away, I, having completed my Colorado Trail hike, moved my hand toward my landline with the idea of calling Curtis to ask if I might know who owned the karmic, if not legal, rights to the *Mountain Gazette*.

As I did so, the phone rang. It was Curtis. Before I could even mouth a polite salutation, he asked, "Have you ever heard of a magazine called the *Mountain Gazette*?"

And the rest is history. Clear up to *right now*. This exact minute. To the book you are now holding in your hands.

With the support of Stranahan, who passed away a couple years ago, gained over the consumption of about 200 Flying Dog beers (George owned Flying Dog Brewery) at the justifiably infamous Woody Creek Tavern (Hunter Thompson's long-time haunt), we agreed to pull out the defibrillators and resuscitate the *Gazette*. Rumors of its death had apparently been greatly exaggerated. Turns out, it had only been resting its eyes for the previous 21 years. Waiting for the right moment to rise again.

And, yes, as Ms. DiFranco crooned in "Hour Follows Hour," everything is indeed governed by the rule of one thing leads to another.

During the multi-month run-up, while searching for a pithy bumpersticker-type slogan, I interviewed David Hiser, a *National Geographic* photographer who was a regular contributor to the *Gazette* in the '70s. I asked if he had any advice for young shooters. His response was "when in doubt, go higher"—meaning, if circumstances are too tight, stand atop a chair or ladder, or hold your camera high above you, to get a different perspective. My jaw dropped. I told him I was going to have to steal that line, which I did. It appeared on the cover of our resurrection issue and has stayed with the magazine ever since.

I received an email from Hiser saying that, well, since I had warned him that I was going to steal his line, he would have mercy and not sully my name in public. I was grateful for that.

The response to the *Gazette*'s rebirth covered a predictable gamut. Some old-time diehards reacted negatively, arguing that we ought to keep the memory of the magazine safely buried. We were accused of robbing a tomb. There were fears that we would corrupt the magazine's sacred memory. Others were guardedly supportive. Others jumped up and down with glee.

From the outset, we faced something of a conceptual conundrum. We wanted to pay justified homage to the giants—Abbey, David Roberts, Galen Rowell, Ned Gillette, John Jerome, Dorworth, George Sibley, et al.—who had laid the foundation upon which we were trying to re-build a magazine in the midst of the emerging internet age.

At the same time, between the two of us, Curtis and I had considerable publishing experience. We felt comfortable applying that experience to the endeavor. While maintaining the core editorial structure of the old *Gazette*—four basic food groups consisting of Mountain Notebook, Reviews, Letters, and long-winded, convoluted features—we added our own side-dish departments, some of which were short-lived failures and some of which, like Obituaries and Cartographic, became popular mainstays.

Unlike the original *Mountain Gazette*, we opted for a free model, printing a shitload of copies and spreading them like wildfire through a distribution network that ended up covering 47 states and more than

1,000 locations.

I know how this is going to sound, but we ended up becoming at least as popular and acclaimed as the original *Gazette*, though, of course, there will always be those who disagree.

Fair enough.

Much as I overall enjoyed the experience of owning and operating the *Mountain Gazette*, and much as that experience came to professionally define me in many ways, I was not put on this earth to be a business person. The pressure of putting out a monthly magazine—of managing employees, dealing with payroll, making sure the print bill got paid on time—while still trying to be a writer, proved too much. After six years, we sold the magazine to a company that ended up selling it to another company that ended up selling it to yet another company, the last of which unceremoniously shut it down.

The second iteration of the *Mountain Gazette* had lasted 12 years—five years longer than the original version.

I stayed on as editor of the *Gazette* for all but one of those 12 years, despite the fact that I had some serious conflicts with the subsequent string of owners, none of whom were versed in even the most rudimentary components of *Gazette* lore and one of whom actually gave me shit one time for not running stories like "The 10 Best Places to Get a Taco After Finishing a River Trip."

I gritted my teeth and persevered.

Because it was important, and not just to me. I had learned that there were a whole lot of folks out there—in the Rockies, in the Cascades and the Sierra Nevada, in the flatlands, in cities, in remote hamlets scattered throughout the country—who *loved* the *Gazette*, who eagerly awaited the release of every new issue, who, like me and my college compadres many years before, appreciated the fact that the *Gazette* was open to content that would have had the editors at *Outside* and *Backpacker* smearing garlic behind their ears and running for cover.

During my editorial tenure, I had perfect strangers walk up to me in mountain town bars and, with tears in their eyes, tell me how much the *Gazette* meant to them. Doug Peacock, the baddest-assed badass I have ever personally known, the man upon whom the Edward Abbey character of Hayduke was based, hugged and kissed me in front of a gaggle of stunned witnesses and thanked me for bringing back "Ed's magazine." I witnessed two people in Steamboat Springs literally having a heated tug-of-war over the last available copy in a gear shop!

Here we finally get to the point of this meandering walk down Memory Lane, where it's time to ask and maybe answer the question I was tasked with addressing in this Introduction: What is it about this offbeat, irreverent exercise in mountain-based literature that inspires near-fanatic devotion that has remained consistent through—now— three iterations since Nixon was in the White House?

I can only speak for myself when I say: Unlike any other publication, the *Mountain Gazette* has always featured not so much articles, but *stories* that, at their core, represent the way many of us want the world to be: forward thinking, but with one foot still anchored in tradition; adventuresome, but circumspect; wild but literate; expertly constructed, but not overly polished; and, most of all, honest.

In a nutshell, it amounts to, well, when in doubt, go higher.

Now, the *Gazette* torch is being held and waved high by Mike Rogge, a savvy businessman and editor who has spearheaded the second resurrection of this venerable exercise in journalistic insanity. Mike is well versed in *Gazette* lore and has brought to bear his own imprint upon the magazine's pages, just like Curtis and I did when George Stranahan gave us leave to bring back a magazine legend back in 2000.

Yes, one thing leads to another.

I still wonder all these long years later, who slid that copy of *Mountain Gazette 30* under my dorm room door 50 years ago. Whoever it was, well, I hope they know the havoc they have wreaked, and the joy that has risen as a result.

1.
Dirty Little Secrets
Written by Tim Cahill

There is a dirty little secret that resides at the core of what has got to be considered a great triumph. It is a matter that I have kept hidden away for over a quarter of a century. Why talk about it out in the open anyway? Nobody cares. So why would I "fess up?"

And then when I was least expecting it-when I figured my friends and I pulled this one off—I got a call from a guy named John Fayhee who asked if I had ever read a publication called *Mountain Gazette*.

"Used to be around in the 70s," I said. "Good magazine. I miss it."

"Well, we're resuscitating it," John said.

He was also putting together an anthology of articles from *Mountain Gazette*, both the old version and new. Would I care to write the foreword?

"Sure," I said, and then months passed and I didn't write the foreword because, I realized, there was no way I could do it without telling my dirty little secret. Right now I'm late with it, Fayhee is screaming and I might as well go ahead and spill the proverbial beans. It was sometime back in 1975, in the *Rolling Stone* offices, back when they were located in the warehouse district in San Francisco. Jann Wenner, the publisher, assigned editors Michael Rogers and Harriet Fier and me to come up with a new magazine idea, one that could be used as a vehicle to sell ads to all these little companies springing up all over that were making sleeping bags and such. Companies with strange names like "Patagonia," and "The North Face." Harriet objected to the concept outright: "You want us to invent a magazine designed to sell ads? That is just not classy." "Then," Jann said, "you make it classy."

We did. We put together *Outside*, a glossy outdoor magazine of acknowledged literary and artistic merit. It was, from the first, a writer's magazine, and writers liked working for us, liked being in the company of other authors they admired But in the early days, we were roundly ridiculed for our efforts. People who went out-doors, media pundits declared, did not read. Outdoorsy folk were knuckle dragging mouth breathers and aesthetic imbeciles, as evidenced by the very fact that they went outdoors. As an editor and writer for that magazine, I sometimes found myself defending it on radio talk shows or TV programs of the "Good Morning Cleveland" variety. I argued, to a succession of hosts, that American literature—from *Moby Dick* through *Huckleberry Finn* through Faulkner and Hemingway—was about the outdoors. We weren't doing something new.

Well, today, the idea seems like a slam dunk, and *Outside* is the only magazine to have ever won the National Magazine Award for General Excellence three times in a row. We, all of us, succeeded in our intention of putting out a literate magazine about the outdoors. We've won all sorts of awards. But here's the dirty little secret: *Mountain Gazette* was doing the same thing—publishing literate writing about the outdoors—and they were doing it years before we at *Outside* ever published our first issue. I can tell you that we were acutely aware of *Mountain Gazette* from the first. In the initial phases of creating the magazine that *Outside* would become, Harriet, Michael and I spent several months reading every outdoor magazine then on the market. Most of what we read was service-oriented, which is to say, if a magazine purported to be about canoeing, it told the reader how to buy and paddle a canoe twelve times a year.

The articles were informational rather than inspiring. But there was one magazine we admired: this dingbat effort out of Denver called *Mountain Gazette*. It was swollen with attitude, arrogant as all hell, and a complete delight to read. They had all these fantastic writers, Ed

Abbey among them, producing stuff that we, the creators of *Outside*, would have been proud to publish. In fact, we did publish those writers later on. Abbey wrote for us, as did Lito Tejada-Flores, Gordon Wiltsie, David Roberts and Doug Robinson. Indeed, it was Doug who taught me to telemark (not his fault I'm so poor at it), and who took me rock climbing in Yosemite. He taught me to see and feel the wilderness in a way I had not imagined before, and I owe him deeply for that, but I think I may be able to get away with buying him a few beers. Later, *Mountain Gazette*'s founding editor came to *Outside*. Mike Moore was a classy guy and what we call in the biz "a tasty editor." What I learned from Mike is invaluable, and I can never repay him, but he probably wouldn't turn down a couple of beers either.

As the years ground on, *Mountain Gazette* began to flounder—I have no idea why—and it died a quiet death in 1979, after seven mostly glorious years. *Outside* was struggling at the time, but it published the work of many *Gazette* alumni. By the late '80s and early '90s, *Outside* was unstoppable: a financial and critical triumph. We were congratulated in the media for our foresight: imagine, a literary outdoor magazine.

Who'd a thunk it? Well, *Mountain Gazette* did, and four or five years before we did. OK. There. I said it. That's my dirty little secret. I feel much better now.

2.
Where's Tonto?
Written by Edward Abbey

Hayduke parked his jeep out of sight among the pines, near the entrance to the Georgia-Pacific logging area. He stationed Bonnie on the hood of the jeep with instructions to keep her eyes open and ears clean. She nodded impatiently. Yes, yes, I know what to do; I'm the best damned lookout you'll ever have, Hayduke.

He put on hard hat, coveralls, gunbelt, gun and leather work gloves, took a small flashlight and his other tools and disappeared from Bonnie's ken into the twilight of the cut-over site, fading like a shadow among the giant machines. She wanted to read but it was already too dark. She sang songs for a while, softly, and listened to the cries of little birds, off in the forest, retreating to their nests for the night, heads nestled under fold of wing, retiring into the simple harmless dreams of avian sleep. (A bird has no cerebrum).

She was aware of tall presences around her, the brooding and transpiring yellow pines, the dark shaggy personalities of the Engelmann spruce and white fir—their high crowns pointed like cathedral spires toward the fireball array of the first-magnitude stars-and off by themselves, an exclusive group, a grove of aspens, slim and white, delicate, gay and ladylike. So I see them, she thought. What is their consciousness of me? Do they give a shit? Bonnie Abbzug, the metaphysical arborologist, philosopher of the psycho-morphology of vascular plants. And other properties. She rolled and lit a joint. Weary and warm in her down-stuffed parka, she nodded for a moment, dozed, woke with a start to find that nothing had happened, nothing had changed except the map of the stars becoming slightly more elaborate.

A small wind rustled through the trees. It sounded so much like human voices that Bonnie looked around for a moment in surprise, expecting to see someone near.

Nobody there; only Hayduke's little light appearing now and then from beneath or from the hulk around the silhouette of some machine.

She sucked on her weed. The wind continued talking with the trees; like the dialogue of dreams—voices far away, not in space or time but out of reach, on the other side of an invisible barrier. Bonnie smiled, subsiding into a warm reverie of oceanic sympathy. We are all ONE, she thought. One what? Who cares? Hayduke however, under the belly of the bulldozer, was tugging at an oversize spanner, trying to open the drainplug in the crankcase of an Allis-Chalmers HD-41, which is merely the biggest tractor Allis-Chalmers makes. His wrench was three feet long—he'd taken it from the tractor's toolbox—but he couldn't turn that square nut. He reached for his cheater, a three-foot length of steel pipe, fit it like a sleeve over the end of the wrench handle and tugged. This time the nut gave—a fraction of a millimeter. All he needed: Hayduke yanked again and the nut began to turn.

So far he'd done nothing dramatic, merely followed routine procedures: cut up wiring, break off cylinder heads, cut hoses, smash instrument gauges, pour shellac into crankcases, destroy air cleaner and oil filter elements, slice fan belts, crack batteries, smash lights, sprinkle emery powder into gearboxes, puncture tires (where applicable) and chisel-punch a few holes into radiator cores. Nothing special. Where possible, as in the case of the HD-41, he drained the crankcase oil as well, planning to start up the engine just before leaving. (Noise factor.) He had no keys but assumed he would find what he needed by breaking into the G-P office, a small house trailer close by.

Another possibility, of course, was fire. Why not as a farewell salute set fire to the tractors, loaders, skidders, et al., et cetera, once and all? Hayduke was a pyromaniac, fond of fire. He liked the warmth and he liked the purity of it, he appreciated fire's quick cleansing action. But he couldn't do it tonight. Not here. Why not? Because George Hayduke, like Smoky the Bear, had a horror of forest fires. Because he, Hayduke, had worked too many summers as a firefighter in too many national parks and forests.

The idea of deliberately setting fire to the number of large oily paint-coated objects upwind from a forest of living trees-even though these objects were set in a clearing, even though he knew the loggers planned to cut most of the trees down anyhow, even though he knew that fires are really good for forests (hadn't Doc Sarvis himself said so and explained, at great and technical length, why it was so?)—despite these considera-tions, George Hayduke could not do it. Could not bring himself.

Another turn on the plug and the oil would begin to drain. Hayduke eased his body out of the way, re-gripped his pipe-handled wrench-and froze.

"How you doin, pard?" said a man's voice, deep and low, from more than 20 feet away.

Hayduke reached for his sidearm.

"Naw, don't do that." The man flicked a switch, training the beam of a powerful electric torch directly into Hayduke's eyes. "I got this," he explained, pushing the muzzle of what certainly looked to be a twelve-gauge double-barrelled shotgun into the light, where Hayduke could see it. "Yeah, it's loaded," he said, "and it's cocked and it's touchy as a rattlesnake."

He paused. Hayduke waited.

"Okay," the man said, "now you go ahead and finish what you're a-doin' under there."

"Finish?"

"Go ahead."

"I was looking for something," Hayduke said.

The man laughed, an easy, soft and pleasant laugh. "Is that right?" he said. "Now what the hell is anybody lookin' for under the crankcase guard of a bulldozer at midnight?"

Hayduke thought carefully. It was a good question. "Well..."

"This oughta be pretty good."

"Yeah. Well, I was looking for—well, I'm writing a book about bulldozers, you see, and thought I ought to see what they look like. Underneath."

"That ain't very good. How do they look?"

"Greasy."

"I coulda told you that, pard, saved you all the trouble. What's that three-foot end wrench for you got in your hands? That what you write your book with?"

Hayduke said nothing.

The man said, "You go ahead and finish your job." Hayduke hesitated. "I mean turn the plug. Let the oil out."

Hayduke did as he was told. The shotgun, after all, like the flashlight, was aimed straight at his face. A shotgun at close range is a perfectly logical argument. He loosened the plug; the oil streamed out, sleek, rich and liberated, onto and into the churned-up soil.

"Now," the man said, "drop the wrench, put your hands behind your head and kinda sidewind outa there on your back."

Hayduke obeyed. Wasn't easy, wriggling out from under a tractor without using the hands. But he did it.

"Now roll over on your face." Hayduke obeyed. The man rose from his squatting position, came close, unholstered Hayduke's gun, stepped back and hunkered down again. "Okay," he said, "you can turn over now and sit up." He examined Hayduke's piece. "357 magnum, Ruger—that's power, boy."

Hayduke faced him. "You don't have to shine that light right in my eyes."

"You're right, pard." The stranger switched off the light. "Sorry about that."

They faced each other in the sudden deep darkness, silent, bashful, each wondering, perhaps, who had the quicker and better night vision. But the stranger had his left thumb on the switch of the flashlight and his right forefinger on the forward trigger of the shotgun.

The stranger cleared his throat. "You sure work slow," he complained. "I been watchin' you for seems like an hour."

Hayduke didn't know what to say.

"But I can see you do a good job. Thorough. I like that." The man spat on the ground. "Not like some of them half-assed dudes I seen up on the Powder River. Or them kids down in Tucson. Or them nuts that derailed—what's your name?"

Hayduke opened his mouth. Henry Lightcap? he thought. Joe Smith? How about...

"Forget it," the man said. "I don't want to know."

Hayduke stared harder at the face before him, 10 feet away in the starlight, gradually becoming clear. He saw at last that the stranger was wearing a mask. Not a black mask over the eyes but simply a big bandana draped outlaw-style over nose, mouth and chin. Above the mask the dark eyes, vaguely shining, peered at him from under the droopy brim of a black slouch hat.

"Who are you?" Hayduke said.

The masked man grinned. "You don't really want to know that," he said. "But I'll tell you this much: they used to call me Kemosabi."

"Who did?"

"Oh that fool of an Indian used to run around with me."

"Tonto?"

"Yeah, that asshole."

"Tonto means fool in Spanish."

"Yeah, he finally caught on. About the same time I learned what Kemosabi really means in Paiute. So we split up. Last I heard old Tonto was hangin' around the United Brethren mission at Elko, hitting the Ripple and the Thunderbird pretty steady. He never was any damn good." The stranger paused, reminiscing, then chuckled. "Bet you thought I was the watchman, didn't you? Made you sweat a little, huh?"

Hayduke was beginning to wish it was the watchman. "Where is the watchman?" he said. (Help!)

"In there." The stranger jerked a thumb toward the office trailer, where a Georgia-Pacific pickup stood parked.

"What's he doing?"

"Nothin'. I got him hogtied and gagged. He's all right. He'll keep till Monday morn-ing. The loggers'll be back and turn him loose."

"Monday morning is tomorrow morning."

"Yeah, I reckon I oughta mosey on outa here."

"Still got your white horse?"

"No, I got rid of him a long time ago. That old Silver, he was just too goddamned conspicuous for this line of work. Got me a big old black gelding now. You wanta see him?"

"What do you mean," Hayduke said, "by this line of work?"

"Same thing you're doin'. You wanta see my horse?"

"No. I want my gun back."

"Okay." The stranger handed it back. "Next time you better keep your lookout a little closer. That girlfriend of yours never seen me nor heard me a-tall."

"Where is she?" Hayduke reholstered his weapon, reluctantly.

"Right on the jeep where you left her, puffing on one of them little Mary Jane cigarettes. Or she was. Probably out there in the dark somewhere now, wonderin' what the hell's a-goin' on here." The stranger waved one hand at the surrounding night. "Here's something else you want too," he said, handing Hayduke a bunch of keys. "Now you can start them starters and burn up them engines real good."

Hayduke looked toward the trailer. "You certain that watchman is secure?"

"I got him handcuffed, hogtied, gagged, dead drunk and locked up."

"Dead drunk?"

"He was half drunk when I got here. After I got the drop on him I made him finish up a pint of bourbon he was suckin' on. He passed out scared and happy."

So that's why nobody squeaked when I knocked on the door. Hayduke looked at the mysterious masked stranger, who was shuffling his feet, apparently eager to leave.

"Where you heading for now?" he asked.

"You don't wanta know, pardner."

A high voice, strained and frightened, came out of the dark. "George—are you all right?"

"I'm all right," he shouted back. "You stay out there, Natalie. Keep watch. Anyway my name is Leopold."

Hayduke jingled the keys, looking at the dark hulk of tractor at his side. "Not sure I know how to start this thing."

The masked man said, "I'll give you a hand. I ain't in that big of a hurry." Off in the woods somewhere a horse stomped, shuffled, nickered. The man listened, turning his head that way. "You be quiet, Sam. I'll come and git you in a minute." He set the (watch-man's) shotgun down and turned back to Hayduke. "Come on."

They climbed to the driver's seat of the tractor. Hayduke found himself faced by an impressive battery of switches, dials and levers.

"Okay, hokay," the stranger began, "What do we got here, a HD-41, right? Okay. First put this here lock lever in neutral position. That ties- in the starter switch circuit."

"I know how to operate a Cat," says Hayduke, "but this one's different."

"It's different, all right. This ain't a Cat, this is a Allis-Chalmers. But these new units is simple to start. Now we pull up this here shutoff knob to RUN position. Got a little release button in the middle, see. You gotta press that first. Yeah. That's right. Now... here's a little light switch under the cowl. Might as well see what we're doin'. Okay. Now the starter switch is this little button right here by the speed shift."

"That's what I thought," Hayduke said. "But when I tried to start it nothing happened."

"I'll show you why," the masked man said. "You didn't have the master switch turned on."

"The master switch?"

"The master switch. Real tricky, them Allis-Chalmers folks."

"Well, where's the master switch?"

The stranger grinned. "Patience, old buddy. I'll show you. Give me the keys again." Hayduke gave him the keys. The stranger examined them under the cowling light, chose one, bent down and unlocked a padlocked access plate on the steel floor of the operator's compartment, behind the braking pedals. Lifting the hinged plate, he showed Hayduke the master switch and turned it to the ON position.

"Now," he said, "the batteries are connected to the electrical system. Now we can start the engine. Push that starter button again."

Hayduke pushed the button. The starter solenoid engaged the starter pinion with the flywheel ring gear: the 12-cylinder 4-cycle turbocharged Cummins diesel coughed into life, 1,710 cubic inches of packed piston power. Hayduke was delighted. He pulled back on the throttle lever and the engine revved up smoothly, ready to work. (But heating rapidly.)

"I'm gonna do something with this machine," he announced to the stranger.

"Yes, you are."

"I'm gonna move things around."

"You better move quick then. It ain't goin' to last but a few minutes." The stranger was eyeing the instrument panel: oil pressure zero, engine temperature rising. An odd unhealthy noise, like the whine of a sick dog, could be heard already.

Hayduke unlocked the lock lever and pulled the speed shift lever into gear. The tractor bucked forward against the lowered dozer blade, shoving a ton of mud and two yellow pine stumps into the Georgia-Pacific office.

"Not that way," the stranger shouted. "There's a man in there!"

"Right." Hayduke stopped the machine, leaving his load piled high against the buckled trailer wall. He shifted into reverse and the tractor backed over the Georgia-Pacific pickup truck; the truck collapsed like a Coors beer can. "So who's next?" Hayduke looked around through the starlight for another target.

"See what you can do with that brand-new Clark Skidder over there," the masked man suggested.

"Check." Hayduke raised the dozer blade, turned the tractor and charged at full throttle-five miles per hour—into the skidder. It crumpled with a rich and satisfying crunch of steel flesh, iron bones. Hayduke buried the wreck under the tracks, squashing it deep into the mud. Now what? He pivoted the tractor 200 degrees, and started for a tanker truck full of diesel fuel.

Somebody was screaming at him. Something was screaming at him. Full throttle forward. The tractor lurched ahead one turn of the sprocket wheels and stopped. The engine block cracked; a jet of steam shot forth whistling from the fissure. The engine fought for life. Something exploded inside the manifold and a gush of blue flame belched from the exhaust stack, launching hot sparks at the stars.

Seized-up tight within their chambers, the 12 pistons became one—wedded and welded—with cylinders and block. All is One. One what? Why, one unified immovable white-hot entropic molecular mass, what else? The screaming in the night.

"She's foundered," the masked man said. "There ain't nothin' we can do." He clambered off over the rear, under the eight-ton rippers. "Come on," he shouted, "there's somebody comin'!" He melted into the darkness.

Hayduke pulled himself together and got off the tractor. He still heard somebody screaming at him. Bonnie.

She yanked at his sleeve, pointing away into the woods. "Can't you see?" she screamed. "Lights, lights! What's the matter with you?" Hayduke stared, then grabbed her arm. "This way."

They ran across the clearing, among the stumps, toward the sweet shelter of the forest as a truck came rumbling into the open area. Headlights flared; a spotlight swept across the open and almost caught them.

Not quite. They were in the woods, among the friendly trees. Feeling their way through the dark in what he thought was the direction of his jeep, Hayduke heard a thunder of mighty hooves and a cry that rang through the night:

"Hi-yo Samuel, awaaaaaaaaaaaaaay..."

The mysterious masked stranger galloped past, his big black horse in a full run. The truck, which had come to a stop beside the whistling bulldozer, discharged some men—one, two, three, impossible to count them in the dark. Hayduke and Abbzug watched the spotlight probing the clearing, the trees, seeking the horse. Again too late: one glimpse of the horseman and he was gone, into the forest and down the road off to the end of the night. A gun barked once, twice, importantly but futile, and relaxed. The hoofbeats faded away. The men at the truck moved to the assistance of somebody inside the office-trailer, who was kicking at the walls. They'd have a tough time getting him out with the load of rubble banked against the door.

Bonnie and George got into their jeep.

"Who in God's name was that?" she demanded.

"The watchman I guess."

"No, I mean the man on the horse."

"Men call him.Kemosabi."

"I'm in no mood for bullshit."

"That's what he said."

"Who was he, goddammit?"

"A man from the past. Shut your door."

Hayduke started the motor.

"They'll hear us," she said.

"Not with that bulldozer howling they won't." He drove without any light but starlight out of the trees, slowly, and onto the main forest road, heading back toward the highway. When he felt he had gone a safe distance he turned on the headlights and stepped on the gas. The well-tuned jeep purred forward, guided by its burning eyebeams, at maximum cruising speed, 55 mph. Sure could use overdrive on this vehicle, Hayduke thought, as he had thought a hundred times before.

"I still want to know who that man was."

"I don't know, sweetheart. All I know is what I told you. He said his name is Kemosabi."

"What kind of name is that?"

"It's a Paiute word."

"Meaning what?"

"Shithead."

"That figures." She huddled closer. "Who was in the truck?"

"I don't know and I didn't want to find out, did you?" He decided to stick it to her.

"Did you, my hotshot lookout?"

"Listen," she said, "don't give me any hard time about that. You wanted me to stay at the jeep and that's what I did. How was I to hear some lunatic on foot creeping around in the dark? I was watching the road like you wanted me to. So shut up."

"Okay."

"And amuse me. I'm bored."

"Okay, okay."

But why, he wondered, did they call him the Lone Ranger, when he had that faithful dumb Indian always at his side? Why? And then the answer came, obvious as the sneer on a racist's face: because a white man with only an Indian for companionship..Yeah...Of course... No wonder they don't come to our Thanksgiving picnics anymore.

"Amuse me," she said again.

"All right," he said, "consider this conundrum."

"Where?"

"Where? What the fuck are you talking about? Now listen carefully: What is the

difference between God and the Lone Ranger?"

The jeep bumbled through the dark of the woods. Bonnie Abbzug thought and thought. At last she said, "What a stupid conundrum. I give up."

Hayduke grinned. "There really is a Lone Ranger."

"I don't understand."

"Forget it." He drove slowly now, looking for a place to camp. He pulled her a little harder against his side. "Those new sleeping bags, you know..."

"Yeah?"

"The fuckers zip together."

"No kidding!"

—*Originally appeared in* Mountain Gazette 28, *1974.*

3.
A Dream of White Horses
Written by Royal Robbins

A Dream of White Horses—one of the great names, fulfilling Geoffrey Dutton's dictum that a name should tell you something about the climb or the way in which it was done. One glance at Leo Dickinson's masterful photograph explains it: that great sheet of spray leaping from the sea, rearing from excited waters like a splendid white stallion, and the two figures fastened to the rock just out of reach of the tormented foam. With its whimsical and romantic overtones, the name appeals perhaps more to the American climber than to his British counterpart. A Dream of White Horses. Drummond, who made the first ascent with Dave Pearce, has a talent for verbal imagery, for metaphorical and poetic phrasing. It's not surprising he should produce such a name. But still—A Dream of White Horses—five words! Turgid with subtle meanings. One of the few long names that succeeds.

Although I knew nothing of the climb, because of that name and that sensational portrait by Dickinson, it was a route I had to do.

A chill, heavy wind flowed from the North Atlantic beneath dark masses of cloud, not rain laden, but casting showers on the soul, dampening the urge, as we stubbed in tight shoes across the barren, heather-covered crown of Holyhead Mountain. The green sea was agitated.

"Lots of white horses today," said Whiz.

"Yea, verily," I replied, suspended in heavy-handed mockery between Shakespeare, St. Paul and Zane Grey, " 'tis a right stamped."

"You know, you shouldn't try to be clever," my friend advised. He has my interests at heart. "You lose points that way. You don't have any judgment about what's clever and what is merely cute. You'll probably put something silly like that in your next article.

You're one who should never digress in your writing. The way you ought to write is this: Open your story in the middle of a pitch, write about that for six pages, and close with the hero (*yourself*, presumably) 10 feet higher. Then you might have an article that people would read."

"Thanks, pal. I'll let you know what's wrong with you, too, as soon as I figure it out." We were soon at the edge, and I was startled by how sharply the green-and-brown slope dipped towards the sea. There was a break in the clouds, and the sun flashed on olive sea and rich, well-watered grass. From the west, a host of albino chargers rushed landward. It was a wind-and-light show and I looked forward to more. The approach was down steep, muddy slopes, the precipice just below. The signals of my mind flashed caution. This wasn't like grit, where one can relax when not actually climbing. On these sea cliffs, you can't afford to stumble.

We came across ropes and packs left by others. Whiz was concerned. "They'll be up to the same thing we are," he assured me. "They've just gone down to check out the wind and wet. We can beat them to the ab and get on the route first."

He talked on in his unique and entertaining fashion, about the likely identity of the others, and about how they didn't know the code, for they had parked in the wrong place. Then he digressed to other subjects: political scandals, rock music, architecture, climbing techniques, photography and the organization and conduct of international mountaineering expeditions. Whiz is an authority on many things. Delivering quick, sometimes harsh judgments, dogmatic, impulsive, abrasive, but often accurate, he is very much alive. So alive that he seems, at times, about to burst with suppressed energy.

A weaker man might have drowned that much painful life force in a sea of bitterness. But Whiz has it pretty well harnessed. He is irritating at times but inspires respect and somehow even a certain affection. But he is a steamroller on the bumpy road of sentimentality, a wine crusher of maudlin grapes, impatient of weakness, scornful of incom-petence, not over worried about people's feelings, a skillful and agile polemicist who usually wins. He comes on strong, and sometimes puts people off with his aggressiveness. But he is not impervious to a slight, or to a well-chosen phrase focused upon a weakness. And he is keenly sensitive to the nuances of status, insisting upon his turn in the front seat.

"Let's just whip over and set up the ab," said Whiz, tripping off. But first I wanted to look at the route, so I scrambled down the steep slope. Four climbers were coming up.

"What are you going to climb?" one shouted through the wind.

"White Horses," I threw back.

"That's what they're doing," he replied, indicating two figures on the wall, halfway between water and grass. I continued down to a promontory which curved and faced the climb across an impatient, foaming gap. Sea spray was dashing against the wall.

What a picture! What a time to be out of film!

Whiz was waving wildly over the shoulder of the slab. I surmised that he desired my presence. I knew he would be thinking: "We mustn't let those 'nods' get ahead of us." (Except for occasional uses of "twit" or "freddie," Whiz, to express disdain, favors words starting with "n" sounds, words like "nod," "gnome," "nurd," "nob," "nibbler," etc.)

I arrived to find him taking great care setting up the "ab ancs." A close friend had recently been killed abseiling, and Whiz didn't want to go the same way. Nor did I. "This is a dangerous place," I said, clipping to the 11-mm runner he had looped over a sturdy block and backed up with two more anchors.

We were now directly above the copulating waters. Whiz threaded the ropes through his brass figure-eight, and was off. The place provoked in me the same feeling I get descending to the notch of the Lost Arrow Spire in Yosemite, with the prospect of falling into the Arrow Chimney. In such places, the recurrent theme of abseiling, that one's eggs are all in a single basket, comes home with special force prompted by the hideous aspect of what one would fall into.

I Dulfer-ed to Whiz who was waiting on a narrow, irregular ledge, just the sort that someone, someday, will fall off. "Just look," he said in a jocular tone, "at that tangled and barking ocean." I missed the allusion to Yeats, but his metaphors seemed nearly right.

The route properly started 70 feet lower, but as the water was only 60 feet down we had to forego the pleasures of the first pitch. We were on Wen Slab. "Slab" in this case doesn't mean low angle, for the rock averages about 80 degrees, and is vertical or overhanging in many places. It is a slab in that it is a single slice of compact rock, forming one wall of a zawn. A zawn is a yawn in a sea cliff, the bottom filled with water.

The outside wall of this zawn is a promontory that juts into the sea and curves toward the south, a sort of pillar the top of which is directly across from, and halfway up, Wen Slab. This pillar is a natural bridge. The waters in their ebb and flow have surgically cut a tunnel through the pillar in an attempt to isolate it and transform it into a sea stack.

Through this tunnel the waters burbled and boiled, forming a counterpoint to the larger boiling flow from the natural mouth into the ocean. I was struck by the savagery of the place, the frothing and sucking, the wind blowing, spindrift flying, the water churning and surging onto the cliff, and the surges breaking and lapping up the wall to hang like lace curtains while slipping back into the sea. Aphrodite, they say, was born of sea foam. But this was a rough sort of love, this mating of water with rock. It was ele-mental, and affected me as do thunderstorms or raging blizzards. I loved the fearful violence of it. In the clash and dash of water, the thundering and pounding, the crashing, breaking din, there was great power, but no evil. It gave pleasure similar to boulder trundling, but touched one's emotions at a deeper level.

I turned my back to the sea and started climbing, moving vertically, following a crack on the right side of the slab. It was steep, but not difficult. All the same, I slotted a wedge and continued up on toes and fingers. The rock there is good for climbing: It doesn't have holds everywhere, but might have holds anywhere. In this respect it is like the rock in the Lakes or the Welsh mountains, but it isn't granite. Such rock offers very good face climbing, but is comparatively rare in the United States. Most of the climbing in the U.S.A. is on "young" granite or sandstone, and generally follows crack systems.

But even in the Shawangunks, where there are few vertical cracks, the complexity of this sort of British rock is lacking. In the Shawangunks there is a certain predictability about what lies ahead. This is not true of places like Craig Gogarth, a fissirostral sea cliff, where it is very difficult to tell from 50 feet away whether a passage is easy or impossible. Or from even closer than that.

I was 40 feet above Whiz. At that point the route traverses left two-and-a-half pitches straight off the cliff. I started, aiming for a crack 50 feet away. There was nothing obvious. A solution had to be found for every foot of progress. The route wasn't going to yield to an aggressive approach. I advanced, tentatively, and the rock revealed some of its secrets. I made further advances, careful but firm. And the rock again yielded, unfurling more, exciting me, raising my hope. There was a bit of a struggle, a setback, a renewed onslaught, and I broke through, confident now and eager for success. But I was stopped cold. False hopes; the damning disappointment of hoping too soon. The next bit was difficult. Should I take a chance and push forward? No, I would have to find the key. I was almost ready to give up. I considered it. But what would Whiz think when I admitted that I couldn't handle this bitch?

Where was the fire? It was cold on the shady slab, with the constant cold wind and the water running down over the holds. The climb was proving cold and contemptible, leading me on, acting easy, then closing the door in my face. Rebuffed, I knocked again.

My eyes scanned the rock, noting every detail. I could take a high line or a low one in an effort to traverse to good jugs and a crack. I chose the low way and descended a bit, fingers feeling the rock, sensitive to every minute variation of texture and contour. I had to be careful, for I was now committed. There was an awkward piece before reaching the crack. I had to restrain myself, to hold back from lunging to escape the tension. But I was getting sick and tired of fiddling around. Finally I found the key and moved into the crack, and up a bit, to a belay where I was to spend the next hour suspended from two chocks and a spike.

I took in the rope. "OK, Come on up." He came up neatly, not fast, but controlled and competent, and soon reached me.

"Found that troublesome, did you?" he asked

"Rather," I admitted. "But good. Real rock-climbing."

"I led that last time," he continued, "and I daresay I found it a sight easier than you did."

"That's nice," I responded. "That's why I come to Britain, you know, to ease the inferiority feelings of you D-team men." Whiz always insists he's strictly D-team. He's kind enough to classify me as B, so it greatly pleases him when he climbs better than I do.

"Well, there's a lot to be said for age and experience," said Whiz, encouragingly.

"But I've yet to learn what it is."

Leaving these words of "whizdom" to rattle around my head, he grabbed the next lead. It was a classic. I longed for my camera. Whiz followed a flake that ran up left, offering good grips, but little for the feet except friction. It was vigorous climbing, different from my tippy toe balance lead. The protection wasn't brilliant, but he made quick work of it, and then took a long while arranging his belay anchors. I like that sort of care.

I followed the flake up and then descended a bit to Whiz's belay and took a gander at the last pitch. I would not have guessed it went that way. It looked like rubble. But not so much rubble, because rubble implies angularity; it was more like Dalinian rub-ble, rubble gone soft like Dali's watches, rubble that had melted and then refrozen, a great dripping morass of melting vanilla ice-cream refrozen in its slopping and plopping descent into the sea. Frozen magically hard. It was uncanny the way some force had cemented those sand grains. First it was sand, then sandstone, and then it was heated and squeezed into super-sandstone: quartzite. Picture the outer walls of a sandcastle that a wave has overrun. The soaked edifice crumbles and melts, but in this case it was caught in mid-melt and rehardened into an extremely durable battlement.

The traverse proved a rare treat. I climbed slowly, savoring it.

Whiz gave me pointers on double-rope technique. Above, the rock overhung, forcing a leftward passage. It overhung below as well, so much so that an unroped climber, slipping from the traverse, would fall 200 feet directly into the water and perhaps escape serious injury!?). I finished in dazzling sunshine, hot in a heavy sweater. Before disappearing up the grass to a belay niche, I looked back along the double ropes across the crumbling wall to Whiz, who had been enjoying my enjoyment of the rock. It was spectacular, and the rays bouncing off the white rock made me squint. White rock. White horses. This route will be a classic.

Whiz walked up the green hill and took off the rope. We coiled it and packed our gear.

"Let's go," said Whiz, his eyes suddenly lighting up with boyish enthusiasm. "I know a great place near here for trundling."

We rushed off, eager for more tumult, forgetting in our haste to retrieve the runner and carabiner we had left for the dreadful abseil.

—*Originally appeared in* Mountain Gazette 28, *1974.*

4.
Mountain Towns
Written by Ted Kerasote

I've lived in a lot of places during the last seven years, probably a dozen towns, many of them in Colorado. Aesthetically, they've been as different as Leadville is different from Aspen, but they've all had one thing in common: somewhere within them I found an apartment, a restaurant, a bar that had a touch of romance and made my life special for a while.

In Aspen it was one room above the Epicure Restaurant at the corner of Mill and Main. From my window I could see the slopes of Aspen Mountain and a good way down the valley of the Roaring Fork. I wrote in the morning and worked in the kitchen of the Hotel Jerome from three to midnight. It was a fine life, though the room was often so cold that I could see my breath, and I would have to wear a down vest while writing.

I had a single electric hot plate on which I cooked my meals, and one day I got the bright idea to put it under my chair as I wrote. Fine idea. The rest of the winter my bottom and the backs of my legs were toasty as I scribed noble stories.

Aspen was a very special time for me, and the hot-plate heater in a freezing writer's garret was only part of the romance. The other part wasn't the skiing, the magical Hansel and Gretel houses, nor the high-stepping ladies. It was the Mesa Store Bakery.

On my one-day-a-week off, I would sometimes write 15 to 20 hours a day, trying to make up for lost time, trying to get out my masterpiece before spring and the melting snow stole the aura of privacy that surrounded me. It was a happy delusion.

At 11:30 on my night off, I would appraise what I had written, and if I deemed it good enough, I would take some change from the ash tray on my dresser and walk slowly up a deserted, snowy Main Street to the bakery. I would buy a large cinnamon cookie and a cup of hot apple cider—my reward for the day—and a small carrot to keep the dream going. Sitting there with my cookie and cider, the backs of my legs still faintly warm from the hot plate, I was the happiest creature on earth—impoverished, proud, my life filled with youthful promise.

Then it was Crested Butte. C.B. and the Wooden Nickel Bar with its worn plank floor, its potbelly stoves, the Victorian sofas and spinsterish lamps out of the age of F.D.R. It also had a greasy kitchen, a cook named Mo, a barmaid with a diamond pin stuck through the left side of her nose, and the best draft beer in Colorado.

That was before skiing began in earnest, before they paved the streets, when the dust still settled behind the jeeps that came down from Kebler Pass. A band would play in the Wooden Nickel during the hot afternoons of September, a band whose name I don't remember, though I recall that there was a drummer and two guitarists. The lead guitarist was black, and his voice was made of silk and sequins and rolling waves.

I used to sit for hours, eating a hamburger and drinking Coors, and listen to him sing of oceans and islands. Then I would go up the mountain to help build the success that ruined the town.

In Silverton, it was the train, and it always will be the train, no matter how camp, hokey and obnoxious a tourist magnet the train becomes. Once in your life you ought to be on the summit of Arrow Peak in the Grenadiers and hear the train whistle from the valley of the Animas, 6,000 feet below you and 10 miles away. You'll be looking out to the deserts of Utah, the Henry Mountains floating on the horizon like the castle of Moroni, and from deep in that valley with the loveliest name in the state, Animas, will come this black eight-wheeler peal, strung out in Doppler, haunting like an elk's bugle, like wind in the crags. That train is how you get into the Grenadiers—it leaves you off at the Needleton Water Tower-and its engineer in coveralls, giving the high sign, its fat conductor calling, "Board," are the lost memories of a time before the automobile.

In October, when the hillsides along the Million Dollar Highway turn to riot, and the train blows its last whistle of the season, Silverton becomes just another mining town—a bit rundown, slightly picturesque, a touch of rustic poetry caught on a weathered sign—in the backwoods of the state

Leadville, on the other hand, is a most unpoetic, unromantic town. A train couldn't save it. The impressive view of the Sawatch has never saved it. A new strike of the rich-est, purest gold ever found wouldn't save it. The only thing that saves Leadville is the El Perdido Bar and the El Metate Restaurant.

They're both under the same dilapidated roof: the lost one and the grinding stone of eternal labor. The Mexican cuisine is not exceptional, no longer even filling. The green felt on the pool tables is getting thin, and there's no more draft beer. In the winter it's cold, in the summer hot. But the atmosphere is so plebeian, so base and no-nonsense, so absolutely and eternally memorable to the passing traveler used to the Ramada Inns of the land, that it couldn't be replicated by 10 Hollywood directors with 10 years and $10 million to spare.

It took Leadville to build the El Perdido Bar and El Metate. It took lots of muddy boots, broken bottles, two-time losers, drunken miners and fighting Chicanos and Mexicans to put the smell of sweat and scams in the backs of the leather chairs. It took a lot of spilled beer and vanished hopes to build the lost one and the grinding stone: the only place in Leadville from which you can look at the shantytowns, the molybdenum mine, the thermometer that says 36 below, and smile like a demon.

One more place: Boulder. More fine running, cycling and climbing, more eateries, more good weather and handsome women than any other town in the West—maybe the country.. maybe the world. Boulder and Leadville: the Beautiful and the Damned It's so chic it's obscene. I think of browsing through plant-filled bookstores, of skiing by deer in Chautauqua Park, or Christmas carols on the mall, of the Green Slab Direct on a spring day, of Eggs Benedict and Fettucine Alfredo, of the best $1.80 Bordeaux purchasable in the United States, of Masi bicycles gleaming with Campi gear.

But, in the end, when I've been on an expedition for a long time and am dreaming of civilization, it's not a single one of those luxurious things I remember. I remember Saturday night and my room. Snuggled under an elkskin bedspread, I read the Atlantic and hear over the stereo the delicate bars of KVOD's "Down to Earth" theme music: the pure notes of a flute and guitar drifting me to moody, cloud-hung places—the sea coast, bracken-covered moors, ice mountains—all far away.

And from my warm bed, close to 90,000 people, I smile nostalgically: the wilderness, like a loved town, will always be sweeter in counterpoint.

—*Originally appeared in* Mountain Gazette 76, *1978/1979.*

5.
The Ride

Written by Katie Lee

It was the hottest day of the year when I decided to do it. Sure as hell it wasn't anything planned in advance. Intuition works best in a case like this. I remember dreaming up something similar a year or so back and threatening that I would do it someday, but the notion didn't even get out of bed with me that morning. I was still deep into the sorrow of loss.

He was such a wonderful friend, such a joyful man, full of life and living it, of love and giving it. He could torch you with his sense of humor-fire your laughter until you peed your pants to put it out. An artist, a sensualist and, I suspect, a creative lover as well. Gentle. A listener. A man who treated women the way he handled his sculptures—molding, caressing, teasing them into creatures of beauty and supple grace until they glowed with a life they didn't know they possessed. I watched that happen with more than one of his many women friends-women he'd never made love to, women he saw every day in his shop, in the shop next door, all around town, really. Everyone knew him. It's a small town, less than 500 of us.

Then, about three years after his move from the Big Rotten Apple to this little burg that he so loved, tiptoeing quietly toward another peak in his creative talent—not with money in mind this time, only love—and with all the freedom to do whatever he chose whenever he wanted and with whomever, his generous heart betrayed him. Harvey up and died!

And the heat moved in.

We held a memorial for him in the park. A big one. Everybody came, brought food, drink and things to say and remember about him. Our town is still one that lets its folks express their grief in their own way, lay it out and mix it up so it doesn't hurt so much. No preachers. Just all of us talking about him, telling stories of our time with him, things he said, things he did, what he meant to us. Harvey's spirit was right there that day, moving among us, telling us to get on with it, laughing at us, caressing us.

And we all knew it. For me it was really tough because I had to sing his favorite song. I ain't no Judy Garland, I can't sob and sing at the same time and I was holding tight to a big aching bubble as I tried to get the words out. Then, I felt Harvey pat me on the bum, right in the middle, right in the hardest part-hardest part of the song, not my bum—and through my tears I almost ended up laughing, which is no better than crying when you're trying to sing

Then the heat bore down.

The first year he was here he was my next door neighbor. I won't forget the day he first walked down the street in front of my gate with a couple of his friends. I was out watering the nematodes that like to make my carrots into funny little men with penises and hair all over them, when he stopped laughing at whatever his friends had said, turned his flax-blue, slightly bulging eyes on me and supposed: "Ooooh! You must be the lovin' lady (lovin' as opposed to lovely I noted right away and he knew that I noted, which is what blew me away), the lady I'm going to live next door to?"

Harvey had class!

I am a lovin' lady, though I try hard to disguise it, which is why lotta people don't call me a "lady." I could care less. (I've always maintained—for those who believe in such messy-physics-moon-shine—that being a Scorpio, right there on the cusp of Libra, the balance of the Scales keeps me from being a total bitch.) Gimme a break. Harvey did.

He sure enough rented the house next door. Every morning from his back deck when I came out with my cup of coffee, he'd wing his sweet morning greeting across my yard, "How-dee-doo, Miss Kitty Lu—you feeling fine today?" He never started working until after nine o'clock because his electric sanders and shapers and drills would make too much noise. (A caring man among his other talents—like he loved music, jazz, folk, Cuban, but he played it benignly, not at 2,000 decibels like some twits in our built-like-a-Greek-auditorium-town do.)

By the time I returned from my morning ride, I'd find him nearly smothered in clouds of alabaster and marble dust, tooling away at some beautiful sculpture he was creating. He'd ask me to come over and check it out—see if it looked all right. Wow!

He sure didn't need my two-bits, his pieces were always elegant. Never mind that it was a media he'd never worked in before—his imagination was limitless, his gift, divine.

Then he bought a broken down little house up the mountain a ways with an outbuilding he could make into a studio, and began its renovation like a doting father building a dollhouse for his beloved daughter. I don't think a nail or a board went into that place without his kiss, or his blessing on it—that it be happy there—happy like he was, and "thank-you-very much for being such a beautiful piece of wood and for coming from such a fine tree in such a lovely forest."

"But where, Harvey?"

"I don't know, but it's a fine tree, just look at that lovely, graceful and oooh ... sensuous grain!"

Key word. Harvey was indeed a sensualist. He had an open Jeep, little runt of a thing it seemed for a guy as big-boned and tall as he was. Drove it with his girlfriend through rain or shine, snow or hail, through forest and desert. In summertime, all over the back roads, windshield down, canvas off, toodling up and down the mountains in his hirsute and shorts, his ponytail straight out in the slipstream—winter it was khakis, jacket and headband, maybe with the top up, maybe not. Rarely did I see the side-curtains except on the floor of his studio.

About a week before he flipped his coin for the "other side," I stopped by his shop with some friends to show them the lovely things he made—I often did that, especially after he'd grown a new wig-bubble and made something that nobody even dreamed about. It was ladders this time. Crazy ladders like some that might have come from a ceremonial kiva back a thousand years ago, except that they were so beautifully and imaginatively carved, they'd have to have been used only by a shaman for special initiation purposes- twining snakes and lizards slithering up the rails and whole Pueblo villages on the rungs that you stepped between as you went up from desert floor to mountains near the top. They were transcendental!

His blue bulbs seemed to be dancing to extra potent jazz that day. He pulled me into a corner and whispered, "Just got back from the Apple, baby, and I dropped a shitload of problems back there that I won't ever have to deal with anymore. I'm never going back. Wow—do I feel great!"

I was so happy for him, knowing how he hated going to New York for anything, except to show his rarefied Arizona girlfriend something she never need worry about missing.

After the memorial, the heat became grotesque.

Nothing short of our Main Street knee deep in rattlesnakes will keep the damn tourists out of here, but the weather that week was proving to be a deterrent of the same magnitude. Shopkeepers were kvetching and moaning "no business"—never mind that most of them came here as artists or Flower Children to enjoy life, grow a little pot on the back deck, and just incidentally make enough to pay the bills, before they opted for a Chamber of Commerce, after which violation, as Ed Abbey said, you can kiss your town goodbye. Friends were snapping at each other like looney birds in a tank of toxins and the humidity was a wet, down comforter under a 110-degree heating pad. Even at eight o'clock in the morning, pulling on my Lycra shorts and top was a sticky chore.

That's when I decided to do it.

I ride my bicycle up the mountain about three miles from the house five days a week, before the traffic gets repulsive, if possible. I've been doing it for almost 30 years, so people are used to it and pay me no mind. (Had the first mountain bike in town—1980, I think, when I was 60 years old—and I took all the outlying cowpaths with the same sort of joy and devil-may-care as Harvey did with his Jeep, 15 years later.) That morning was no different with regard to the joie-de-vivre. I always love the ride because of the canyon, once I get above town. The rocks are so beautifully cruel; deep maroon, red and orange and pale sheeny-green in ragged pinnacles and spires, spit from the pit of the earth into great ridges and crevasses that time can't seem to smooth over. The smell of juniper and mountain earth is heady under early morning sun before cars and motorcycles take over the highway with their noxious fumes, and there's a sometime-creek rippling below the winding road where canyon wrens sing their sweet song down the scale. All this adds up to perfection, or as close as you can get to it— on a paved road.

It's my meditation time, too, that ride. I sort out everything for the day, the week, sometimes the month. It's where I learn the lyrics to new songs—up, on up, to a rhythm of the pedal's turning—where I find inspiration for a story, a show, a letter or a melody.

And the reward! All downhill at 25 to 30 mph-cooling the sweat, blowing through my helmet, down my back and neck, even through my shoes! Ya-hooooo!

So... 8:00. I got on my Trek and pedaled up through town. Didn't stop at the P.O. for my mail, it wasn't in yet; besides which, I was looking very hard for special little nooks and hidey-holes that could assist me on the way back down. My heart was beating a bit faster than usual—the adrenaline of anticipation already started.

I must not have been paying close attention to everything like I usually do, because the "beep" from behind startled me. After 30 years I can hear cars coming both ways before they get anywhere near me—it's an acoustic mountain—I can identify locals from tourists and tune in the driving "mood of the day." There is one, you know—fast or slow, frantic or relaxed—it infects the whole road like a virus. That day it was relaxed, nobody on the road but me. The beeper wasn't a local—they don't beep—so I looked in my bike mirror and saw... Harvey's Jeep!

I'd been thinking about him so hard, my sadness turning to giggles as I rode, picturing what a hoot he would get out of this caper, that for a second I just accepted it.

When I remembered him being gone, I nearly fell off my bike. But it wasn't his Jeep, just some slow-driving, far-more than-ordinarily polite dude trying not to run over me.

I got to my rock under the tree, ducked in, sat down and poured half the water bottle over my head. Cooling down, I rested there in the shade for about fifteen minutes.

Even so, my heartbeat was much faster than usual.

So... 9:15. I had chosen my spot on the way up.

As I zoomed down the mountain and through the upper residential section to the turnoff that goes to the open pit, I was so exhilarated, so hyperventilated, that the wind made me shiver. No one in front of me—good. No one behind—even better. Very few cars on Main Street (the only level spot in town) and I didn't see anyone walking the street.

I darted in behind Robby's antique ore truck-yanked off my Lycra, everything but helmet-socks-shoes, mounted the Trek, buckass, and pedaled furiously through the center of town, past the P.O., past the shops, the bars, Town Hall, Police office... Oh-oh!..never had I seen our Town Marshal (as he liked to be called) out in front of the cop shop, but there he was, in a blur, talking with someone beside him. He looked up, automatically began a wave... Hull... ohh, (double take) Kay—t-e-e-eeee?!

I was gone!

Faster then, working the brakes, no more level ground. As I passed Harvey's empty shop, I looked up and cried out—"Harvey... this is for you, Harvey, Bye-bye!" The last half-mile to my front gate, I was laughing so hard I could hardly steer and hoping to hell no one would pull out in front of me, when up came Wally, one of our town crew, in the frontloader. You got this? These are no-passing, two-lane roads, barely, and behind him was a whole string of tourists, 10 or more cars long, chugging along at 3 miles per hour.

Hoo-eee! What an opportunity!

"Ole!" I yelled, as I sailed by, "Welcome to _____! (You cannot have the name, you won't like it here.)

In my mirror, I saw arms flapping out windows and a couple got out and stared downhill, not at all sure of what they'd just seen.

My uproarious laughter had turned to streaming tears and coughing by the time I hooked a U-ie in front of my gate, hauled in, decked the bike and headed for the shower, where I sat down under the spray and howled.

Still wired and laughing, my tummy sore from it, I dressed, got in the car and drove up town. I knocked on the Police Chief's door, walked in and said, "You wanna arrest me, Ray?"

He just looked at me, shook his head and sucked in the corners of his mouth to keep from laughing. "I thought about that," he said, "but what exactly would I do?"

"Yeah, that could pose a problem," I answered—picturing him chasing me down with the cop car, getting out, yanking me off the bike, steering me onto the seat, nude-o, and driving me up to the office.

"Phones are ringing like crazy (as was his), you certainly gave the town something to talk about."

"That was the object of the exercise, Ray. Everybody's so damn glum they need something to distract them; besides, hardly anybody saw me, there weren't more than three or four people on the street."

"Enough. I took a consensus and asked them, 'Well, is anyone deeply offended?'

Only the retarded son of one of our emporium owners raised his hand and said, 'I am,' so I told him to go chase you down the hill and tell you so."

His phone was still ringing. Ray ignored it. "You going to make this an annual event?" he queried.

"Absolutely not. I like to quit when I'm ahead..meanwhile I'm going to enjoy what all the hardnoses have to say—the old farts who need their blood stirred up. As for my friends, they'll just laugh their butts off."

There was, as expected, quite a reaction-notes, phone calls and letters—only one anonymous, which wasn't really bad. The next day, tacked up on the post office bulletin board, there appeared an Ode to me and my stunt, and folks were smiling again.

The town had lightened up, and I had purged the heavy loss of our dear Harvey.

Before the weekend, it rained and cooled the town down right smart. I ran into friend Mod-Bob at the P.O. and stopped to chat. Underplaying it, he eyed me sideways from beneath his brows, and sneaky-like, whispered, "I saw ya."

"Oh, yeah? I didn't see you—where were you?"

"Sittin' on the bench in front.out there...by the Nellie Bly," he misered it out, one word at a time, "Hollered...but you weren't lookin'."

"Nope," I laughed, "I was in kind of a hurry."

"Uh-hh... ya think anybody got any photos?"

"Gawd, I sure hope not!"

"Yeah..uhhright." Then he looks at me straight on, eyes dancing, his face nearly fractured by his smile, and says, "B'cause I thought you had... your backpack on backwards."

The nerve of that boy!!

—*Originally appeared in* Mountain Gazette 78, *2000.*

6.
The Guardian of Sleep
Written by Jeremy Bernstein

"The interpretation of dreams is the royal road to a knowledge of the unconscious activities of the mind."
—Sigmund Freud

1.

It is Paris. It is winter. We have just made love. It has been a failure. Our separation has been too long and our reunion too painful. It is early afternoon.

She is next to me in bed, her face buried in a pillow and her naked back curled into a question mark. I know what she would say if I were to ask her what was the matter. She would say, "I have no feelings." She would not say, "I have no feelings for you." This would end our love affair and, as yet, neither of us has had enough courage to do that. How can one end so many months of experience shared?

Each corner of Paris contains memories for both of us. I can hardly think of any street without thinking of her. I cannot imagine a future for myself which does not include her. She has gotten out of bed and I can hear the water running in the bath. I can imagine her settling herself in the bathtub and covering herself with warm water like a blan-ket. I find myself staring out the window at grey Parisian sky—the jigsaw roofs of Paris.

I feel like a small child being punished for something he can vaguely perceive but cannot understand. What is it like to have "no feelings?" I can only think of people who die by freezing. First they are in pain and then they become numb. The danger for people exposed to extreme cold is that when they start to become numb they lose all will to resist. They do not want to return to life and they die peacefully. I have heard of such people in the mountains. They must be aroused-often brutally shaken and even slapped until they return to life, often against their will. Perhaps I should shake her and return her to life. But what kind of life would it be and would I be part of it? Freud once wrote that every sexual act was a "process in which four persons are involved." Who were the other two in bed with us this afternoon? Does she have a lover or were the others simply memories of what each of us had once been to each other?

2.

I have been having a recurrent dream. In it I am to give a lecture or take part in a play. She will be there and I have promised to save her a place in the theatre. She has arrived and I am trying to find the place I have saved for her. My search takes me farther and farther from the stage and becomes more and more futile. From time to time I remember that I am to deliver some sort of speech from the stage. The notes for my speech are in a briefcase that I am carrying. I have not had time to look at them and have no idea what it is that I am supposed to say from the stage. I will have no time to look at them because of the search for the missing place. As we get farther from the stage she becomes more and more scornful and eventually vanishes. Freud once described dreams as the "guardians of sleep." I have often wondered just what he meant.

After having read Freud I picture dreams like watchdogs perched beside my bed as I sleep. But what are they supposed to frighten away? What is more frightening than the dreams themselves? What is it that the dreams are guarding us from?

3.

It is winter. It is Chamonix. I have told my friends that I have come to Chamonix to go skiing. It is true that I have brought my skis to Chamonix. I had a friend once who came to Chamonix to "go skiing." He was an expert mountaineer and knew every glacier in Chamonix like a brother. He took the cable car to the top of the Aiguille du Midi to ski down the Valée Blanche. He had skied down the Valée Blanche a hundred times and knew the glacier like a friend. The tracks of his skis disappeared at the edge of a large crevasse— perhaps 300 feet deep. They never found the body. They said it was an "accident." I knew better. A few days before he left he had come to see me. He had been having severe recurrent headaches for nearly a year. Much of the time he was unable to work. He told me he was going to Chamonix because even though the medical specialists had been able to find nothing wrong with him and no cure, he was sure that in the high altitudes and pure air he would discover a way to stop his headaches. As far as I know Freud never addressed himself to the physical aspects of skiing so that we are free to make of it what we will.

4.

The water has long since stopped running in the bathtub. She has taken her bath, gotten dressed and is ready to go out. I am to walk her from the Left Bank where I live to the Right Bank where she works. It is a walk we have taken hundreds of times. We will pass by the Ile de la Cité and stop for a moment or two on the banks of the Seine. In earlier days, we would walk arm in arm. She would, from time to time, nuzzle against my shoulder like a gentle grazing animal. We would say nothing because nothing needed to be said. Today we will say nothing because nothing can be said. We have taken the steps down to the banks of the Seine. From underneath a nearby bridge there emerges a small band of young people each carrying a flower. One of the girls is laughing but each time she laughs too hard she sits down in the middle of the walk and sobs uncontrollably. They are having difficulty walking straight and I am afraid that one of them will fall into the river. They have all passed by except for one boy who has stopped to stare at us, his eyes wide open, like two great lamps. He looks extremely cold, his thin body barely covered in jeans and a tattered jacket.

First he studies one of us and then the other. Nothing has been said and we are all transfixed in each other's eyes. Finally he leans forward to whisper in my ear. He points at her with his finger and whispers, "*Elle—elle est trop bien pour toi*," and disappears after his friends. "What did he say?" she asks. "I couldn't understand his French," I lie. "He must have been taking drugs."

5.

In 1907 in his "Obsessive Actions and Religious Practices," Freud describes a woman of about 30 who had been separated from her husband for several years. (In these descriptions we are never told the color of the woman's hair or if she liked music or even what first attracted her to her husband, unless these are somehow specifically relevant to the analysis.) Several times a day this woman would run from her own room to another in which there was a large table with a tablecloth on it. She would arrange the tablecloth in such a way that a prominent stain on it would be most visi-ble. She would then ring for the maid and send her out on some trivial errand, always making sure that the maid had seen the stain on the tablecloth. Freud discovered that on their wedding night the woman's husband had been impotent and had come running into her room several times to try to make love but to no avail. (Why, on their wedding night, they had separate rooms is not explained.) In the morning, he was so ashamed of himself that he had stained the sheet with red ink so that the maid might think the marriage had been consummated. Freud concluded that the woman's obsessive act was still an attempt to justify to the maid the behavior of her husband on his wedding night.

I find this analysis convincing but incomplete. I would like to know the feelings of the maid. Was she able to wash out the ink stain or did she simply throw away the sheet? What were her thoughts when she was summoned again and again to look at a stain on the tablecloth? If it were me, I would have taken the tablecloth and thrown it out the window. Although born in 1856 to a family in modest circumstances, by 1907, Freud had entered the professional middle class. He too, no doubt, had maidservants who came and went, clearing away the dinner dishes. We are all mired in the limitations of our environments.

6.

It is late afternoon in Chamonix. I have taken one of the last cable cars to the Aiguille du Midi carrying my skis. There are no other skiers in the cable car. No one would run the Valée Blanche on skis at such a late hour. I explained, when asked, that I was going up for the view and taking my skis so that they would not be stolen during my absence from the valley. We have reached the top and I have walked through the small tunnel leading from the cable car to the snow outside. Lights have been turned on in the restaurant above the cable car station. The cold is intense, and my lips and cheeks burn like fire. The wind whips needles of snow and ice into my eyes. I look down over the Valée Blanche. On the track there are long patches of blue ice with crevasses on either side. To ski on ice requires a special technique. One must traverse across the ice leaning down away from the mountain. This will make the edges of the ski grip and cut grooves in the ice. One must struggle against one's natural instinct to lean into the mountain—to hold it, to embrace it. This will only make the skis slip sideways along the ice—to become detached from the mountain and lead to a certain fall. Once a fall on ice begins on a mountain like this, one cannot stop himself.

7.

Some days have passed since we were last together in Paris and some days are still to come before I go to Chamonix. We have not spoken since our afternoon in bed. From time to time I reach for the telephone to call her only to find that somehow one of the digits in her telephone number has slipped my mind. By the time I have looked up the number in my book I no longer have the courage to call. She has not called either. This morning a letter from her has arrived. As usual it contains no name or return address on the back of the envelope. She used to say that she did this so that I would be happily surprised when I opened the envelope. By now the handwriting is so familiar that it is its own return address. I feel, before I open the letter, that I know what it will say. For some time I do not open the envelope. I am tempted to write on it, "No longer at this address—present address unknown," and to put her address on it and send it back.

Finally, I open the envelope. Her handwriting is very neat and bold. She is given to short sentences and brief letters. "You must know that there is nothing more between us.

During our last separation I met someone and have now decided to move to London with him. I do not regret the last two years. I hope you feel the same. Fondly.." A tidal wave of melancholy sweeps over me. I see an endless row of empty days and nights before me, aligned like unlit candles. My strongest urge is to sleep for days and to wake up somewhere else as someone else. I have told my friends that I am leaving Paris for a while to go skiing in Chamonix; to change air—*ça fait du bien.*

8.

In 1915, Freud wrote his celebrated paper "Mourning and Melancholia." The melancholic is often subjected to rages sometimes against others and frequently against himself. One of Freud's more famous patients-the Rat Man, so called because of a sordid fantasy he had involving rats—had been abandoned by a lady.

"On the day of her departure he knocked his foot against a stone lying in the road, and was obliged to put it out of the way by the side of the road, because the idea struck him that her carriage might be driving along the same road in a few hours' time and might come to grief against this stone. But a few minutes later it occurred to him that this was absurd, and he was obliged to go back and replace the stone in its original position in the middle of the road."

Freud points out that this behavior is more complex than might appear at first sight. To begin to comprehend it one must take into account the fact that the Rat Man replaced the stone at just the place where he thought the carriage of his lady "might come to grief." He was torn between the desire to injure his lady and to protect her.

Frequently the melancholic becomes partially identified with the loved one now lost.

His rage turns against himself in his identification with the lost object. In Freud's famous phrase, "The shadow of the object fell upon the ego."

9.

It is clear what I have come up here to do. All that is needed is to put on the skis, to point them down toward the Valée Blanche and to let myself go. Once on the ice there will be, there can be, no turning back. I cannot do it! It is not exactly fear of death.

I envisage death in the snow as a long sleep; numb with no feeling. It is the fact that she, in London with her lover, might never know or hardly care. I have collapsed onto the snow and have begun to weep uncontrollably. Two men have come out of the restau-rant, through the tunnel and toward me in the snow. Each takes an arm and partially carries me towards the warmth of the restaurant. As we go through the tunnel, one says to the other, "These Parisians—the thin air up here makes them a little crazy."

—*Originally appeared in* Mountain Gazette 9, *1973*.

7.
Hallucinations

Written by Barry Corbet

I have a friend who saved for long years to buy a sailboat. The sailboat was to give him freedom. About the time he had accumulated enough money to buy the boat, he discovered that there was no place to go. That was a colossal disap-pointment, he said.

Last May, I had accumulated enough time to go somewhere for three weeks. I had no sail-boat, so I pondered where to go. To my colossal disappointment, I could find no place to go.

In front of me is an Executive Planner. It has few entries because I normally am so overwhelmed by executing that I have no energy for planning. A notation for Saturday, May 25, says "Go to cabin?" I suppose that some crazy evening I must have actually decided to spend three weeks by myself in a one room cabin in headlong retreat from phone, liquor, electricity, running water and relationships—all the scary things in my life.

I looked forward to this trip as I energetically met film deadlines, overreacted and, in general, indulged in a manic speed trip. No matter—I knew I was soon to be going no place with nothing to do.

The rules:
- Take two serious books for edification and reflection, but not for entertainment.
- No dope, pets, or people.

- No music-making, writing, painting, photography or other habit forming activity.
- Go somewhere and live with yourself.

I cheated. I took three liters of red wine, one for each week. I took my Executive Planner, in which I sometimes wrote a maximum of 2 column inches a day. The books I took were *The Lazy Man's Guide to Enlightenment* and *Cutting Through Spiritual Materialism*. I would prefer not to tell you that, but I have no choice. I cheated further by taking *A Field Guide to Rocky Mountain Wildflowers*.

I feel that I should tell you why I made this decision to disappear for a while: I felt pressed by professional and domestic conflicts, and I wanted to suspend them for long enough to see if either my problems or my sense of being victimized by them would go away. I also lusted after Sensible Alternatives. The following is inflated from my Planner.

Day l: cabin. A stupefying hangover prevails, because friends had dropped in on the eve of my departure to celebrate my foolishness. Everything happened last night; nothing is happening today. I'm content, since I know how good things are going to get.

I worry about the overlay of Eastern mystique that hangs around things like this. I think there's both a mystery and a message in my solo, but it's all so damn trippy that it seems sort of precious. Mystery + message - mystique.

I wrote the account of my 22 days at the cabin just recently, three months after the fact. To put the experience into a more "worldly" context, I've added another 22 days to the mix. There was no attempt at consecutive ordering made here. These are just some of my days, without the mystique.

Day l: world. A client finds out his contract doesn't include something big that he's already promised to his management. How could he be so naïve? Am I the keeper of my brother's illusions? I am.

I speed to the downtown office, attempt to reconcile my various prose styles, research all the ingredients carefully and write a letter that refuses to choose between alternatives. It scathes and consoles. It's an onslaught of good will, right thought, venom and threat. They'll love it because I'm in the right. So are they, but that's their problem.

Day 2: cabin. Evidently, nothing happens again. There is no entry in my Executive Planner.

Day 2: world. Yesterday's problem client calls to express his good feelings, and I wish I hadn't written. But he frees me to do what I do, which is edit film.

But this film appalls. All of our films are misleading in one way or another, but this one is 18k raunch. Funded by a Midwestern bank, its warped objective is to depict the good life as perceived by the bank's loan officers.

It's the good life for the teeming blacks and Polacks because of all the socially redeeming industry that exists to employ them into grateful consumers. It's good for industry because of all the toilet trained labor that consumerism makes available.

Highly-Semi-Skilled Hype. Good for the bank because of loans to labor and industry alike. How beautiful is the garden...

Day 3: cabin. Memorial Day. Visitors. A young couple on horses. A strident voice from a concealed man in a wheelchair (me):

"Would you mind going back the way you came?"

"Private property?"

"Yup."

They wheel their horses in acknowledgment of Private Property Rights. Aghast at

myself and then at them, I return to the vigil. Repression.

More visitors. Two men and a daughter approach on horses. A voice from the woods once again requests withdrawal. This time, an adult in very full chaps detaches himself and lopes voiceward to parley. Intimidation: big horse, small wheelchair.

"You own this place?"

"Yup."

"I live in Paradise Hills."

"Great."

"You can ride from here all the way to Central City."

"Mmmm."

"You all alone here? Why do you want to be alone?"

"Religious reasons." (Holy, holy.)

"What's your religion?"

How the hell should I know? I decline to answer.

"There's no 'No Trespassing' sign up there."

He's right. "I know—I'm sorry to do this to you, but I really need to be alone."

"I'm sorry you feel that way."

"So'm I."

He leaves, without sensing that I admire his good balance in the face of hardship. He pauses to explain this unexpected turn of events to friend and daughter, then moves off toward the end of the trail.

It's still Day 3, a long day. More visitors. This time two four-wheel-drive pickups clatter importantly toward me. I am mindblown, outraged, undone—for the enemy is here. A redneck father and semi-longhaired teenage son occupy the first cab, and I'm out of words:

"I really don't like people driving over this land. I just don't like it."

"How'd you get here?"

"I drove."

"Well, I've been trying for three years to find a way from here down into Clear Creek, and I thought this might be the way," he says like some nouveau Vasco de Gama.

"It's not. U.S. 6 goes there."

"Listen, I'm willing to talk to anybody, mister, but I want him to meet me halfway.

I mean. I want him to be friendly." He says this defensively, eyeing his young son as if he's looking in a mirror.

"Look, I'm really sorry that I'm not being friendly (true becoming false), but I just

don't want trucks down here."

"Listen, we didn't hurt your goddam road at all. Not one goddam bit," he says in triumph, and backs up to confer with his friends. They talk for a long, long time, produce no rifles and leave.

What should I learn from these encounters? Who was worse? Is it wrong to want to be alone? Is it wrong to hatefully and unjustly assume that all people in four wheel-drive pickups are mobile insults?

I take a felt pen, a shingle and a 2x2; and I make a sign that says:

PLEASE
PRIVATE PROPERTY
NO HORSES, JEEPS, ETC.
NO THROUGH ROAD OR PATH
NO BULL!
NO OFFENSE?
THANKS

I drive to the cattleguard and plant the sign. I guess it's significant that I have no more gate-crashers during the remainder of the three weeks. Holy, holy.

I also have time to decide on this long day that there are only two kinds of films: Films to persuade. Films to open.

This consideration seems important. I also consider, with coaching from *Cutting Through*, that my thought patterns act as excellent ego-defenses.

Day 3: world. I ply my trade, converting footage into film. This film I struggle with is persuasive if you don't see the relationships involved, or naïve if you do. I derive perverse pleasure, an opening experience of sorts, by cutting the chrome and glass and steel of modern buildings to Bach's Third Suite. The cutting of visuals can reflect the tempo and mood (and even the intent?) of the composer so accurately that Bach seems to exalt what man hath wrought in downtown Milwaukee.

Alchemy.

Day 4: cabin. All-out war on overlapping thought patterns in an effort to be alone, to be nowhere. It's discouraging to find that the mind natters incessantly as if it had an audience.

I sit for a time in a swale filled with flowering dandelions and consider this thing.

As I sit, I feel some love, although it may be only an affinity for dandelions. I call it a technical success, and take the money and run. Exploitation, beauty, peace and awareness have no real collateral.

Day 4: world. Trade-plying. Vaguely pleasant. I put off my partner, who is returning from New York tonight and who might want to stop for a drink. Why does that make me feel guilty? Wanting to be alone is tantamount to being unfriendly. And, for that mat-ter, I don't even know why I want to be alone tonight. To write this? To be free not to cope? The fear of invasion of privacy is the fear of being discovered. I hide. The only thing worse than being discovered is being discovered hiding. The risks compound.

On Gaffer Tape: *Gaffer tape is a wide, gray, sticky substance used to pack or secure film equipment. It resembles duct-tape, but is much stickier. Gaffer tape is exceedingly sticky. You can attach anything to anything with gaffer tape. It always stays stuck. Very sticky stuff. Insatiably glommy. It's a very comforting product, for it sticks your stuff together.*

Now, as you become older and wiser, you watch your personal drama unfold with less and less cohe-sion. You lose what you had, you gain what you don't need, and you require more energy to remain in place.

You acquire so much information and concomitant interpretive baggage and opinions and openness to new opinions that nothing can be guaranteed to be right. Absolutes fall away like flies, the reality depends upon the perceiver and nothing can be believed with confidence. This is a definite problem for beings.

The answer is gaffer tape. Gaffer tape enables you to enlist all the fine properties of stickiness in your own favor—just take all the fractured elements and stick them together in any old order. Doing that creates a cohesive entity that can be identified and therefore related to in safety. Maybe that's how we stick it to ourselves. We try too hard to keep it all together. There should be some way to neutralize the use of gaffer tape, or at least keep it judicious. Fly-paper is useful for catching flies, but you want to be able to step out of it if you fall in yourself.

The only clue I have to this dilemma, and I find the idea troublesome, is that Time is quite a lot like gaffer tape. They're both useful ways of arranging events.

Day 5: cabin. Excess baggage—more travail with the Dread Natterer.
Natterer: Regretful Rehasher—"Look what I've done."
Coach and Commentator—"Look what I'm doing."
Future Fantasist: "Look what I'll do."
Nasty Natterer.

Day 5: world. My enthusiasm for this piece has waned, and I've taken a week off from my book of days. Why publish this drivel? That's *Mountain Gazette*'s problem. Given a publisher, one publishes. Who's at fault?

Day 6: cabin. Milarepa, a 10th-century Tibetan yogi, encountered demons that had "bodies big as thumbs and heads like plates." Demons, to Milarepa, were manifestations of his own negative energies.

My demons are also as big as a thumb, and they manifest as bumblebees. They cruise in and out in amiable stupidity. Battering from surface to surface like bumpercars, and I struggle with my noisy demons. I feel possessed.

With nothing to do, I try really and truly to do nothing. I can't. I'm trying to stop trying. I need a gap.

Day 6: world. Five separate films, and their sponsors, nag me with disruptive detail This wall of trivia needs to be dispersed before craft can proceed.

If the mind is spared conflicting commands for a while, if it can relax and sense the overlapping qualities and similarities of the diverse material, then the elements of a film magically determine their own structure by being allowed to. Once the material makes its proper arrangement known to him, the editor is just a functionary who can splice. That's Phase One.

Phase Two is manipulative. After structured integrity is allowed to develop, then insidious intent runs wild, and the editor can challenge, threaten, stroke, alienate, seduce or coerce without either jeopardizing or enhancing the film's sound structure.

Structure is hardest, because it can depend upon tempo, mood, texture, story, shock, thesis, antithesis or nothing—or all of these things. It has to reflect what's there.

It requires a discovery.

Interpretation is the most fun, because you can use technique— like putting English on your serve.

Workability is a mixed bag in which you jiggle the objectives, prejudices, persistence and clout of the various forces involved in the film. The biggest force is usually the guy paying the bill.

Then you stick all those little stop-frames together, twenty-four to the second, and you watch the photons of your ego bursting all over the silver screen until they bounce back, repulsed, seeping like spilled milk onto the shag rug of the screening room ... such wretched excess.

Day 7: cabin. The Dread Natterer is perceived as an enzyme of insanity. Physical and mental defection. Eyes hurt and closely watched breathing scours the underbelly of my brain. I'm caught up with this nonsense and can't relax with it. This is the first time I've been worried.

Claustrophobia. It's too deep to breathe in.

Wine day! Wine is nice. The flight of the self vindicator.

Wine is nice, and, being newly unaccustomed, it makes me want to try things I wouldn't always do, such as dive naked into ant hills. It makes me euphoric and communicative. Loving. It allows examination of concepts, or non-concepts, unavailable to me when I'm deep throating the dharma. It gives me time.

Day 7: world. I took Willi Unsoeld back to the airport this morning and am left in contemplative shock. It's bizarre, after not seeing him for four years, to find how very much of our lives are common ground. Just one person acting out two fantasies. It's been years since I've felt like discussing my magnificent and crummy past with anyone, but Willi's past is mine and mine is his, and talking about it is like one ego getting off on the antics of its various aspects.

We use each other as mirror, blackboard, stimulant and antidote.

It's scary to ask myself if I have this relationship, latent or developed, recognized or not, with untold numbers of people. Hideous. Our Karass is in a sling. Let us go then, you and I, for we have no choice.

Day 8: cabin. Still driving wedges into my brain. Painful, powerful and scary. I chastise another bumblebee. A CAT! I see an enormous Siamese, or a puny Puma, slinky and beautiful, gliding between trees.

Day 8: world. Nothing much happened today, which is a relief.

Day 9: cabin. "Try to be as simple as you can," I tell my Planner. Minimum impact.

Day 9: world. Attending to busy-ness, and nothing gets done. I am irritated by the dedication required to maintain my speed and by the uselessness of speed maintained.

Day 10: cabin. At 4 p.m., I am stalked by CAT. While sitting, absorbed in other things, I have a peripheral flash that tells me CAT is crouched six feet away and working closer. I think of Castaneda and his friendly coyote. I think of madness and its messengers. For lack of communication, I think of conversation: "Hello, Pussy!"

Pussy bounds down the slope. I came to get empty, i.e., to become a suitable terminal for communication, and I can't even hold my tongue in front of the most quiet of animals.

I have a sense of aggression and speed refusing to slow down. Or of hope and fear refusing to strike a bargain. The cat is out of the bag and the fix is on. We are separate.

Day 10: world. If alienation stopped being bad, would sunsets stop being good?

Without expectation, can alienation exist? Without alienation, can dualism exist?

Without dualism, can sunsets exist? Hello, Pussy.

Day 11: cabin. It's a quieter, better day. I'm doing nothing in a more businesslike fash-ion, accepting it as hard work (does nothing need to be done?) instead of harboring anticipations of the beneficial results of doing nothing. Nothing times nothing is nothing and yields nothing. Except that the Natterer editorializes. Simplicity is no longer a consideration. Business as usual.

Day 11: world. Solar extravaganza. Red skies, red earth; alpenglow lights the powerline and Mother Cabrini's shrine. Would sunsets stop being good? Enigma pie.

Day 12: cabin. Depressed. Technique and dedication have failed utterly. One cannot be dedicated to nothing. Each thought pattern has its friends and relations.

Wine. Bad wine. For a while, I sit outside with bottle and glass on a stump, trying to feel the dignity of the occasion, but it's just bad wine. I go inside in time to witness a tableau. A teenage couple is passing by the cabin. The boy prances and makes insistent animal sounds. The girl, unamused, repeatedly screams, "Don't!" The charade is real, though they seem physically apart. "Don't, don't!" she cries, pleasantly terrified. The boy sees me leering from the window, waves with a high good humor as if we share a conspiracy, and continues the ritual. "Don'ts" echo from the forest as the couple proceeds.

I turn to serious matters.

Why, I thought, am I drinking lousy wine alone, trying to do nothing and indulging

in voyeurism? These were my reasons:

1) I want to create or experience a gap in the constant rush of thought and emotions with which I fill my days. Sub-reasons:

a. To let intuition get an anti-thought in edgewise.

b. To develop a sense of space, which in turn is (I'm told) characterized by enhanced awareness and compassion for self and others. I especially like *Cutting Through*'s notion of making friends with oneself.

2) I also want to reconcile form, or phenomena, with undifferentiated space. This subject is appallingly vast, unless (I'm told) you understand it. I don't. Why do I call it a subject if the object is to transcend the subject-object? I know nothing. I can't do nothing. I can't even experience nothing. When I die, I'll be a beginner at that too. Where should I start?

Day 12: world. Counterpoint: empty times playing against the sting of being alive. I convince myself that this thought is creative, not morbid.

Day 13: cabin. I have a moral hangover from last night's excesses. Speculation is not my strong suit, and I really feel I'm getting too serious about all this.

I wheel to the spring, scoop a hole in the mud and wait for the little pool to clear. A robin bathes first, then it's my turn for a cleansing. It rains. Everything feels good, as if good things are going to happen.

Day 13: world. A nice piece of relationship takes place today, and I feel cheerfully uncritical. I'm alone tonight for the first time in a week, and I have a rush of expectation at having no expectations.

Day 14: world. Lunched with a client. He was pleased with the commercials I'd made for him, and confirmed his euphoria with gin. Afterward, the color and whereabouts of his rental car had slipped his mind. I repeated directions to the airport and left him car-less, for I am not my client's keeper.

Day 15: cabin. Snow all day long on June 8. A beautiful, nice day. Neurological Buzz. It's easier to do nothing when it's so busy outside. If phenomenal flux were more constantly apparent, perhaps emotions would subside. In a snowstorm, it's hard to know which snowflake to focus on.

Day 15: world. Last night's emotional encounter caused today's hangover. Didn't it?

My goodness, I've been in the over-indulgence business for eighteen years, not knowing that I could do myself such a disservice.

Day 16: cabin. Wind and sun. Painful sunburn. I love it.

Day 16: world. Halloween. I masked off the screen on my editing table with gaffer tape to simulate a wide screen. I masked my feelings about Michigan spectator sports with devilishly clever cutting, and about a client who hasn't paid with hypocrisy. Children I know and love well arrived in monster masks clearly showing their true natures. Their chaperones arrived straight, unmasked, and seemed to be in relative drag. Who was that masked man?

Day 17: cabin. My eyes still hurt, as if I were breathing through them. If one seeks to prevent pain with each breath, one is busy as hell.

The understanding improves, but the condition prevails.

Last wine day. This wine is truly pigshit. As always, it triggers considerations, this time about my psychological set. This set is derived from the books I am reading, and from deep dissatisfactions that seem too close to the surface.

As I am trying to learn to see it, here's the scam:
- We are alienated from ourselves (i.e., rendered neurotic) by dualism, a mode of perception and intellectual thought that characterizes Ego. Neither dualism nor ego exist as things, but like a politician's media campaign, once they're postulated, their notions serve to influence and confuse.
- Ego perpetrates the dualist mode. Dualism serves ego. A circle jerk.
- At another level, dualism is the description of phenomena, space and whatever else exists, as either subject or object. Since this arbitrary separation helps ego see itself as discreet from whatever is not included in its own definition of self, ego and the dual-istic mode become inseparable. Ego is the tendency; dualism is the process. Perhaps.

- Since ego constantly changes its estimate of what's inside self and what's left over—the penchant being to assimilate as much as possible and to increase the Empire-the dualistic effort of data-processing becomes confused and erratic. The Peter Principle, over extended
- This erratic confusion generated by tendency and process creates malaise, which preoccupies us so intensely and painfully that we fortify our Private Ground (holy) against this suffering. But suffering is a basic condition of dualistic logic. Dualism is conflict. Conflict is suffering. Suffering is ego, the battleground mentality of subject-object departmentalization. Our fascination with suffering drives us to struggle against it. The struggle is the struggle.
- All we have to do, obviously, is to quit.
- Is that ALL?

It's very bad wine, and I plagiarize shamelessly. The people from whom I plagiarize probably don't care.

Day 17: world. I resigned from the American Alpine Club today.

Day 18: cabin. A good day, a good supper-why is this evening so bottom-line bad? No one is here, nothing is wrong, and my bummer is demonic and complete.

I didn't know I could do that all by myself.

I've read a Tibetan parable of a monkey locked in a house of his own creation. He experiences various states of despair and elation as he tries to escape his condition, but nothing really works. He's still imprisoned by his hallucinations. The solution, the tale goes, is to recognize and laugh at the hallucinations.

I take comfort in the notion of laughing my way through the hallucinations, but comfort is undoubtedly a cruel hoax. Still, the idea appeals.

Day 18: world. I had an easy and disappointing day today. I showed our client in Michigan his new film depicting the pathetic emptiness-yea, vicariousness-of a tourist's activities in his state. He was pleased by the accuracy of our statement, sure that Michigan's flagging tourism industry would be forever revitalized. I was pleased that this ugly duckling of a film had won his approval.

My related despondency stems from the idea that we pool our mediocrity. My client and me, we're proud to share the total pointlessness of what we say and do because we know that nobody will object. We're just playing the game, and you can tell the best players by their colorful uniforms...

Day 19: cabin. Uppers and downers. It's hard to laugh at the hallucinations. Laugh and the world laughs at you.

Today's hallucination is frustration. Vibrating intimately with frustration is frus-trating. Who could laugh except a frustrated cynic? I yearn tragically for a more convenient hallucination—perhaps I'll be a fireman when I grow up.

Day 19: world. I had an easy and disappointing day. I showed our client in Alberta his new film depicting the utter tragedy of marketing his beautiful province to the global letch for uncluttered real estate. He loved it, so we found ourselves in agreement.

We both get paid for what we do.

The reason the monkey is supposed to laugh his way through the hallucinations is that they're his own creations. Why would I make such a mess? How could I be so creative?

Day 20: cabin. Nothing.

Day 20: world. My dog cries outside this shed where I write. She doesn't like to be alone. She has a dream house of her own, and I'm IT.

Day 21: cabin. Pretty boring day. I'm sure getting ready to leave this place.

Day 21: world. Just finished *Tales of Power*. Castaneda makes me laugh and cry more than any other author. At the end, it's all warm tears. "We're all alone, Carlitos," don Genaro said softly, "that's our condition."

Castaneda makes me think longingly of sitting alone on a desert peak, waiting patiently to see the "lines of the Earth."

Day 22: cabin. What the hell is this? I arrived on a Saturday, left three Saturdays later, and it's one day more than three weeks. I've been cheated, detained by order of the hallucinator general, who can't even count.

In fact, this whole excursion seems like a dream, a hallucination of insight into insightlessness. There have been isolated instances of apparent timelessness, but these too are gone, safely gaffer-taped into continuity.

Day 22: world. I can't say that any one series of days was better, harder, spacier or more instructive than the other. I'm not sure that one even influenced the other. They're just days, without any psychological or moral valence. While I vividly remember occasional yearnings for convenience and companionship while I was gone, I now find myself subject to periodic urges to disappear again.

I'm glad I went away, and I know I'll do it again. I have no idea where I'll go next time, or what I'll set out to accomplish. If I'm lucky, of course, there will be no place to go and nothing to do.

I'm looking forward to it immensely.

—*Originally appeared in* Mountain Gazette 33, *1975.*

8.
Hanging Around
Written by David Roberts

"This is all very different from the South Col!" you can remark crisply, as you watch bikini-clad girls swarming over the rocks like chameleons.
—Tom Patey, The Art of Climbing Down Gracefully

One cringes at belaboring the obvious. But every once in a while the need for such an article as this arises. Traditions grow fuzzy, and the legends of one generation need footnoting in the next. In my recent rambles around the climbing world, a melancholy fact has gradually nagged its way into my consciousness.

The fact is this: There is emerging upon us right now a whole new crop—one would be tempted to call them a "school," but for their woeful ignorance—of young, dedicated climbers who have got the most central tenet of mountaineering ass-backwards. For their benefit, and at the risk of sounding pontifical, I here reaffirm that tenet. Namely, that the very object and essence of mountaineering, its be-all and end-all, is Hanging Around. All else is peripheral, a distraction.

The youngsters, it grieves me to report, can be seen everywhere these days obtusely infringing upon the long-established convention of Hanging Around. Some of them, for instance, behave in a climbing store as if it existed in order to sell them equipment to go out and abuse the cliffs with-not as a hanging-around scene for its own sake, sufficient unto itself. Others can be observed leaving a bar at 10 p.m. in order to get "an early start" in the morning. Some actually come to slide shows to get ideas for expeditions. I do not exaggerate. In general, there is a disturbing tendency among the young generation to take climbing itself altogether too seriously-which cannot but lead to a deplorable loss of finesse and subtlety when it comes to Hanging Around.

For their sake, then, and for the sake of posterity, which seems to have a knack for losing track of the most obvious facts of the past—it takes My Secret Life, for example, to remind us that English women wore no underpants before the 1870s—I shall set down here in cold print the hows and whys of Hanging Around, as it was practiced in the golden heyday of mountaineering, by the best climbers in every civilized nation, some few of whom I was privileged to loiter and vegetate with in their best days.

The Climbing Store. It is important to realize that the climbing store exists not to sell equipment but as a mutual sniffing ground in which mountaineers establish their credentials. The essence of proper behavior, as in so many climbing scenes, is not to try too hard. The climbing store is particularly effective in allowing the local talent to size up the visiting outsider, and vice versa. The game is harder to play for the outsider, since indifference and disdain come automatically to the proprietors, who are sick to death of selling kiddie-packs and freeze-dried lasagna. There are a few tricks, however.

For instance, in Southern California you can usually get away with talking tents.

A successful dialogue might proceed as follows:

Customer (musing over the store's own design, prominently pitched in the front foyer): Very pretty. Nice colors.

Owner: Notice the extra-long sleeve door. And optional mosquito netting Customer (With a chuckle): Ah, yes, mosquito netting. What won't they think of?

I was wondering if you have something with a ridge pole, you know, a little sturdier?

(At this point it doesn't hurt to push skeptically against the tent wall.)

Owner: We do sell the Glacier Designs four-man. It's very popular with Sierra Club outings.

Customer: I was thinking, really, of a two-man. With snow flaps.

Owner: I see. For winter use...

Customer: Well, yes, of course, but really for next summer. Up North. I hate to spend so much money, but my old Alp Sport's in tatters.

And so on. In the East, talk jumars vs. Gibbs ascenders. In Boulder, cagoules. In Jasper, bivouac hammocks.

In the climbing store, of course, it is essential not to hang around too long. Twelve to eighteen minutes is about right. Longer brands you an equipment freak. And, of course, one does not browse among the books (implying unfamiliarity with the few good ones), but only among the magazines (implying that you would never subscribe to one).

Another gambit is to dash in and ask abruptly for a very specific item. Half a dozen nuts of the same size, say. If questioned, it is legitimate to mumble something about "taking the aid out of Steppenwolf"—but never volunteer this information.

It goes without saying that proper attire is vital. The sort of fellow who shows up in a climbing store with a nylon runner for a belt has blown it irrevocably. Likewise with worn climbing shoes, frayed knickers, or too conspicuous cuts and scratches on the backs of the hands. Greasy down jackets, however, are OK.

The Local Climbing Area. Here the important thing is not to get conned into climbing anything hard. A once-clever gimmick, now ruined by over-use, is to show up in sandals. (Future guidebooks will list first sandal-ed ascents; the standards are already tough.) However, fresh variations on the nonchalant just-happened-to-drop-by approach still work. A friend of mine recently scored valuable points at Carderock (near Washington, D.C.) by becoming the object of awe-struck whisperings: "You know ____? He doesn't even use chalk."

In the old days, a favorite way of beefing up local prestige was to take the visiting celebrity out to the local area, ostensibly "Just for a little climbing," but really to see what the hot-shot could handle. It's sad to reflect that even champions like Terray and Robbins fell for this trick, and struggled valiantly on 5.10s some local wizard had spent the last half-year perfecting. By now, of course, the visitor knows that all the hardest local climbs are hopelessly beyond him, and that the way to play the game is with studied magnanimity. Thus, the locals are in danger of blowing it themselves—as happened here a year or two ago, when, following a visit by Chouinard and Frost to the nearby climbing area, the local store wore its hero worship on its sleeve, immortalizing the visit in a poster-board display (photos of Chouinard's shoe poised exquisitely on a foothold) and repeating fervently to all who would listen Frost's assessment of a 15-foot aid climb.

"Yessiree, we don't do much in the valley that's that hard."

The local climbing area is an ideal place to show up with an ulterior motive: say, hustling a touch football game, or (although this is a trickier tack to take) soliciting information about the big climb planned for the next weekend at The Gunks. "Anybody know about the top pitch of Carcinoma? How's the protection?" The danger, of course, is that someone there will have done Carcinoma, or that someone else will remember two weeks later that you were going to do it last weekend.

If forced to climb, it is best to wander absent mindedly along traverses five feet off the ground. If you fall off, you can usually imply that you were trying it one handed.

Never bring a rope. The reason for not soloing climbs, naturally, is for fear of encouraging beginners who may not know any better. Groups of beginners have other uses, too: You can often claim that you showed up (and can persuade others to join you) just to watch the University Outing Club practicing prussiking.

The AAC Board of Directors Meeting. A very strange scene, one which, for better or worse, most mountaineers will never be privy to. The weekend of a directors meeting begins with a Friday evening cocktail party. The principle of the disguise, developed originally for use in climbing stores, seems to have reached macabre perfection here.

Most of the directors show up in business suits, wearing shiny black shoes, carrying attaché cases, talking committee reports. At the party, after hearty back-slapping, they drink—not beer or cheap wine, as in campgrounds the world over—but real cocktails, scotch-on-the-rocks in hefty belts.

The next day, during the business meeting, the directors continue the masterly charade. All of them display an astonishing familiarity with parliamentary procedure, and they sling around with Congressional pomp phrases like, "If the chair can prevail upon the head of the Rocky Mountain Section to instruct his membership that..." They seem to know about budgets.

There used to be a dangerous pressure at directors meetings to knock off Sunday and go climbing together. Fortunately, the business of the club has grown to such proportions that it can be counted on to spill generously over into Sunday afternoon. Thus the Board need not be haunted by the specter of an aging director securing the token Yosemite youngster with a classic European over-the-shoulder standing belay, or of a boozy ex-hard man developing sewing machine leg on a 5.4 move the day after a hard night arguing membership qualification standards for the AAC.

The Slide Show. Slide shows used to be fun, easy going. No longer. There was a time when you could get away with sunsets. Tilted climbing shots. Under-exposed bad-weather shots. There used to be a gentle give-and-take; the audience was on your side.

In fact, I can remember the hoary days when you could get a chuckle out of old chestnuts like, "The belay I gave Joe was a strictly psychological one," or, "Ten minutes after we climbed this slope it was swept by an avalanche."

Nowadays a slide show audience is hostile in proportion to its sophistication. This makes it very hard to give slide shows. Good photos are suspect; if you have time and the weather to take a beautiful picture, obviously it was posed, or at least you weren't spending all the effort you should have getting on with the desperate business at hand. Bad photos (poorly centered, out of focus, dusty, over-exposed) have their integrity. In fact, the perfect slide show, like Apollinaire's perfect poem, would have no pictures in it.

The right tone is extremely difficult to strike. One must imply that he is somewhat bewildered by all the fuss being made about some climb he and his buddies happened to blunder up last summer, that he is quite astounded to find anyone interested in the fact that he woke up one morning last January to discover himself in Patagonia at the base of Cerro Torre. The "what am I doing here?" tone is best, which modulates easily into, "Wouldn't it be more fun if we all went out to the local bar?" tone, which lends itself admirably to a transition to:

The Climbers' Bar. The bar, it is understood, is the place one goes to commiserate with other climbers when, darn it all, the awful weather has spoiled the climbing. Like the climbing store, it also serves as a mutual sniffing ground. Here the game is to figure out what route the other guys have up their sleeves, or, failing that, to imply that you have their much-coveted route up your own sleeve. I recall a conversation in a brightly lit bar in Banff (all Canadian bars are brightly lit) a few years ago with the resident master, who was quite suspicious of our plans. After the ritual pleasantries, he said:"Well, what brings you chaps up here?"

"Oh, nothing much," we answered cheerfully. "Some of the classic routes. Robson, maybe."

"Lovely mountain. We had a great weekend there in May."

Thus we had established that we were both after the same new route. Now the sniting got sharp. After half an hour's banter, we managed to compliment the old hand's route of a few years before on our intended mountain's north face. "Must have been a fine climb," we said.

"Nothing special."

"That route up the middle of the face would be something else. Scary, I'll bet." His eyes glinted. "Suicide, I suspect. When we were on our route, we saw this huge bloody rockfall sweep the whole thing."

He had scored there. We must have betrayed a little panic. "That's what I figured," one of our group managed lamely. "Anyway, after all this weather, a thing like that wouldn't be in shape till August. If then."

"Maybe not too hard a climb," the master said as he got up to play shuffleboard.

"Just suicidal."

That we were out the next day, nursing our hangovers on the hike in, was irrelevant.

The essential battle had been fought the night before. The master had won, by insinuating that we were crazy if we tried the route and chicken if we didn't.

Bars, too, serve as scenes for epic gross-outs and obscene displays. These are a specialty of the British. A rule of thumb to follow is, if you can't be spectacularly offensive, then get quietly drunk in your corner. Anything in between is bad form and smacks of seeking attention

Corollaries: Make sure you show up in the bar on marginal days—defined as days with any clouds in the sky. Only perfect weather, you want to imply, will lure you into attempting a scheme of the boldness of the one you and your cronies have been hatch-ing. And you need a few days of sun to get "the summit snowfields" in shape. There is a whole style of slouching, of brooding pensively, that reeks of hoarding strength and of building up psychologically. Cultivate it.

Bush-pilot Hangars. A scene requiring very adroit one upsmanship. The politics of hangar-waiting in Alaska, for example, during the mandatory three-day storm after arrival, are fairly subtle. One tries to imply an old friendship with the pilot, leading to the automatic assumption that he will take your party in first as soon as the weather clears, no matter when you showed up. Meanwhile, an air of calm confidence attends your perusal of the other groups' gear. The Japanese in Alaska always used to provide a few laughs. "Very interesting pickets," you would say, grinning, as you dubiously flexed their hopelessly flimsy stakes. "Pickets, yes," the Japanese would grin back.

"Much snow McKinley."

In Don Sheldon's hangar there were archaeological layers of leftover rations from past expeditions. There, behind the cartons of Pepsi, were Terray's lemon drops; and, yes, under them, could those be some of Cassin's meat bars? One liked to strike a pose of being willing to donate, say, an extra loaf of logan bread to that food museum.

Relations with the pilot himself are carefully ritualized. Self-evidently gauche is any palaver about how-soon-do-you-think-you-can-take-us-in—in a category of crudeness, really, only with haggling over rates. On those rare occasions when the man himself comes into view, one hallos out a hearty greeting, as if you are quite surprised to find him there, in the middle of your summer's food-boxing and equipment-puttering. Most coveted of all: the special invitation to have dinner in the pilot's own house, there beside the air strip. The green looks of envy on the others' faces, as they labor over the Sveas, are worth a whole expedition.

Finally: The International Scene. Having never climbed in the Alps, I consulted a friend just back from three years in Europe about the international scene. He had done some of his best hanging around in Chamonix. I was curious to know whether European climbers understood the traditions of the activity as well as Americans do. He was reassuring.

"Basically, in Chamonix," he told me, "the scene centers around two bars: the 'Nash,' or Bar National, and Le Drug Store. Only the English hang out at the Nash, which is a pretty raunchy place, small and seedy, with a foosball game and a one-eyed waiter named Maurice. At Le Drug Store, you find all nationalities. That's where the English go when they're looking for a fight."

"A fight?" Never in my climbing days had I seen a fight. American climbers are pacifists.

"Yeah. They hate the French. They get drunk and stand up on the tables and sing songs like, 'If you've never fucked a Liverpool man, you've never fucked at all. One day I was walking to this climb with some English guys, and they saw two other climbers in the distance. Naturally, they assume they're French. So they shout out, in inimitable Cockney, *'S'enculer!'*"

"Which means?"

"Roughly translated, 'Up yours!' There's a pause. Back comes a voice in inimitable French, 'Sheeet!"

"Why do they hate each other?"

"God knows. They're English. It's English to hate the French.

When I was there, I helped them heist a table from Le Drug Store to take out to their campground."

"A whole table?"

"Yeah. They camp on this private land owned by Snell's, the local climbing store. Snell's has a tacit agreement with the English: They can camp on the company's land, and in return they won't shoplift from the store."

"Weird. What about the others? Say, the Germans?"

"Oh, the Germans. They all camp in another campground, tents in perfect rows, neat and tidy. And the climbers are all very hardy looking, neatly dressed."

"But they hang out at Le Drug Store."

"Yeah. All except the Japanese, who are far too serious for the bars. The Japanese only know two words in English: 'North Wall."

"Not like the old Japanese in Alaska."

"Nope. A different generation."

"How about Americans? Besides yourself."

"Oh, there's a typical kid from Washington who's done all the 5.9s in the Seattle area. He's come over to do the Bonatti Pillar. The day after he gets there he hears two people are killed in the approach couloir. He manages to sprain his ankle falling off the boulder in the campground parking lot."

"I see why you associated with the English."

"Yeah. Hey, did I ever tell you the story of how MacInnes inherited Terray's down jacket after he fell off the statue and broke his leg?"

At least the English, I concluded, have the proper respect for the grand traditions of Hanging Around. While we were talking, a 15-year-old kid had just made the crux move on Amanita. Two 17-year-olds beside us were planning their expedition to Nuptse. An eight year-old girl in tennis shoes was perusing a well-thumbed guidebook.

We shook our heads, finished our peanut-butter sandwiches and headed down to Ramon's for a morning beer.

—*Originally appeared in* Mountain Gazette 19, *1974.*

9.
Crooked Road to the Far North
For Ajila, Whose Name Means Life
Written by Lito Tejada-Flores

At a beer garden in Berkeley, putting down a pint with my old friend, Chris Jones, the subject of summer climbing trips came up, and that's how I got back on the road. Chris had planned a mini-expedition to the Devil's Thumb, a redoubtable granite spire in Southeastern Alaska, with two Salt Lake City climbers, George and Jeff Lowe. Something had come up, Jeff couldn't go. Did I want to come? Sure.

The juke box was blaring out Elton John, the air warm with summer and tasty with pizza smell, students and freaks and half-naked chicks swirled around us; through the open patio, the popcorn machine was spitting and the avant-garde cinema beside us disgorged its Fellini-eyed crowd into the night. Not exactly an atmosphere for reflection but perhaps "up there" would be more real than "down here." Sure. We left La Val's drunk and enthusiastic. Chris and George would drive most of the way, via Salt Lake and Canada, as far as Prince Rupert. I would go by bus to Seattle, then ferryboat to Petersburg, Alaska, and meet them there. We'd fly into our mountain, air-drop our gear, and climb it, even if it took us a month.

We were laughing and joking, and it wasn't really too clear just what I was getting into. (On a last minute practice climb before leaving, I discovered how out of shape I was, and a real anxiety about the climb began to build up inside me.) But one thing was sure: Before I knew it, I'd be traveling again, stepping out, in the grip of strange currents again, and it felt good.

So it's starting again:
Once more, the mad
last-minute dash,
hastily packed bags,
smokey white tiles of
Greyhound waiting rooms.
Once more, the motives
are uncertain & the means
confused with the ends. Only
the need to go (but where?)
to do (but what?) to feel
again (but why?) is real.
So it's starting again:
Once more, my mind overflows
with debris from the future,
with scraps from the past:
sleepless nights, narrow seats,
wide country, endless roads...
Somewhere in the far north
a mountain will do for a goal.
And perhaps this time
the crooked road
will lead me straight,
instead of sending me off
again in search of myself,
starting again & again ...

Early in the morning in Seattle, bleary-eyed and loaded down with ragged old duffel bags, I find my way down to Pier 48. False front of wood and plastic, giant Indian totem designs, yellow and blue Alaska Marine Highway signs. Right away, I've got a problem: The list of walk-on passengers is full, closed. No, we don't make reservations, but all these folks came in yesterday; first time ever; we'll put your name on the standby list; yes, we'll know around three or four this afternoon. A helluva note. Only one boat a week from Seattle, and my friends up there waiting. Screwed. Well, what can I do but trust my Karma, again and always? Leave my pack and bags at the feet of a giant stuffed Kodiak bear in the waiting room and go out to see Seattle.

After an endless walk in cowboy boots, I decide to eat lunch at The Prague, a gallery/restaurant in a waterfront district of run-down brick buildings, slowly being remodeled into a funky, posh shopping area. I know it's overpriced but shrug my shoul-ders: There won't be anything like this up north...

> *Prague or Seattle, it's all the same,*
> *only the mind travels ... only the feeling*
> *that something is about to happen (or*
> *just has or is, right now, around*
> *the corner) counts. Why search for*
> *Gothic images here? Steinbruke or Golem?*
> *A skid-row panhandler meets me at the door*
> *& dust-mote light pours down green vines,*
> *shines the wooden floor, dusts old brick walls,*
> *starkly hung with post-Klee prints:*
> *this is post-Kafka Prague, post-Dubcek too.*
> *Only the mind travels... Beside my soup*
> *spotlights hit exploded heads, magic wheels,*
> *spikey suns & transcendental paddle boats*
> *gliding through intaglio seas of scratchy green:*
> *horses & priests & life & death & sex,*
> *safely under glass frames from West Germany.*
> *Waitresses without breasts shuffle by*
> *On three- inch cork heels... Only the mind travels!*

Lunch is good: watermelon and fruit, cold meat and cheese, a mysterious central European soup to go with the tangled images on the wall. It's two o'clock. Time to say goodbye to Kafka and Klee, Telemann and Bach on the stereo, time to say goodbye to Prague and

Seattle and, somehow, get on that boat to Alaska.

Back in the ferry terminal, the situation has deteriorated: There are now some 90 frustrated, confused people on the stand-by list (and a few really angry ones). Their story is the same: We telephoned from Tucson, drove all the way from L.A.; no plane till Wednesday; they promised; I told my husband, planned this trip for three months; they'll tell us at 4:00 a.m., no, at 5:00 a.m....

In the middle of this displaced-persons atmosphere is a lovely slender girl, tallish, in faded jeans and a big, loose Levi jacket. How do we begin talking? An unimportant, impersonal remark addressed at random to the milling crowd. A minute later she is say-ing, with a smile: Want to hitch-hike north with me if we don't get on? Inside me a small voice is already shouting yes, yes! I am surprised at myself. She has a little child and an enormous duffel bag. We compare luggage, miles, laugh at the impossibility of it.

Don't worry, we'll get on!..A long conversation begins. Something else has begun.

Her daughter's name is Ajila—a lovely smiling face, a snub turned-up nose, short blond pigtails. She sits between us on the high ticket counter and draws with a ballpoint pen on application blanks for MasterCharge cards. We exchange names, fascinating bits of information that unfold and unfold: Kathleen, unlike her daughter, has dark wavy hair pulled way back, a pale oval face with only two spots of color on her cheeks, prominent without being high-boned. A tiny gold dot in a pierced nostril makes me think of gypsies, central Europe, faraway places. She is beautiful without being beauti-ful. She doesn't sparkle, she glows. But she's real, she's tired, has real problems, a real mixed-up past, her own crooked road leading her north. She's going to Ketchikan to meet her old man, they'll travel, work, she's not sure, maybe she'll wind up working as a nurse as she did in Crescent City... Her dreams are close to the surface: She talks about going to South America someday, adopting a lot of kids... Ajila? It's an Arabic name, her father studied Arabic, no someone else, she married him to keep him out of the Army...

Around us people fester and complain. Behind the counter, the harassed clerks with their gold and blue ALASKA HOST pins pretend not to notice the people on the other side. But eventually the purser's list arrives with 96 free places: room for everyone, I think. My own name is third on the list. I buy my ticket and stagger to the gangplank under my enormous bags.

The M.V. Malaspina is so big that its levels, decks and passageways seem, at first, a labyrinth. I lug my duffel bags in relays to the solarium on the top rear deck of the big blue and white boat. This is home. What next? Look for Kathleen, of course. I meet her at the top of the stairway from the car deck; her bags are down there, so we go down again and I carry them up on deck. We're still amazed at having got on board at all. And we sit down, out of breath, and stare at Seattle, rising up the hill behind the waterfront in grey tiers of freeways and office buildings, a grey city under a cloudy sky. It looks like rain.

We relax, the three of us, on a wooden box-seat full of life preservers, peeling oranges while Kathleen makes cheese sandwiches from the food left in her old carpet bag. A bushy-whiskered, prophet-like figure of a man walks by (prospector? recluse? hermit?) dressed in Army fatigue pants and an old brown sweatshirt. Are you hungry?

Would you like some? Kathleen knows, offers, dispenses, smiles. Strange easy-going vibes are all around her, all around us.

Paul is, indeed, an old recluse with a philosophical bent, going up to Wrangell to "work in the woods." He takes me down to the deck below to show me a part of the ship he has "captured," hanging a large blue and orange tarp across a corner of the covered walkway. Beneath it are his incredibly worn-looking possessions and his pride and joy, a big black iron pot. He pulls two beers from a paper bag. One for your wife. No, she's only my friend. A strange rush of emotion that will be explained later, or never.

When we get back to the solarium, the ship is just casting off; silently, imperceptibly at first, the long wharves slide away from us, gathering momentum as the whole panorama of Seattle distorts, expands, recedes… It takes a long time to lose the city astern, but already we're in a new space. The North is already more real, our day-to-day lives already half-forgotten. Under threatening skies we enter another world:

Bluegreen water
beside
Greygreen forests
beneath
yellowgrey clouds
thru
The sundeck roof
where
Raindrops dance
on the grey
Plexiglass windows
& the grey
Velvet fabric
of dreams.

The solarium is full of backpackers, young people, freaks. Kelty packs and down sleeping bags are everywhere. Paul spreads a 100-year-old, hand-embroidered quilt on a kind of raised dais, like a legendary bearded pasha out of the Arabian Nights. Down inside the boat, there is a second scramble for the remaining staterooms. The other walk-on passengers, those of a certain age, or a certain lifestyle, will be spending the night stiffly upright in airplane-type lounge chairs. They don't look very comfortable, or very happy...

The evening is forever. Already the northern latitude gives us more daylight than we're used to. It's a late long twilight, the lamps are on, Kathleen and Ajila are tucked under a forest-green sleeping bag. I lie on my stomach on a deck chair beside her, and we talk, ask, answer, tell: What kind of women do you get involved with? A funny question, women like you. (My words surprise me, the feeling doesn't.)

Our talk takes us back to our other lives, takes us forward to the edge of the Far North, the edge of our own dreams. We surprise each other by talking of death, finding that we've both met it, thought about it, made a temporary truce with it. Kathleen has put a degree of order into a confused life. She talks of her "life plan," a good one if slightly impossible, as anything must be that makes sense. She asks me questions that stop my standard answers cold. Her face is full of possible answers. Her beauty is as hard to understand as my reasons for taking this trip, or wanting to climb that moun-tain. I fall asleep beside her with an open heart.

Tomorrow we'll wake up to the same gentle motion, the same heavy clouds, anonymous forest channels moving mysteriously past.

The boat glides on and on
shedding an outworn skin of miles
behind it, while I too
wriggle painfully forward
out of my own past,
leaving the transparent scales
of a hot California summer
shimmering in the wake...
And so we drift North
through the fog
toward a second summer
and a new skin.

The next day was long and lazy, monotonously beautiful, and at the same time full of a quiet excitement that had nothing to do with the scenery—the low forested hills sliding by on either side, the stark rocky inlets, isolated homesteads, tiny lighthouses, lonely channel markers on a lost spit of granite, sudden waterfalls cascading out of the clouds into the inky blue of the strait.

We walked and read, and even ventured into the high-priced world of the ship's cafeteria for coffee and hot chocolate for Ajila. We met our fellow vagabonds on the rear deck, and talked about their trips, and their scenes. The real landscape of people and faces began to take shape. There were climbing boots to grease and free hot showers to enjoy, and the lazy quiet flow of water on every side to pace us through the day. In the evening I wrote a small poem for Kathleen and gave it to her:

Frontiers are places so beautiful,
and so empty, that men

have to fill them with dreams.
Frontier women, too, have
calm deep faces that
make men dream...
It's good to know
that both still exist,
and that you're
one.

Her smiles went through me like knives. Wherever she went on board, the air would ripple around her. I enjoyed watching her random movement on our deckside world: finding her and losing her, smiling, exchanging private glances, watching her disappear around a bulkhead, spotting her through a window, noticing how other people were attracted into her orbit, coming up to her to offer their smiles, their gifts, listening to Ajila play with the other kids on board, only smiling when I noticed that her mother wasn't really as beautiful as she seemed to be... Her beauty was beneath and behind beauty. I was in love with a gentle dark-haired puzzle in faded blue jeans.

Everyone in the solarium that evening looked hungry. In any case, no one could afford to eat in the cafeteria, much less the dining room. The prices were unbelievable.

Someone, I think one of the kids on a bicycle trip from Seattle, suggested pooling our food for a community dinner. (Some hadn't thought to go shopping before our depar-ture, and others, caught in the stand-by list, hadn't had time.) It was a huge success, a feast, not a dinner. Food appeared from everywhere: bread, cheese, sardines, celery, fruit, peanut butter, cold meats, cookies... I bought some Rainier beer and Jay, the neuropsychologist whose daughter played with Ajila, contributed some wine. We were already drunk without it. Serious bearded faces, young hairless ones, homely girls beginning to look pretty because they were having such a good time. Paul was there, beaming like a prophet; and the art school teacher from the East Coast who had sketched Kathleen resting against her duffel bag; two teenaged boys from Maine who looked as if they hadn't eaten for days; pint-sized tousleheaded Ray, a diminutive chain-smoking

16-year-old whose dad was a steward on the ferry, on his way back to Alaska after a year in an "institution" for some adolescent craziness, smiling and stuffing his face like the rest of us. Ajila was kneeling at her mother's side. Incongruously, older "straight" people were drawn into the warm circle of our picnic on the floating bank of this endless winding ocean highway.

After dinner we borrowed the ship's vacuum for our crumbs, then played charades till midnight, laughing, jumping up, crying out, losing track again and again, still drunk with each other, coming down slowly, slowly, like the long pale northern evening, reluctant to give up the last light in the sky, or in each other's faces...

Fatigue finally triumphed. The kids were already asleep. Ajila was a blonde Muslim angel under her green nylon sleeping bag. Lounge chairs were pulled out flat to sleep on. Kathleen and I headed below decks for a midnight drink in the ship's bar. A perfect day, perfect evening. I wanted to stretch it out, talk to her until the words dried up until there was nothing left to say—knowing that in a life you hardly begin, that one more evening wasn't even time to begin...

In the bar we talked, drank Scotch because neither of us could think of anything else to order, listened to a guy in the booth across the way thump out a bluegrass polka on his banjo, laughed when two of the cyclists from Washington, brother and sister, started to dance crazily up and down the narrow aisle. Out of breath from dancing, Mike came over to sit with us: his hair sticking out in all directions, his chambray shirt pulled out, his thick smiling lips covered with fever blisters (beautiful people, we learn, don't have to be too beautiful). And out of the blue, he delivered a crazy, moving, totally disarming speech about Kathleen and me, about having watched us on the ship, about the way we stayed together without grabbing onto each other, about watching the way Kathleen treated her little girl with such respect, letting her choose what to do next, what clothes to wear in the morning... And going on to talk about himself, his efforts to find himself, not to be possessive with girlfriends, with people... And he said a lot more, but what moved us was how he said it. Letting the barrier between himself, his ego and his words become eggshell-thin, exposing himself in a strange trusting way to talk to us like that, so that we learned more from where the words were coming than from the words themselves. At any rate, we blushed when he talked about the two of us, but he was right: Our bond in the present was so real we hadn't even begun to hold onto each other for an imaginary tomorrow.

There you are. Happiness, desire, perfection. Where, if not inside you? Who, if not us now? When, if not here now? We fell asleep, warm on the cold deck, arms outside our sleeping bags, hands clasped.

Reborn under dazzling blue skies. They stole the clouds during the night. Nothing to do. A million things to do. Time rushes forward out of control. Before we can adjust, Ketchikan is swimming into view like a postcard of some far Norwegian village. The dark blue water is full of pale white jellyfish. At the railing, Ajila has a tearful moment, imagining that we'll have to swim ashore. No, it's not like that at all. Minutes later I'm carrying their duffel bag downstairs and across the ramp to Ketchikan. Farewell is a little picnic on the rocky bank, a few words, Ajila crying out: Oh, mommy, you kissed him!

And an incredible knot of emotions in my stomach. Kathleen's old man, the fellow she's been living with for two years, should be arriving on the afternoon ferry from the north, and the three of them will have to begin the business of making a new life. All my con-cern, my good wishes, for her, for them, seem superfluous; of course, it will work.

Back on board, I remember my Solzhenitsyn novel, The Cancer Ward, that she was reading, find it in my pack, and manage to run ashore at the very last minute to give it to her. An extra farewell, stolen kisses. Kathleen and Ajila running out to the dock's end as the Malaspina pulls slowly away. My eyes are full of tears. I've just lived through something unbelievable. Paul is standing beside me at the rail. Whatever he is saying seems to make sense, with such a long grey beard he must have lived through all this, too... The knot in my stomach starts to untie itself, we're still moving north.

Back on top deck I find my friends the bicycle-campers and a few others sitting around in shorts and cut-offs, having (in the simplest possible way, and so unself-consciously) a kind of Quaker-like Sunday-morning communion, sharing a giant hunk of rye-crisp, taking a few moments to think about it and share their thoughts.

*Breaking bread
with brothers and sisters
sitting in sunshine
sharing white wine
sharing our weakness
warm in the sunshine
feeling our strength
not yours nor mine
quiet communion
on a grey steel deck
taking our turns
talking of love
listening by turns
to brother and sister
sitting in sunshine
breaking bread.*

Everything that's happened so far has made us all high, and that's the way it stays, all day. Paul leaves us at Wrangell, the next port, with his incredible collection of surplus equipment and his beautiful antique quilt. Hot-rodding teenagers are driving motor boats through the pilings of the pier, and one runs headlong into a cement footing, flips 20 feet into the water and emerges unhurt. A carnival atmosphere with everything but flags fluttering in the breeze. But the magnet keeps pulling us, we keep on moving North.

*Perhaps this is the Far North:
The water opens and islands
pull back their forest tongues
for us to pass... Overhead
black and white clouds are fighting
their ancient Taoist battle
(summer's victory a fragile truce).
In the distance now, rain streaks
are staining the pale sky with rust.
White mountains rear up, like*

welcoming ghosts or new friends
on the far edge of our dreams.
Wrangell Narrows swallows our boat.
Rainbows welcome us to the Far North.

Time to repack my bags. We're almost to Petersburg. The northern sunset has just begun in a high-contrast battle of burnished gold and inky blue. Someone says: Look, your mountain! Yes, there it is all right, even though it isn't mine. The incredible Devil's Thumb, even this far away, it's overwhelming! I wonder how we'll ever find the courage to climb it, but I know we will. It always feels like this. Kevin, one of the cyclists, gives me a small card, a poem that a friend had written for him a long time ago. Here, take this, for the summit...

"It's the time you have wasted for your rose that makes it so important."

Thank you. Thanks for everything. It seems impossible that I'll ever forget all this: today, this evening, these people, Kathleen and Ajila, reading poetry on the rear deck, sharing our food, such perfect uncomplicated love. I didn't come North to find this, I have almost forgotten why I came, what was behind it all, luring me up here.

Behind snowy coastal ranges,
behind the cobalt blue
of Fredrick Sound evening,
the crackerbox waterfront
of smalltown Petersburg,
behind all this there's only
a granite dream at sunset,
too icy perfect to believe in
but just real enough
to pull me off this boat...
And all our island friendship
and ferryboat love
becomes one last shout
from ship to shore
and back...

I gather up the echoes
in my rucksack
and promise myself
to spread them around,
promise to pass them on...

II

In literature things end. Stories end. Poems end. But in real life (as they say) things and people and events go on and on, world without end, forever and ever, amen. In real life you never reach the end of the crooked road. In real life there is always a part two.

For, of course, getting there is only a part of the story. There one is, there you are, here I am, but yet not completely here. I'm still traveling, or else a part of me has already moved on, and ultimately I'll look back to realize that I left without ever completely arriving.. And the Far North is not different. The Far North: dream image, typewriter cliché, dimestore poetry, five-and-dime metaphysics.

But I did get here. What now? What next? Now that I'm back in charge of my own life, at least temporarily, at least partially... The present is Petersburg. The immediate future is the mountain, lonely and frightening on the horizon, really a thumb-like Thumb-poking up into an 11 p.m. sunset or hidden in rain and clouds, but still waiting. And the far and future future? Out there somewhere, behind the Devil's Thumb and those long snowy ridges, invisible guesswork.

Things change, time is no longer a slow crystal river.
But there are still new friends, events, poems:
This is the calm before the storm:
an extra day, waiting for friends,
down by the public float, where
spikey boats thrust long trolling poles
up into the low clouds. The seiners

*are coming home tonight, the tenders
will be here in an hour, and the girls
who work in the egg room
are having one last cup of coffee
before reporting to their Japanese foremen.*

*Alaskan summer: reflections in green water
a simple life (here too, brothers and sisters),
the circus scene of snow and trees and boats.
Hippies migrating north for cannery jobs
have come to civilize this hard wet land
with their gentle talk and long wavy hair.*

*Even the clouds look friendly now,
and the next cloudburst, when it comes,
will only lay more dust in my heart.
A float-plane takes off with a roar,
buzz saws whine, below my feet
an old hull is being scraped on the grid,
overhead: eagles, gulls, giant ravens
circle together, scream, fight and wait.
The sunshine is supercharged with mist
and the clouds are shot full of holes,
torn by sundrop, scattered by rainbeam.*

*I'm soaked to the skin and don't care.
Surely, this is the storm before the calm.
Afterwards will be time enough
to grab a paintbrush, tear fish from nets,
finish this life or start a new one.
This must really be the Far North,
and from here the only way is down,
all roads lead back to the world,
lead south and home... Yes, surely,
this is the storm before the calm.*

It passes quickly. It takes forever. The people of Petersburg are my clock. It's always raining, it's always cloudy, the mountain has disappeared for good. I am happy here and at peace.

The telegram reads: CAR PROBLEM ARRIVE FRIDAY EVENING PLEASE GET BATTERY CHRIS CALGARY ALBERTA. So I have an extra week to wait. I can wait.

Secretly I hope they never get here, I know they will. And sure enough, when they do, a whole lifetime has passed, the rain stops, the clouds lift enough for us to fly in, drop our gear, land at the lake. And we're right on schedule again, the real schedule.

The weather keeps improving, luring us on in two days over a high pass toward the Devil's Thumb. Chris Jones, my old mate from Fitz Roy, lean and cunning, witty and optimistic. George Lowe, old friend but new companion, smiling tousle-headed physi-cist, full of power and quiet strength. Me and my doubts, still glad to be here, glad that it's started, that it's happening to me, this incredible scene: the ice and granite battlefield of the Witches' Cauldron, the spire-like satellite peaks, the overwhelming bulk of the Thumb itself, this mad adventure unfolding.

The weather gets better and better. Two days of rough packing to Base Camp.

Collecting our fluorescent orange air-drop boxes, strung out across the glacier. Dazzling white snow, dazzling blue sky, hard-edge sunshine. There will be no rest day tomorrow.

Such weather is too good and too rare to waste. We have to start tomorrow and scramble to get ready. The Thumb towers overhead.

Magic mountain—
in all probability
we are enchanted
& not the mountain.
Let's hope this magic
pulling us up there
will bring us down
again.

The rock begins tricky, stays tricky: slantwise traversing pitches, awkward leading. awkward hauling, awkward following. George and Chris are full of fire and energy, but still they move up oh-so-slowly. At the bottom of such a great granite face, I feel—as I must have known I would—overwhelmed by the situation. A voice inside me is saying this is no place to get in shape for hard climbing and today I manage to lead only one pitch; it will be my only real lead of the climb. Uncomfortable about contributing so little to the pointed end of the rope, I knock myself out trying to clean the pitches fast and efficiently. We do six or seven pitches gaining the shattered diagonal ramp system that leads up across the face. A square turret-like buttress does for a bivouac platform.

We're in the clouds now. The Thumb is claiming us for its own.

The next day takes us on up into the clouds, into the upper face, even into the long final summit dihedral, but also into the rain. Only a drizzle at first, but it doesn't feel healthy. It's almost midnight when Chris rappels back down out of the mist after fixing two more ropelengths above our ledge. We have an impossible time wriggling into our sleeping bags in the dark, everything wet, boots still on, eating a small snack, shouting across to George on a ledge 30 feet away, trying to sleep sitting up on our miniature ledge, fumbling with our anchor slings, waiting for dawn.

Ice cliffs crack & groan:
huddled on a tiny ledge,
damp climbers moan & dream
of warmer places, of
lovers' faces that seem just
out of reach & each one
wonders why he came
& how long it will last.
In the night
enormous sheets of mist
& rain blow slowly past.

New morning: drizzling first, then rain, then snow, whipping along in the wind, fat wet snowflakes. George and Chris are cold and wet, but still optimistic. They look up, push on back up last night's fixed ropes.

This is the low point of my climb: Alone with the hauling bag and a giant wet pack, I feel sick, weak, lost. It's really snowing now. The rock is turning white. My friends are out of sight, somewhere above. For a minute I find the voice to question our judgment in going on under such deteriorating conditions, but George calls down that everything's OK. What can I do? Push off the ledge, pendulum across and start prusiking up the long thin nine-millimeter rope. Part way up, I feel my tail rope jammed behind me, back across the traverse. I have to jumar down and back across to free the rope. I want to cry or curse or hit something out of frustration, but save my strength for going back up...

An incredible day: Everything goes slowly, awkwardly. Our dihedral world, our long vertical rock corner is half white with snow, wind begins to whistle up the slot. Near disasters follow each other like desperate warnings shouted in vain at the deaf and dumb. I reach a tiny belay ledge and reach out to steady myself against our big hauling bag. It starts to topple slowly off the ledge—my god! The knot in the tie in sling has come undone. I only just barely catch it. All our food, sleeping bags, everything, a few more inches... don't think of it!

I'm slowly cleaning the pins from a steep pitch at the top of the dihedral, but below me the rope jams again: I rappel down to free it and start back up on stirrups and jumar ascenders. Sudden rumble/explosion: the rope has dislodged a cluster of big flakey blocks, they cascade down on my head. By the time I can duck it's over, I'm only scratched-but no, don't move! There is one more block, a big one, teetering some fifteen feet above me, pinned, held in place by the rope I'm standing on. I hold my breath.

If it falls and cuts the rope, well... George is just above on a small snow-covered stance; he sees, understands, throws me the end of another rope. That way they can't both be cut if the rock comes down. I tie on, still holding my breath, then slowly shift my weight to the other stirrup. Oof—the block tumbles, hits me in the face, falls into my arms. I manage to hold on to it, turn in my slings and heave it off, safely beyond our ropes. My gloves are red with blood, but it's only a cut lip. On we go...

Just below the summit, standing in a kind of notch out of the wind, roaring up the dihedral at gale force. We're soaked and shivering and we have to take our sweaters off to wring out the sleeves. We lower George into a gully, he disappears around the corner and ultimately, the hauling line leads up at a cockeyed angle over an immense overhang.

I'm too tired and impatient to be careful and when I swing out on it, I find myself hanging 5-feet from the wall and screwed up higher than Hogan's goat: I've rigged everything wrong, my slings are so short I can't move, my safety loops are somehow clipped into each other and not the rope... It takes a while to get everything straightened out, but I do, and now moving slowly up this yellow-green thread into the sky I get another nasty surprise. The rope is icing up and time and again my jumar clamps suddenly come loose, dropping me with a thump, so that only the extra Gibbs ascender clipped on top of everything just in case keeps me from dropping to the end of the rope every few feet.

It's too much, I'm really getting psyched out and call up for a top rope just in case. Once more George saves the day, although it's probably all psychological.

Chris has been waiting in the wind through all this, and now he's too cold to lead on, so George takes the last pitch, disappears over the black, hoar-frosted summit ridge.

We're up. I'm the last one off the face. The rope is an icy white cable. As I clean the pitch there is a momentary clearing, the mist parts below me. A surrealistic vision: snow-plastered slabs dropping into the Witches' Cauldron, the giant twin Cat's Ears spires rising out of the gloom under my feet, so cold, so hostile, so beautiful.

The clouds close back in. On the other side of the summit ridge, George and Chris are shoveling out a bivouac ledge like demons, clouds of spindrift pour over them, a snowslope shelves steeply off into the greyness. The summit is up there in the mist but it looks easy, we're here, we're up, and tomorrow...

No summit
   no mountain
   no earth
   only
   three shadows
   walking
   on top of
   mother of pearl
   clouds
   no climbers
   no climb
   no victory
   no defeat

Afterward came another wet cold bivouac, another day, another bivouac, another day. Our fiberfilled sleeping bags, soaked and frozen, somehow keeping us warm and alive. Our soggy feet and hands carry us, lowering us, carrying us again, over the top and down, and down, and down.

A few moments snatched out of the mist: the top or thereabouts (a series of bumps on a long thin ridge, who knows which?) where we spent an hour or two moving above the clouds. Our shadows accompanied us on the clouds some few hundred feet below, each inside its own rainbow halo, Brocken's specter.

There was our happiness at finding two of Fred Becky's old rappel rings from his first ascent of the mountain in '48. Just to think that somebody else... And then at last the glacier, an out-of-focus world of subtle shades of grey:

Cloudwalkers,
or fallen angels,
we stumble forward
across the
uncertain interface
of snow and sky.
Why escape?

*We may already
have left the earth
far below us
to keep company
with invisible gods,
tramping silent circles
thru the infinite
white on white
of endless clouds.*

It was whiteout city, but we just kept on trucking. And sure enough there was an end to it. The edge of the high Stikine plateau, the escape route into and through the ice fall; and four-thousand feet lower down, after we'd run like madmen under the last ice cliff, jumped the last crevasse, our beautiful blue tent was still waiting for us.

After six long days, we took off our rope, threw off our packs on the moraine, kicked off our wet boots and smiled at each other and the world. This time the crooked road had led us straight. We'd been to the Far North and back. The journey was over and no longer mattered. That too was OK, and still is.

*Thank you, Lord, for rest days:
for sun on the boulders,
for camp in disorder
with drying ropes and
clothes and bags and all
our rainbow colored junk
spread out around us.*

*Thank you for this lonely place
for these empty miles
of cracked glacier tongues,
for these stark grey walls
towering into the clouds,
for letting us be here
where we don't belong.*

Thank you for these safe sounds:
the rain on our tent fly,
and not on our faces
under soaked bivy sheets,
the roar of ice cliffs
collapsing high above
and far away.

Thank you for our mountain
which frightened us
but didn't kill us,
for a safe route down,
a world to return to,
friends and women to love,
for today and tomorrow.

—*Originally appeared in* Mountain Gazette 15, *1973.*

10.
Alaska: Journey by Land

Written by Galen Rowell

He was walking down the road in a drizzle, a few miles from Watson Lake in the Yukon. An ageless Indian. Maybe 50, more like 30. We couldn't tell, and it made no difference; he put out his thumb and we stopped. Now there were five of us plus a thousand pounds of gear in the station wagon.

It wallowed around curves like a waterbed on roller skates and bounced over chuckholes with the shock of a steel ball rolling down stairs.

The Indian was quiet and oblivious, eyes focused at infinity. His twisted Asian face seemed incongruous above Western cowboy clothing. His nose had been broken, and when he turned my direction it still pointed at 10 o'clock. We asked him questions and he answered in a guttural, barely intelligible monotone. What did he do? Worked in a motel part-time and lived off the land. Trapping, shooting game. Suddenly the dam opened and information poured forth, almost too predictably. Many brothers. Hard winters on the trap lines. Constant referrals to boozing. All the stereotypes of the Northern Indians. We began to wonder, was this all for our benefit? Was he just telling us what we wanted to hear, guarding his private life in a last vestige of dignity? Or was he for real?

We asked him his name. He looked at me intently: "Just call me the Black-Haired Yukon Kid."

We took the Kid to the bar of his choice in town. It smelled of beer and piss. An imaginary Mason-Dixon line separated the Indians and the Whites. Ours was the only integrated table. The Kid was on edge. Conversation flowed, but not in a stream.

Rather, it resembled a canal system with locks that ended abruptly before a change to a different level. He didn't tell stories, he dropped fragments, and unlike a skilled politi-cian, he made no attempt to tie them together.

Realizing the window of his soul was closed to us, we began to talk about our trip Halfway up the Alaska Highway. Six hundred miles through the dirt and 600 more to the border. We talked about glaciers, wildlife and all the things we expected to see in Alaska. Our palms sweated when we talked about climbing; each of us was unsure how we would perform on 5,000 feet of granite in the Alaska Range in May. The Kid was drunk. Something roared up inside of him and he yelled at us.

Screamed. Bellowed. Just as quickly his anger subsided and he began to sing a weird improvisation of primitive sounds and modern jazz. He sang of his family and his mother and just as suddenly he stopped. It wasn't embarrassment. Maybe pride and anger for having given us an inch of his soul. The window closed; he clammed up for good.

Communication dwindled to awkward tense stares. We gulped our beers and left him sitting there.

We drove two blocks from the highway in the center of the town of 500 people, parked the car, walked 50 feet and slept in boreal forest. It was twilight at midnight and sunny at three.

We were back on the highway at 6 a.m. When passing cars we kept our windows rolled tight and the heater fan on high to prevent dust from sifting through every nook and cranny. Trucks were a different matter. At the beginning of the highway, near Dawson Creek, a passing truck had unleashed a rock that hit our windshield like a bul-let. It was the first of seven breaks. But the dust was more dangerous.

Winnebagos and Aristocrats crammed with American geriatrics crawled along the road at 30 mph-pathetic products of the Affluent

Society whose only touch with the environment was an occasional forage for food, gas or souvenirs. But the truckers drove the road at 60 to 70, leaving a wake of dust and gravel that defies the imagination, until you try to pass one.

Fifty miles from Whitehorse we were cruising at a comfortable 65 mph, raising an opaque cloud behind us. Wisps of dust, at first barely noticeable, began to appear on the road in front of us, like cirrus streamers before a storm. Soon, thick dust surrounded us on all sides, pierced only by the bouncing taillights of a charter bus, glowing an eerie maroon through the murk. We followed it for miles. I couldn't decide whether to pass, stop and wait, or hang behind in the dusty pall. The bus was traveling a consistent 60 mph and would be much more difficult to pass than the shorter, slower houses-on-wheels. I made up my mind to pass after I chugged behind the bus at 20 mph as it climbed out of a ravine. When a half-mile straightaway appeared, I pulled out to pass and found myself going 75 to get around the accelerating bus. Gravel from its tires rattled off the station wagon like machine gun fire. Forward vision was totally obscured when we came abreast of the wheels. I determined my position on the road only by watching the side of the bus. Suddenly the strafing ceased, vision returned, dust began to settle in the car. We breathed a sigh of relief. But the dusty wisps continued on the road in front of us. A minute later we encountered another set of maroon taillights in another murky cloud. The passing scene repeated itself, but to our horror we were behind a third tour bus. The view through the windshield was a continuing explosion, and the rear view mirror was filled with the front of the second bus. Smog and the Manhattan rush hour seemed placid by comparison.

In Whitehorse we replaced our third tire. All three steel-corded radials had burst in about the same place on the sidewalls, while a rayon tire rolled along just fine. We would never know why. It was like the story of the plastic Jesus still standing upright on the dashboard of a demolished car.

Whitehorse is on the railroad, the highway and the Yukon River. It is the transportation and tourist center as well as the capital of the Yukon. Winnebagos and clicking shutters surround dead hulks of old sternwheelers, beached near the middle of the city. Neon and Mounties and Pavement.

The Alaska Highway was built across Canada by the U.S. Army Corps of Engineers during World War II. After Pearl Harbor, the Pentagon boys decided that having the Japanese in the Aleutian Islands without a supply road to Alaska was not a good thing So they told the Corps to get with it. Nothing beats Hard Work and American Dollars, so tens of thousands of people and dollars were sent to the North along with a suitable number of bulldozers. The effort began in March 1942, with crews working from both ends toward the middle. On September 2, 1942, the bulldozers met at Contact Creek in the Yukon near Watson Lake. Never before had so many bulldozed so far so quickly—1,200 miles in less than six months.

Unlike more habitable places—such as Southern California—the Yukon has not been quickly populated in the wake of the road builders. Even today, the entire population of the Yukon is only 18,000 in a land larger than California. A boom may be coming, however. Mineral exploration has tripled in the past five years. Two new national parks will bring in more tourists, but only in the summer. A record temperature of -81° Fahrenheit was recorded in the town of Snag in 1946.

Near Whitehorse we visited the Yukon Game Farm, which advertised "Wild Animals of the Yukon in Their Natural Setting." For two bucks we drove our car past some sickly Dall sheep and caged predators. A golden eagle tried to flap its wings in a cage the size of a closet made of cyclone fence. A wolverine slobbered and grunted on a half-chewed piece of plywood inside a similar enclosure.

We imagined how a family might tour the farm. Mom and Dad would gaze through dusty windows, commenting ecstatically at real wildlife, while sitting in the rear of the mobile home, the children might possibly view a scene closer to reality by watching "Wild Kingdom" on Whitehorse TV.

A hundred miles past Whitehorse we reached the shore of Kluane Lake, more than 75 miles long at the foot of the St. Elias Mountains. The big peaks were hidden from view by a front range of mountains under 10,000 feet. Even so, the monotony of the relentless boreal forest was broken by views of glaciers, green fell fields and the giant, still-frozen lake. At the lake's inlet, white dust clouds blew across the flood plains. The dust was glacial milk, but it gave the place the impression of an alkaline desert.

We were on the edge of Kluane National Park, second largest in the Western and the Manhattan rush hour seemed placid by comparison.Hemisphere. We talked to one of the two park wardens and found out that the entire population of the park at that time, including tourists, was probably less than 10.

There are no roads and no facilities in the park. More than half of its 8,500 square miles lie under ice. Mt. Logan, Canada's highest peak, rises to nearly 20,000 feet in a remote section of the park. When it was first ascended in 1925, the party spent 70 days installing supply caches over 130 miles of the route in winter, because the terrain was too rough to pass with pack animals in summer. When horses could go no further, they guided dog teams over the snow-covered ice fields in 50-below-zero weather. We felt pretty insignificant complaining about the dust and the chips in the windshield.

At the edge of the lake, a sign next to the highway proclaimed "Sheep Mountain." It was a beautiful setting. Sun, wind, ice, green hillsides and white Dall sheep. But here, in a land where the human population was less than one person for every 10 square miles, the sheep were adversely affected by people in many ways. As the sun and the temperature dropped on a May afternoon, we were not alone scrambling on the hillsides for a closer view. Many tourists stop at the sign, and the area is mentioned in most travel guides. The sheep's normal predators, wolves, bears, eagles, were greatly reduced by hunting and trapping. Gradually the sheep lost much of their fear of the approach of large mammals, developed over eons of time when life hung on the thread of seeing and escaping enemies without being seen themselves. They have little use for their powerful telephoto vision, often likened to 6X binoculars. A chink was missing from their bold-ness, and they lay on the hillsides like bundles of inanimate white wool, moving only when I approached them very closely. I might have had stunning photographs except for the fact that some self-centered biologist had hung collars on many of the animals. The old ram with huge horns wore the latest in wide natural leather, while an adolescent yearling was attired in a Day-Glo pink. I could not explain why I found the collars such a flagrant affront to my senses. I have not felt that way about tags on the ears of campground bears in national parks. It is more like the hatred I would have if I visited New Guinea and found the tribesmen primitive except for Sears Roebuck tennis shoes—an unnecessary, degrading intrusion of the modern world into one of the last strongholds of wildness. I wondered why the study of wildlife is so often pushed so far that it robs the very wildness it seeks to comprehend.

After hours on the hillsides, we squeezed into the car and drove along the lake. We had traveled more than a thousand miles on the dirt, and it began to seem like home. We now expected dust and rumbles under the car. The road is perhaps the best unpaved highway in the world, carefully maintained by large crews that constantly repair the frost-buckling, chuckholes and wash-outs.

The original course of the road was not intended for modern tourists and truckers. Quite the opposite. It was purposely twisting and winding to safeguard military convoys from aerial gunfire. Even across flatlands, the highway meanders. Many of the winding sections are being slowly replaced with modern straight roads and wide right-of-ways. Pavement is one step closer.

The dirt road—almost continuous for 1,200 miles except for small sections through towns—was something we originally dreaded. We thought to ourselves how easy and pleasurable our journey might be if those miles were only paved.

We drove through the long hours of subarctic twilight. After midnight we reached the Alaskan border. The U.S.A. and asphalt roads beckoned on the other side of the customs building. A small but determined customs agent searched our car, sure that our youth, laughter and long hair meant illegal drugs. He looked serious, dedicated and definitely unhappy when his search was fruitless. Like big game trophies on a hunter's walls, the waiting room was adorned with drug oriented spoils: elaborate pipes, bags, bottles, etc., mounted in locked glass cases.

We rolled out on pavement. The end of the dirt and dust. But the road was worse! More curves. Poor banking. Harder to drive. Frost-buckled pavement caused us to hit more bumps in the first five miles than on all the miles of dirt. The bumps were severe and unpredictable; but the worst thing about the pavement was insidious. We sensed it but could not express it. An element was gone from the Alaska Highway mystique. Finally, after an hour of winding through the mountains next to double yellow lines, someone said what we all felt, "It doesn't seem like wilderness anymore. It's just like any other paved road in any other mountains."

After a long day on asphalt, we reached the end of the drive. Talkeetna, Alaska. Fifty three people, two airstrips, hundreds of dogs, uncounted drunken Eskimos and two bush pilots who refused to speak to each other. It was truly the Last Frontier. We watched two young men in buckskins walk through town, carrying rifles and knives.

Ever-present Winnebagos occasionally rolled past, turned around at the dead end, and rolled out again. Grotesque, dusty, myopic eyes of our times, unable to focus at one point longer than the time required to stick a decal onto a window. Behind the first row of houses a man dressed totally in leather negotiated with a bush pilot to be airlifted, with his dog team and canoe, to a very remote lake. He talked only about one-way terms; no mention was made of coming out.

GOLD
GOLD
GOLD Alaska is
GOLD   the place to go!

I found this inscription on a men's room wall in a Winnemucca casino, but in Alaska I saw the other side of the coin. Rising gold prices have brought would-be prospectors back to the North. On the airstrip a man with tomorrow in his eyes thrust a chunk of rusty metamorphic rock in my hand. "Gold," he said simply. "It assays at over $200 a ton, but I've got to fly it out. I'd be rich if only there was a road." That night he was dead drunk in the Fairview Inn.

At 10 in the morning the main street looked like a typical western town in the 1950s. Two-lane road. Dirt shoulders. Neon yet to come. Outside the Fairview sat two young men—one wearing Levis, a sweatshirt and a crewcut; the other with a Hell's Angels style vest, cowboy hat and gun belt. Rattling the doorknob of the closed tavern was a wizened, almost blind Eskimo, leaning heavily on his cane. Age, booze and 20 hours of daylight had obscured his awareness of time.

At the corner of the building, a chattering group of Japanese, wearing double boots and bright parkas, busily crammed equipment into the rear of a brand new van. In the distance, far beyond the railroad, the river and the spruce forests, the Alaska Range loomed above the horizon. A 40-minute plane ride would transmute us into an Ice-Age scenario. Like a shabby time warp in a cheap movie, we would find ourselves in a primeval, uninhabited land, staring alternately at unclimbed, unnamed mountains and at our mound of tents, skis, beer, freeze-dried food, paperbacks and week-old newspapers. We had arrived.

—*Originally appeared in* Mountain Gazette 17, *1974.*

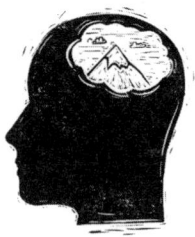

11.
Growing Up High

Written by Randy LaChapelle

During the International Geophysical Year (1957–1958) my father initiated a research project on the Blue Glacier. The Blue Glacier lies on Mount Olympus, part of Olympic National Park in Washington State. A 16x24-foot field station was erected on a rock outcropping adjacent to the Snow Dome. This was to be my summer home from age 5 until I was 16.

That time spent living on the mountain has never left me. I find myself driven back to those memories. The experience looms inside of me, a psychic presence of great power. I return to cleanse my past and dwell in peace with my mountain parentage.

Each summer morning, I would awaken and walk outside to see the mountain. On clear days I would walk the horizon on a radiance of light. The glacier was sharp as the shale beneath my bare feet. The air was unburdened, carrying only the cold and light. It would pass as a breath of wind, barely noticed, leaving the mountain to touch me unhindered. On cloudy mornings the island of rock around the cabin was the extent of my world. Dimly felt shapes would press against the clouds, hinting at the world I knew to be there. The focal point of the mountain constantly changed. I have grown a whole mythology of remembrance around the view from the glacier. Vast distances and oppressive nearness were the gods of my life.

I used to climb to the top of a small peak behind the cabin and look out over the valleys below. The horizon extended from the Cascades in the east to the Pacific in the west. To the north lay Vancouver Island and the peaks of the Coast Range in British Columbia. I had the entire c as the crucible for my imagination. I have difficulty filling the vacancy such space has left me in life—it has been a Promethean wound.

Often I would sit on the peak and stare out into the valleys below, from which the wind carried the smells of the forest upward to my resting place. Unexpected openings in the currents of air revealed whole meadows. The smells were over-rich in the mountain air. I could see one particular valley from the peak, which fascinated me. It would usually melt out by the middle of July. Four small lakes lay on the floor of the valley. I was the hermit of the valley and had responsibility for the adventures that took place there. I peopled the valley with my fantasies. I have often intended to visit the valley in person, but never have. It remains sacred to the visitations of a child.

My day was at the mercy of the mountain. Drifting patches of clouds raced their shadows across the snowfields and enveloped me. The sun wandered across the sky and my body simultaneously. I was overly sensitive to the lighting and mood of the glacier.

I was content to live in a child's eternity, with the peaks as my companions. No brothers or sisters, no playmates to seduce me from the mountain. It was an innocence that had its own ecology. The research station and its debris were as natural as any other part of my glacier life. I suppose now I could find the rationale of protest. I could disapprove of such wilderness contaminations. But it would be a lie. My emotions cling to the unchangeable unity of my childhood.

My earliest memories come from when I was two years old. At that time we lived in tents on the moraine of the lower Blue Glacier.

The tents were strung out along a thin rocky top. Heather and a few wildflowers grew among the glacial debris. I remember it as being always foggy. The glacier and the fog intermingled, creating a uniform world of white. The dim forms of trees could be seen downslope from the moraine. Looking upward the snow blended into the sky. Out of that mingling of heaven and earth, climbers would occasionally appear. I remember having an unquenchable awe for the bundled men who went high above my world.

The peak-shaped, six-man army tents, filled with the incense of Coleman stove gas and musty canvas, were my personal temples. They took on a substantiality that seemed to magnify their interiors beyond all reason. All the space in the world could fit, together with my sense of security, inside those tents. My staple food in those days was peanut butter and logan bread. I burnt out on both. Even now peanut butter has little hold over me. I grew up being the kid who didn't like peanut butter—a stigma which would set me apart. One of the many ways the mountain separated me from my age. I was timeless, with no need to grow up, or change, or be any different than I was. That eternal time sense lingers on, subtly conditioning my world even now.

I had few toys then. A red ball was my prized possession. One day I lost it, the ball rolling down into the glacier and then disappearing into the icefield. I still distrust that icefield. I feel cheated by the convolutions that robbed me of my toy. I can watch that ball disappear endlessly in the inattentiveness of my life. The glacier is my silent answer, the judge of my willfulness to find my lost possession and pick up the pieces of my craft.

I was 2 when I made the first walk up the Hoh River Trail to the glacier. My only memory of that particular hike is of my father coming to meet my mother and me three-quarters of the way up the trail. He had come down from the camp on the moraine. I remember him bouncing along the trail, tanned and full of energy. His presence was overwhelming. I was captivated by my father, transformed as he was into an emissary of the mountain.

The bridge where we met was the demarcation point between the valley floor and the climb upward. The area of the bridge has always transfixed me. It spans the Hoh River as it meets Glacier Creek. The

Hoh runs in a deep chasm at this point. The boiling water in the narrow canyon was mesmerizing. The water welled up in massive spirals. A deep green movement muted with the glacial dust. An overpowering urge to jump would strike me like a disease. It was with little surprise that I learned of a suicide from the bridge a few years ago.

The trail upward reads clearly in my memory. The slow places, the first view of the mountain, avenues of moss and the lake all appear when called upon. The personality that emerges along the trail is as complete as any other part of my glacier life. The steady fall of footsteps measured off the thoughts and feelings of the journey. Always there was the image of the mountain that displaced the monotony. The clear crunch of snow underfoot echoed along the hot, mosquito-paved way. The other worlds of snow and ice haunted the footfalls of the forest.

Such comparative spaces are the legacy of the mountain. To have lived in the highlands has rendered the lowlands incomplete. My intellect rebels at such thoughts, but in my heart I feel it to be true. I am inflated by the mountain. Tendrils of perfection reach out from my past, usurping the present.

Time is elastic. It stretched to break a child's patience, riding the eternal presence of the mountain. The coming and going of the sun was the heartbeat of glacial time. During the long periods of storm, the days would lengthen into boredom. The four walls of the cabin were the measure of my sanity. Among my refuges were cases of army survival rations that had been airdropped at the start of the project. They were intended as a stock of emergency food; instead they became part of my personal domain. Opening all of the carefully packaged food, uncovering treasure after treasure, had its own delight. A six-year-old can of fruit cocktail may not seem luxuriant, but entwined in the ritual of my childhood, it was pure ambrosia.

Tiring of the usual cabin occupations, I would sit and watch the fog blow past the window. Cunning wisps of cloud streamed from the wet rocks. It was as if the sea had risen and was seething in phantom shapes, turning the valleys into cauldrons. The presence of something just beyond reach often came to me. There was a pregnant depth to the storm that fascinated me. Even though it might be sleeting or snowing, there was an indefinite heat that seemed to flow from the greys and whites of the storm. It was the incarnation of storm demons, and my fascinated stare struggled to uncover their birth.

More often than not, a child's boredom quenched the mystic in me, and I would turn to the cabin for amusement once again. The opiate of card games, books and food shut out the storm.

During the earlier years of the project I often flew into the glacier on the supply plane. It was a small ski plane with a payload of three hundred pounds. It seems incredible to me that one small plane supplied the vast machinery of the project. Yet I know the vastness I conceived is a product of a child's vision. There was a self-contained quality to the station that assumed the weight of my whole world. In actuality the project was run, after an initial investment of $60,000 on $15,000 to $20,000 dollars a year (with the majority of that going to salaries). A paltry sum for financing a whole world.

I remember spending hours at the Clallam County Airport waiting for the supplies to be organized for the flight in. The airport was an old World War Il fighter strip. It was absurdly large for the small aircraft that flew out of it. I filled some of the space by learning to ride a bicycle on the acres of unused pavement. Those times at the airport were gilded with the edge of anticipation. The subtle warmth of knowing I was on the edge of another way of life.

For the flight in, I was seat-belted and then surrounded with the rest of the bag-gage. I would wrap the plane around me like a chrysalis and wait to emerge on the mountain. Invariably, I was confounded by the terrain on the way in. As the plane climbed, a snow massif would appear that looked deceptively like the Blue Glacier. I would be amazed at the speed of the flight, but a little disappointed in the shabbiness of the vision before me. This mountain was spectacular, but did not have the aura of the glacier. I would resign myself to the counterfeit and then the plane would pass beyond, revealing the real thing. The Blue Glacier quickly filled the gaps in my memory with the ease of recalled landmarks. I was navigating again in the security of the past. The plane would land and I would stagger out, ducking to avoid the blow of light. But there was no escaping the radiance of the mountain; I was home.

The safety record of the station underscores the sense of security I had about the place. In the 17 years of its existence, the only injuries there were a sprained knee and a mild case of food poisoning. Often I played at the cliff's edge, cautious but unafraid. I had an inner freedom that betrayed an unsaid bond between the mountain and me. There was trust between us.

I learned a subtle secret of movement in those early years of scrambling over the rotten Olympic rock. The secret was to trust the mountain and move as low in my body weight as I could. There is a touch that sustains you when you abandon yourself to a mountain. Some days I could move unencumbered within my body—an effortless flow from somewhere around my waist. There was no separation between who I was and where I wanted to be. I travel in the mountains now and am amazed at how some people move through the land. They appear to walk from somewhere in their throat or chest and have to constantly readjust their balance as a result. "Come down," I want to tell them, "relax and walk with the mountain."

The early ease of the glacier has left me in a naivete about mountains in general. I could easily disappear into strange and shoes. My conditioning draws me to high places, but leaves me unprepared—a traitorous beguilement.

Watching the sun set was sacred to the glacier ritual. I doubt if I have forgotten any of the thousands of nightfalls I have seen. As the air stilled countless times on the point of the setting sun, I traveled the length of the Puget Basin in the stillness. The lights of Victoria and Vancouver would gradually emerge. The Pacific coastline sometimes broke free of fog, the Tatoosh Island echoing the constancy of my sunset awareness. My vision could be entirely different each time, and yet the same mood would flow over me—the sense of being on the edge of eternal time.

I felt a peculiar attraction to the cities at night. The cold of the evenings would come up fast, biting through my parka, but often I stayed and lingered in the after-colors of the sun. And I would gaze out toward the cities. I treasured the presence of other people. The lonely place in me that was an only child on the glacier took comfort in the distant lights. Vancouver and Victoria have always been my favorite cities.

The only times I can remember feeling a sense of acute danger on the glacier is when I journeyed into a crevasse field. The really large crevasses, the ones that could swallow several buildings easily, petrified me. I would creep downhill to the edge and look in. I could never dismiss the glacier when it opened itself with such massive wounds. The crevasses always chilled me. It could be a hot day, and I would still get a cold shiver looking into the ice shadows. On either side of the prominence where the cabin was situated, there were large crevasses-catchment basins, should I ever slip and try for the valley floor. They were the watchdogs of my world. In my mind I have fallen many times, the result of these musings being hours of imaginative attempts to extricate myself from the glacier. Candy for a child's mind.

As the summer deepened, the sun cups on the glacier surface would grow more profuse. If they became too large they would endanger the landing of the ski plane. I can remember many times trudging out after dinner to do battle with the sun cups. It was glacial housekeeping. We would carefully shovel the top layer of snow away from the landing zone, leaving a strip of cleaner, less-contorted surface behind. It always seemed futile to me, rearranging a small patch of the glacier in hopes of fooling the sun for a few more days. It was like scratching the back of an enormous beast so our gnat of an airplane could land.

The ice worms came out in profusion during the evening hours. Every shovel of snow was peopled by sun cups and little black worms. I learned much about the tenacity of life by digging down through layers of algae and ice worms, uncovering the thin layer of life that the glacier begrudgingly sustained. Throwing ice worms into the sun, I would watch the day end.

The glacier was an ocean. Whenever I stepped off the rocks and headed onto the snowfield, it was an entrance into another medium. In the morning, the crust would be peaks [...] with nothing more than a shirt, pants unyielding, demanding a tight, controlled step to navigate between cups-like walking on a thin membrane of tension, protecting me from the deeper currents of the ice-field. I was always amazed at the distances I could cover in the early morning. As the sun rose higher, the glacier gradually sucked at my feet. Footholds had an ephemeral existence as the soft snow gave way under my weight. Distances would drag out the glare and heat of the snow. The glacier could be a desert, an ocean and an icefield, all within the change of a few degrees of the sun. The sun molded the substance of my world-shaping it and giving it color and tone. The ocean of snow was extremely sensitive to the slightest change in the environment. It was a resonant membrane that suffered us to walk on it.

Scientifically, much of the early research conducted on the mountain was to determine the energy exchange of the glacier. Instruments were set up to monitor the incoming and outgoing radiation. Thermocouples monitored the air temperature over the snow surface. Anemometers measured the wind flow. The microclimate of the glacier was constantly logged. The living movement of the glacier was transposed into dots and lines of yards of recorder paper.

There was an interesting progression of research over the years. The initial experiments studied the energy exchange on the surface of the glacier. The surface was mapped and survey points were established. Sites were picked for ablation measure-ments. The glacier was monitored for extremely subtle changes. As the years passed, there was more concern with the internal structure. Hot-point drills wormed their way down to measure the depth. Pits and tunnels grew larger and deeper. The hardware associated with the research transformed; electronics gave way to air compressors and jack hammers. The permutations of gravity as it played within the ice animated the gla-cier. The life of the glacier was communicated in plastic flow. The mechanism of that flow was the focus of attention for the research.

Science was a ritual that I took for granted. It was something automatically done when confronted with something as mysterious as a glacier. I knew that all the instruments and all the experiments would never really unmask the mountain, but the ritual was important. There was a subterranean purpose behind the daily tasks of the project. Even now, I have only a fleeting glimpse of that purpose in my mind, enough of a view to know that science really was a sacred approach to the mountain—a way of expressing the connection of man with the mountain.

The last year I spent on the glacier was the year of the great tunnel dig. An ice tunnel was bored into the western ice fall. The effort involved fourteen people. An unheard-of population for the station. The silence of the mountain was pushed into the background with the intensity of the activity.

The tunnel, when completed, reached to bedrock. One section of the tunnel deformed so quickly that it repeatedly had to be dug out. The tunnel bisected several small crevasses. It afforded the interesting comfort of being able to look up a crevasse while secure within it. The end of the tunnel revealed the soul of the glacier. The ice was exposed in its massive response to gravity. Long feathers of ice peeled away from the ice-rock contact. There actually was considerable space between the two mediums at various points. I always felt, standing at the tunnel's end, that I was intruding on some private relationship between the glacier and the earth. I would catch the movement of the glacier in the transitory light of a flashlight. An intrusion of human perception that violated the time sense of the glacier.

The psychological space of the project was far different than during any previous year. The drama of living together with fourteen people in a small mountain cabin became more interesting than the physical surroundings. An example of the change was the transformation of one of my favorite scrambling areas into an arena of competition. I joined with the others in trying to make it up impossible routes. The old ease with the mountain was gone. The freedom of scrambling was caught in personality structures. I was growing up, into the world of adults. It was fascinating, but it was also drowning out my connection with the mountain.

My descent into adulthood has been arduous. No climb in any of my glacier years can match the shock of having to grow up. I no longer have the psychological edge of the mountain. I am stripped of my uniqueness, my mountain overrun with hundreds of climbers. I have been forced to let go of the inviolate sanctuary of my youth. The memory vault has opened, and everything the mountain was pours out, demanding a new reconciliation. The power of my connection with it emerges despite the saccharine memories with which I cloak it. Going back to these memories has liberated the real mountain of my youth. This dual vision, of wishful memories and real power, is my legacy of childhood in the peaks.

—*Originally appeared in* Mountain Gazette 40, *1975.*

12.
Fear

Written by David Roberts

Buddhists know that the *duhkha* of this world—the suffering, discontent, anxiety—outweighs the joy in it. And I knew it, too, during those early June days in 1963, as I watched the mud and dust of the Alaska Highway reel past from the back of our VW bus. I was afraid of Alaska, where I had never been; I was afraid of McKinley, a mountain, I was sure, too formidable for my three short years of climbing. But in 1963, I would not have said so. Then I might have seen in the gloom of the spruce trees plodding past our window only an uneasy regret that I wasn't spending my summer as I had the previous one: working construction in my home town and dating old high school girlfriends. Where were the grassy parks and blue lakes of my native Colorado? The highway was not even mountainous. Instead, a gauntlet of gravel-lot gas stations, expensive stale hamburgers, generators chugging all night; in the cafe kitchens, prim Canadian radio voices through a fog of oatmeal and bacon. And between oases, those endless stands of shaggy spruce, with hardly a glimpse of a view.

But it was not the scenery I was afraid of, not nights without girls and beer. In the threat of those somber woods, of those dismal gas stations, there was something all tied up with our plans for the

Wickersham Wall. I was afraid—like all climbers, though I didn't know it then—of getting killed. I had never seen an avalanche, never stepped across a crevasse. We were too brash, I thought, seven college kids blundering into water over our heads.

On the way up, as we drove along, I'd argued with Hank Abrons about danger. Mouthing Rébuffat, I'd contended that we would enjoy climbing all the better if it were perfectly safe; we seek out difficulty, I quoted, not danger. Too naïve, said Hank. Without risk, there'd be nothing to it: Climbing would be reduced to a game. I was sure at the time that he was wrong. I wanted him to be wrong. Like brash college kids, we climbed our route gaily and fast without a real mishap.

When you got down to it, when you stared an avalanche slope or a crevasse field in the face, it lost much of its terror. Notice, we would say, that the slope only slides after 10:00 a.m.; in this part of the glacier, we observed, the crevasses are pretty regular. The only close calls—a few falling rocks and a river-crossing—were over before we could work up a healthy fear; and bravado, we found, was a more effective weapon against them. At McKinley Park Hotel, we were received as conquering heroes, and so we began to believe we were.

Yet 11 years later, I remember my depression before and during that expedition better than I do the feeling of triumph afterwards. It claimed me in the wee hours as we traversed the Denali Highway, when I shivered even in the driver's seat, at a mere 2,000 feet, and stared at the unsympathetic plains of tundra to the left and right. It emerged while we waited, for four days, most of them sunny, for Sheldon to deliver our air-drop at base camp, 35 miles in. We heard imaginary planes, played cards and dice and read out loud to kill the time, cutting back at last to two meals a day, the "what-if he-doesn't..." never quite spoken. During storms, too: my first taste of them, of the insidious, clammy waiting for three days in a sleeping bag, watching the tent walls frost, sponging the floor. Twinges, twenty days in, at the thought of fresh bread and salad and oranges. The gloom depended on standing still, or lying still, waiting and wondering. Once in motion, I was safe.

What sticks in my memory about McKinley is that first perception—which I'd never had in Colorado—of a natural world to which I did not belong. There was too little order to those highway forests, and the dreary lives led in those well-spaced truck stops somehow reflected that fact. There was a hugeness on both sides in which mere human travel seemed inconsequential. The mountain made more sense than the tundra; the hike in was coherent because it led to the climb. All around the edges of the mountains lay a world we specialists would not define. Why did the river wander there? Where did the silt in the sandbar come from? Better hidden, but there just as surely, the sense of the alien lurked on the mountain itself, to be glimpsed in those quiet, depressed moments of waiting. It made no difference to the wind if it blew for a day or a week. The snow turned to ice randomly, not for our step-kicking convenience. The mountain knew nothing about routes.

Six years later, on the north face of Mt. Temple in the Canadian Rockies, I thought there was a fairly good chance of getting killed. I was with Hank again, and Denny Eberl, whom I'd never climbed with before. It was about four in the afternoon of a late June day; we were three-quarters of the way up the 4,500-foot face. We'd gone up impatiently the day after a long storm, climbed the lower wall fast, and now, with simple logic, the snow was beginning to slide in the afternoon sun. There was no ledge to hide on, no going down.

I'd seen avalanches, I thought—from the safety of base camp below McKinley, on adjacent walls on Deborah. But not up close like this. An hour before they had begun, little sloughing trickles of wet snow presaged by runnels of powder. A deterioration in the texture underfoot. Now they were in earnest, and fear and bravado seemed equallyimpotent to cope with them. I watched as a big one piled over the short cliff we crouched under, only a hundred feet to our left; tons of wet snow dumping noisily into view, gathering force and size downward, for all the world like the cement I watched as a kid pouring out of mixers down a wooden trough.

We did what climbers must always do when their real urge is panic: climbed as fast as we could upward, yelling advice, skipping belays, moving desperately. Over the cliff, up into the bright sun on the steep, long slope where all the danger was focused. Like cement,

I kept imaging, and us with no anchor to hold us on, no roof to keep ourselves dry. The grace and naturalness of avalanches seen from the valley floor reduced to a squat, heavy, gouging ugliness up close. Here, too, was proof that we did not belong.

Denny was leading. I went last. In the middle of the slides, starting his own little ones, he plowed through the deep snow upward, as fast as he could move, at a snail's pace. With time to look around, I spotted an escape route left. Five minutes of extreme danger, then safety. I shouted up; Denny yelled back "no." Maniacal, he drove himself straight up, toward steeper snow and an ice cliff. I knew my way was better. I yelled again, told Denny to wait. The three of us assembled, stood on a rotten snow platform, and harangued each other. I thought of unroping and deserting Denny. Hank tried to mediate. All three of us pictured the absurd possibility of being swept off while we stood there arguing.

At last, Hank voted with me; Denny grudgingly gave in. I led the dangerous traverse; in 10 minutes, perhaps, we were safe. The rest of the way up to the summit, I walked in a euphoric stupor, prickling with apology toward Denny, yet glad-oh, how glad—to be alive. Hours later I realized, with a chill, that what must have driven Denny upward was the abstract image of our route, the straight line on the photo. We had traversed off, cheated, lost the true first ascent. At the edge of easy and obvious death, the game had still mattered to him, the line of the route, the human imposition of purpose on a place that mocked purpose. Was he the fanatic, or was I the coward?

A year ago I went to Arizona, alone, during March. It was a deliberately structured trip: eight days alone in the unfamiliar terrain of sandstone buttes and arches and pin-nacles. A calculated way of forcing a new experience upon myself: I didn't know the desert, in fourteen years of climbing I had never spent more than two days in a row alone. To upset my habits further, I would define for myself no goal, no arbitrary point to reach; I would simply wander. And I would leave my camera at home.

It was, I knew, a safe experiment (that too was calculated). I would do no climbing, only hiking: I had gear to stay warm in a Colorado winter, plenty of food, good maps. I worried more about snakebite than frostbite, Navajo laws than safety rules. To be sure, I could slip, break an ankle and die before anyone found me. But I was safer in the desert than driving there.

It snowed the whole time. The country seemed strange, depressingly so, illogical to my mountain-trained mind. But traveling in it was so like winter camping that I found myself oppressed with familiarity. Juniper, it was true, burned smokier than sub-alpine fir; north was less obvious than in a timberline cirque. But lighting the stove, cooking the usual glop, pitching my tent, finding water: all the rituals of camping seemed dead-endingly habitual.

Only the solitude was new, and I was surprised to discover how it frightened me. I could rationalize that the discomfort of the storm made life miserable; but it was not so much a damp sleeping bag that disheartened me as the poverty of myself, the emptiness of waiting and being alone. I turned for solace to my habits. The watch on my wrist became my most valuable piece of gear, for it measured out the pieces of time that I could sanely squander on each necessary task. Time: too much of it, the nights too long, eight days an eternity. If I started to cook breakfast at 7:30, it might last till 8:30, then packing up would take half an hour. Two-and-a-half hours of hiking to an early lunch; by 12:15, chilliness would drive me on. I was tired by 3:00, but it seemed too soon to camp. Perhaps I could eke out the day till 4:00 by angling up this side canyon. The tent up by 4:30, dinner over at 5:30—depressingly early. My diary wasted an hour, then reading by candlelight until 8:00. But I could seldom sleep before 10:00.

My habits were my only companions. I leaned on them, taking a meager comfort from the just-so placing of my boots beside my sleeping bag, the efficiency of Jell-O cooling while the glop was on the stove. I missed my camera, paid less attention than ever to my surroundings. As long as there was a trivial chore to do, I fought off the fear: even gathering wood or sweeping out the tent. But if I tried to sit and reflect and hear the silence and watch the snowflakes fall, I recovered my misery. Even writing in my diary, where I tried to explain the fear, kept the fear away: It was the purposeful act of moving the pen, filling the pages, accounting for my time, that gave the time meaning.

The country had made sense beforehand. There were jumbled chaoses of contour lines I had longed to investigate, claustrophobic canyons to explore. But in the deep snow, most such goals were too far away. I confined myself to a timid circle, and decided, on the fifth day, to go out.

It felt like cheating, there was no denying that, no matter how I rationalized my decision. On the last day, it cleared suddenly, confronting me all the more squarely with my defection. It was truly beautiful here, the red sandstone hissing dry in the dazzling sun; but beautiful also was the prospect of car and town and newspapers. I edged past the smoking hogans and hostile dogs of the Navajo, whom I never saw, and unlocked my car with a sense of relief.

As I drove into Gallup, the thought occurred to me that, in a deliberate attempt to upset my habits, to force myself into new ways of knowing the wilderness, I had only reinforced the old ways, discovered how much I needed habit and ritual. And I knew disquietingly that already the comforts I had longed so to get to were dwindling in value: that however familiar the sliding of tent pole in nylon sleeve was to me, the clink of a quarter in a Coke machine was more so.

In the summer of 1974, I found, with a kind of pleasure, that the fear was still there, as naïve and presumptuous as ever. A few miles south of McKinley, Galen Rowell and Ed Ward and I were climbing on our second day on a 5,000-foot face of Mt. Dickey. Part of the fear came from knowing that this was, simply, the hardest climb of my life. The mist had closed in at dawn; now it seemed certain that a storm would follow. The trick was to get high enough to be okay when the storm came. But, of course, the higher we got the harder it would be to back off. Already a labyrinth of potential rappels lay below us, invisible in the mist.

The granite had to be read in code: orange meant good, white bad. The pitches twisted, traversed deviously; rope drag was a personifiable enemy. All through the day ran the motive thread of fear—subsumed by our skill, tamed by precaution. I grew to hate the feel of carabiner and jumar handle. I kept my mind on a mental abstraction of our route that I could collate with the Washburn photo in my pocket.

Then there would come one of those moments for which the only apt word is *augenblick*—the blink of the eyes signalling the absurdity of the self-evident perception, *yes, here, I am indeed here, exactly here, here rather than any other place*. Absurd, because it was as clear to me in this twelfth straight year of climbing in Alaska as it had been on the drive to McKinley-that here we do not belong

Safety: the imaginary line leading up through the bad white rock; the point of the climb, the definition of the game. Against its purposefulness, those existential *augenblicke* that catch me at a loss to understand what I am doing, and a running commentary of pious fears, like half-remembered nursery rhymes: "And if this rope should break, or if that rock should fall..." "Down will come..."

Now, five days later, the route successfully behind us, I sit alone on the Ruth Glacier, waiting for Sheldon to fly me out, and begin to write this essay. Galen and Ed got out yesterday; this morning, when it was to be my turn, there was a thin drizzle, and Sheldon did not appear. For all those 12 years of Alaska, waiting is as intolerable as ever, and I wonder why. We are sate now; the white rock cannot collapse above us. I have no duties but to cook myself three meals a day, and wait. But I lose interest in the books I pick up, I eat too much, and the rest of the time I catch myself listening for that distant, lovely whine of the plane.

What puzzle is working itself out in me? Which me does the fear define? Am I the same person here, on Mt. Dickey, as I am in an armchair at home? I think now that I am not. But as long as I continue to climb, I cannot separate the various strands of my ego, or figure out how to splice them together.

I know now that Hank was right. Without fear it would be nothing, or little—another game. I have always loved games, loved winning, and I know that much of my urge to climb comes from that: For whenever I see the kind of wilderness that defies route finding, I see it with a heavy heart. The unclimbable exfoliated north wall just opposite Mt. Dickey, for instance, or some of those aimless canyons in Arizona. But why does the game, if that is all it is, continue to vitalize me? I know by now how good or bad I am at other games; I know winning is a dead end. But at the top of our wall on Dickey there was all the violent relief and joy there ever had been, the victory (or escape) as gratifying as ever.

Then why do I so wish, right now, that I were off this glacier? Why does the thought of a beer in the Fairview Inn or a magazine stand in Anchorage hold out all the false promise of civilization, even though I should know better?

The fear connects with, is implicit with, the waiting. An allegory occurs to me: This waiting for salvation by airplane is, in its temporary way, not unlike the waiting of our years for that archangelical moment of death—so much of life is spent impatiently, waiting in lines, for vacations, for quitting time, for that favorite theme in the last movement.

The fear I felt on Temple, on Dickey, however, had the power to transform 15 hours of hard work into an almost timeless, unified day, a day when there was no urge to look at the watch, no need to eat or even sip from the water bottle. And the ironic moment of the Augenblick—does it not give the illusion of time stopped, seized, photographed?

Yes, to all that; but still, why me? If I need the fear, why don't others? Why aren't other lives barren or tawdry for the absence of it? Could I change? Learn to live less mechanistically with others (for climbing is mechanistic), sensitize myself to weakness and love as I have to strength and passion? Could I learn that Buddhist calm that would forever make climbing unnecessary?

But it is almost time for dinner. The clouds are lifting over the Southeast Spur, yet it looks foggy down-glacier. I think he'll fly in tomorrow morning. I really think he will.

—*Originally appeared in* Mountain Gazette 25, *1974.*

13.
Flat Mountain
Written by Charles Bowden

She tells me the garden grabs at her as if the tangle of trees and shrubs were trying to take her down. She just arrived a moment ago and told me crisply that she had once met me briefly at a bookstore in some scattered moment I can't remember. And I am hardly aware of her at this moment. I've been up since dawn chopping celery, onions, carrots and garlic, tossing in a dash of thyme, the zest of a lime, pepper and salt. For days, I've collected veal shanks, a material far more difficult to obtain in my town than cocaine. About six a.m. I fell into my work and by eight the shanks were browned, the vegetables minced and sautéed, the broth simmering and the ossobuco safe within two iron pots, lids on, placed on the lower level of the 350-degree oven. The day before I'd made noodles, carefully drying them on the table. I'm full of this cookery, plus some of the wine I opened to splash into the broth and then sucked down the fumes as the alcohol sizzled off.

The woman is the waif that we beckon to our tables on holidays, an acquaintance of my mother's who has hit a bad patch. She enters like a wind, takes in the glass wall that forms the south of the house, and suddenly she is in the tatters of the garden and walking down the path. She moves with girlish speed. She is in her late seventies and in a few months she will be dead. She was told this a few weeks ago. Her face is lined, browned from the sun, and her thinning hair bristles from its short cropping. She wears sensible slacks and shoes. She has that assurance the old earn when all the fires are banked and gone cold and nothing really matters anymore. Her body is disintegrating as she wanders the garden with the thorny trees grabbing at her clothes. The garden has no straight paths. I do not trust straight things.

We sit in the living room sipping glasses of wine, there are about a half dozen of us. The talk is brittle and to no point, remarks about the mild weather, comments on the fire. Around us the city is silent, dead with the languor of the holiday. The mountains framing the valley hold in the smog. They stand mute and dumb and pocked with pines and patches of snow. I used to climb them until I learned that the top led to nowhere. Now I stay in the flat pan of the desert where I can't look down on things. I am tired of cooking and anxious to eat. For hours, I have thought of the veal slowly leaking its richmarrow into the sauce. I resent the wait, the talk, the sputtering fire, the sparkling wine in the flute in my hand. The food is ready and I want to savor it at its peak. I hate the holiday and everything about it. This whole dinner happens with my resentment. I want to scream leave me alone, I'm sick of people. I want to simply devour the meal and have silence return. The aged woman with one foot in the grave is a nuisance whom I barely acknowledge or listen to.

She begins to cough and then this racking comes from deep within her. She rises, excuses herself, and slips out the front door. My mother, eighty-five and recovering from a stroke, says, with disapproval, "She is going to sneak a cigarette."

I nod.

Finally, she returns and we sit down to eat.

The meal flows with platters of ossobuco, noodles, a salad, and a Norwegian sweet bread the woman has baked from some ancient family recipe. The wine glasses fill and refill. A numbness descends from the food and idle chatter, the great calm of feasts that have been observed for centuries and from this long march of gluttony have created their own rhythms and silences. I am counting the minutes until this will all end. Light floods in from the garden, and the only movement there comes from dozens of birds darting on and off the feeders.

Would you like some more wine?

The old woman considers and nods. I fill the glass like a robot.

"I remember when my husband retired from the military and the party we threw," she says suddenly. "It was the best hangover of my life."

The light pouring in through the glass wall catches those outlaw hairs that sprout on the chins of old women.

She speaks in a soft voice with a sharp undertone, a vinegar lacing through the soft petals of her words. She is back in Wisconsin and she is coming home from college in the Fox River Valley. A huge storm sweeps off the plains. She and the other passengers spent the night snowbound in the rail car and then when she gets to her town, she must walk a mile to her parents' house through the drifts. She is wearing high heels and nylons, it is just after the Second World War, and the cold goes to her bones. And my God, when she finally makes it home, her parents are without food, the storm, you know, so she changes and puts on her skis and glides into the village market. The thing that keeps her going then is theater, the arts and she loves the theater so much that when people listen to her they think she must be part of a company, but it is all really in her dreams. She saves and in '48 takes a vacation in Europe. And, she laughs, she does not come home for three years because she meets a soldier boy, and then come the three children, the moving from base to base, that wild retirement party, my God, when she came down the following morning with that huge hangover, the living room was a shambles and after she passed out the night before, the drunken revelers blowing out the candles had gotten red wax everywhere, even on the walls. The marriage lasted forty-eight years, and she still drives his big Chrysler, he insisted on solid and large automobiles.

I can smell the whiskey and cigarettes of those barracks days. The aroma of the ossobuco has filled the house for hours, the rich scent of bone marrow and meat and wine clogging my senses. But now the whiskey and the smoke knife through this aroma, and there is lipstick on the tumblers, red lipstick smiling from the rim of the glasses where the ice slowly melts and slowly lightens the amber glow of the drink. And I don't ask about the three children, there is nothing to ask since she is alone on a holiday and eating at a stranger's house and dying at a rapid clip. I can see the snow clinging to her young strong legs, clinging to the nylons with a dark seam etched along her leg. I can see her dreams where she is painting sets and cueing actors and dancing on table tops after openings in New York where the war hangs like smoke and is slowly blown away by the post-war boom. She is cross-country skiing across continents and oceans, tossing down a drink now and then, peeling her nylons off as she sits on the bed with only a low light glowing in a strange and hopeful hotel room. And she is not alone in that room and the heat rises off her.

She begins to cough again, that bad cough that says I am not a cold, I am not bron-chitis. The cough that leads to a rattle in the throat and then to nothing at all. She excuses herself and says, "I must go out to the car for my medicine."

As soon as the door closes behind her, the rest of the table drifts into the mutterings about the cough, about concerns, compassion, how brave she is, all the small notes we make to avoid the short word: death. The mutterings all say: we are sorry. And the mutterings never say what we are sorry about. Because that would ruin all the meals.

And then, she is in her chair, as if she silently glided back to the table on skis schussing through perfect snow.

It is time for coffee. We are full. The old woman's eyes seem to float over the walls and the walls are cluttered with photographs, paintings, masks, fetishes, amulets, prayer sticks, a visual noise that makes me calm. I cannot abide orderly walls or any form of symmetry. Order terrifies me, like a hand choking me to death. Suddenly, her eyes alight on a Dorothea Lange print, a shot of an Okie mother in a California camp of the Depression, an image that has come to be seen as the Migrant Mother, a kind of Madonna of that dark and deep economic trough.

She says, "I love that photograph, that is my favorite image."

Her voice rises, there is vivacity, the guileless energy and appetite of a girl in a college classroom, a girl fresh off some farm, who has just had the hand of this thing called art touch her breast for the very first time. I look at her, the wrinkled face, the hairs sprouting on the chin, I sputter something about the history of the photo, how it was taken at the end of a long day, how Lange almost did not go down the road to the camp, how she was tired and it was late in the day and she saw the turnoff and said the hell with it and then twenty miles later felt this nagging, this sense of missing out on some-thing, and wheeled around, went off the side road, got out of her car, and only spent 10 minutes, took but five shots, how she stumbled on the woman being devoured by her children like a sow in a farrowing pen, how the contact sheets reveal the way Lange slowly zeroed in on the famous image, the shots distant, then closer, the baby sucking at the white tit, then the camera waiting for the tiny mouth to release the nipple, the blouse sheltering the breast again, the children flowing around the mother like a flood of flesh, and then click, this icon imprinted in our minds that says hunger and fatigue and the flesh willing us to march on and damn the reason why. And it almost didn't happen, just a happenstance, a trip taken with surprises.

"I love it," she says simply.

We all sag from eating too much. The words float away, their enthusiasm alien to our stupor. The meal begins to break apart. My mother, full of years, must go home, the dark hours will come soon and she does not drive at night. And since the stroke, mornings are her best time and the afternoons are more of a struggle against fatigue. The old woman too must drive and beat the setting of the sun. And there is the cough to constantly rein in, the medicine to swallow. I'm tired also, I've been over my pots and kettles for hours, and there is a table to clear, china and crystal to put away. I want everyone gone, just the fire flickering and then I'll drink all the open bottles until empty, drink them dry and hear the glass clink as I toss them one by one into the trash.

I walk the old woman out. She gets into her big Chrysler, talks about how she knows she should trade it in and get a smaller car, but you know, she continues, they're not safe, nothing but damn little shoe boxes. So she'll stick with his car even though it is an ugly brown, she couldn't talk him out of the color. I watch her drive away.

Then I empty the bottles. The wine tastes so rich I think a carpet of just stomped pulp flows across my tongue. The bitterness lingers like a gift as I swirl the cabernet in my mouth. I am through with the peaks. I tell you it is all a flat mountain. The peaks are a lie, or at best a fantasy. The skis glide, the smells hit the face, the hotel rooms glow with weak light, the lipstick smears the rim of the whiskey tumbler. A hand is on the body, the buttons come undone and the skis keep gliding, silently gliding, and the peaks are never apparent until long after they are passed. The seam of the nylon snaking down the creamy skin of young fresh legs, breath hanging in the frozen air and blinding light. And the mother, that cracker face, staring straight at the camera, unsmiling, as the children take her down in the undertow. Drove by and almost did not come back. Just 10 minutes for five quick shots.

The best hangover of my life, the red wax even on the walls.

———

—*Originally appeared in* Mountain Gazette 79, *2001.*

14.
The Impsons, Ed & Ma'am
Written by John Peters, M.D.

Christmas Eve, 1961: a holiday at home for most folks, but it was the night Lydia Impson walked five miles through a raging blizzard to get help for her dying husband, Ed.

Five miles in that savage storm would have been an ordeal for a trained mountaineer in the prime of life. But imagine an 81-year-old woman, crippled with arthritis and almost blind. It sounds impossible, but then, you didn't know Lydia Impson. She may have been nearly unable to walk, and well-nigh sightless, but her spirit was as strong as the mountains.

Ed had "taken sick" about two weeks before Christmas and had gotten progressively worse. He was having trouble breathing, his legs were swollen, he had a high fever, and he was passing blood and pus in his urine. To make things worse, the Impsons didn't have a phone, and their nearest neighbors were five miles away, down a dirt road blocked in winter by drifting snow. And their only transportation was Sally, an ancient brown mare that hadn't been ridden in years.

Ed stoically took stock of his situation and told Lydia it was no use, that there was nothing she could do. No one could help. "Ceptin' me," she said later, proud but matter-of-fact. Over Ed's protests she put on her "shawl and greatcoat," as she put it, and headed out into the storm. She went to the barn and got Sally out of her stall. "I couldn't sit on no horse, 'cause of the arthritis in my hip," she said. "So I just grabbed onto Sally's tail, and headed her down the road toward

Bob's place. I knowed Ed was a-dyin', and I knowed there was a purty good chance I was goin' to die too. I've been livin' in these mountains for nigh onto 75 years, an' I've helped bury more than a few young, strong folks who got themselves caught out in storms like this 'un. But I figgered, if I don't go, Ed's gonna die. And if he dies, ain't much use in me goin' on either.

"Ain't neither of us afraid a dyin'," she smiled a tranquil smile. "It's close to our time anyways."

So the old horse and the old woman plodded on through the storm. Sally forced her way through two, three-foot high drifts for five miles that night, along that old river road, avoiding the steep dropoff on one side. One misstep would have sent them both plunging into the icy river below... but their steps were sure.

No one knows how long they were out in that storm. As crippled as Lydia was, it must have taken them eight, 10 hours. "That cold wind was a-bitin' right through me. And these old hips and knees, they felt like they was gonna freeze up solid," Lydia smiled. "I could only go a little ways, and then I'd pull on ol' Sally's tail, and we'd stop and rest for a while, and then we'd go on. We kept doin' it till we got there."

Around midnight, Bob Magnus, the game warden, heard a sound on his front porch. He went outside and found Lydia collapsed on his doorstep, nearly dead from exhaustion and hypothermia. The faithful Sally stood a few feet away, watching over her. Bob carried Lydia inside and phoned me.

"Hey, Doc, I've got Mrs. Impson down here at my place. She's been out in this storm, and she's in pretty bad shape. My wife and I are trying to get her warmed up, but all she keeps saying is, 'Don't bother about me. Ed's back up at the house, and I think he's dying. You've got to help.' If you can get down here right away, we'll take my Jeep and try to make it back up to the Impson place."

"I'll be right there."

It took me almost half an hour to make the seven-mile trip. The storm hadn't slacked off a bit; if anything, it was coming in harder. The snow was still falling and the wind was up, causing whiteouts that reduced visibility to a foot in front of the wind-shield. After many a white-knuckled moment, I pulled up in front of Bob's.

The first thing I did was give Lydia a quick exam, over her protests. "Don't you worry about me," she scolded. "It's Ed who's the sick one, Doc. He's got the fever and the cough, and he's peein' blood. He's real short of breath, and he's swole up like a poisoned pup. He's probably dead by now—it took me so long ta get here," she sniffled

"It's a miracle you made it here at all," I said, patting her on the shoulder. "Listen, Bob and I are going to head up right now and check on Ed. Don't worry."

"I'm a-goin' with you," she said determinedly.

"Lydia, you almost froze to death tonight. Wouldn't it be better if you stayed here with Mrs. Magnus and rested up a little more?"

"No sir. My place is with my Ed. If he's still alive, he'll be a-needin' me. He's blind, see, and can't do for himself. Just pack an extra blanket or two and I'll ride in back, out a the way of you menfolk. But I ain't takin' no for an answer."

Well, that was that.

It took us nearly an hour to get back up to the Impson place, in four-wheel-drive with chains on all four wheels. How an old horse and an 81-year-old woman ever did it on foot is beyond comprehension. I guess love does have unseen powers.

The Impson house was an old-fashioned earthen-walled place with a sod roof. As we stepped in the rough-hewn wooden door, I could immediately see Ed was in bad shape. He was sitting up in an overstuffed chair, puffing for air with waterlogged lungs. His legs and feet were horribly swollen, like the limbs of an agonized giant. He was coughing up blood. There was a milk bottle on the floor next to him, half full of an unholy mixture of urine, puss and blood. Ed had a deadly combination of heart failure, pneumonia and a severe kidney infection. Thrice-deadly, really: any of the three was enough to kill a man in his 80s. Ed really needed to be in a hospital, in intensive care, and even there his chances of survival would be poor.

"Ed, I'm going to give you a shot of penicillin and something else to strengthen your heart and get rid of the fluid in your lungs. Then we're going to get you out of here and down to the hospital."

I began to prepare the injection. As I did, he reached over and squeezed my arm gently.

"Doc, I sure do appreciate you comin' out in this weather, and I don't mean to be disrespectful, but I really don't want to go to no hospital. I won't." All this was said with painful effort, like a man pushing a boulder up a steep mountainside. Before I could say anything, he continued. "Soon as I leave here, somebody's gonna steal my ranch."

The Impsons "ranch" consisted of a few acres of hardscrabble mountain terrain, with hardly enough flatland to make a pool table out of, buried in snow seven months out of the year; but to an old-time Westerner like Ed Impson, it was "his spread." And beyond price.

"Who's going to steal your ranch?" I asked gently.

"Don't matter who. Someone," he rasped. "And I ain't leavin.'"

"You may die if you don't go to the hospital, Ed."

"Then that's what I'll do."

"You mean go to the hospital?"

"No, I mean I'll die."

Just then I felt a tug on my shirtsleeve. It was Lydia. She drew me aside and whis-pered, "If Ed says he ain't a-goin', he ain't a-goin'. And don't be thinkin' of tryin' to make him go, neither. He may be 86 years old and blind as a Pharisee, but he's still got that ol' Colt 44 six-gun in that coat hangin' on his chair."

"Thanks for the advice," I said. "But don't worry. I don't ever try to make anyone do anything they don't want to. But I'll tell you, I'll do everything I can for him right here, but I don't think he has much of a chance if he stays."

I was, as you will see, wrong...

Bob Magnus and I stayed with Ed and Lydia that stormy night. I gave Ed a shot of penicillin every four hours, plus heart stimulants and diuretics. In between, we talked with the tireless Lydia, who insisted on staying up with us. I'd noticed a big scar on Ed's right groin, and the fact that his right testicle was missing. I asked her if he'd lost it in some kind of accident.

"No, Doc," she said matter-of-factly. "He lost that nut o' his back in 1898. We'd been married about a year, when Ed went and got himself a bad case of the mumps. Well sir, the mumps went right down him, the way they'll do, and they settled right in that nut o' his.

"We were livin' up on Lizard Head Pass at the time. I loaded him in the buckboard and took him down to the hospital in Telluride. He was in that hospital for 'bout four days and that nut just kept gettin' bigger and bigger. It was hurtin' him something awful. So Ed called me over to his bed. 'Ma'am,' he said—he always called me Ma'am-Go hitch up the team and bring the buckboard around. Take me on home. I asked the doc here to cut the damn thing off, but he won't do it. Says it'll get better by itself. But it's plain to see, it just keeps gettin' bigger and bigger, and I'm afraid it's gonna burst. I'm gonna have you take care of it.'

"Now I was gettin' a might nervous. 'I don't know if I can do it, Ed, I told him. 'Sure you can, Ma'am, he said. 'You watched them cowboys castratin' them steers last year. Just do the same thing to me.'

"So that's what I did. We went home. Ed sharpened up his hunting knife, and then fired it up till it was redhot. Said it wouldn't bleed so bad if it got seared while it got cut. Then he took the Bible to bite on whilst I cut off that bad nut."

Thank God the story was over! I was sweating just thinking about someone performing a semi-castration on me with a hot knife and no anesthetic. I looked over at Magnus; his face was a sickly shade of green. Lydia smiled beautifully at us.

Well, ol' Ed went through a crisis that stormy night, but by morning he had made it through and was beginning to make a miraculous recovery. Bob Magnus and I checked on him every day for the next three weeks. He was completely well in a month. Like I said, I was wrong, thank God.

There was just one more installment in Ed's medicinal story. On one of my visits, he beckoned me to come close, and confided in me in a low voice: "Doc, Ma'am told me you talked 'bout me losin' that right nut o' mine. I guess my left kept workin' purty good, 'cause she gave me a baby boy two years after that. And it kept workin' good till about a year ago. Maybe it's 'cause I'm gettin' a might old, but me and Ma'am can only make love about twicet a week now. It's beginnin' to worry both of us. There was a time when twicet a day weren't enough. And now, here we are, down to twicet a week," he said mournfully.

"Ma'am works with me most every night, but I can only get hard enough to please her a coupla times a week," he went on. "I'm beginnin' to feel like I'm only half a man, Doc. Next time you come down, can you bring one of them testyrone shots I heard about?" I did what he asked, and, placebo effect or not, it sure seemed to work. He asked me to keep giving him the "testyrone" every time I came. By that time I was only seeing Ed every few days, and if I was a day or two late Ed would be beside himself with concern. "Thank God ya got here in time, Doc! We were afraid that testyrone was a-fixin' to wear off!"

Several years later, Ma'am broke her hip. It never really healed right. She never was able to walk again, and went into a nursing home. Ed tried to stay home by himself; he hired a nephew to stay with him, but it didn't work out. Within two days he was out of his head, screaming, hallucinating, threatening to kill himself and everyone else within range of his Colt 44. He just missed Ma'am so much he couldn't take it. We had to arrange for him to stay in the nursing home with Ma'am. As soon as he heard her voice, he was fine. Love conquers, and cures, all. They had a rule back then that males and females had to stay on different floors in nursing homes, even if they were married. Soon after he arrived the nurse on duty called me. She was upset, to put it mildly: "I can't keep Mr. Impson out of Mrs. Impson's room! And he's always trying to have"—I could actually hear her blushing over the phone—"intercourse with her!"

I tried not to chuckle as I replied. "Mr. and Mrs. Impson have been making love at least twice a week for over 70 years. I guess they're just luckier than you or me and our spouses. Now listen, I want you to tell your administrators to change the rules for the Impsons. Put them in the same room, and keep the door closed if real lovemaking bothers you. And tell your administrator if he doesn't do it, I'm gonna come down there and when I'm through with him he won't be able to have intercourse for six months. If that doesn't work, I'll move the Impsons to another nursing home, and he can kiss that income goodbye."

The nurse laughed nervously. "You're joking, aren't you, Doctor?"
"Of course," I said. "But don't tell him that, okay?"
"Okay. There's just one more thing."

"What's that?"

"Well, Mr. Impson has some kind of padded belt on. He won't let us take it off him, even when he's bathing. Could you talk to him about it?"

"I'll be down there in a couple of days, and I'll see what I can do."

The padded belt turned out to be Ed's money belt; and it was stuffed with $32,000 in medium to large bills. I persuaded him to let an attorney put it in the bank for him.

Ed then told me he had another $120,000 in cash, that he and Ma'am had buried in coffee cans under their old house: this was "the ranch" he was so worried about somebody stealing. I immediately called the San Miguel County Sheriff, and he went right out to the Impsons' place. Ed's fears proved correct. The floor was ripped up, and there were empty coffee cans strewn around...

Ed died at the ripe old age of 101; Lydia died a few weeks before he did, 96 years old.

Ed probably could have lived forever, but when his wife died, he decided to die too. Yep, decided: He just stopped eating and drinking, there was nothing anyone could or should have done about it, till he quietly passed away.

And the thieves who stole their money? Well, in an intimate place like San Miguel County, we had a pretty good idea who they were. And frontier justice had a way of making things right in those days. But that's a story for another time—when the statute of limitations on certain "crimes" runs out...

―*Originally appeared in* Mountain Gazette 79, *2001*

15.
On the Frontier

Written by Steve Wishart

"Does ropin' really beat dopin'? I wonder."
  Luckily Shady's mother decided not to make the trip.

I had been trying to get someone to go to Cheyenne Frontier Days with me for weeks. And while everybody flushed enthusiastic at first, they all tended to have second thoughts about going up there for six days of ritual red-necking in the end. While there were more than enough wild stories about the rodeo, they usually ended with someone in jail or on the wrong side of some cowboy's idea of what constitutes good behavior.

I was beginning to grasp at straws for companionship in what my paranoid mind had escalated into a fearful, sweaty excursion into the World Out There.

I knew those people were different from me, and I was worried. But Shady Lane's mother? The idea just didn't set right, especially after he'd told me that she hadn't said anything all winter.

It was while he went around telling whoever would listen that I had refused to drive his mother to Cheyenne that it first occurred to me that Shady's mother was... ah, no longer among the living. All along he had wanted me to escort a small box of ashes back to Friendly

Soil, the family's ancestral home, Cheyenne.

But sober morning thought convinced Shady that a beat-up pickup, loaded down with the refuse of my manner of traveling, was not the suitable vehicle for such a delicate mission, and I was spared the problem of having to explain just why I was toting around somebody else's mother's ashes. I mean, what if the memorial park had decided not to take them? ("Listen, buddy, no telling who's in that box. And besides, you don't look like you belong in Cheyenne, anyway. WHO ARE YOU?")

No, I was going to have to do this one alone.

Cheyenne Frontier Days—The Big Daddy of Them All. Packing them in since 1897. The best riders on the best animals at the best rodeo, competing for huge amounts of prize money. And all of this was about to be covered by the least experienced Rodeo Reporter in the western United States.

My past trips into the world of rodeo had been limited to the Hotel Jerome Bar in Aspen, listening to one of my fellow bartenders run on about his roping horse, Jack. But I knew the feeling ran deep, because he was housing his family in a log cabin, and his idea of a vacation was an all-night drive to Muckstick, Nebraska, for three days of roping school... with Jack.

New Boy in the Press Room. After negotiating myself up to Cheyenne and into the only available motel room—and judging from the price of my accommodations, the management was only too aware of this fact—I called Press Central.

Oh yes, they had received the letter of introduction but, uh, blanket press passes were very tight and if I would see them tomorrow, they would see what they could do for me.

I had been told very seriously before I left that if I wanted to "get along in Cheyenne" I would need "a pair of boots and a good straw." I had the boots, holdovers from my cowboy days in college in New York City, but decided my old Lyndon Baines Johnson white felt would have to do for a head-piece.

I could have used the straw.

I could also have used one of those shirts with the pearly buttons. And a four-pound, silver bucking-bronc belt buckle. And something other than my octagonal purple sunglasses.

Understand, it wasn't outright hostility that greeted me when I showed up in the press room for my credentials. Rather, it was a certain wariness. A silly reaction on their part, I thought. Hell, I didn't go up there to savage their cowboys. On the contrary, I was afraid those cowboys were going to savage me.

After a little fencing with good ol' boy Tracy, my main contact at the press office, it was decided that I would be given a daily pass to the VIP press box. This cat-bird seat was tucked under the eaves of the grandstand across from the chutes. While it lacked the immediacy of the old press box adjacent to the chutes, it did provide the best all around view of the spectacle, and that's what I was seeking—the entire, majestic sweep.

(An aside on the press relations: toward the end of the week, a friend, attractively female, showed up in Cheyenne and when she accompanied me to the press room, my stock rose sharply. The next morning, when I showed up with two lovely ladies—-the second one our photographer-it absolutely skyrocketed. One of the previously unavailable magic blue "blanket" press buttons appeared for the photographer, and I finally was admitted to the old press box next to the chutes. As in most places, tits and ass are still coin of the realm in Cheyenne.)

Back to Day One. With press pass in hand, I made my way up and up into the grand-stand, stopping only for beer and a little grease for sustenance... up past the Burns boys and out onto the catwalk toward the press box. Suddenly it dawned on me why I had long ago given up wearing cowboy boots (except when I visited the West End Bar): Cowboy boots hurt when you walk. Which makes sense, because they were designed for wearing astride a horse. But why were all these other people wearing them? Wobbling along, I wondered if they all felt as conspicuous as I did.

I finally made it to an empty seat, set out my afternoon's food and beer, stacked up a couple of chairs to lounge on and got ready to enjoy the show.

On the first day, the show began, as it would every day, with the grand opening cer-emony—enter all the dandies of the "Daddy of Them All." Below me, astride good-look-ing horses, I saw about forty ladies and as many different shades of matching pastel hats, coats, pants, boots and sashes—the latter proclaiming things like "Miss Routt County Whoopie Days." Lots of flags and every name in the parade announced. And bringing up the rear, the Ogalala Sioux of the Teton-Dakota Nation. The only walkers.

An interesting show, one time out, but after that first day, I took to sitting in one of the beer tents on the Midway, downing a brew and reading the paper until I heard the call for contestants' events.

I Have to Admit that I Developed a Taste for Certain Parts of the Rodeo. This, in spite of some of the cruelty and violence. Or, maybe, because of it—but we don't have to get into that... do we, Herr Doctor Krafft-Ebing?

Take the brahma bull event. Actually, bull-riding doesn't sound too hard to take at first: just some guy trying to stay on top of a very large animal for eight seconds. But how angry this large animal can get quickly becomes apparent. And an angry bull rarely is satisfied merely to rid himself of his baggage. He often wants to put his rider on his horns, as well.

Since the bulls seem pretty docile in their pens, it's hard to figure the hostility one of these 1,500-pound beasts will exhibit in the arena toward the mere fly of a man on its back..unless you know about the flank strap, that is. (In bull- and bronc-riding events, a leather strap is noosed around the lower stomach of the animal and cinched sharply just as rider and mount exit from the chute. A veritable pinching of the balls. It makes all the animosity understandable.)

Following the brahma-bull event, I got my first taste of steer-roping—and I found it a bit gut wrenching. It goes something like this: A steer is released from a pen at one end of the arena and given a 30-foot lead before a lone rider chases him down, puts a rope cleanly around both horns and then rides by at full gallop. The animal usually is lifted entirely off its feet as the rope goes taut between horse and steer.

Seeing that first steer ripped off its feet sent a chill up my spine. (Anyone who has ever suffered a serious neck injury probably would recoil.) The chill returned a while later when one steer got up with its head cranked crookedly toward the sky, trying to run away, yet veering again and again into the arena wall.

But after the initial shock, the cruelty doesn't seem to bother the sensitivities much. Along with that one broken neck, I saw perhaps four animals break a leg. I also saw lots of flanks bloodied by spurs. But it was all tolerable in context: Rodeo, after all, is a direct link to the working cowboy, who had behind him the whole tradition of honest labor. The cruelty of making the whole thing a sport is thus softened. It's not at all like bear-baiting or cock-fighting—or pro football. There are, in fact, several events in which the animals have a fair chance of winning. About half the cowboys in the bucking events gimped back to the chutes, and several had to be helped off the ground.

After steer-roping came steer-wrestling—definitely the brass-balls event. If you've never seen it, picture a large beast flying out of a chute, followed seconds later by a rider armed only with his bare hands. The cowboy runs down the steer, leaps off his mount onto the animal's horns, stops the charging brute, and if all goes well, throws him on his back. It is a little life-and-death tableau that lasts perhaps 25 seconds and was repeated before my eyes about 20 times every afternoon. No doubt because of my own days as a wrestler, I was completely caught up in this event. I felt like Norman Mailer vicariously enjoying a boxing match. No—I felt like I was out there. If the steer put up a solid resistance, I was fighting him, too, knocking over chairs in the press box, digging my heels into the floor. On a good toss, my head would snap to the scoreboard at one with the cowboy's. Yeah! Together we were delighting in a little one-to-one combat of man against beast.

Except for steer wrestling, my enthusiasm for most of the events was pretty general. I enjoyed watching them, but I never got so deeply into any of them that I followed the standings. It's the kind of pick-and-choose entertainment where you can appreciate a good performance here and then move on to something interesting over there. A rodeo, in fact, is just like a circus.

The Analogy of The Circus Runs Throughout. All the events are structured so that there is always something going on. Your attention is constantly courted. If things start to slow down, on come the clowns or in march the Indians.

Some of the make-up events were classics. Like the Dinner-Bell Derby. I prefer to call it the Tit Race. Visualize a half-dozen mares with their unweaned colts: mother and child are separated from each other and moved to opposite ends of the grandstand. The colts are released. Well... you get the picture. The winner, of course, is the first colt to hit the right tit. I'm not sure what bothered me about this particular event. Was it demeaning to the horses? Latently sexist? In the end, it just seemed stupid.

After the first day, I became acutely aware of the repetitions. All the jokes were old and the gags the same: "She must have been a welder's daughter... she had a set of lean legs..."

But, happily, there were also some rare moments of unplanned humor-like the afternoon Monte Montana was out on the track, doing his grand finale, roping five riders at once with a great loop. He's spread the loop-some 20 feet in diameter-across the track and was earnestly heading toward the riders when he was brought up short by a track official caught up in the other end of the rope. Just as the five riders thundered by. Monte was yanked from his saddle and did a flip over his end of the loop while the sport-coated official at the other end went flying. It was pure Keystone. The move won the biggest hand of the day.

The Indians, On the Other Hand, Were Pretty Depressing. I know they've performed at rodeos for years. They're a stock act, brought in to evoke memories of the cowboys and Indians of the Old West. But it all seems so wrong, especially in this day. At Cheyenne, they trooped out to do a few steps in the afternoons, walked in the parades, danced at night and starred in hundreds of snapshots. They were the trained bears of the rodeo.

Women aren't treated much differently. I suppose it should come as no great surprise that the Great Awakening hasn't hit Cheyenne with full force just yet. (N.O.W. was represented with a float in the parade, but carried a decidedly mild message about equal rights under law.)

No, the rodeo is a man's world, and it has enough tradition behind it to cause change to come slowly. So the rodeo woman finds her role pretty clearly staked out: barrel-racing, pony bronc-riding and, of course, beauty queening. This year's Miss Frontier Days, Beth Murry, had ridden in the pony bucking contest previously, but to continue as part of the rodeo world, she eventually had to make the shift from participant to object.

This is also reflected in the fashions in Cheyenne. That chic thinness that passes for beauty in all the right places hasn't made many inroads in Wyoming. Those men still like their stock corn-fed. Shapely, yes... but substantial. Most of the older women were on the large side and relatively unself-conscious about how they looked. In fact, it seemed the men were much more into their image than the women: It wasn't uncommon to find a slim gent with his hat cocked just-so and his pants razor-creased, sitting next to a woman in curlers and pedal pushers. I didn't see too many halter tops in Cheyenne, either. Rather, those pointy bras that aim a little too high and sensible shoes were the style. (A substantially built cowgirl at full gallop probably would look a little sloppy without a bra.) But I digress.

Every afternoon the rodeo ended with a little bit of insanity sponsored by *The Denver Post*, called the Wild Horse race. Ten teams of three men each were given a haltered, unbroken horse with instructions to saddle it, get a man in the saddle and then get both man and animal around the track. An event for the crazies. It wasn't necessarily a team's own horse that caused the greatest problems, however... it was those nine others.

Usually, just as one team succeeded in quieting its steed and stood numbly arranging the saddle, another horse inevitably careened toward them, dragging with it some fool with visions of money impressed too strongly in his head to let go. That kicked off a reaction in the first horse, soon sending cowboys flying in all directions. A race by fiat. Aside from the delicious confusion, I liked this event because the horses were decidedly in control.

But It Does Make You Wonder Why They Do It All. Why were those people out there competing in the first place? There is some money involved, to be sure. But according to the Rodeo Cowboys Association, only 100 of the professionals win a pile of it in a season.

At Cheyenne, more than 1,000 contestants paid $75 or $100 apiece to enter each event. With a misdirected flick of the wrist they could throw away that money in mere seconds in an event like the calf-roping contest. Of course, if they hit, they stood to make a lot of money quickly. And we all love a gamble. But the risks involved are very real, and to most of us, they would hardly seem worth the relatively small return.

I don't know why they do it. Maybe there are mystical reasons. A group of outlaws on the fringe, living a free life that always has been associated with the best in the American Character. With the mechanization of ranching today, our stereotyped cowboy is fast becoming obsolete. But he can live on at the rodeo.

As a nation, we seem to need a stiff-lipped, independent, macho type as a part of our collective psyche. Look at all those cigarettes Marlboro sells. And why not? It is a romantic life, a cut above the one most of us lead. I need those fantasies myself to help get me through the week. I can do without the lumps and bruises. But I'll buy a ticket and all the fantasies that come with it.

One Afternoon I Was Sitting in the Press Box Watching Quail Dobbs Shoot Wilbur Plaguer in the Ass with a Shotgun, just like he did every afternoon about that time, when an official-looking type came up and asked me if I was "working press." Paranoid, I reached into my pocket for the piece of paper that attested to that fact, when he said, "No, no. I mean, do you want to come to a press conference for Danny Davis?"

Seeing my duty clearly, I nodded, and after the rodeo, headed for the Rouge Room at the Little America Motel and Country Club to meet my first Cowboy. Or so I thought.

After we media people had settled around the table, a "cowboy"—in matching robin's-egg-blue shirt and pants-walked in, with 15 pounds of turquoise and silver around his neck. As the conference progressed, it became apparent that Danny Davis was from Massachusetts, by way of Nashville, was heavily into the Music Business and hadn't had cow shit on his shoes for quite a while. Danny Davis and his group, Nashville Brass, had played hundreds of fairs and rodeos. The music they played for the four big night shows at the arena was much like the people who attended them: straight, if a little country, easy to understand and essentially harmless. Doc Severinsen and the Now Generation Brass, The Loretta Lynn Show with the Coal Miners, Hank Thompson, Jr. and the Brazos Valley Boys—and Danny Davis and the Nashville Brass. Even the names didn't threaten—unlike Traffic, Chicago, War, and Blood, Sweat and Tears. But the music, if a little bland, was very professional, as itshould have been. Because playing fairs and rodeos is Big Business.

Danny Davis is a case in point. The Nashville Brass has recorded 16 albums, each one of which has sold at least 100,000 records. Each one of those records is a catalogue seller, which means that the longer it's out, the more records it sells. And now about all the group does is make records and play at fairs.

Danny seems to have a sense of what he's doing. The Nashville Brass is solidly musical (of the nine musicians, five have doctorates and two have masters' degrees, and Davis himself is the only one without a degree); but it is also something of a novelty act.

Because they do have a limited audience appeal they push hard. They make all those shows in their own plane, with a traveling group of 17. The plane has two bars and originally was designed for 54 people, so I guess being on the road isn't too uncomfortable.

Our press conference ended when the road manager, a former rodeo rider himself, came in to ask what "uniform" the band was going to be wearing. "Did we wear the wine last night..? Well, let's go with the blues." All the way to the bank.

Nighttime shows were held at the arena and lasted about four hours. As with the rodeos, they were orchestrated like a circus; any time the action slowed down, on came the clown with his dogs or Miss Something-or-Other, shooting down the track, flicking sharp salutes off the brim of her color-coordinated cowboy hat.

After the nightly chuckwagon races and some Roman riding by the sequin girls, on rolled the stage. This was a stage mounted on wheels and pulled onto the track like some musical ark. By this time, it was completely dark and the stage became a strange island of light and music out in the void. It was about my favorite part of the rodeo, sitting up in the press booth slowly sipping beer and looking out at those little figures below on the island while the spotlight beside me hissed and smoked...

But the music was bland and the audiences were, too. The real night spectacle wasn't out there. It was beyond the stage, in the distance, where Cheyenne pulsed and shimmered in the blackness, sucking you in. The real action was downtown.

It Goes Something Like This: "You know, I had just turned 14, and I was a rangy sort of kid to begin with, but nobody seemed to care. Frontier Days was really wide open then, with gambling and drinking right on the street. The only thing they cared about was whether you were able to reach that money up to the top of the bar. Well, I sauntered into the Mayflower and found a stool at the end of the bar. When the bartender finally got down to me, I was so nervous all I could think to order was gin and Seven-Up, which gives you an idea of how sophisticated I was. I didn't care, though, what I was drinking, never having done much of it before, and being so thrilled to be in there with all those real men, tossing them down just like the cowboys. Needless to say, I got a little carried away, and after about a dozen drinks, my critical judgment was somewhat impaired. You can imagine my surprise when I looked up and saw what appeared to be a band marching down the bar. Not only that, but it seemed to be a very small band.

"Now, there was this typical cowboy-type sitting next to me. We hadn't exchanged a word, but I figured I just had to find out about this decidedly midget band that was making its way toward me. I asked him if there was anything unusual about the band, and he turned around and took a look, turned back and said, 'Nope.' Getting a little panicky, I figured I better put it a little stronger: 'I mean, do they seem a little small to you?' He fixed me with a hard stare and told me, 'They seem perfectly normal to me.'

"For about a year after that I stayed away from gin. I figured midget bands marching down the bar was what happened when you got drunk."

That was the sort of experience I was looking for when I went to Cheyenne. I've always had a taste for the bizarre and what better place to look than in a town full of raving drunks, midgets and girls?

Curiously, the Mayflower was something of a letdown. It was big, for sure—three long rooms packed with sweating bodies, the beer lapping at my ankles—but it was also predictable. Like a big fraternity party where everybody gets loaded in a crowd and seethes around. The non-stop country music in one room was too loud, there were periodic fights, girls puking and guys passed out in the corners. OK... but all that does begin to pale a little when you get much beyond 25.

Also, things apparently were toned down this year because of a heavy rash of vandalism in previous years. The Mayflower crowd spilled out into the street and onto adjacent cars, but was pretty well beered into submission.

Sleaze, On The Other Hand, Was Certainly To Be Had. On my first night in town, I made a tentative circuit of the bars and was heading back to the motel when I passed a window that sported a sign imploring: "Girls Wanted." Rounding the corner and cutting through the lobby of the Palace Hotel, I came on a sight for sorely demented eyes.

Up on the bar of Sam's Place was a vision in pink chiffon and pale flesh—a vast expanse of pale flesh. A modified-bee-hived blonde was up there grinding away to "C and W," her head a few inches from the ceiling and her bare thighs a like distance from the brims of a line of straws. It wasn't a midget band, but it filled the bill.

I slid onto the first vacant bar stool and ordered up. The place was a study in contrasts: the bartender couldn't have been more than 20; she was dressed to the teeth and looked like nothing so much as a nervous high school queen—as opposed, say, to some very professionally-at-ease women at the other end of the bar. Aside from her lack of dancing ability, the dancer also had to contend with six pool tables in the other room. I remember thinking, "She's competing against high drama on the green felt and she's losing."

But not for long. She was dressed in a Barbie-Doll type top (one wished it left more to the imagination) and a matching pair of panties. As old Playboy-type pin-ups were flashed on the opposite wall, she started to roll down the panties, letting a hint of pubichair hang out, galvanizing every weathered eye in the place-and the battle was won.

Sam's Place also was the center of hustle in Cheyenne. There was some serious pool being played in the other room and a lot of obviously idle women were milling around The place became my own "Outlaw Bar" in the town. I felt pretty comfortable there because it's the kind of outlawry I'm used to. While I was sitting there, two cowboys gave each other the soul/freak thumb-shake, a couple of black pimps paraded through in platform heels and pink denim pants-and jacket outfits and a chorus of ladies in too much makeup successfully steered drunks in and out the door.

I Moved On to Another Kind of Nightlife. An evening far from the downtown section, at the Little America Motel and Country Club, convinced me that my stereotyped view of the cowboys and loners hovering on the fringes of respectability was, perhaps, bullshit. If anything, a large segment of the rodeo crowd is conservative and actively upward-mobile.

The two bars with the most authentically cowboy-rancher crowds were the Holiday Inn and Little America. We all know what the Holiday Inn is like; Little America is a giant place with hundreds of rooms all done in red brick, mock-Williamsburg Colonial. Inside the Manor House, looming in the middle of the com-pound, are the lobby, coffee shops, nightclub and a fancy restaurant, all reminiscent of a country club in an old Fred Astaire-Ginger Rogers movie.

One night my companions and I went to Little America for the Big Dinner. Aside from the obvious ego-boost of squiring two ladies around, I found my presence was apparently more acceptable in the company of such presentable women. We were ushered into a room literally saturated with red plush and crystal, those seemingly univer sal synonyms of taste that always give me a feeling of having stepped into a showroom for Castro Convertible furniture. It occurred to me that the red velvet booth we were sitting in probably folded down into a bed. But, hopefully, not during dinner.

The food was OK, just missing it all the way down the line. The only thing extravagant about it was the price. Still this was, we had been assured, the place for a fancy meal in Cheyenne, and the ranching crowd was out in force, particularly in the nightclub (the next room). Out in force, but not very lively. A group of the good burghers out for a good time. Hats and boots, but clean hats and shiny boots. The Marlboro man would have been appalled.

Wednesday Already? Time Begins to Fade and My Perceptions Blur. It's been too many afternoons of beer and foot-long hot dogs and being given the announcer's count of how many cars are in the parking lot from Nevada or Colorado or Maine. (He went through every state in the Union every day.) If I was going to take four more days of this, I needed some calculated diversion: the Carney.

I know all about carneys. They're all rip-offs. They always extract 50 cents from you and get you into some dumb tent to find-nothing. But I always go. I love it. Especially when you can say "screw it" and blow $10 going into every shuck show on the Midway. trying to guess just how you are going to be ripped off.

Even big Chloe. A very slick come-on, that lady. She had me on the ropes. Larger-than-lite pictures depicting an Amazon telling her discoverers to "take me to your leader." A taped introduction explaining how she had been contracted for over $10,000 to appear with this fair, how she was "almost 10 feet tall." How could a man of my diminutive stature (five feet, three inches) resist? The Ultimate Woman. I'd be able to gaze levelly, right into her navel.

Naturally, throughout the entire spiel, Chloe was always referred to in the present tense, a living, breathing monstrosity right in that tent, Rube. She was in there, all right. All 10 feet of mummified bones. I came out whistling. Not a bad scam, I told the fat, bleary-faced ticket-seller. When he realized I wasn't going to demand my money back, a spark of recognition flashed into his one good eye. "Ah, so you can appreciate a good joke, my friend."

And so it went, right down the Midway. One folly after another. I saw the dog with skin like an elephant; the baby with two heads, four arms and three legs (mercifully, in a jar, since I don't think I could have handled that one alive); the chamber of tortures featuring "Slaves of Love." I saw everything, in fact, except one spook house. Nothing was going to get me in there. I had been in one of them at Excelsior Park in Deephaven, Minnesota—and I knew those things could scare you.

I really like carneys and the atmosphere around them. It's a speeded-up version of the old American Sell. All those people with angles trying to separate you from the long green. "Hey, Mountain Climber (a day pack over my shoulder), come over here. I want to talk to you." The Cosmic Guesser: "Just give me the first initial and I will guess the name of your girlfriend, your horse, your mother-in-law's birth sign..." That was pretty good, too. For $1 you could fool the Cosmic Guesser and have your choice of a rack of prizes, any of them easily worth 25 cents.

As The Week Drew to a Close, The Complexion of The Crowd Changed. There were just as many straight country folk as before, but there were more halter tops and hats made out of Budweiser cans. The number of dazed, vacant faces increased and drunks stumbled among the flow of humanity coming out of the stadium and heading for the parking lots, like salmon fighting upstream.

It was like a human demonstration of Brownian motion: in a given crowd, a certain number of people would collide with a predictable frequency.

After Big Chloe, I swore off carney women—until I saw Patti the drummer. Over in the beer hall, there were two bands alternating day and night. One was the weirdest country band I've ever seen: a giant black drummer who looked like he probably straightened auto bumpers with his bare hands when he wasn't drumming, but who sang in a soft, Charley Pride voice, backed by a stringy-haired freak on guitar and a raw-boned, slouch-hatted, straight-out-of-the-bayou type on fiddle.

Patti played with the other group. The Speed Brothers, with little Patti up there pounding the skins. She was a vision behind those drums: a purple satin halter top and matching mini-skirt, her straight black hair flowing down to meet her high, black vinyl boots. No matter that the two brothers were so wired that every time they announced a song, it came out unintelligibly through gritted teeth. Patti could play the drums, and she looked far out of place in the crowd of punk cowboys and beer-soddened college kids.

My palms began to itch about the fourth day. All that grease was beginning to seep out of my system through my hands. One too many corn dogs and more beer than I had consumed in the previous year. I don't normally drink beer, but when it's the only game in town and the combination was beginning to get to me.

In fact, I was reaching a very perverse point when I met the Crazy Whistle Man. He put everything into perspective for me. My first encounter with the Crazy Whistle Man was on Tuesday. After that, he became a daily ritual. I would hear a dissonant whistling and popping coming from the crowd below the stadium, and like a transfixed rat, followed the music until I could watch the act.

Usually surrounded by delighted kids and skeptical adults, a full-grown man was grotesquely distorting his face to create a whistling/singing sound with some kind of diaphragm in his mouth. He punctuated the whole thing by snapping his suspenders, popping his dunce cap up and down and grinning oddly. Certainly a man not of this world. His scam was selling those whistles at 25 cents a hit.

It's hard to approach your gods, but one morning, sitting in Your

Father's Moustache, I did. After the crowds had cleared the tent and moved into the stands, the Crazy Whistle Man came in and sat down. He had a broad, Teutonic face and his neck had been ravaged by something like smallpox, but the overall image was of a warm per-son. For the last 17 years he had been the Crazy Whistle Man. It was his life.

"It offers me the freedom to do what I want. My family is here with me... my wife is over there in that hot dog stand and my son is selling ice cream."

With a sense of disappointment, he told me how he had just sent his other son back to school. "He doesn't like all this, he wants to be a surveyor." Hard for a man to figure, when the only life he has known since he was 14 is this one.

"I got tired of working for that." He gestured toward the Midway. "I wanted something of my own." The American Dream. But who else would want to be the Crazy Whistle Man except him?.. and maybe me.

"It gets to you, let me tell you—after 17 years, the same song gets to you. But you come in, have a few brews and a little conversation, and go out and hit it again."

—*Originally appeared in* Mountain Gazette 26, *1974.*

16.
Where the Trees Walk
Written by Harvey Manning

What my childhood would have been without Sax Rohmer there's no way of knowing. Had I read nothing but adventures of the Rover Boys and Tom Swift and Dave Porter at Yale, my experience of evil would have been limited to the sort of the naïve nastiness exemplified by the neighborhood bully. However, I strayed into pages of the Saturday Evening Post and got so sweaty about the unspeakable Dr. Fu Manchu that to this day I'm uneasy in a Chinese restaurant.

Rohmer's most devastating attack on my nerves, though, was a story centered on the Middle East. An outbreak of Arab unrest was suspected as being fomented by a sinister force, unknown. Simultaneously, British diplomats and generals and financiers were being murdered, one after another, under identical and baffling circumstances. In each case the victim, just before locking himself, alone, in a room whose windows were too small for a human to squeeze through, had been delivered a package a foot square on the end and three feet long. Hours or days later, when concerned family or staff battered down the door, they found the mutilated corpse, no sign of the killer, and the package—open and empty.

The hero-detective astutely discerned the packages were the key to the puzzle and patiently traced them to their common source-the Middle East. Instantly he realized his familiar antagonist, the fabled Old Man of the Mountains, was again plotting to conquer the world. He tracked the evil genius to his lair, or rather was lured there, whereupon the Old Man was delighted to explain how he had stolen babies and raised them on a diet of hashish, which stunted their growth and made them homicidal maniacs. He sent packages to leaders of the British Empire, with covering messages cryptically declaring the contents were to be revealed solely to the inner circle of the ruling class.

Open the package and out leapt a drug crazed dwarf waving a scimitar and snicker-snack and that was that. The assassin exited via the room's tiny window.

The bragging monster grew careless and the final hope of the Empire and the Western World saw a chance and cut out. The last scene, I remember vividly, is the hero running through the desert night pursued by a pack of little hashish fiends. He got away, of course, but then so did the Old Man of the Mountains.

One night while walking home along a country road I heard a noise behind me, looked back, and spotted a movement in roadside shadows. I kept walking—and heard footsteps. Another look back—a wiggling of bushes, as if someone had hastily jumped in. I broke into a run and now I had no leisure to glance over my shoulder, and no need. The hashish fiends were gaining and 100 yards from the house, I started yelling "MOTHER! MOTHER!" and she opened the door in the nick of time.

Country nights are dark, very dark, and a country boy cannot confine his travels to day. Often, far from safety when light failed, I ran for my life, the thud-thud-thud of little feet spurring me to great speeds. Only when I moved to the city to attend college did the fiends abandon the chase.

Comparable to Sax Rohmer as a molester of my childhood were

preachers. Frequently I awoke screaming from a dream in which I was trapped in the basement of a house we lived in when I was six years old. If I could get to the steps leading upstairs, I was okay, but barring the way, crouched by the furnace that was his passage from Hell, was the grinning red Devil. I grew out of that dream and that terror, becoming convinced God was as good as everybody said and therefore He'd not tolerate a Devil in His world. Eventually, however, following the line of thought to the logical end, I realized elimination of the Devil left only one source of evil, and I was terrified by God. I decided Christianity was altogether too scary and gave it up for naturalism, which postulates a single order of reality, one not mechanically materialistically simple and certainly not all good, but with everything out in the open, no spooks. The belief has since served me very well—the daylight and/or in a group.

Wilderness nights alone are something else.

I wish the hashish fiends were still with me on the dark trails. I'd welcome the thudding of their little feet. But they were scared off by the Others.

One spring, I was the first hiker of the year up the East Fork Dosewallips River Trail. At Camp Marion, sitting by the fire, I heard voices in the forest and shone my flashlight down the trail, happy at the prospect of company. No hikers arrived. Who, then, was talking? Where? The "who" was unknowable but I discovered the "where." The voices were in the river. Listening intently, I caught occasional words, portions of phrases-and over and over again, my name. And hideous chuckles.

In the morning, plugging steps up snowfields from Dosemeadows to Lost Pass, I found the memory amusing. But not that night. I returned to Camp Marion, listening and watching through the long black hours. Nor the next night at Dose Forks, where I'd planned to camp before starting up the West Fork to Anderson Pass. With the first mention of my name I hoisted pack and fled to the road, pursued by the pounding Others, infinitely more dreadful than my old hashish fiends.

Not for some time did I again dare a wilderness night alone, not until I reflected that never, except beside loud rivers in black forests, had I been menaced. Thereafter, always camping in high meadows with a clear view in every direction, I enjoyed many a serene night.

Blithely, therefore, I left Cascade Pass late on a July afternoon and ascended Mixup Arm and the Cache Glacier, attaining shadowed Cache Col as sunset rays were streaming from behind huge Johannesburg, pinkening the narrow shelf holding Kool Aid Lake. In twilight, I reached the lake, cooked supper on heat tabs, and—wood lacking for a campfire—crawled in the sack to read a while by flashlight.

So calm was the weather I hadn't rigged a tarp and lay in the open, vision unobstructed over the meadow bench. The night was eerily quiet. Downslope breezes were soft, not even stirring heather bells. The outlet creek, beyond a knoll, was a voiceless murmur, as was the far-below Middle Fork Cascade River. Starlight vaguely outlined moraines and the scattering of small alpine trees—wind-sculpted shrubs, really.

Peaceful, perfectly peaceful. Why wasn't I? Silence rang in ears. Eyes ran over print, fingers flipped pages, but no words penetrated brain. Scanning the surrounding tundra, I sensed some subtle change.

I noticed a shrub framed by the starlit glaciers of Formidable. Something was wrong with that tree. I focused on the book—and abruptly looked up. The tree was closer.

I checked the other direction and a tree there also had moved. I swept the circle continuously holding back the trees, which stayed put when I was watching, just as the hashish fiends used to dive off the road when I glanced over my shoulder.

Heartbeat by heartbeat I fought my lonely battle. Then, horrified, I saw Formidable's glaciers and cliffs were pressing steadily nearer from the south and Mixup and Johannesburg from the north. Hurryup and Magic, above the lake, were leaning outward, outward, into a virtual overhang. And the stars were lowering.

Mercifully, the eastern sky lightened, stars blinked out, peaks and trees retreated to daytime positions, and I slept, exhausted.

Never after did I feel secure alone in a mountain night. Boulders, sharp-edged and inert by day, became shifting, seething blobs. Creeklets giggled my name, ripples of tarns whispered threats. Bambi, soft-eyed in the sun, pawed turf under the moon, grinding his teeth.

My sanity may seem questionable, insisting as I do on repeatedly placing myself in mortal peril. It is, however, essential. I know, now, who the Others are, and understand that if I don't face Them in the wilderness, soon enough They'll crowd around my house, and some night when the family is away, will come right through the walls.

Last spring, I deliberately walked into a trap, hiking from the Stehekin River up Bridge Creek. As night fell the nearest humans were miles distant and I was cut off from mankind in both directions by torrents difficult to ford by day, fatal to attempt in blind panic. Escape by running was impossible. I had no choice but to stand my ground—in the worst imaginable spot for a confrontation.

Dense forest and cloud-heavy sky merged into total blackness. The voices in snowmelt thundering Bride Creek were the most savage I'd ever heard. In treetops, moaned wind, and in bushes and duff rattled and splatted rain. The entire night was bellowing, groaning, babbling, cackling. And from the woods came a periodic thumping—when I shone my flashlight there I saw two balls of hellish green flame.

Yet I had not come to this test defenseless. My enormous fire thrust blackness back, back into forest, across the river, and above tree crowns toward swift rolling clouds. And I'd heeded the teaching of Robert Burns:

"Wi' tippenny, we fear nae evil;
Wi unsquabae, we'll face the Devil!"

Beside the roaring fire, rain splashing my face, I listened, tense, sipping lemonade. A power grew within me and I progressed from sipping to swilling. Bring on the hashish fiends! Bring on the damn Devil! I began answering the river shout for shout and by midnight was offering to rassle Them, one by one or in a bunch, I didn't give a shit. The later stages are hazy. I do remember that eventually we weren't so much yelling as laughing, and that in the end we agreed to continue the discussion another night.

Now, I've not the slightest desire to be the prophet of a new religion—or better say, of the most ancient of religions. Even a minimal organization, as implied by a "prophet," would ruin the whole thing. Each individual, if he chooses to go walking alone in wilderness—-which is by no means compulsory—must find his own personally proper relationship with the Old Ones.

To none but the truly desperate do I suggest the Rites of Bridge Creek. Next morning the celebrant is sorry not to have been struck dead in the night. And over a period of time an excess of conversation with a river, whatever the benefits to the spirit, surely is injurious to the liver.

—*Originally appeared in* Mountain Gazette 19, *1974.*

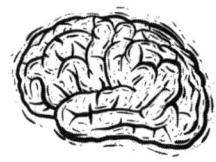

17.
Breaking Free from the Human Potential Movement
Written by Mike Moore

I went the full week without getting touched, felt or laid. So if you find that what I have to say about the Association of Humanistic Psychology and its 13th annual convention in Estes Park, Colorado, sounds at times a little grumpy, well, you already know the reason why.

I went there, let me admit right away, with a fistful of prejudgments, hellbent on writing a frolicsome satire that... who knows?... might even have found its way into Tom Wolfe's next anthology of "the new journalism." I went there thinking that this was just the right combination of mountains, people and madness for a *Mountain Gazette* article.

I also went there with a certain amount of fear in my heart. The prospect of spending five days—alone—with a gaggle of massage persons, transcendentalists, Rogerians (they don't even talk), Frommists, Zen Buddhists, nudists, sexual acrobats, Sufi dancers, acid heads, Jungians and existentialists, lesbians, pederasts and feminists, brainwave synchronizers, Rolfers, seers and magicians and god-knows-what new variations on your basic Elmer Gantry theme... well, I was afraid—afraid they might get me!

And maybe, in a way, they did.

WHO ARE THESE GUYS?

"Somewhere, there has got to be a psychology that includes poetry, art and a movement toward social justice that will also help me understand myself—and nowhere does it exist, even beginningly—outside the Association of Humanistic Psychology."

—Rollo May

The first night of the convention I dropped into the Dunraven Inn, the only bar within easy range of our dry campus—the Y-Camp-for a bit of liquid inspiration before that night's activity, a pair of keynote addresses.

I sat down next to a grim-faced young man, who I later learned was a Vietnam veteran from western Kentucky. He had been living in Estes Park for the past six months, and he worked in a nearby meat-packing plant. He was drinking Wild Turkey, fast and straight.

I've had a little barroom experience, enough to know that grim-faced young men who pop their Wild Turkey in that manner can easily become volatile, dangerous. So I sat silently, staring into my own drink, and tried to listen in on the conversation at the table behind me. It was an interesting one, about the Delancey Street Project in San Francisco.

I turned to find my stoolmate staring at the badge I had neglected to remove from my chest. "What the hell is the 'AP,' anyway?" he demanded. "At first I thought it was a bunch of A&P grocers, but Jesus, these people can't be grocers!" (Our $50 paper badges actually said "AHP," but there was a good reason to miss the "H." Some oh-so-clever graphic artist had reduced that letter to a single line running between the "A" and the "P." Just as with those silhouette drawings in which you see what you want to see—a vase or a pair of faces—so with the AHP logo. The "H" for *humanistic* could be there, or not there, depending upon how you looked at it. Several times during the week I was to ponder on the symbolic genius of that artist.)

"You're right," I told my new friend. "These people aren't grocers. They are humanistic psychologists."

"They're *what*? They look like a bunch of fairies to me," as he nodded in the direction of two middle-aged gentlemen, both attired in denim and soft, blousy flower shirts, one sporting a long, gray ponytail. "And all these women with their tits hanging out. You say they're *psychologists*?"

I tried to explain to him what was going on at the Y-Camp, who these people were, but I don't think I got the job done. My friend had his own idea of what a psychologist should look, act and dress like, and these people simply didn't fit his bill.

But it was a good enough question.

And it would have been an easy one to answer 10 years ago when the movement—and that's what it is, a movement—first got under way. In the beginning, they were a band of rebels, led by Abraham Maslow, Carl Rogers, Rollo May and a few others. They set themselves off against the behaviorists and the mechanistic experimenters who then owned-and pretty much still do—the departments of psychology at virtually every major college and university in the country. They were existentialists, phenomenolo-gists and humanists, opposed to the cold, rigid determinism of the stimulus-response, reward-punishment school of mind control. To a lesser extent, they were also in philosophical opposition to what they considered to be the overly structured methods of Freudian psychoanalysis.

The Esalen Institute in Big Sur, California, became the proving ground for experiments in the new therapy: encounter, Gestalt, mediation, the healing baths and the sen-suous massage—all that we called "touchie-feelie" a few years ago.

Humanistic psychology—the human potential movement—is getting more, not less, complex. No longer firebrand rebels, the AHP has been accepted into the American Psychological Association as a "legitimate" discipline, and that has set them to the task of building their own edifice, with a theory, a methodology—no mean chore for a bunch of radicals who built their revolt upon open-endess, experiment, the "holistic" approach, a kind of joyful anarchy.

While the founding fathers are today talking about responsibility and epistemology, there is a new, more radical idea building within the human potential movement. It is a turn, not toward the left, but toward the East. In seeking a resolution to the old mind-body dichotomy, the new therapist is turning more and more toward spiritualism and transcendentalism. The mystics and the non-mystics were still talking to each other in Estes Park, but that split could finally prove to be the greatest dichotomy of them all.

SOME PEOPLE HAVE IT AND SOME DON'T

"Gatsby believed in the green light, the orgiastic future that year by year recedes before us. It eluded us then, but that's no matter—tomorrow we will run faster, stretch out our arms farther... And one fine morning..."
—F. Scott Fitzgerald

That I spent the entire week of the convention untouched, unfelt and unloved would appear to be my own fault. But I'd rather blame it on Rollo May.

I went up there prepared to take off my clothes, spread mayonnaise all over my body and climb trees if that was what was required to get inside the story. I went to Estes Park not knowing what to expect, and expecting just about anything.

Had I, on that first morning, passed by May's talk on American myth, and gone instead to the workshop of "Play, Games and Self-Awareness" or "Advances in Transactional Analysis: Regressive Techniques in Outpatient Group Psychotherapy," I would no doubt have written a much different report on the conference. I would also have missed my own "peak experience" of the week.

I suppose the idea of myth is largely Jung's legacy to humanistic psychology. I kept hearing the word "myth." It may be one of those 20 or so words-"space," "center" and "centered," "share," "stroke" are others—which at times that week seemed to make up the entire *language* of the human potential movement. In the hands of Rollo May, myth was something else again. He told us some nice stories: the story of Orestes; the story of Gatsby. (Great God, *The Great Gatsby*! The first morning of the touchie-feelie conference and I'm getting off on Gatsby!) (It is May's contention that Fitzgerald's Gatsby, and not Horatio Alger, is the true American mythic hero.)

Rollo May talked softly, unassumingly, but like an artist he made

Jung and Spengler and even Kierkegaard come alive and dance. May's message was complex, and I'll probably destroy it in the translation. But I think he was telling us that we have no more myths. We still need them..need them badly. We are "crazy" (not May's word) without them. We make them up. ("Everything takes on a mythic quality when myth is denied," said May.) But these new myths are hollow, empty, useless, not the real stuff. May told us that we must become reconciled to living in this time of mythlessness. He also told us that we would have to go and meet our gods on the inside-inside ourselves.

I left the Rollo May sessions with a slightly spinning head. While I had come expecting "anything," I never quite expected this. I didn't recover from it all week. I stayed up there in the loft regions for five days instead of rolling around in the grass along with everybody else

There was no way to actually cover this convention, to really report on it. There were as many as 20 workshops going on at any given time. You had to choose one.

And I made some pretty bad choices.

I fell asleep during Ida Rolf's lecture on structural integration—rolfing. She opened her talk with a history of physics—she was up to Einstein's relativity and Planck's quantum work when I nodded off. When I woke up, almost half an hour later, she was talking about gravity as something to be avoided. Sometime during the void I assume she built a "scientific" foundation on which to stand her Rolfing technique.

I did look around the room and observed that quite a few people had their eyes closed and their mouths open, and while some of them may have been in deep concentration on Ida's every word, a few others were audibly snoring.

I fell in love with Barry Stevens. The close associate of the late Fritz Perls, she is perhaps the *grande dame* of the human potential movement. A beautiful old Zen monk is what she is. Barry Stevens has it—the mysterious "it" that everybody in town that week seemed to be looking for.

Outfitted in her customary straw hat and smock, she stood in the center of a circle within a circle—the outer circle, a ring of impressive mountains; the inner circle several hundred friends, admirers and some people like me, there by accident, really, to experience this lady for the first time. Barry Stevens paced the center-calm, but full of energy, happy, funny, often throwing out enigmatic Zen conundrums, talking casually, conver-sationally, sometimes very intimately with us all. I remember thinking that this must be *real* Zen, or something close to it. It wasn't even necessary to listen to her words.

People kept asking her questions, about her life, her current thinking, wanting to know how she'd solved her own riddle, as she so obviously had. One fellow yelled out,"Hey, Barry, I just like watching you." She laughed and threw her arms up over head as if to say, "Yeah, I know you do."

I also went to hear Werner Erhard talk about *est (Erhard Seminars Training)*, and I got the living shit scared out of me—but that's a story in itself. One I'll try to deal with a little later on.

NARCISSUS FOR PRESIDENT

"Today our revolutions are against limitation of personal rights, the right of individuals at all social and economic levels to create, to chose, to achieve and fulfill, to realize their fullest humanity."
—*AHP Program*

"A liberal is a Marxist with two kids."

The Estes Park convention was billed as a political event. But politics—just as you might expect with a group of more than 2,000 people seeking self-cure, self-mastery, enlightenment, personal growth, spiritual development-didn't come up very often.

Indeed, political discussion seemed to be allotted to a single evening, the night of the keynote addresses. That night, John Vasconcellos, a state assemblyman from California, called the convention nothing less than "the most important political event of the year." George Leonard followed him, and with Kennedy-like fervor, asked the audience: "Are you willing to get in touch with yourself and use our best and fullest powers to bring about political change?" He also suggested the price: "We must be willing to lay down our lives, our careers, our ease." (Ask not what the human potential movement can do for you. Ask rather what you can do for the human potential movement.)

There is a gaping paradox that lies at the bottom of a "politics of personal growth" and George Leonard went sailing over it like it was not there at all. I tried to ride with him as far as I could, but I finally sat scratching my head, wondering if I was hearing the politics of Freud or the psychology of Marx.

In the end, I decided I was hearing neither, but instead a kind of grand, sweeping defense mechanism at work. While there may have been a few people in the room that night who were totally apolitical and self-involved, my own guess is that the large majority of them own a Volvo, vote Democratic, oppose foreign interventions and bleed over social injustice and world hunger. They are, almost exclusively, white, educated, middle-class and guilty. They are already politically active, involved.

Yet as a movement, not as individuals, they are accused of self-indulgence, of avoiding the large and critical political issues that face the species. These accusations hit home and they hurt—largely, I think, because of their accuracy. So we listened to a couple of speeches on politics, and never mind the leaps that had to be made in talking about a "politics" of "self." It made everybody feel better and quieted the noisy con-sciences. Therapy, they call it.

Or maybe George Leonard really does think self-actualization is going to save the world and that we should all set about organizing (however you do that) this universal self-awareness.

I heard Charles Hampden-Turner ask the day before, in a completely different con-text, "Are we to always wander in the wilderness—existential arrows, Lone Rangers of the Astroturf?" Well. why not? The best of the human potential is sifting down to the society and having a significant effect. Some are now beginning to argue, and with elo-quence, that too much has sifted down. In any event, it seems contradictory, even absurd, to package something so private and personal into a political club and go running with it into the arena.

But politics was just an aside in Estes Park. The action was elsewhere, and I missed most of it.

NO NUDES IS BAD NUDES

"And what is the point of revolution
Without general copulation."
         —Weiss

Estes Park, a friend of mine said, is the Okies' Aspen. (I realize that is a rather snobbish way to describe the place, but we do have our symbols, and that one seems to work pretty well. Besides, the remark came from a local, Steve Komito, an enterprising moun-taineer/businessman/bootmaker with ambitions of running for mayor of Estes Park. And if he can say it...)

The people attending the convention tended to look upon Estes Park as a cultural backwater, largely, I think, because of the state of shock the management at the Y-Camp (where the event was held) slipped into over the scattered incidents of nudity and random cavorting. (Komito quickly came to the defense of his town when he heard the "backwater" charge leveled by a pair of conferees in a bar one afternoon. "Listen," he said, "You're having your convention at the Y-Camp. That's Y-M-C-A. Those letters stand for Young Men's Christian Association. They have one of those in San Francisco, too. Go try screwing in the lobby there and see what happens.")

I saw a lot of *near* naked people almost everywhere I looked. But no dreaded penile member, not a single mound of Venus. I heard stories, though. Of maids stumbling over copulating couples in the fields while on their way to make beds in the scattered cabins; and maybe stumbling into some really bizarre California fetishes once inside the cabins.

But, by and large, the conferees were much more.well, dignified than I expected or even wanted them to be. While the Y-Camp management quietly made the decision not to invite the AHP for another convention, I would speculate that their decision was based on the very general demeanor of the participants and not on any particular acts of outrageous behavior. I would also speculate that most of the conferees wouldn't return to the Y-camp even if invited.

This was a convention, and in many ways no different than a gathering of, say, a bunch of hardware manufacturers or ski-equipment merchandisers. They came to talk shop, have fun, get laid.

The sexual opportunities were perhaps greater here than at most conventions.

There was a balance of the sexes-with women conferees perhaps slightly outnumbering men—that you don't find at most conventions. These 2,000 people count themselves as among the most "liberated" in the country, you must remember. And, if those aren't enough reasons, consider that they look upon sex as therapy.

Most of the people I talked with, including a couple of AHP officials, were very open in telling me that, while the opportunity for sexual encounters wasn't the only reason they came to the gathering, it was certainly one of them. To have spent that entire week at the Y-Camp without a piece of some kind of action... well, that could well have brought on horrible traumas, deep feelings of inferiority and self worthlessness. I managed to avoid the conflict—and the fun—by commuting to Estes Park. long, late hours on the lonely highway contemplating Rollo May's myth of mythlessness.

On the other hand, this group didn't seem to drink like conventioneers usually do. There was, no doubt, a preference for other drugs, but I also noted a specific disdain for alcohol. That's just as well, because the campus itself was bone-dry, and despite what thousands of beer swilling college kids may tell you, Estes Park is no drinking man's town.

Indeed, the only half-interesting bar in town is The Wheel. But that one can get pretty interesting. I spent two hours in there one night drinking with a pair of the most decadent old men I've encountered in a long while. I walked out of the place thinking The Wheel must be where Tennessee Williams comes for his material.

But that's getting off the subject. And despite what a humanistic psychologist might tell you, free association can be abusive.

And I've yet to talk about the single most disturbing event of the week.

THE HENRY FORD OF HUMAN POTENTIAL

"When Mrs. Pattycake comes to us to be taught, turn that wandering doubt in her eye into a fixed, dedicated glare and she'll win and we'll all win. Humor her and we will all die a little."
—*L. Ron Hubbard (Founder, Scientology)*

"They wanted someone to set matters right again, to tell them what to do, and it did not matter how that was done, or who did it, or what it required them to believe."
—*Peter Marin*

One of the best-attended workshops at the conference was Werner Erhard's session on "est," Erhard Seminars Training.

Est was a point of major controversy at the AHP convention. The first day, at the opening workshop, I heard Rollo May take a public position against est, calling it just the sort of "anti-humanistic" approach to therapy that the organization should be standing against. He wondered aloud why Erhard had even been invited.

That night, George Leonard, ex-Esalen vice-president, ex-*Look* magazine editor, author of several books, including *Education and Ecstasy*, delivered the convention's keynote address. In his speech, he said that the AHP should be open to new concepts, dynamic ideas, like Werner Erhard's "est." (Leonard has taken the training.)

By now it was mid-week and I was a reporter without a story. I thought I might be able to make one up by putting Rollo May and George Leonard together at a table, throw est out in front of them, and just write down what happened. It was my feeling that such a mini-debate, however contrived, could stand well enough to symbolize the intellectual push and pull, the search for identity and purpose, that is now going on within the human potential movement.

I asked an AHP official if he could help me set up such a meeting. He raised his eyebrows and said he would try. In the next few hours I was approached by several people from the AHP office, warning me off the topic of est. The next day I was hosted to an impromptu roundtable of AHP directors, all trying to dissuade me from focusing on est in any article I might finally write.

This little gathering backfired, actually. Three of the four officials had taken the est course, and for a while, they spent as much time defending Erhard as they did in arguing that Erhard has "nothing, absolutely nothing" to do with the AHP. "Werner Erhard has been a good friend of AHP and that is all," I was told. "We certainly don't endorse est by having him here. There is a genuine and valid curiosity about his techniques among our membership."

There certainly is. Est has taken off like a missile, and at a time when Esalen and some of the more established institutions in the field are having trouble attracting needy psyches, Erhard appears to be turning them away by the hundreds. He says he is. Although for a vendor that is "temporarily sold out," he continues to do a remarkable job of rather sophisticated high-pressure marketing

I was never able to arrange the date. May was willing and Leonard sounded like he might have been willing as well, but he had to leave the same day I approached him.

Werner Erhard scares me. I didn't like the idea of est before I listened to him that week. I'm even more uncomfortable about it, having heard him speak.

My familiarity with est comes from reading and from long conversations with several friends who have taken the training. I also attended what they call a guest seminar in preparation for the convention, but you learn next to nothing about est at one of those—except of course, that it is a mystery, a mystery that will cost you $250 to solve.

Erhard, and everybody who has taken the training, would also tell me that I have no right to write on the subject of est until I have been through it. It's not something that can be explained, we are told, but only experienced. We were treated to the analogy of the chocolate sundae at the guest seminar. How could we explain the chocolate sundae to someone who had never seen or tasted a chocolate sundae? How indeed? But then, the same problem would exist if we were talking about, say, a lobotomy. And I think then is the time to start trying to express the phenomenon in words and to hell with the experience.

I'm not equating est and lobotomy, understand. But on a scale between a chocolate sundae and lobotomy, est is closer to the latter than the former.

A fellow named Mark Brewer ate the sundae and didn't much like it. He wrote a very tough piece on est which was published in Psychology Today. (While Brewer was strikingly negative about the Erhard methods, the real force of the piece was in revealing, in some detail, what actually goes on at an est production. He lifted the veil on the mystic. And mystery has been an important factor in the success of est.)

I have a good friend who went through est the year it was started. My friend had his problems. He is a diagnosed psychotic. When this fact was "uncovered" during the training, he was quietly shown the door. (Est is not for the sick, the truly ill. They openly acknowledge that they screen out people with serious mental and emotional problems.) Anyway, my friend often speaks with an almost frightening clarity, and one day, in such a mood, he gave me his own three-sentence description of est, I liked the simplicity of it, and I pass it on for what it's worth: "They simply drag you down to the bottom of the hill, to the edge of the abyss, kicking you all the way. Just when you are feeling, or think you are feeling, worse than you've ever felt in your life, then *zoooommmm*, they send you rocketing back up. You come out of these dancing; you've never felt better; and you've completely forgotten that you didn't feel all that bad when you went there in the first place.

"The est package is a complex stew, and a person could get heartburn trying to identify its many ingredients. I thought I recognized some borrowings from French existentialism (vague notions of "self-responsibility," the existential present, and "good faith"..but no mention, interestingly, of the idea of existential responsibility to the larger community). There is certainly some

Buddhism (the idea of "no-self" and a jet-age ride to enlightenment). There may be some Wittgenstein (there are certainly a lot of tricks with the language). There's a great deal of Dale Carnegie ("you're perfect just the way you are.").

Also important is Erhard's own background in encyclopedia sales—he trained salesmen. That's a tough world, a world in which only the true geniuses of the flimflam survive. Erhard has been *training* people for a long time.

Erhard also has some experience in scientology. The scientologists, in fact, have lately been accusing him of having stolen their own system out from under them. Erhard laughs at this. In Estes Park he told us, "They'll call anything scientology if it works."

I knew next to nothing about scientology, save that they use tin-cans hooked up to simplified lie-detector arrangements (they call them "E-meters") to bring true confessions pouring from their subjects (they are called "preclears"). The system is the invention of a fellow named L. Ron Hubbard. With these tin cans he built a multi-million-dollar empire. Hubbard now lives at sea, on one of his yachts. He's been hounded with legal difficulties, and there are many shores on which his ships cannot land.

Coming back from Estes Park, I picked up a book called *Inside Scientology* by Robert Kaufman (Olympia Press). Another exposé, this time by a guy who'd "had it" for a while, but finally decided he'd been had.

In reading the book, I found what seemed to be a number of very evident parallels between est and scientology. In some ways est appears to be little more than scientology without the tin cans and all the sci-fi horseshit that Hubbard indulges in.

(Pondering all this at 3 a.m. one morning, I had a true paranoid's fantasy. I saw Werner Erhard as the creation of L. Ron Hubbard. Est was dreamed up, designed, on one of his yachts at sea. Erhard enters, Manchurian Candidate-like, to give the world the next, higher stage of Hubbard's forever evolving dianetics. That they appear at odds today is merely a clever cover to conceal the true origins of est. It didn't end there. That night I went on to dream that Werner Erhard was elected president of the United States.)

But enough of these dismal fantasies. The reality is dismal enough. Besides, I'm doing the same thing Werner Erhard does, which is to talk all around est, but never about it.

Let me list a few of the known facts: An est course costs $250. That's a fact. (Just for sake of comparison, that can be looked upon as a great savings over Hubbard's old ladder to enlightenment, which retailed for about $500 a rung. A committed seeker could lay out 15 grand getting to the top of that one.)

Erhard is working another side of the street—numbers, mass production. A son of Henry Ford. He may charge you only $250 to go straight to enlightenment, but you're not alone... There are as many as 250 other people making the trip with you. There are supposed to be—so far—about 40,000 est graduates at large in the world. Just run the math on that one.

But the money thing is pretty obvious, and Erhard is always ready for it. His tech-nique, when challenged on money—or any other difficult question—is to disarm with candidness, openness. Sure, he says. You get help from me and you pay for it. With money. I'm not doing this to be a hero. The hero, he says, always gets killed.

Okay, you've made your investment. We can all agree that $250 is a small price to pay for enlightenment, after all. And maybe you're already well along on your way to a cure—because you aren't going to leave without getting your money's worth, are you? (But doctor, that placebo *worked*!)

The scene now becomes a large room. You are with your 250 fellow travelers. You will spend four days, about 15 hours a day over two consecutive weekends, in that room. The environment is very structured. You cannot, for example, get up and go to the john except at an appointed time. (There are two reasons for this, Erhard told us. It would break the group's concentration if people were constantly up and down. And, then, some people like to take off at just that critical moment when they are about to confront the truth about themselves: When the going gets tough, the clever duck out.)

But it is also part of the larger humiliation process. You are now officially an "asshole" (their word). You may think that $250 is a lot to pay to be called an "asshole." But, eventually, you'll "get it" (their phrase). You will "get it" by doing a lot of ridiculous things; by being ordered around, stared at and lectured to. Soon enough you will understand what you are supposed to be doing. You are supposed to be working on the dismantling of your value system, your belief structure, all of those ideals-notions of right and wrong, good and evil-that have been screwing up your life all these years. You haven't been aware of this, but you'll "get it," you'll "get it." Just throw away all that intellectual baggage, all those cumbersome values. Look past them. *Transcend* them.

Est employs several techniques to aid you in your breakthrough. There are a number of "processes" (a word, and a device, used in scientology) in which the "trainer" takes you through a series of standardized exercises, most of them a form of directed meditation.

Another technique is called "sharing." That is simply getting up before your fellow trainees and talking. Perhaps you'll want to share how you are benefiting from the training. Or maybe you'll want to confess—I mean share—what you see as your deepest personality flaws. ("Get rid of your shit, you asshole.") A reward, a "nice stroke," comes with it. When you share you get a round of applause from the room. It is not required that you share, "but just about everybody does, eventually..."

I was in an Aspen bar one night when an est program ended, just before midnight. I noticed that the bar immediately cleared of all the happy alcoholics who had been laughing there all night. There was a real change in the mood of the place. Anyway, a woman sat down at the table next to me. She was very high, almost giddy. She was still talking about her "sharing" of the hour before. She had "shared her experiences in the womb." (For that, I thought, she must have been given a standing ovation).

Erhard doesn't want to wipe out your belief system so that he can replace it with another; he will assure you of that. He's not Hitler, out to set the world on fire. No. He will convince you he's the Buddha instead, out to light a small flame in your heart. But he's careful not to oversell this Eastern mystical thing; he doesn't like all those associations—those crazy kids in airport lobbies with their saffron robes and shaved heads selling "The Godhead." That could drive away customers. Est gives you the best of both worlds. You can have your karma and your station wagon too.

An Erhard graduate, the fellow who led the guest seminar I attended, kept making these same vague nods toward the East that Erhard makes. Yet he would also make snide cracks about the poor devil who wanders his entire life with a begging bowl seeking the Truth. He kept saying it's right there for the picking, the Truth..."I've got it." I asked him if he really thought it was the same piece of truth that the Buddha was spending his life looking for. Was he even asking the same questions? He was a man on the go, he said (he was an airline pilot) and he didn't have time to screw around trying to find that out. Est got him there in a hurry and that, in itself, was one good reason to take the trip. Erhard says some of the things the Buddhists say: "It is not what you know, but how you know it." But, then, I can say that, too. And *to say it is not to know it.*

Erhard is slick. He is very intelligent. He is very quick. He is probably quicker than thou. He is certainly quicker than me. He exploits language with art. He can transform a question before you finish asking it... or make it disappear altogether.

In Estes Park, for the first two hours—the first half of his talk—he fell into some of the most inarticulate gibberish I've ever heard. He was facing a crowd of 800 people... intelligent, educated, humanistic... the great majority of them his natural enemies.

He made a rule: In the first half of my lecture I'm going to give a talk, and if you have any questions, they must pertain directly to what I have to say or I will not answer them. Then, in the second half of the session you can ask me anything you want.

Then he let loose with this drivel, this jabberwocky. People would ask questions. He would refuse to answer them. People began to leave the room. They left laughing at Erhard. Their curiosity was satisfied. They had met the devil and he was a straw man. A hustler without a brain. No threat at all.

Hell, Erhard *designed* it that way. I hung around even though I wanted to get away from him, too. I'm glad I did or I would have missed the show. He came back a new man. There was a much smaller crowd. Maybe half of them were est graduates, on hand to pay homage and get their batteries recharged. And the new man was in high gear. Swinging. Still inscrutable, but now happily, aggressively, confidently inscrutable.

The new man. That's a lot of what est is about and a lot of what Werner Hans Erhard is about too. His name used to be Jack Rosenberg. He left his wife and four children in Philadelphia-ran away with a woman named Ellen-and changed his name. That piece of biography was in the *Psychology Today* article. And it came up again at Estes Park. A young psychotherapist, himself Jewish, was intrigued by the name change—not just the obvious implications of a Jew denying his Jewishness, but the heavier implications of a Jew going for a loaded title like Werner Hans Erhard.

So he asked him. And Erhard responded, like he did to every tough question, directly, smoothly, happily. I was never a Jew, Erhard said. I was not raised as a Jew and I had no Jewishness to deny. He said he pulled the name out of an Esquire flying across the country to his new life.

Neat. Rosenberg was never a Jew. But he had to have been somebody. He was denying something. His past, his personal history, his self. All the stuff that Erhard, the healer, now tells us is in our way.

And it is a fantasy we all have. The fresh start. The resurrection. The new man. That is a lot of what 'est' is about.

The feeling keeps creeping over me that all this polemic is..well, a hell of a lot of ado about very little. Werner Hans Erhard is hardly a national menace. That guy Kaufman, he thought Ron Hubbard was going to take over the world. I once had a friend who sat on the edge of paranoia his every waking moment, certain that Billy Graham was about to take the government by force. Mark Twain thought the Christian Scientists were spreading across the land and would rob us all of our minds, our culture, our humanity.

But then I keep thinking of the potential size of this thing—the implications if the grass fire spreads too far; the fervor of the est graduates—they're not proselytizers, they're zealots.

In Aspen, where they have one of the most politically liberal county governments in the country, all three of the county commissioners are est graduates. Earlier this year, the commissioners proposed that the county pay half the cost for any of its employees who would take the training. There were cries of "church and state" in Aspen, where est has almost divided a small town into warring factions. But Erhard has trained California schoolchildren under a Federal grant, and he is looking for business like that.

The est people see no conflicts in the training being used by political agencies. They say it's apolitical. And indeed it is. An est graduate can be a better Nazi, a better com-munist, a better candlestickmaker. An est graduate, a young woman, came up to me at the guest seminar and, with all the style and grace of a Los Angeles used-car mover, tried to get my name on a contract. She was as inarticulate as all est graduates finally are in trying to state her gains from the training. She ended by saying: "It's like this. I run a lodge in Aspen. And before I took the training, I couldn't look my customers in the eye. When I showed them a room, I was always looking down at the floor. Now I can look them square in the eye!" When I suggested that, if her prices were comparable to the prices of other Aspen lodges, she was quite right not to be able to look people in the eyes, she moved on without so much as a "thank you" or a smile.

There is common sense good in almost all psychologies, and est is no exception. But I keep feeling that, with this one, there comes more harm than good. I'm no card-carry-ing humanistic psychologist, but I see Erhard's est coming down on the wrong side of the line that divides freedom from determinism.

I just thought I would *share* that with you.

HUMANISTS CAN BE HUMAN, TOO

"If we would have pure knowledge of anything, we must be quit of the body."
—*Plato*

"Apart from the body, life is an illusion."
—*Alexander Lowen*

"I want to warn you Indians that honesty is the last weapon of a desperate man."

—*William Eastlake*

There exists in all of us a mind-body dichotomy. As a society, we are generally out of touch with our bodies. This I believe. Most of the time I cannot find my own, I will freely admit.

But still... I had expected, even anticipated, the communal love that was all around me at the Y-camp that week. People didn't just say hello to one another, they embraced, fondled kissed, touched, felt. But even expecting this, I found myself to be a little troubled by these displays. I kept wondering, if this is how they say "hello," what do they have left when they want to express something a little deeper, to make a gesture of real intimacy? There was, finally, something contrived, forced, phony about it all. And something pass-ing, ephemeral, about it, too...like the "love generation" of a decade ago.

This was illustrated in a way by the relatively high incidence of small-scale emotional "breakdowns" I witnessed walking the grounds. I recall one young lady falling quite apart—weeping and moaning—when she discovered she had lost her program. She was immediately swarmed by people, all strangers I'm sure, who smothered her with embraces, comfort and kindness. That seemed to help. Oddly, nobody thought of simply getting her a new program. Similar incidents of coming apart seemed to be happening all around me, I suppose because there was so much help everywhere you turned (I was reminded of a day when my own youngest daughter cracked up on her bike. First, she looked around to see if there had been witnesses. Seeing none, she shook off the hurt and remounted her machine. She had only pedaled a few turns when she spotted me and, of course, immediately broke into tears.)

This aid-and-comfort approach was even institutionalized in the form of an ongoing "nourishing Touch Program—for people who want caring." You could just drop by and get a hug whenever you needed one.

At a workshop on creative anger—a workshop that was apparently panned by many of the professionals present, but one which I thoroughly enjoyed—there were perhaps 200 of us, gathered outdoors. We were using techniques designed to bring out suppressed anger—a most useful therapy for depression. With the first technique, we were to go back in time, to again become three or four years old, and to throw a fine, bloody tantrum. One young man got deeply into his own three-year-oldness, or seemed to, and put on a magnificent display of screaming and shouting. He kept getting louder and louder. The people around him stopped their own kicking and ranting to watch him in wonder. Soon, all 200 of us were craning to see into the center of the circle where the young man had by now lost all control and was in a full rage. Jesus. We were worried, concerned, that some deep place had been touched in this young man, some horrible wound opened up. One of the therapist team—a big, strong, gentle guy—went to the now weeping child and held him tightly, speaking to him softly. He was calmed.

We were all moved and rather impressed by the experience.

But with the very next technique—we became dogs and cats, a hundred of each, and made aggressive and menacing gestures toward one another-the same kid did it again. He was no cat. He became a roaring, mad lion. And at that point he also began to lose his audience. Muted word passed among us: "Oh, he's just a primal."

He proved to be a very bad actor. He'd lost his audience but would not stop his performance. By the end of the session, he was still carrying on in a highly exaggerated fashion, but he was ignored by us all. In fact, he had won our hostility. He was an embarrassment. And we were resentful about having been taken in the first place.

It's just a feeling I have (after spending a week with the human potential folks, there is in me an irrepressible urge to express my feelings), but I sensed an emptiness while walking among all those joyful, happy, feeling people. In reaching so far to reaffirm their bodies, their spirits, their human playfulness, many of them seemed to have over-reached. They've come to deny their equally human minds, their sadness, their aloneness. And perhaps they are now feeling the loss of these things as deeply as, before, they felt the distance from their bodies. Or maybe they are simply trying too hard; try-ing so hard because they sense the therapy isn't really working.

In all their talk of "peak experiences" the human potential folks seemed to pass by the notion that in order to have a peak you must also have a valley. In order to reach a great height of joy, or anything else, you must necessarily come out of the darker places down below. Not depression or despair. But just plain old human hard times, sadness, the blues.

The people I talked with in Estes Park—many of them, certainly not all of them—seem to be trying to make life on the summit. They want to stay up there-high up—in a state of near-continual bliss. My own feeling is that it's a nice place to visit but...

AND THAT'S NOT THE HALF OF IT

"Consciousness is a congenital hallucination."
—*Blaise Cendrars*

As I said, I missed a lot of what was going on that week in Estes Park... maybe most of it. ("Or all of it," I can hear Werner Erhard saying.)

I missed the magic. I've since read in *Rolling Stone* that, while the conference was going on there, the First World Congress of Sorcery was being held in Bogotá, Colombia. Stanley Krippner and some parapsychologists in Estes Park tried to put themselves in telepathic contact with colleagues in Bogotá. Rolling Thunder, a Shoshone medicine man, was somewhere in Nevada trying to plug into the Colorado/Colombia circuit. I missed that one completely.

I also missed The Women. Or, rather, I saw them only out of the corner of my eye. I felt their presence, but I didn't give them my full attention. I should have. The Women were probably the most important thing going on at the AHP conference. They seemed to be a step away from power there; or maybe they already have it. I had a murky view of strong, attractive and self-possessed women and meek, powerless men. That's both a vague and a mighty generalization, of course. And here's another one: it seemed in Estes Park as though the sexes had not met together in that valley of hoped for harmony; but had simply passed by one another on the trail... the women on their way up the moun-tain, of course. I should have watched that one.

I also missed the star attraction of the week—Jonas Salk. Or rather, I went to hear him talk, but missed much of what he was saying. Jonas Salk was not in town with a vaccine for loneliness, but something almost as far removed from "basic medicine." Salk has worked out a large and ambitious theory of biological evolution that would appear to explain the transition the world seems to be undergoing at present. It's a complex and interesting theory, and I don't dare go further into it without reading his book on.

I also missed Hearts and Minds, a film that was exhibited several times during the conference week. But I'd already seen it. It's a powerful piece of film, and I talked to a number of people who were thoroughly shaken by it. That was the true "political event" of the week.

Finally, it was those two men who were the focus of "my" conference. There was Rollo May-who might be called the dinosaur of the human potential movement, because so much of the movement seems to be away from what he stands for-telling us that we must know ourselves through our own histories, through the histories of the civilizations that came before us; telling us that we are all imperfect, flawed—but to be otherwise is to be against ourselves, to be inhuman.

And there was Werner Erhard-call him the serpent of the human potential move-ment—telling us that we must deny our histories, both cultural and personal, telling us that we are perfect just the way we are.

I had already written this story when the October issue of *Harper's* appeared. In that issue is an article titled "The New Narcissism" by Peter Marin. I mention it here because I think it is a very important piece of writing, and I recommend it. While I think Marin goes too far in his criticism of the human potential movement—he leaves no room for May, for Stevens, for the obvious good that has come with self-discovery—he talks clearly, eloquently about the inherent dangers in the movement, "the ways in which selfishness and moral blindness now assert themselves in the larger culture as enlightenment and health." He talks about "the warm winds of forced simplicity blowing away the tag ends of conscience and shame." He writes: "We proclaim our grief-stricken narcissism to be a form of liberation; we define as enlightenment our broken faith with the world. Already forgetful of what it means to be fully human, we sip still again from Lethe, the river of forgetfulness, hoping to erase even the memory of pain. Lethe, lethal, lethargy—all of those words suggest a kind of death, one that in religious usage is sometimes called acci-die. It is a condition one can find in many places and in many ages, but only in America, and only recently, have we begun to confuse it with a state of grace."

I think he's "got it" there.

—Originally appeared in Mountain Gazette 38, 1975.

18.
Wild Red Dharma Pickup Truck
Written by Lacey Story

Prologue: This is for the mystery mechanic in loving memory of my last truck, a '91 Toyota 4WD 4Runner, which he repaired and shored up through its dying days. She thankfully retired on top of Baldy Mountain at 12,000 feet in the company of a Tibetan Buddhist monk while looking for retreats way back. My mechanic just might, maybe, appreciate the contagious lure of the Wild and the religious ecstasy of backcountry fervor in any season. He should know, even though unbelievable, I am the shyest of the very shyest New Hampshire small town farm girls underneath the false bravado of title, occasional sparkle, and survival personality. I am pathologically shy, even, and don't take to parties and never, ever, ask any man out, even for skiing, with only one exception in my life before Xmas this year. This would take too much of a shift and the fear of rejection is far too strong. I travel alone, study alone, work alone and get right into the wilderness at every possible moment. So I related to his dog, Sara, instantly, with her shy girl wildflower way, and when I looked at her looking away quickly with her head down I looked at myself. I thought that if Sara could find love maybe I could, too, if I ever dared to consider the possibility.

However, I was not born a dog in Summit County. Wild can be introverted although that's not the usual association. The mystery mechanic should not be intimidated by any wordsmanship here knowing that a quivering aspen leaf of a girl who spooks easily in social settings wrote this. If he ever looked at me straight in the eye, if I could ever look back, he'd see things that perhaps could write another vignette, a tale of far off places from another time, or a tale that only he knows deeply in his heart. Somewhere there is a connection. Hey, listen, I'm trying here.

It's not important to know what it is, perhaps, but maybe it is to him, so I warmly welcome his response. He will do with this as he wishes. What follows is a disclaimer. He should not, under any circumstances, take this personally or deduce this means any-thing, because, after all things are examined it really doesn't matter in light of the Greater View. Be forewarned. Inspiration is the head of literary free rein. Artistic license gives one enough rope to choke oneself with and that would be missing the point entirely. This writing is neither true nor not true. It walks the Middle Way on its own, on the razor's edge. Have courage. Think Red. Enjoy the journey. It never ends.

My longest relationships are with pickup trucks. Four wheel drives usually last the longest. A vintage 1985 red Toyota, extra cab with a topper is the current flame. Red enough to create passion off road even with a stick shift and a thick pile of topo maps between you and a likely hard core companion (preferably a mechanic with tools, long hair and a few days growth to tickle tender, soft flesh). Red enough to go all the way. Up the mountains, across the divide, higher and higher to highest. Red enough to handle a scattering of spark plug boxes, emptied Chinese deer antler and Chang Bai Mountain ant extract bottles on the floorboards interspersed with Tibetan language tapes, empty Mountain Sun organic raspberry juice containers and a used up Big Daddy Red lipstick case. Red enough to know that pink satin thongs, a kiss me relative of red, are the correct attire under jeans for steep boulder-littered climbs to the secret cabin in the woods. The only better moment for wearing them is with a tan, a thin white wet T-shirt under a waterfall on a summer day near a rock big enough for two. Add blue columbines, a liter of rhodiola tea, a fresh watercress salad, venison sand-wiches, and voila, you have an afternoon. This is never far from red: action. Enough to make Padmasambhava beam. Even beyond Red, just beyond to the Land of No Return, to the farthest shore. Let's make it deliriously excitable and a true out-of-body experience.

It is winter. These are the days to add snowmobiles to the list of other ways into the backcountry just to spice things up in an already perfect and committed relationship with one's truck. Envision reclining back on the extended black leather seat with the trees as a backdrop to the perfect entry of hard deep unzipped bliss, the snowflakes gently released from high spruce boughs falling onto his long hair tied back with a black and white bandana. If you think about it too much at all, the opportunity vanishes. The rule is non-attachment. The method is volition. The path to heaven plays a catchy tune sung as a mantra that chants the words "I give up" in the repeating stanza. Surrender completely and the world is your oyster. Loosen into the genital groove of all that is or ever will be. A physical consort is better than none at all. The liquid light of unconditional love unravels any preconceptions or obstacles that you might be carrying around like lodestones. Fruition comes only through letting go. Lighten up.

Alas, men do not come in four wheel drive anymore. Let alone with split shift. A manual model is becoming obsolete. No computer chips for me. No automatics. No preprogrammed undesirability. Something you can touch, feel and are partial to lovingly caress all Sunday afternoon is a requirement for total satisfaction. Years of devotion build the greatest of loves. I prefer four, preferably five, on the floor with a good heater and a sturdy body that withstands a few dents and branch scrapes, definitely capable of enduring an equal amount of days without a shower or an oil change.

Things are better in the woods. Water is sweeter. Men are wilder. And it's pickup trucks that get us there. To the back bowls, to the

Divide, to that nameless peak along the gulch road. Edward Abbey says, "Wilderness is the only thing left worth saving." That includes me and you, wildness embodied in human form. Read and you discover that the Wild is strong in the equation of biological imperative. It's the primitive, dark horse deep river, the pheromal unpredictable lucky star, that wins the evolutionary race to transcendence and the perpetuation of thankful genetic shifts nearing the Ultimate Sphere. Everything I've ever loved has happened in the wilderness, in remote cabin shangri-las or in pickup trucks. Some fortunate beings are even conceived in pickups, the most auspicious vehicle for the continuation of our species. In New Mexico, if you're really onto lightning bolt luck, you find a box canyon or a ghost town with a perfect ledge to line up tin cans and plink at them with a 357 and a case of .38s for the second best part of an afternoon. The reverberation in your cerebrum induces ecstasy if taken with scent of after-the-rain sagebrush. The echo lasts forever. The flash of rapture ricochets in your cavernous mind like a pinball wizard's eternal game. The tailgate is down. The passenger door is open to the Indian blanketed full front seat. All things holy happen here. The music of the celestial spheres seduces you with enchantment and beckons you in with a warm embrace. View the Sangre de Cristos from a remote access dead end off Buckman's Road to the Rio Grande through the thick willows. Don't even think you've ever heard of clothes on the sandbars a few miles in towards Jaconita. Here, eagles pronounce your name in an accent you recognize from past lives together. In a pinch, Moab, specifically White Rim, will do. The deserted cabins in Futurity, Colorado, are a close third. A yearning curiosity arises for the inner sanctum lakes of the Gore Range and Holy Cross is looking better and better these days. Awaiting spring thaw seems to be an eternity. I simply cannot confide the true number-one locations. Find your own, sweetheart.

Rename some mountains and some creeks. Make them yours. The geographic change will do you a lot of good. This simple act provides for a vacation on your own turf. An understanding of impermanence is pivotal for the necessary changes we need moment to moment. Baldy is Grizzly now. Copper is still Copper. Wise is still Wise. Santa Fe can still be Santa Fe, if only for the vestigial memory that Canyon

Road was once hard packed red dirt without the sort of folks that are there now. Illinois is now Sugar just because we all need a Sugar Mountain. Deer Creek can stay the same, as can North, South and Middle Forks. Every mountain and creek has the unique privilege to have secret names, like old Navajo clans or Tibetan Deities. Mountain of the Lotus Born, Flicker Breath Canyon, Buddha Fingers Creek, Guru Rinpoche Gulch; Yeshe's Pool of Transcendence, a bottomless well as black as jaguars. Never say their secret names aloud. Keep the noble silence. Be breathless at the mere thought of their existence in the same life as yours. When nightfall comes, rename the stars. Your secret name is written in the sky in case you never noticed. Create a new mythology, a legendary saga for every year you've journeyed around the sun.

 I graduated Most Unpredictable with high honors. Translation: Most Likely to Be in the Woods or somewhere maybe on the Tibetan Plateau in a Mongolian ger drinking fermented yak milk and listening to Russian tunes on the accordion. Somewhere in Montezuma or Sts. John out of cell-phone range contentedly in a twin-zip sleeping bag with no one anyone would imagine me with, a regular reformed badboy quiet homeboy with the spirit of a deep river current. Deer Creek is as close as I can come these days. As a young girl I was happiest in a meadow clearing, lying on my back, surrounded by princess pine or in the white birch grove amongst intoxicating Mayflowers by the hidden spring. I was so quiet, so small, so blended in energetically that the deer would browse within a few feet of a barely breathing body. Tread lightly with Indian moccasins as supple as baby white oak leaves in the spring. Later on was the discovery of friction climbing Pawtuckaway Ledges for a view of the hawk migration and thousands of orange-bellied salamanders, Franconia Brooks Falls and haunts where you can still find picture agate on Hurricane Mountain. My graduate thesis was in Comparative Geographic Hideouts. Today I specialize in Rocky Mountain ghost mining towns. Always the wilderness, the Shambala. Always the driving force to keep the wild still wild. Still. Wild. Silent and Wild.

 The best sex is in trucks. A five-star rating often includes a Vietnam Vet point man from the Texas panhandle or an off-the-map

Oklahoma ranch near Antlers. His name is sometimes initialized, like R.J. or J.R. An evening of sunset teasing in a split window '49 flatbed Ford is a good beginning to the discovery of how good it can get. No need for dual 36, cherry glass pack mufflers. Add 10,000 points for every 1,000 feet over 8,000, up to 14,000, not that you need to attach a number. Adorn the rear-view mirror with a red lace bra and the door handle with unmatching flutter panties. Consider the perfect red polish, chipped to just enough near imperfection on your toenails, an old jean jacket with a Nirvana Now pin, a pair of worn elkskin boots with a riding heel and a delightfully sheer voile dress on and off again. Honey dust and royal jelly are always welcome. A bonus gift includes the scent of pine needles and spruce anointed way up, between the legs. Mingle it with manly musk.

The best relationships require a perfect balance of body, mind and spirit. You know it in your brain, taste it always as the nectar of immortality deep back in your mouth (a personal favorite place) and feel it in your heart as one with the infinite expanse. The recurring pattern of continual quivering occurs when the mixture takes on alchemical consum-mation. Hear the bells. Take a red pickup truck and balance it with trees, mountains, sun, sky and water, and you have perfection. All five elements in harmony. Metal, Wood, Fire (red), Water and Earth. Take spruce trees, tall ancient sentinels of wisdom and combine with compassion, the emptiness of spacious clear blue sky. The Wilderness Drive-In movie is playing The Six plus Four Perfections. Generosity in sparing no cost in truck mainte-nance. Joy in truck ownership. Energy enough to change a flat on uneven ground in the dark. Wisdom in carrying emergency fan belts and flashlights with working batteries. Meditation upon envisioning the truck upright and in good form. Discipline with carburetor adjustment and the right amount of air in tires. Right means in choosing the path that gets you to the most perfect of perfect places. Vows to maintain the truck in peak condition and honor the pristine environment. The manifestation of the 10 powers in getting you out into the backcountry with a snap of the fingers, and finally, the knowl edge of true truck dharmas. The Six plus Four shows every day at the perpetually spontaneous matinee in your mind. Instant replay insures achievement of enlightened truckness.

Correct view is the paramount star. Always, in all ways, seek the Wild. Add a creek, hot springs or river bed and fuse them with your awareness. Open sesame. Abracadabra. This is it. That Such-ness, That Which is That Dharmakaya Being with Light. This is it. Right Now. Love the moment. Paint it in the rainbow body shop a pure red. Watch it glow in the dark and light up the sky on full moon nights as you ride, ride, ride to the highest heights. The vehicle of your dreams takes you There, Right Here, to the Now Tao of 4WD Truck Delight, the Abode of Pure Visions. Truck body, truck mind, truck spirit.

These days I am truckless. Each night before I go to sleep I pray for truckfull-ness in physical form. Perhaps tomorrow, if I just let go of today, it will appear outside my cabin window in grateful union with a big red bow, a single red rose and a small card addressed "For Lacey." On its trailer is another guiding star, a Polaris snowmobile, just for diversity, just to keep things spicy. If you're feeling plush, throw in a CD player with "Days of Future Passed" and Lucy Laplansky's "Secret Journey." Remember the bumpersticker "No rules over 10,000 feet." It is not an option. Maybe even add an invisible "If you're not the lead dog, the view never changes," in memoriam to a past truck love. Stick it on, then quickly take it off. A bell, prism, hawk feather and Tibetan turquoise on rawhide adds a nice touch to the rearview mirror. The keys are on the seat. The keyring has your number on it.

It reads a scrawled, "Call me. Now." I decode intentions encrypted in the handwriting analysis. Be reality in a dream and a dream in reality. This is my prayer. I beseech the Powers That Be to deliver the red 4WD pickup truck, to make manifest the vehicle of bliss, heaven sent, maybe, even, from you. Screw love. Give me a truck. Truck Love Lasts. I call it Supreme Joy. I ride the Red Road. Come and join me. My refuge name is Unity. My secret name is Lucky. My truly secret of secrets name, unspoken, is Wild. Going my way?

With thanks to R.J. in 1967, a psychedelic Oklahoma rancher, who taught me to ride tough in the saddle, roll my own while four wheeling in the driver's seat of a dilapidated excuse of a truck, read the *Tibetan Book of the Dead* and Kerouac to me on LSD-25, never complain when your hair's full of hayseed and your hands full of grease and who first planted the gentle hint that what I wanted to be when I grew up was enlightened. I am happily ever after.

———————

—*Originally appeared in* Mountain Gazette 81, *2001.*

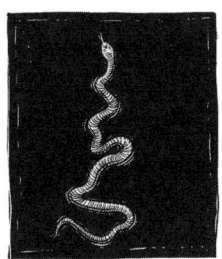

19.
There Was a River
Written by Bruce Berger

The following records a two-week trip through Glen Canyon in October, 1962, months before a dedication ceremony for a dam served simultaneously as a canyon's obituary. The journal also records, less explicitly, a discovery of the English language which, like many things we accept from birth, we only find again with a kind of surprise. My rivermates took snide notice of my scribbling while grease hardened on the dishes it was my function to wash, and even made nasty asides while parching for pothole coffee water as I tried to snag metaphors before they disappeared.

Typing it fresh took my mind off a week of diarrhea contracted the last day from settled river water, when potholes ran out, and I revised once, a year later. But I could think of no interested publisher, and my stupor continued into my second year's subscription of *Mountain Gazette*, over a decade later, when a piece on the desert brought home the obvious: that they weren't hemmed in by the mountains. I have since tried to render some baby fat, but have had to stop short of rewriting a subject which is gone forever. So the narrative should be seen from its occurrence in 1962.

October 6

Beginnings are a bore. If a trip really begins from the first blow to the brain, the memory begins with the push-off: The preliminaries make dull reading even if one is lashing balsa logs on the slopes of western Peru. As it was, we made most of our preparations in a supermarket in Grand Junction, Colorado. Perhaps, as the world is leveled for their bene-fit, it is in the supermarket that our future adventures lie. Suffice to say that it carried everything from bonito flakes to a 60-cent copy of The Celtic Twilight, that I bought the lat-ter, and that we wound up with $80 worth of green stamps, a sales receipt over six feet long on which I was able to write a very newsy letter and an acute case of museum feet.

The idea of the trip was simple—four of us were to float approximately 120 miles down the Colorado River, entirely within the confines of Southwestern Utah. The distance in a straight line would be considerably less, since rivers never aim where they're headed, but our own distance would be more, following curiosity as well as gravity. Calm water, uninhabited land—all of our passage was scheduled for inundation by Glen Canyon Dam at the close of a year that was already nearly over. I was prepared for beauty and desolation, and felt privileged to see it before it was destroyed. What I didn't know was that the trip was to bring so much into focus, to tinge its pleasure so strongly with the bittersweet.

Three quarters of our party drove from Grand Junction to Blanding, Utah, to pick up the supplies not destined to be eaten. It was an improbable trio for that dusty Chevrolet. From my own driver's license: male, 24 years old, blond hair, blue eyes not permitted to drive without corrective eye lenses.

The leader of the expedition was Miss Katie Lee, a professional folk singer who had already traveled the river 14 times and acted as if she owned it. She has explored many of the Glen's side canyons, and given 25 of them the names that appear on the map. She got her start folk-singing by learning the guitar as she waited to perform bit parts on Hollywood sets; when it became possible to make a living in the real world, she evacuated. She crested a vogue of sick songs—a brief period when people enjoyed Freud as much in the night club as on the couch—but came into her own singing songs of the West, improper ballads, and Spanish songs that allow her to show that, unlike most folk singers, she can play the guitar. Her temperament is volatile, by turns gentle, amused, bitter and impossible. I recall a period when she tried to water down her vocabulary and wound up saying things like "Oh shit! I mean hell." She was unquestionably in charge, and the rest of us, more quiet by nature, were able to absorb her fire and be warmed by it. One of my favorite people.

Natalie Gignoux (the name is Huguenot and pronounced jih-NOO, like French for the knees) was in the process of selling the hugely successful taxi business she started in Aspen, against the wisdom of those who told her that, a) the town didn't need a taxi business, and, b) it couldn't be run by a woman if it did. She took tourists on Jeep trips into the high country, managed a staff of unpredictable drivers who would have preferred to find their salaries floating in bottles down fishing streams, and specialized in civilizing the impossible. She is as strong-willed as Katie, but is more likely to have her way by just sauntering off and having it. Also one of my favorites.

Since Leo was described to me as a river rat, I looked unwittingly for the rodent, and found it. He is tall with a face that accentuates the vertical, but his close-cropped hair and roundness of feature-including a small mouth and two prominent front teeth—add a certain woodchuck inquisitiveness. He looks like Humphrey Bogart.

Leo works as a garage mechanic in Riley, Kansas, but his job is merely a springboard for the next leap. Last year, Leo hunted jade in Wyoming and discovered the second largest piece ever found in the United States—2,200 pounds. He propels his own life as if it will never shake the world, neither will his world fall to pieces. Next year perhaps Baja, California. Lotta country out there a fella might look into…We picked up the raft, the cook box and other equipment from a good friend of Katie's who runs a weather station in Blanding between trips through the Glen and Grand canyons. We passed up his invitation to stay the night, for a neutral and deserted motel. We wished to say goodbye slowly to a tile bathroom…

October 7

We meandered the road from Blanding to White Canyon (pop. 2), approximately 90 miles of sandstone and sagebrush in endlessly refocusing patterns. The pavement gave out after 10 miles. We passed the turn-off to Natural Bridges National Monument, and the road continued like a bad scar. We bounced up and down in the seat and mentally I rerouted the road in straighter lines, wondering vaguely why it went where it did, knowing there was some not very interesting reason. Roads like that set you adrift.

We rounded another crest, and there was the river. It was about what I expected—a width of muddy brown water flowing through one more depression in sandstone, this one a bit deeper, lined with a vibrant and shocking green. Save for the vegetation it was neither inspiring nor breathtaking; it was merely there.

October 9

Two days late, we have finally blown up the raft, labeled all the cans with magic marker in case the paper soaks off (four successive cans of peaches were labeled Peaches, More Peaches, Still More Peaches, Peaches Goddammit), piled box upon box on the raft and—best of all—shoved off. The raft, the apparent property of the Museum of Northern Arizona, is a 16-foot monster of billowing black rubber, shapeless as a dead whale. An interior skeleton of wood has been improvised to hold the motor, so that the bulbous mass remains rigid, fends off water and doesn't buckle in the middle. There is a constant pull and give between the rubber and boards, as if a fat woman had swallowed her corset. It is designed as a 12-man raft, but with the heaping gear there is only space to seat two abreast on each side between the supplies and the 35 horsepower outboard Otherwise one must move about the rim or jump in the river.

October 10

The mellowness of the night before was rudely shattered by a trio of blunders that gave us a sickening first-morning-out-in-an-awfully-long-parade sort of feeling. The campfire flames leapt up to the bacon grease and made the grill look like the Chicago fire as Nat sweated blood for every charred hotcake. As we pushed off the propeller fell off the motor, and for half an hour we waded in icy water scouring the mud with our feet, performing a sort of bump-and-grind through the ooze. After we covered the same area three times Leo put on our only spare, and we would have to accept whatever its fate. Off for the second time, Nat's hat blew into the water, and we barely pulled the raft around in time to retrieve it. We hoped it was true that mishaps stop after three.

We spent most of the day drifting on the river I have put off describing because it is so difficult. And so simple: a flow of brown between sandstone cliffs, with strips of willow and tamarisk along the banks. That is all—and nothing. First light brands the rim-rock with cayenne, then bleaches—depending on time and the locale-through saffron, peach, salmon, sienna and rust. Light slants deeper into the bas-relief, trapping shadows between illusions of free-standing figures. The sun climbs, light flattens. Glossy streaks of dark, shining blue in the sun, plunge from the rim and sweep like murals of Spanish moss. Called desert varnish as a phenomenon, tapestry walls as an effect, it forms as water seeps from the rim, leaving streamers of lichen and deposited minerals.

And below all this moves the endless serpent of water, remixing each eddy and back-wash, running coffee, chestnut and sable into caught blues, receiving the sky and tossing it back mottled in beige.

Between water and stone lies a brief transition, a talus crumbled from the heights and projecting like toes of balance for the sheer walls. The oldest of this debris has broken into loam for the willow and tamarisk that line the banks. This green, so shocking in contrast, sheers water from rock the way the horizon sheers rock from sky. All landscapes interlock, but here each piece is also honed to a unit.

From the shore Glen Canyon is spectacle, but floating in passage it invades the five senses. A 35 horsepower motor sounds aggressive, but in deep current it provided little speed. Its function was rather direction, to avoid the thrashing of canoe paddles while guiding us to campsites and side canyons. Still, the scream of gears deadened the river's voice, along with our own. If one had to communicate one began with the hands and concluded with a voice pitched for hog-calling.

But if the river by-passed our ears, beneath we could always feel the swell and slide, the meanders and eddies where power insists. It assaults even the nose with a penetration of slurry and mud. One is forced into the landscape until it evicts the self and becomes, as Eliot said of strong sensation, "...music heard so deeply / That it is not heard at all, but you are the music / While the music lasts."

The river has doubtless been sharply defined by minds down it many times. Side canyons become known, formations stand out as landmarks, all is anticipated. One knows to look up when old granaries merge with the rock, when tributaries loom. But I will know it once, and am glad now to be worn out. My senses are exhausted, grateful for simple flames, hot rum and a swelling moon...

October 12

We spent the day exploring areas that promised Moqui ruins. If the destruction is weeks away, this is the last chance. We tried a bluff that seemed to retreat along a shelf, hiding the wall behind it, thinking it a spot likely to have been missed. What we found was very much alive: a two-point deer. Mixed with my thrill was a burst of ego, since Katie had never spotted one during her 14 ferret-eyed trips on the river. But up ahead Leo gestured to us frantically, and two more bounded gracefully from beneath his perch. We watched them leap and freeze, leap and freeze till they disappeared. Several minutes later we glanced back and caught their heads arching silently over the current as they swam the river.

We climbed to Leo's perch and found the deer had been startled from a beautiful emerald pool. Katie announced it was movie time, so we waited while she returned for the cameras. After they were dutifully arranged she descended to swim the icy waters, while we worked the machines from above, ringed on the upper tier like med students at an operation. (As it turned out, the operation was successful.)

We named the pool Two Deer Spring, though it seemed ludicrous to label a spot anonymous for millennia and fated to succumb within the year. We rounded a bend and came upon another sight that had nothing to do with ruins. We suddenly found ourselves dwarfed by an enormous hollowed-out dome with a round window on top, a sandstone Pantheon, plunging to crazy formations like lava frozen into basins and whirlpools. Around the dome was a faint seepage of water from which fell a delicate band of maidenhair fern, repeating its motif like decorations for a Pompeiian dining room. It was cool and damp as a wine cellar and secret from the river. I have decided that to really see it one must walk up and down both banks, which would be physically impossible even if there were time. No wonder we are about to lose this—how can you tell people when you can't even find it yourself?

October 15

For once we spent the day entirely on our feet, exploring the opposite bank. Our first destination was a place called Music Temple, a cavernous room that opens dramatically from a brief and narrow canyon. The floor is a pool that mirrors a hemisphere of black rock, and the only exit is a cleft that begins 75 feet above the floor and reaches the sky through hundreds of feet of twisting precipice that must assemble in the mind from one glimpse below. But its greatest qualities are not visual.

Katie stationed herself against one wall and began to strum her guitar. The whole canyon suddenly filled with the sound of vibrating strings, as if the single guitar had gained the resonance of an orchestra. Her voice entered and bloomed with its own reso-nance, yet never blurred with echoes and overtones. The music, like the light, came from nowhere, but filled the whole canyon with the body of its sound, as if Katie's song swelled from the canyon's own throat. (It must be the distemper of the times that Utah, with Music Temple and the

Mormon Tabernacle securing its primacy in acoustics, glo-rities what it built and shrugs off what it was given.)

On the way back, Nat and Katie climbed toward the back of Music Temple to see if they could look into the chamber where Katie sang this morning, but they found another chamber in the way, hanging in mid-distance. They returned to Leo and myself, and we began the descent. All of us suddenly realized how tired we were, and Nat was so abandoned she started sliding on the sandstone, missing an occasional Moqui step, and caused the rest of us to miss an occasional heartbeat. When we got back we were so worn out we nearly had seconds on the rum I could down five any night, but the supply doesn't permit loose behavior). As final proof of weariness Katie, for the first night, did not sing Yet even in stupor it is amazing how much less time it takes to do things than at first. Campsites become home in a hurry. After the non-humanity of so much stone, we wallow in the domesticity of a well-screened grate and selected bedsites. The firelight itself throws up walls one must brave, in opposite directions, to get or pass water.

Tonight, everyone works like cogs of a greased machine. Crass orders are still sometimes the rule, but no one in the party would dream of bristling under crassness. Part of it, of course, is knowing when to stay out of the way. One does not impede Nat while she is cooking unless she wants something, in which case you better jump like now. But out here in this physical and mental health I'm getting so that I relish the wood-gathering and dishwashing, the way others enjoy cooking, mechanics and bartending. It works—tonight we are in bed by 7:30.

Mend my holey pocket
And I'll caulk your leaky bucket;
Life's a mutual fixit Or a universal fucket.

October 17

After nearly 10 hours of untroubled sleep, I woke to find it still dark and a soft rain falling, the sort of rain sometimes referred to as

Scottish mist. Sometimes even in clear weather we waken late if there is a high wall to the east, but with no clarity to lure, you could spend the whole day curled in your bag, avoiding the chill where the rain has seeped in, wallowing in your imagination.

We all felt slightly sodden at breakfast, and lingered over coffee making snide remarks. (What did you use for a coffee pot, Paracutin? It must have a hardness of seven. And that old standby, it's like the Missouri River—too thick to drink, too thin to plow.) Katie looked up at a raincloud and said, "I don't think this is a 24-hour rain. I think this is a 48-hour rain."

Leo looked at her blankly and said, "In that case, ah think ah'll draw the string to my poncho."

When we finished stalling for dry weather, we crossed the river to Twilight Canyon and spread our sleeping bags out to dry under a broad dome. From there we hiked the canyon turn after turn, unable to stop, because one must always see around the next turn, even if it's only another turn. At last our feet, exhausted from clawing their way over boulders, informed us it was the end. When we got back to the dome we ran excitedly to our sleeping bags and found them still soggy and rank.

After lunch, the old routine—look for one thing, find another. We climbed to a notch reputed to hold a scaffold house built by the Moquis, and caught no trace of it. Gazing casually across the river our eyes were stopped instead by an enormous rock perched on the wall's edge, greyish green, nearly round with an elongation toward the vertical.

Elephant Ass Rock became the subject of much speculation. The binoculars revealed a surface of strange cracks almost like canals that laced it like a roadmap.

Perhaps a relic from some earlier age, like so many of the smaller ones caught in pockets of all strata, it looked more like a space ship about to take off. Katie swore she was going to get up there the next day to investigate, but on reconsidering our schedule, our devotion to science waned. You can't expect to understand everything.

We intended to push on as far as Forbidding Canyon so that Nat and I could hike up to Rainbow Bridge the next day. It is the only well-known spot on the river, being a National Monument, and we had it in our minds that we really ought to see it. We already knew what it looked like from many pictures, and it hadn't the glamor in our minds of the little-known side canyons. Katie, by small remarks, let it be clearly understood that she wanted to sail on past it, but we pretended not to notice and dutifully pulled up at the campground. There was man-sign, the first real evidence we'd seen since we started. We could make out two outhouses (his and hers? guests and guides?) and a tent where tourists could stay for the night. Yes, real tourists; they are transported by commercial launch from downstream at Kane Creek so they can hike to the bridge, then repose in comfort—a soft touch from our point of view, rugged for modern tourism. We beached timidly downstream, and Katie went up to arrange for one of the guides to give assurance of our approach to the people who were to meet us at Kane Creek next Sunday. Meanwhile the rest of us began to have some doubts about wanting to stay. The outhouses glimmered ominously. Katie returned.

"What news?" asked Nat.

"There's two fat bitches, a drunk and a cretin and another party coming in at nine

Tomorrow"

"Let's get outta here!" It came out like a chorus.

"Ha-hooooo!" shrieked Katie. She leapt, scissored, fell back into the raft and we

shoved off. We camped at the edge of a broad soggy beach, farther than we wanted to from our rubber beast, the weather still bleak. After dinner, the stars came out and once more we thought the storm was over. Katie sang her first concert in three nights. By bedtime the sky was black again, but we were grateful to have sailed on from our glimpse of civiliza-tion. It left a bad taste in Katie's mouth, and we newly valued our own small tribe. I have wondered since whether the people were as nasty as they looked to Katie, and whether the peace and stability of the river wouldn't have shown any visitors in an unfavorable light. The trouble with mental health is that it finally makes the entire world look sick. Perhaps the river will make misanthropes of us all...

October 20

Day dawns in a dozen shades of deepening blue—last night's blood and thunder was the storm's farewell. As the trip neared an end, our thoughts turned to a suitable finale for Nat's movies. The scenario: a shot of Nat cooking breakfast, the camera zeroes in on the skillet, the spatula turns over a pancake on which is written THE END, Nat flings it over her shoulder into the river, the camera pans it as it floats downstream, the muddy water washes over it and slowly engulfs the writing as it vanishes. We fried a pancake till it was brittle and wrote THE END on it in magic marker. The camera began to roll. A close-up of Nat turning the pancake over. It says THE END. With a look of utter nonchalance she flips it over her shoulder and out of range. The camera swings wildly, fishing for it, finds it floating face down in the river. It sinks. We push off for our last complete day on the river forever.

We spent most of it making our way up the right fork of Dangling Rope Canyon, another canyon Katie named and would be saying farewell to. By this point our methods of getting up canyons defy English prose—though perhaps Oriental characters could suggest some of the possibilities. Foot-feeling, ass-wedging, straddling, jimmying, spread-eagling, hand-stirruping, knee-boosting, shoulder-bracing; scaling rocks, trees and each other: After two weeks we move like a team of polished contortionists.

On April 11, 1956, with a grin, President Eisenhower triggered the first blast, and on January 21, 1963, the dedication was celebrated by the Bureau of Reclamation's Floyd Dominy, with the Sierra Club's chagrined David Brower in attendance (those interested in that moment are referred to a delicious description in "Encounters with the Archdruid," a three-part *New Yorker* profile on Brower by John McPhee). But even completion of the dam did not end the bickering. As it filled, the Lower Basin states complained they weren't getting their share, Udall opened the floodgates, the Upper Basin threatened to sue if they didn't get their water back, the Lower Basin threatened to countersue, and so on.

It is said that if the world were reduced to the size of an orange it would be still smoother. But to us, the specks that crawl its surface, it is full of staggering peaks and chasms, towering bluffs and shoreless oceans. These are the places we love and return to, that we will walk, drive or climb miles to see, and carry them home inside us. With their sense of the past stretching beyond us and transforming under our eyes, we watch in them the same process that flows in our blood. When we destroy them it is part of ourselves we freeze. It was years before I could bring myself to go back, and see firsthand the slow encroachment of Lake Powell. But as the world's new comfort is enforced, we become desperate for the wild remains. So I have been back to hike what's left, up from the lake or toward it from the rim, unable to avoid the slow erasing of Glen Canyon.

Its veins bleed out beneath
A winding sheet of water. Here and there
Cottonwoods grapple for air
In side canyons, their leafless tops
More like upturned roots, and a few trapped deer
Come to the end and stare
As the cool impartial waters rise
And include their terror-stricken eyes.
The rest is rippled stone
As the new creatures water-ski
Over the mask of death—
Though doubtless some catfish still ask where
Such rapturous mud has gone,
And sandstone, if it remembers, still
Dreams a return of the sea.

—*Originally appeared in* Mountain Gazette 31, *1975.*

20.
For the Sport of It?
Written by Gaylord Guenin

My daily official duties are such that, after completing them, any more writing is a painful labor; but yet, in view of the fact that I take a deep interest in all legitimate matters connected with fly fishing; that I have been a lifelong lover, and for very many years a keen follower, of the gentle sport; and further, that I am indebted to you personally for several nice suggestions or hints in your writings, I feel that it would be simply churlish of me not to give you a few words in reply to your courteous letter of inquiry. However, I shall ask you to give full credit to my statements as to lack of time, and consequently to make due allowance for haste, condition, and brevity.

—*From* Favorite Flies and Their Histories, *Mary Orvis Marbury, original printing 1892.*

The above is a portion of a letter from Gen. O.D. Green, Fort Leavenworth, Kansas, to Charles F. Orvis, and it also expresses the sentiment of this writer.

Like a ginseng root, the old man, so weathered and bent. He was a Montanan, perhaps the first Montanan. At least the second. In the early 1900s, maybe before, he filled huge cans with fingerling trout fish and mule-packed them into the high mountain lakes above his valley. He loved the mountains, the lakes, the trouts, and the sport of it. Before the ginseng root, there had been no fish in those lakes. Now there were, and the Finlanders and squareheads, when they were not digging coal and dying, tossed dynamite into those lakes and blew the trout fish out and mule-packed them back down to the valley to be salted and dried and eaten when it was time. It was their way, to blast the fish, when times were hard, when times were good, whenever it was time. But the lakes did not die, nor did all of the fish, and the old man who looked like a root always returned for the sport of it. Even then in the early 1900s, or maybe before.

And he showed others, and he showed me, and it was for the sport of it.

THIRTY-ONE: A week later, Lobo Neves was appointed governor of a province. I clung to the hope that the decree would be dated the 13th. However, it was dated the 31st, and the digits, by this simple transposition, lost their influence. How deep are the forces that control our lives!
—*Chapter 110 (In its entirety)* Epitaph of A Small Winner, Joaquim Maria Machado de Assis

But first, for me, was my grandfather, a hunting and fishing guide and a dedicated fly-fisherman, and my father, not a guide but no less dedicated to fly-fishing.

So count three reasons for my lack of success-three fly-fishermen, one who looked like a root, set me on this trail. While other five-year-olds were being schooled in the fine art of war profiteering and influence peddling, I was receiving instruction in the business of fly-fishing, for the non-profit love of the sport of it.

The reader is burdened with that background information only to demonstrate that I am not a Johnny-come-lately to trout-fish killing. It should not, however, be concluded that a Johnny-come-early to a specific endeavor is necessarily an expert.

What I know about this is what I know. Undoubtedly, others may know far more, and they can kindly keep that fact to themselves. In truth, this article will offer little instruction in the business of trout-fish killing. Anyone who can master a peg board can capture trouts. I have waded Montana and Wyoming streams for more than 30 years, which is, I agree, an excessive and unnecessary amount of sloshing about. But it is done and during that time, I acquired an hysterical fear of water, a festering suspicion that in the next world anglers will have to account for all of the trout fish killed in the name of sport, and an uneasy fondness for the same bugs that trouts love to eat, and those bugs are more or less what this article is all about, more or less.

Caddisflies, craneflies, dragonflies, damselflies, Mayflies, stoneflies, no-see-ums, mosquitoes, springtails, gnats, midges, moths, back swimmers, water scorpions, and god only knows what else, make up the list of these mountain bugs. Most of them, the most beloved, are aquatic insects, and in truth they are not singularly mountain dwellers, but it should do no great harm if we think of them as mountain bugs, for a while at least, for the sport of it. We hunt the trout fish because it allows us to go to the mountain, that is what I remember. There is no redemption if the trout fish is hunted away from the mountains.

A place to begin?

With the salmon fly! That should be obvious.

Western anglers call them salmon flies, willow flies and, on occasion, trout flies.

The smart asses in the lab say they are Pteronarcys californica, and they are members of the stonefly family.

> *"Yis, Henry, that's it; and queer enough it seems to a man of the woods. Lord! I guided a man a year or two ago that knowed everything that books could tell a mortal. He was a full of figgers and facts as a hedge-hog is of quills, and if ye poked him up a leetle with a question or two, he'd shed 'em faster than ye could pick 'em up. But when ye got him right down to it, he didn't know nothin', Henry"*
>
> —Adirondack Tales, *W.H.H. Murray*

Baby salmon flies (nymphs) are called hellgrammites, which is actually the nymph of the dobsonfly, but who really cares? The nymphs are ugly as sin. If you were unfamiliar with them and found one in your bed, your heart would turn cold and pump wet fear. The nymphs, however, are not dangerous, they will not attack, or bark, or bite, or form a subversive political group, or even cause a rash.

Their fame, and they are famous in angling circles, is not due to anything they have ever accomplished. Caddisfly larvae are more deserving of fame. They are extremely clever architects, building tiny stream-bottom homes out of sand, bits of gravel, fragments of wood, and pieces of root. But the salmon fly has our attention because of its size—it may grow to two inches or longer-and because it appears in such huge numbers.

Adult salmon flies are called adults, the first practical name the smart asses in the lab have ever come up with. The adults have wings, the nymphs have none, which is true of most aquatic insects.

The nymphs live in clean, well oxygenated streams, mostly under rocks, for about two or three years before hatching. When the time comes, they crawl from the stream, shed their nymph uniforms and become adults. As a bonus, they get their wings. The whole affair, which normally occurs in June, improves their looks.

Outdoor and fishing editors are inclined to write things such as this about salmon flies: "Then he said I should pick some of the big natural willow flies off the bushes along the stream, tear the wings off, bait them on a hook and throw the affair out so that it would drift back into the deep holes but near the bank of the river."

Tear the wings off! Jesus Christ!

After the bugs become adults they hunker around the stream, sit on bushes and twigs, fly around a bit, crawl into your ears and down your back, mess up windshields, mate, drop their eggs into the stream, and die.

Not much of a life but no less futile than that of the trout-fish killers who thunder from stream to stream in hopes of becoming a part of it.

So when you are going after the large trout when the willow flies are hatching, which is the same thing as your salmon fly, you will find that the trout much prefer the female flies as bait.

—More outdoor editor talk

Female salmon flies are likely to be loaded with tiny eggs that resemble caviar but taste like something an insect would lay.

But the finest characteristic of the salmon fly is that it does not become something else if you happen to be on drugs, or some of Austin Nichol's excellent Turkey, or are troubled by visions.

A friend of mine in Montana used to get into LSD now and then before he went trout-fish killing (honestly), and I once found him curled up in a hollow stump babbling about things that were after his salmon fly. Sure as hell, he had a salmon fly cupped under his tongue, offering it protection, I assume.

One once saved my life, but I can't tell you about that.

During a major hatch, there may be millions of the bugs in the air. The Minneapolis-vacationing-musician-trout-fish-killer came stumbling up a path. He wasn't running but it was obvious he was escaping. He had been fishing the Yellowstone near Big Timber when the salmon flies began to move and now he was tumbling and swatting and trying to understand it all.

First memories—my dad had walked upstream and I was fishing out of sight below him when the flies began to move. I didn't know what in the hell they were and most certainly did not want them crawling all over me, which is precisely what they wanted to do. I did not know it was for the sport of it.

The escapee-to-be wanted to know what the bugs were. I wanted to say they were flying Rocky Mountain spotted fever ticks so his heart would stop and I could have the Orvis rod he was carrying, but I didn't. We told him we didn't know what they were because we wanted him to leave. We were off to a trout-fish kill of our own. Some of the Chinese who lived in a nearby railroad town had the habit of placing illegal set lines in the river, heavy lines that you weight and bait and leave overnight. We, a friend and myself, were off to see if we might pilfer a few trouts from those sets.

The root would have approved. My father and grandfather would not have approved of the set lines, or our cleaning the trouts off of them. The Chinese anglers would have been appalled at such a crime.

But that was long ago.

Mrs. Little Kid's Neighbor Lady Who Was Nice always said,

"Insects are our friends." She always shook her finger in your face when she said that and she always said that after she had caught us with a jar full of bees, which we were shaking as hard as we could, or when we were jamming a water hose into an ant pile, or putting a spider into the same jar as a lady bug. She used to let us eat rhubarb out of her garden. She was the only lady in the neighborhood who would. But we still never swallowed the stuff about insects being our friends. Until later.

Maybe it was an accumulation of Turkey in my blood and brain, maybe it was the ginseng root's attitude towards things natural, maybe it was my father's belief that even trout fish and things such as salmon flies, like buffalo and grizzly bears, would not last forever, not even for the sport of it, but whatever it was, something brought about a change.

Salmon flies cannot be domesticated. They do not live long enough. But no matter. They won't hurt you. None of the under-the-rock-in-the-stream-bugs will. Fish feed on them. It is the natural way. Trout-fish killers use some of the bugs as live bait and would probably use more if they realized their potential...

"Next spring, I intend to send you an insect we call here the salmon fly. It is mostly killing bait, and it ought to make a very successful fly."
— Written about 1889 by a Montana Angler,
Favorite Flies and Their Histories, *Mary Orvis Marbury*

...but most of them don't. Anyway, the majority of the nymphs are too small to be shoved on a hook and they are difficult to catch in quantity without a partner.

Hey! You really don't have to catch them and stick them on hooks. If trout-fish killing does enhance the soul as poets and presidents and philosophers have claimed, then it can be fully accomplished without ripping wings off bugs and shoving hooks through their bodies.

"Oh the gallant fisher's life,
It is the best of any,
Tis full of pleasure, void of strife, And 't is beloved
of many:

> *Other joyes*
> *Are but toyes,*
> *Only this*
> *Lawful is, For our skil*
> *Breeds no ill,*
> *But content and pleasure"*
>
> —Izaak Walton, 1593-1683

Bullshit!

For the sport of it. The ginseng root saw no contradictions there. Perhaps there are none in the sport of it. It just seems there should be, somewhere.

It was, for them, socially important. The trout fish brought home, the size, the num-ber, were important. They put on their man clothes for the weekend and Winnebago-packed their way to the high mountains, taking their busy with them, the first thing that should have been left behind. Fight for a parking place, rush to the stream, hate the angler there before you, curse the bugs that swarm around your head, damn the wind blowing down the canyon, the damp that seeps into your sleeping bag, the tick sucking on your thigh, the skunk that got your dog, the leader that broke, the rain that brought lightning, and goddamn and goddamn and goddamn those trouts you cannot kill.

Gather up your busy and Winnebago-pack it back to town.

Man pants off, patio groovies on. Trout fish killed and counted are now to be bragged about over cocktails, to be discussed for the sport of it. No recall of graceful Mayflies, of the smell of the rain that brought the lightning, of weird bugs drifting by in the stream, of tiny mushrooms beside a dead tree, of the things the root always remembered.

But he never took his busy into the mountains. He could go trout-fish killing and never bother with it, spending time just sitting and watching whatever it was he saw, and feeling whatever it was he felt, and he always came back with more than anyone.

The Winnebago-packers returned with nothing but numbers—inches and pounds.

They attacked it for the sport of it like a golf foursome or a bowling team, keeping score but nothing else.

Lord, keep my memory green.

The tourists in camp (and me, too) were always in a rush to get on with the fish killing each morning. Grandfather and his partner were easy. It took a long, long, long time before I understood their ease, their relaxed, studied approach to the day. There had to be time to see the day before you jumped into it so that you could remember what it was when the time came to jump out of it. The sport of it was not in the killing of the trouts alone, as it is in bowling a 300 or shooting sub-par rounds, but I didn't understand that then.

Rock Creek near Missoula was overrun with vehicles and anglers. The word was out that the salmon flies were hatching.

Big browns and rainbows were rolling to the surface everywhere but they would not take the adult salmon flies we were using as bait. We gathered some large nymphs from under the overhang near the stream and placed two or three on our hooks, adding a couple of small splitshot. It worked like mad.

—More outdoor editor talk

Big trout-fish killers were rolling up and down the road in their cars but they would not take our bait. We gathered some shotguns and placed them in the hands of a crazed ecologist we found under the overhang near the stream. It worked like mad.

—Indoor editor fantasy

The damselfly nymph is more attractive than the salmon fly nymph. It is about the only nymph that is attractive. You might call it almost sexy, but you would never be able to convince a doctor as to why you almost called it that. Damselflies are found in quiet water, such as ponds and lakes. They are long and slender. Unfortunately, some varieties are said to be cannibals, a thought that tends to make them somewhat less attractive, but they remain a delight to watch.

The contradiction exists. Trout-fish killing, for the sport of it, becomes more enjoyable as you reduce your participation, as you spend more time watching those things the root watched, and hearing what he heard, and being easy in the mountains.

You don't have to keep score anymore, just for the sport of it.

The legal limit was 10 trout. Being a good sportsman, NRA member and all that, plus being a sniveling coward, the local trout-fish killer would not have thought of being caught with more than his limit. So he played a little game: when he had nine fish in his creel, he would throw the smallest fish he had caught into the bushes if number 10 were larger. It was an endless scene—keeping number 10, if it were large enough, and reducing his total catch to nine by chucking the smallest dead trout fish into the weeds.

He was an obscene, 20th century Johnny Appleseed, skipping along the banks of Montana streams and scattering dead trout everywhere he passed.

He also was a greedy bastard, but he considered himself to be a good sportsman.

This sport breeds greed. Really! You have to fight it. Always!

Spirit of Pitsford Mills, Royal Wulff, Queen of the Waters, Rat Faced McDougal, Beaverkill, Wichams Fancy, Greenwell's Glory, Whirling Dun, Badger Spider, Royal Coachman, Iron Blue, Cahill, Gray Fox Variant, Breadcrust, Zug Bug, March Brown, Strawman, Isonychia, Martinez Black, Quill Gordon, Carrot, Jock Scott, Popham, Black Doctor, Red Ibis, Green Weaver, Gracle, Hill Fly, Mooselucmaguntic, Parmacheene Belle, Oquossoc, Silver Doctor, Seth Green, Saranac, The Time, Sheenan, Ben Bent, Bluebottle, Bissett, Cinnamon, Cow Dung, Equinox Gnat, Esmeralda, Furnace, Ethel Man, Gosling. Golden-eyed Gauze Wing, Great Dun, Golden Monkey, General Hooker, Hare's Ear Imbrie, Jungle Cock, Jenny Lind Blue Wing, Lady Sue, Neversink, Prime Gnat, Cisco, Puffer, Blue Professor, Quack Doctor, Silver Horns, Widow, Welshman's Button, Hammond's Adopted, Silver Sedge, Academy, Cracker, Beaufort Moth, Dark Flaggon, De Gem, Golden Dustman, Polka, Max Von Dem Borne, Toddle-Bug, Premier, Maid of the Mill.

Just names. All names of flies used for trout and bass fish. Nothing very important. Call it a diversion, something to get my mind off greedy good sportsmen.

This article lacks substance, so maybe it is time for some standard, outdoor-writer-type-article information. Here it is: the most dangerous animal you are apt to meet while trout-fishing in North America (excluding North Americans) is the cow. Honest to god, it is. Moose, bears, wolverines, rattlesnakes, chipmunks, turtles, etc., etc., are really overrated. For one thing, if you are in the woods, you should be aware that things live there that may not welcome you, but who in the hell is ever going to suspect a cow?

I have seen guys knocked down by cows, chased out of fields and shoved into ditches by cows, and I mean cows, not bulls. Nothing could be more nerve wracking than having three or four stupid cows following you—they don't growl, or bare their teeth, or hiss, or rear up on their hind legs, or do anything else to give you fair warning they are about to attack. They simply give you the standard, dumb, contented cow look, and then, before you know it, one of them may be standing on your foot or attempting to shove you down a bank. Oh, they do give one warning. If a cow sticks its tail straight up in the air, you know it is going to take a dump, so don't stand behind it.

Beware of cows! Consider that a tip from the wild woods.

Reduce your participation by increasing your participation at another level. Less casting and catching for the sport of it, and increase your joy of it.

The contradiction lives.

K-Mart stores furnish the trout-fish killing kits and Ford urges you to the open road with pleas such as this: "Travel in your own motel-on-wheels! The Econoline ourtmakes just the camper you want—equipped just the way you want it."

Who supplies the ethics? Woolco? Sears? K-Mart? Ford? GMC? Nixon? CBS?

McDonalds Hamburgers? Ron Ziegler? Head Komics?

They are all scorekeepers.

Don't keep score.

Not for the sport of it.

Trout-fish killing needs more losers.

Little trout fish, particularly little brook trouts, are excellent eating. Most trouts, how-ever, have flesh that tastes like attic must. A little lemon, salt, wine, Wild Turkey, pepper, mushrooms, onions, will correct the taste. Trouts that maintain a diet of freshwater shrimp, which are not shrimp, by the way, but scuds, according to the smart asses in the lab, usually have an excellent taste and bright, pink meat. Hatchery trout taste like mud.

The girls, college age, were skinny dipping in a large pool on Lolo Creek. Trout-fish killing was immediately forgotten. Mad rushes of evil acts overwhelmed both of our imaginations.

This was trout-fish killing at its finest. Hiding in the trees, lusting. God, it was open mouth breathing time. But what to do? Action as well as caution was required.

Should we strip and charge out of the woods in full rape? Should we casually stroll upon the scene, act surprised and embarrassed and attempt to apologize our way into a relationship? Should we sneak closer and just keep up our voyeurism? (At this point in my life, I was a sophomore in college and had spent three years in the Marine Corps, my sexual experiences and carnal knowledge amounted to little more than a few giggles.) Should we it didn't matter now. Our hesitation was our downfall. While we pondered it all, the girls had put on their jeans and were walking away from the stream. My fishing companion, also a sophomore in college and life, was outraged at the girls. He erupted, suddenly screaming vile accusations at the girls, who stopped and turned to see a fly-rod-waving-chest-waders-and-fishing-vest-wearing-out-of-control maniac accusing them of being whores and teases and bitches and sluts. I wonder if those girls ever understood why they were the targets of such abuse.

Nevertheless, it was a memorable day. Can you hear me, Izaak Walton? It was one hell of a fine day.

Oh, the brave fisher's life
It is the best of any,
'Tis full of pleasure, void of strife,

and 't is beloved of many...

And we didn't even bruise a trout.

This-is-my-most-favorite-sport-of-all historians seek the superlative, assuming that all is well with their sport because all has always been well, they think:

This is one of the oldest and perhaps the most artistic forms of sport fishing in the world."
—From the introduction to the chapter on "Fly Fishing" in McClane's Standard Fishing Encyclopedia and International Angling Guide.

Those same historians can tell you about men who wrote of fishing with the bait fallacious before the birth of Christ.

So, we know trout-fish killing pre-dates rock. But who supplies the ethic?

The ginseng root is gone, and he was one of few who understood that the sport of trout-fish killing requires very little killing for the sport of it.

"In 1969, 29,855,000 fishing licenses were sold in the United States. The cost to the anglers was $87,501,000."
—Pocket Data Book USA 1971, *United States Department of Commerce Publication*

Who supplies the ethic? Trout Unlimited? The Justice Department? Mother Bell? The NFL? The Upper Clark Fork and Vagabond Inn Seal Hunters Society? The salmon fly?

Maybe the salmon fly, or the Mayfly, or the caddisfly, or the damselfly. Maybe they will, maybe they won't.

The root seldom said anything, but I remember once that he said of his mountains, and lakes, and trouts, "It's a nice day." We were sitting in his tent, above timberline, camped on the Hellroaring Plateau, shivering. Outside it was cold, raining and blowing. No trout-fish killing this day, not even the squareheads would have been out, if any of them still lived.

He was right, it was a nice day. A gentle day for the trout fishes, a learning day for the trout-fish killers.

Don't keep score!

―*Originally appeared in* Mountain Gazette 11, *1973*.

21.
Confessions of a Butterfly Chaser
Written by Rob Pudim

I should have gone to work. I should be doing a lot of things. But here I am, Monday morning, chugging up the mountains, not for anything dramatic such as rock climbing or wrestling a grizzly bear. I am chugging up the mountains in front of a dust cloud to chase butterflies. I should be working.

Being a collector of anything is strange unless you do it for money.

A garbage collector collects garbage because people pay him to do it. People are happy to pay him to collect trash. In cities like New York, not only is he paid well to collect garbage, but during hot stretches in July, citizens gratefully make special donations of filthy lucre in plain, brown wrappers to their garbage collectors. There is so much money to be made collecting garbage that the Mafia has muscled in on it.

People collect paintings, coins, stamps and certain butterflies because they can turn them into cold cash. There are dimes worth $30,000. Ratty purple stamps, poorly printed, can bring a half million. Who would not collect them? From this perspective, there are good financial reasons for collecting campaign buttons, comic books, jewelry or antiques.

Recognition, speculation, and greed are pure, simple and understandable. The problem is how to understand those who are interested only in the collecting, not in the money. Try, for instance, to explain how somebody comes to collect dinosaur shit—excuse me, coprolites. The essential point is that most collectors of this sort do not choose to be collectors. You do not choose to be a butterfly collector and willingly trot around in public with a net in hot pursuit of an essentially worthless, inedible bug.

Who, given all the rational alternatives, would choose to look for petrified dinosaur road apples? Nobody chooses to be a collector. Perhaps the collecting urge is caused by cosmic rays.

Somewhere in the human brain, among our 10 billion neurons, the grey-matter givers of consciousness, is some DNA. When the DNA is cosmic-ray zapped, it rearranges itself slightly. The altered DNA in the brain cell begins ordering its 20 million or so messenger RNA slaves into producing new proteins. These proteins, in turn, effect transmitter molecules in the synaptic cleft between neurons. New links and pathways are created among the 60,000 to 300,000 nearby neurons and something happens.

The zapped DNA produces strange proteins which slightly alter normal human brain holograms. This newly created hologram is identical to those found in animals that compulsively collect things—animals like magpies, octopuses and pack rats. It causes heretofore normal people to compulsively assemble, classify and store all sorts of godawful stuff. They get zapped, and their brain begins to change. They become like freshly hatched ducklings wandering about waiting to be imprinted. A duckling will accept the first thing that moves as being its mother. A recently zapped human will collect the first thing it sees.

Zap! A butterfly collector.

Zap! A dinosaur turd collector.

Deep down other people know collectors have a medical problem and know collectors cannot help themselves. They know that at any moment they, too, can get zapped. They laugh at butterfly collectors, ball-of-string collectors, empty-beer can and tinfoil collectors. But they know that there, but for the grace of God or chance or a random cosmic ray, go they.

The bog I have driven to lays between two mountains, just below the tree line. The mid-summer winds coming over the bare peaks have a wintry smell. It never vanishes.

You have to haul ass into the high bogs to get there in time. Too early and there is a glaze of ice around the grass hummocks. Too late and the clouds build up to the west and the sun disappears. In between there is a brief time when the sun warms the bog and small brown butterflies and flashy blues and sulfurs emerge.

I put on my Mekong Delta swamp boots, one of the few good things to come out of Vietnam. The Vibram soles are good for walking and the holes in the side of them allow water to run in and out. The nylon-net sides permit your feet and socks to dry once you are out of the bog. They are also cheap.

I put glassine envelopes in a shirt pocket, drape a forceps on a chain around my neck and assemble my net. I look carefully around, not for butterflies but for people. light a cigar. I tell myself that it keeps the mosquitoes away, but I know it is to show I am a macho sonuvabitch should anyone happen to see me. The full beard adds to the effect.

There is nothing dumber and sillier than a butterfly collector. Hundreds of cartoons testify to the character, armed with a net, traipsing around a meadow in foolish pursuit of a Painted Lady. Any real man would be pursuing real painted ladies in downtown New York or Las Vegas. There would be dignity traipsing around that same meadow, armed with a rifle, in hot pursuit of a defenseless, inedible crow instead of a defenseless, inedible bug. Hundreds of movies testify that butterfly collectors are batty in a pleasant sort of English way and, without exception, they are males who speak with a high voice and gesticulate with a slightly limp wrist. The outfit is usually a safari jacket, shorts, a Boy Scout hat and thick glasses.

Every butterfly collector is embarrassed about being a butterfly collector. People are embarrassed for you when they discover you do it.

Collecting butterflies is something like masturbating. Each time you do it you feel relieved and somewhat ill at ease. You try to do it in private, away from roads, from peo-ple, from casual on-lookers. You would never do it at a party or in a stadium except in the most extraordinary circumstances. The rationalization is that you want to collect butterflies in untouched areas, areas unaffected by man's pollution and presence. The truth is you would rather not be seen collecting butterflies by other people. And the worst part of all is that after you are finished collecting, like masturbating, you know you are going to do it again.

This may be why butterfly collectors like to call themselves lepidopterists. They think they can hide behind the Greek roots *lepid* or *lepis*—"scale"—and *pteron*—"wing"—and be something dignified. Deep down lepidopterists know that a scaly-winger is a butterfly collector. The rose is not going to smell any sweeter because it is given Greek roots.

Butterfly catchers never talk about the pleasure they derive from butterflies and the joy and satisfaction they get from the pursuit of them. They talk a lot about embarrassing situations—about the time a moth flew in their ear and they had to go to an emergency room to have it removed, about the time a rancher caught them sneaking up on some fresh cow patties and no butterfly was in sight. They talk about where they have been and the dangers of rain forests in New Guinea, high mountain passes in Alaska, or jungles of the Amazon. They talk about everything but pleasure, joy and satisfaction.

This is not exactly true. There is an exception.

"This is ecstasy," Vladimir Nabokov once wrote about standing in green woods among rare butterflies. "Behind the ecstasy is something else which is hard to explain. It is like the momentary vacuum into which rushes all that I love. A sense of oneness with sun and stone. A thrill of gratitude to whom it may concern—the contrapuntal genius of human fate or to the tender ghosts humoring the lucky mortal."

I never felt this when collecting butterflies—even in the presence of a rare one. I am not sure I know what the hell he is saying. I have felt something connected with a sense of oneness with sun and stone. But that has occurred a lot of times under a number of different circumstances.

I remember the first time I caught a certain black swallowtail in my net. It was not rare but I had tried to get one a number of times. Holding a swallowtail between your thumb and forefinger, there is a tremor like a low-grade electric current. It buzzes silently at the end of your fingers as the muscles beneath the hard exterior skeleton try to drive the wings to flight.

The sunlight as it strikes the compound eyes reveals deep inside a honeycomb pat-tern, magnified and moiréd as the insect is turned. The eye is alive and completely alien, like a wite's eyes during a divorce proceeding.

Held between your fingers, there is a thick and pungent smell of freshly crushed parsley. It is as much a smell of summer to me as creosote from July railroad ties or an asphalt pavement in August is to others.

But like a good collector, I am prowling the swamp catching small brown butter-flies. I am swearing a lot. To catch the little bastards, I have to watch them, not taking my eyes from them as I trot after them to where they land. This means tripping over hummocks a lot and, once and a while, stumbling into a bog hole or creek up to my ass.

Tree line water is cold. Elephant hunting would be a helluva lot easier.

When you are up to your ass in a swamp, it is hard to remember the object of the exercise is to empty the bog of butterflies. Some conservationists and the Department of Interior do have a Genghis Khan fantasy about unfortunate, zapped collectors like myself. The fantasy starts with equating butterflies with Bengal tigers or African elephants.

> *"Butterflies First: Butterflies are the first insects to join the ranks of the U.S. Endangered Species List. Of the 700 kinds of butterflies in the U.S., the Department of the Interior has put 41 on its list of threatened and endangered species. This marks the first step toward protecting the butterflies from interstate shipment, commercial sale, and mass collecting."*
> —NWF Conservation News: 5-15-76

Until recently we worried about such vertebrates as whooping cranes, whales and bald eagles. Now, in addition to the more than 100 kinds of vertebrates on the Endangered Species List, there are some invertebrates on it, and things will never be the same. Invertebrate preservation poses a unique set of problems to the conservationist. It is a set of problems which the current set of vertebrate answers do not satisfy.

It is difficult to make an insect extinct. This is not to say they have not become extinct. The fossil record proves they have. There are no longer dragonflies around with 12-inch wingspreads. But there are only two known cases—one in America and one in Europe—of insects becoming extinct because of man.

No insect has become extinct or even been threatened by extinction because it has become part of man's menu or wardrobe. It has not been threatened by over-collection, natural predators, artificial insecticides or insect diseases, or because it has been stomped on in enormous numbers. As a matter of fact, the insecticides, such as DDT, have done more harm to animals and birds higher on the food chain than they have to the roaches, mosquitoes or beetles against which the poisons are directed.

Given high birth rates and short life spans, invertebrates like butterflies are adapted to life in short-term environments such as the brief sub-alpine summer or the growing period of a specific plant. Their population explodes to take advantage of brief but favorable conditions. This also allows them to evolve defenses rapidly to counter the punches man throws at them. As long as they are in some sort of equilibrium with their food and predators, they can adapt and survive.

Remove the predators, and insects increase in numbers and devour their food plants at such a rate that starvation follows. Some survive, the plants recover, the predators catch up and the equilibrium returns. This cycle occurs regularly in the Painted Lady butterfly (Vanessa cardui), and the mountains are treated to enormous northern migrations as the adults seek their food plants elsewhere.

Add predators—this includes humans-with all their ingenious devices for attacking bugs—and insect numbers are kept to manageable numbers and an acceptable level of food plant destruction. The predator-prey balance is healthy for the survival of insects. After all, the butterfly is both prey and predator simultaneously—the former in all stages of its development and the latter in the voracious caterpillar stage.

Fluctuations in numbers of insects-enormous fluctuations

by vertebrate standards—are normal and are usually due to environmental changes. Some of these changes are due to natural events and others are due to human impact.

It has been said by a number of biologists that butterflies are barometers of industrial civilization and man's burgeoning numbers. They are, for example, indicators of atmospheric pollution. There is a phenomenon called "industrial melanism" that describes the darkening of wings in response to dirty air. It has been observed in places as separate as Manchester, England, and Pittsburgh, Pennsylvania. One Pennsylvania moth, for example, had gray wings to match the tree trunks upon which it landed.

These wings darkened, becoming almost black, to match the soft coal begrimed trees and buildings in the Pittsburgh region. Now, after the antipollution program has cleaned things a little, a lighter form of the moth is becoming characteristic of the area.

The Xerces blue did not fare as well. A decade ago developers bulldozed land in the San Francisco Bay Area for housing sites and tore up a wild lotus native to the place, which was the food plant of the Bay Area Xerces (*Glaucopsyche xerces*), a small butterfly first described in the early 1800s by Jean-Baptiste Boisduval. The wild lotus disappeared. The blue disappeared.

Commercial sales did not do it. Over-collecting and interstate shipment did not do it. Something as ordinary as a housing development, a shopping center and a parking lot made the Xerces blue the first insect in North America to become extinct as a direct result of human impact.

In England, another butterfly, a large copper (*Lycaena dispar*) became extinct in the latter part of the 19th Century. Again, the culprit was not over-collection. The destroyer was a human need for peat, a need that required draining the bogs in which the butterfly lived.

The historical message is clear. If the habitat of a species is destroyed, that species will disappear, no matter what steps are taken to preserve individuals of that species. The general truth invertebrates teach us, according to Lee D. Miller, is this: Habitat preservation without restrictions assures the survival of the species, but prohibitions without habitat maintenance assures extinction.

Miller, as a lepidopterist, is aware of a paradoxical thing about butterflies. Most butterflies are rare in spite of their adaptability and prodigious birth rate. A butterfly's occurrence is local and restricted. Most butterflies are delicately adjusted to their immediate environment and bound to a single food plant. A single female can produce several hundred offspring. A few thousand females in a few summer weeks can create a population of millions of adult offspring—but all will be found along a single mountain chain, or on a single island in the Gulf of Mexico or in one bay on the California coast. The unusual butterflies—such as the Cabbage white or the Painted Lady—are those with a wide range and numerous kinds of food plants.

The Department of the Interior does not need an Office of Endangered Species, it needs an Office of Endangered Habitats. Butterflies are telling us that habitats are being destroyed, but that they and other animals can adapt to an altered habitat if the changes are gradual.

Butterflies are also telling us about the shortcomings of having an Endangered Species List and its protections and not an Endangered Habitats List. This can be further illustrated in the recent attempt of the Bureau of Land Management to save a butterfly, the *Nokomis fritillary*.

To quote from the Spring 1976 issue of *Our Public Lands*: "The species is dependent on a particular violet (*Viola nephrapaylla*) that grows in steep meadows on National Resource Lands in BLM's Grand Junction District in Colorado. The female lays her eggs on the leaves of the violet, and the emerging larva feeds on the leaves while waiting for metamorphosis."

Habitat restrictions make Nokomis extremely vulnerable to certain kinds of development of National Resource Lands. Springs that feed the seep meadows are sometimes tapped to provide water for man or livestock. When this is done, the meadows dry up and the violet cannot grow in the drier soil. In some cases, whole colonies of Nokomis have been wiped out.

Studies are now being made to determine if Nokomis should be included on the list of endangered species. If it is placed on that list, definite parameters will be set on any management decision affecting the butterfly or its habitat.

Tom Owens, a BLM district manager, is quoted later as saying, "I never thought the day would come when butterflies would be one of my problems." Butterflies such as *Speyeria nokomis* are not Owens' problem. Owens' problem is, and always was, an endangered habitat.

Reading the article, one would never realize that a butterfly is a basic link in a food chain, not at the end but in the middle. The butterfly's prodigious reproductive capacity is not meant to produce caterpillars to eat violets, but to provide other insects, birds, frogs, toads, lizards, spiders and even small mammals a food supply. The *Nokomis fritillary* may be important because it is food to another invertebrate with an even more restricted range.

Moreover, there is little reason to believe Nokomis could be included on the list since there are flourishing colonies of it elsewhere. The whitewater area in question may not have many *Nokomis fritillaries*, but this is by no means the limit of its range. Thus, no parameters can be set on this particular habitat to preserve it.

This example also illustrates that even saving the endangered habitats of a single species may be too optimistic an endeavor. Emphasis on rare and endangered species has resulted in several land reserves for the protection of individual animals. This emphasis—for instance on the Whooping Crane—ignores the more common plants and animals. This is an expensive program. A bog in Gilpin County, Colorado, some prairie land in Weld County, the southeast corner of Middle Park—it would run into millions of dollars to save only three modest butterflies in one state, Colorado. It is one thing to persuade people to preserve at astronomical cost a large and easily recognized bird like a Whooper or a plant like a Joshua tree. Whether the same people will be willing to underwrite ambitious programs to preserve brown dingy butterflies is another thing.

What the butterflies are telling us is that we need to preserve communities—an assemblage of a population of plants, animals, bacteria and fungi that live in an environment and interact with one another, forming together a distinct living system with its own composition, structure, environmental relations, development and function.

Evolution does not normally carry a species toward domination of its environment. If this were true the world would be overrun by a number of successful animals like roaches, sharks or butterflies. The goal of evolution is not the survival of the fittest species in a dog-eat-dog world. The goal of evolution is the persistence of a species in an ecosystem. Evolution does not produce butterflies or horses; it produces communities of living things in equilibrium with the inorganic world around them.

The way to preserve communities is through the concept of the "megazoo"—a concept advanced two years ago in an article in Science by A.K. Sullivan and M.L. Shaffer.

Sullivan and Shaffer argue that we need to look at a system of primary wildland reserves to ensure a diversity of plant and animal life in the future. Existing reserves are presently inadequate in size and number and are clumped in one geographical region. The megazoo approach would provide a planned network with several levels of reserves of varying size, starting with first and second order watersheds large enough to support stable populations of large carnivores. The megazoo reserves can effectively cut the per-species cost of preservation. The price will still be considerable, and it will not be easy to sell to a large segment of the populace. The megazoo concept offers the best and only chance for the continuation of many species that otherwise will become extinct in our country.

The presently conceived regulations to preserve butterflies and habitats are unlikely to succeed. Similar regulations do not work well for the vertebrates, for whom they were formulated. The Xerces blue experience is warning us that the way to save the timber wolf is not to save the wolf but the timber and all the animals and plants in the food chain for which the wolf is the endpoint.

There is a passage in W.J. Holland's *The Moth Book*, published in 1903, which expresses a notion we all have in the backs of our minds: "When the moon shall have faded out from the sky, and the sun shall shine at noonday a cherry-red, and the seas shall be frozen over, and the ice cap shall have crept downward to the equator from either pole, and no keels shall cut the waters, nor wheels turn in mills, when all cities shall have long been dead and crumbled into dust, and all life shall be on the very last verge of extinction on this globe; then, on a bit of lichen, growing on the bald rocks beside the eternal snows of Panama, shall be seated a tiny insect, preening its antennae in the glow of the worn-out sun, representing the sole survival of animal life on this our earth—a melancholy 'bug."

This is turn-of-the-century romantic nonsense and ignorance we must purge from our minds. When man goes, he is going to take everything with him. And being the gentleman to the end that he is, it will be the birds, mammals and butterflies first.

As you look across a meadow, seeing a butterfly is both a commonplace and remarkable event.

Butterflies are showy animals. They are common animals found all over the world. There are a lot of different kinds of them. Next to the beetles, they are the second largest order in the animal kingdom.

Butterflies have no aggressive characteristics. They do not bite, sting, puncture, pinch or tear. Their defense is flight or protective camouflage, coupled with complex behavior patterns or, occasionally, distasteful body juices.

That butterflies have survived so long so well with so little is remarkable. They were there before the first fish stuck his head into the poisonous atmosphere and decided it was better than the terrors of the deep. They watched the disappearance of the dinosaurs with the same dispassionate stare that watched the arrival of humans.

But in truth, that is a romantic notion. The insects are no more aware of our presence than they were of the stegosaurus' disappearance. In the shifting kaleidoscope world of their compound eyes, humans, the dinosaur and the Kenworth tractor are no more than a mosaic patter of ultraviolet light. Humans do not see the same wavelengths as butterflies, they do not hear the same sound frequencies, they do not taste the same chemicals or feel the same touch.

Humans forget that reality, the real world, is the creation of a nervous system, be it a few fiber-connected neurons as in insects, or an elaborate tangle perched on the neck of a man. Reality, this creation of our nervous system, is a paradigm, a pattern of a possible world. Reality is an invention that allows a nervous system to handle the enormous amount of information it receives and processes.

According to K.J.W. Craik, an English psychologist, this is the nature of explanation. The "true" or "real" world is specific to the species sensing it and dependent on how its brain and neurons work.

Robert Pirsig, in *Zen and the Art of Motorcycle Maintenance*, talks a lot about the classical and Apollonian in contrast to the romantic Dionysian concepts of reality in humans. This is a penny-ante distinction compared to the perceptual worlds of butterflies and men. The German biologist, Jakob Johann von Uexkull, argued that the work of the brain was to create a model of a possible world and transmit to the mind a world that is metaphysically true. Different worlds are constructed by different species and they are all true worlds.

Butterflies do not have much of a brain, but the butterfly's world is no less real than man's. It is not more true or more false when compared with "reality." It is devoid of human beings and the contrived order we have discovered in the randomness around us. Someone once pointed out that all ordered relationships are merely a subset of total randomness or, saying it another way, order is a special kind of chaos. The disturbing thing about butterflies for us is that, despite all our ordering, thinking, planning and calculating, we are a haphazard event in a butterfly's life. The gridwork cities, the ordered rows of crops and the systematic use of pesticides surrounding the butterfly do not exist in that butterfly's reality.

From this, an observation about life on Mars or on planets of other stars can be made. It has been said that we may not be able to recognize life elsewhere because it may be different. It might be silicon based instead of carbon based; it might use ammonia instead of water; it might be energetic instead of material; it might be asymmetrical rather than symmetrical. But behind all this is the assumption that even if we do not recognize the beastie, we will recognize his communication.

We listen to the voices of the stars at the hydrogen wavelength for a signal from them, confident we will recognize it as a signal because it will be repetitive, intentional and meaningful in some way.

The irony is that an extraterrestrial's choice of pattern may be indistinguishable to our nervous system from the chaos around us— just as dit...dit dit ...dit dit dit...is patternless to a butterfly. It may very well be that other intelligences are transmitting messages but all we perceive is a hiss from space, a white noise from multicolored stars.

There is one more observation to be made. The more advanced and sophisticated a society is, the more random its order becomes. To the Chinese all Western music sounds like a thump thump march. The regular beat in Western music is seldom found in the complicated beat patterns of Indian ragas. They also have more tones, so that Indian and Chinese music is closer to modern electronic music with its bleeps, wheezes and burps than it is to Stravinsky or Beethoven.

Language has evolved from sounds to a written code of symbols that have little or no relationship to the sounds. "A" has a number of sounds associated with it, some of which are identical to "U" or "O" symbol sounds. These symbols, in turn, have been converted to pulses on a wire or to electromagnetic frequencies, modulations, or amplitude variations. Bursts of laser light or the warble of satellite radio telemetry is random sound or a flickering light to a primitive man.

Thus the music of the spheres the ancients talked about and the hiss of space the astrophysicists hear may be the same thing. While the cricket hears it through his leg and saws his wings in time, a man merely listens, shakes his head and feels alone.

—*Originally appeared in* Mountain Gazette 54, *1977.*

22.
The South Side of the New England Soul
Written by John Skow

There is no sense to maple-syrup making, no sense at all. I am not sure, but that may be its attraction. What I know is that if you want gentle exercise in the open air, stump-pulling is less strenuous, and if profit is your goal, the shell-and-pea game is a far sounder investment. If all you are after is syrup to put on your pancakes, the only sane course is to humble yourself, stop at a roadside stand in New Hampshire or Vermont, and buy a quart. The cost will be absurdly high, but it is a near certainty that the callused philosopher who sells it to you will be losing money at that price.

If the philosopher has made the stuff himself, however, he will have gained something more valuable than money, and if I think for a moment I will remember what it is. Self respect? No, a man who has satisfied himself for the 20* or even the 40* year in a row that he is a damn fool (syrup-makers are long-lived and stubborn) does not speak willingly of self-respect. Self-knowledge is another matter. The syrup-maker had more of this commodity than he needs, and in March and April he sometimes shares the excess, at the top of his voice, with his dog, his sap buckets, his snowshoes, his sap-sloshed boots and pantlegs, and the trees themselves. A good deal of winter weight swearing gets done in spring in a sugarbush.

All very true. Yet I have never heard of a New Englander who, having made syrup once, did not go on to make it, muttering to himself, year after year. Until very recently, a man in my New Hampshire town led his oxen out on the lake each January, and, using a big crosscut saw, cut himself a year's supply of ice. This rite was much respected by the rest of us (as it was intended to be), and although the man owned a perfectly good electric icebox and freezer, no one thought him strange. Ice-making was what you did in January, never mind the sense of it. And syrup making is what you do in the spring, when a combination of cold nights and hot days causes a watery, almost tasteless fluid to run in astonishing quantities through the white sapwood of the rock maple tree.

This is not good city logic, but by last winter I had enough of cities, having strayed from New Hampshire, by mistake, to live in one of them. I told some friends back home that I would help work their sugarbush. On March 9, I left the city to its own burned-out devices, and the next morning at 9 a.m. I reported for work. I was the first soul at the sugar camp. New Hampshire, a state of bluff, honest motel owners, no longer keeps farmer's hours.

A farmer once owned this sugarbush, and doubtless had his sugarhouse where the present one is, sheltered below a steep hill of maples. A sugarhouse, where the boiling is done, is always below, and a clever man does not need more than five minutes of lugging sap buckets to see why.

Sugarhouses burn down with some regularity, because of the great wood fires that roar beneath the evaporating pans, and because carbon cakes up inside the sheet-iron chimneys and burns, and because boiling syrup itself can catch fire just when you don't want it to. One that stood on this spot burned down—or sideways, since the shed end wasn't touched—and after that a big oil-fired evaporator was installed. It hasn't paid for itself yet, in terms of gallons of syrup produced, but it hasn't set the sugarhouse on fire either. This is as far ahead of the game as the syrup business lets you get.

The sugarhouse that burned was almost certainly not the original, or even a first cousin of the original, but in any case the farmer who once owned the sugarbush was not around to care. His dwelling house, not below the hill but triumphantly at the top of it, burned at the beginning of the century, and what remains is a cellar hole, grown with saplings, and a well, still good. Not thinking about it, working out a series of switchbacks to let my new snowshoes take me to the top of the hill, I arrive near the place where I found the cellar and the well one afternoon three years ago. I think I have found it again, but there is three feet of snow now, and it is hard to be sure.

A yell from below; my friend John is here with the rest of the free labor. John is a prep-school teacher who has volunteered for extra duty; he is teaching a term-end "mini-course" in the economics of syrup making. Clever students will discover—although not, John hopes, before some work is gotten out of them—that the granite underpinning of syrup-making in New Hampshire is free labor.

One hundred years ago on this spot it was the free labor of the farmer and his family, who had little else to do in March except the chores.

Now the owners sneak off from work to lug buckets—John's brother Bill also teaches, and their father is a surgeon—and recommend the sport of syrup making to their friends, who show up dependably on sunny Sunday afternoons, but not in any quantity on rainy Wednesday mornings. As a hobby, sugarbush owning is not more expensive than yacht-racing, and it has this advantage: when it is finished, everyone gets some syrup. (It is said that in Vermont and New York, large syrup combines make a profit and pay their labor, but in New Hampshire these rumors are widely unbelieved.)

Now in a syrup class there is much to be learned. A boy whose home is in Florida learns to his surprise that he can move in an upward direction with a stack of 20 sapbuckets on his back. Then he learns that on the third or fourth step the snow crust breaks, one leg drops out of sight, and the buckets roll down the hill. Back for snow-shoes. This time he reaches what he started out for, a clump of maples where we have started tapping.

I appoint myself chief tapper and learn that a 20-pound gasoline drill gains so much weight in an hour that a man is reluctant to pick it up. There are other sub-tleties. The south side of a tree flows first.

Tap under a limb and about two inches deep, the old-timers say. Don't tap at a comfortable chest height, because when the snow you are standing on melts, the sap bucket will dangle over your head, and people will laugh when you walk into the drug store to buy your paper. Watch what you tap; your maple might be an oak or a beech. I pass the gas drill to a student who looks as if he needs instruction.

The day has been fairly cold, and my first tap showed only a promising wetness gathering at the edge of the wood. Now, toward noon, it has warmed, and when the drill binds in a hole and stalls, there is a small new sound in the air: this slow plink and answering plunk-pink of sap beginning to drop into empty 16-quart buckets. Then a yell brings everyone skidding down the hill to the sugarhouse; John's wife Sue has turned up with a grill, charcoal and hamburgers.

During lunch, a problem that has been skulking about the edges of the sugarbush all morning comes into plain view and leers at us. The fact is that no one knows exactly where the pipeline is. Snow is not a total surprise to New Englanders, and there are stakes to mark the pipeline that is supposed to carry sap to the sugarhouse, but this year's snow has been unusually deep and persistent, and most of the stakes are buried. A search party is sent out to take soundings. There is much to be done. The fittings where the big 36-quart funnels will be screwed in must be dug free, and the pipes must be flushed with hot water and checked for leaks. There is no telling how much time we have. The sap running now could run all night, or stop in an hour. But already some of the buckets have stopped plunk-plunking. Sap is falling quietly into sap.

Up to this point the syrup making class has been a success. The boy from Florida, for instance, has responded well to what educationists call the learning situation. He has worked hard, watched closely, asked questions, and now he feels that he understands how to tap a sugarbush. Good, his quick mind tells him, on to the next lesson. And sure enough, the sugarbush has not run out of things to teach.

The new lesson, however, is that the old lesson will continue. The boy from Florida finds this idea difficult to grasp. Yes, he is told, there is a fine grove through the juniper pasture over the top of the hill, and then when we finish the home orchard, we follow the road for about three-quarters of a mile tapping both sides, and then there is a sugarbush on the backside of the property that you get to through a swamp. We have hung something like 200 buckets, with perhaps twice that many to go. To improve his spirits, I let him work the gasoline drill, which has not gotten any lighter. A short while afterward a cheer arises. The Florida boy, in his agitation, has tapped a beech. But the hooting dies quickly. We have all snowshoed up and down the hill too many times to laugh much. When we quit, a few minutes after four, talk is brief.

Tiredness: the distance runner floats loose above his body, the tennis player feels pleasantly done in, and the golfer's unused muscles are not so much tired as bored to distraction. But the tiredness of syrup making is, after that of mountain-climbing, the most agreeable I know. This is because it is rotten with self-satisfaction. The syrup-maker's carcass, normally city-bound, has put in a day's work. It feels proud of itself.

By morning, some of the self-satisfaction has been replaced by stiffness, but the sun is hot and there is a great rush of life in the sugarbush. The snow is still deep, but beneath it there is the quickening sound of water pouring down the rocky hill. The sap, which stopped during the night, is running again. It is shirtsleeve weather, if a man keeps moving. Stiffness does not matter.

For reasons no better than sun and sap and the fact that the earth is turning—for no reason at all—there is excitement in the air. The pipeline still is buried, and there are still 200 or 300 holes to be drilled, galvanized iron spikes, or spouts, to be knocked into the holes, hooks to be hung on the spikes, and buckets to be hung on the hooks. Yesterday afternoon, our mood was edging toward mutiny. Now we are all loony with cheerfulness.

By mid-afternoon, most of the buckets are hung, and one branch of the pipeline has been excavated. The other branch is found, and hot water poured through it. The water does not reach the holding tank at the bottom. We dig to find the break, down through last week's eight inches of snow, now melted to four, through layers that mark the monstrous storms of February and January, down to the fossil snow of the November storm that started it all. A 20-foot section of galvanized pipe has split lengthwise. We wrench it out and replace it with plastic tubing. I am glad, with my city man's stern sense of New Hampshire tradition, that there is no more plastic in this sugarbush. Some nervously up to-date syrup makers have used plastic to eliminate buckets and sap-carrying altogether. They run the transparent tubes from their pipelines all the way to the drill holes in the maples. Deer and snowmobile delinquents sometimes knock down the tubes, but except for repairs, the up-to-date operator had little need to round up free labor. And has not much fun either, would be my guess. Such a man runs a danger of making a profit; he might as well be running a frozen orange juice factory.

By late afternoon, although there is no need for it, since no bucket is more than half full, we gather our first sap. It is clear and tasteless. A thirsty man can drink it. It gurgles down the pipelines to the holding tanks with a sound like the rush of water beneath the snow.

We talk of boiling. But the next day no sap runs, and the day afterward almost none. It is hard to say why; the motives of maple trees are as murky as those of the syrup makers. A reference work written 50 years ago offers the information that what makes sap rise during some periods of cold nights and warm days, but not during oth-ers, and indeed what makes it rise at all, is not fully understood. More recent reports assert confidently that some trees are more productive than others, but add that why this is so is not yet known.

This murkiness is one of the most pleasant aspects of syrup making, because it means that one man's opinion is as good as another's. Both opinions may be worth-less, but no one can say for sure, and the citified newcomer who at the beginning of March desperately seeks advice will be lecturing confidently to tourists by the end of the month.

For two days, the sap refuses to run. Then it begins, slowly. Now, five days after we started work, the holding tanks are full, the buckets are filling, and my friends John and Bill are ready to fire up the big evaporator. And I must leave New Hampshire to keep a journalistic appointment. That is the trouble with free labor.

When I am able to return, three weeks later, I still have not tasted a drop of syrup, but everyone else has had more than enough of it. The chart tacked on the sugarhouse wall records the production of 80 gallons. This is far less than in other years. For some reason, the sap flow has been thin. Still, since about 40 gallons of sap must be boiled down to make one gallon of syrup, my friends have poured some 3,200 gallons of sap, weighing about 15 tons, down the pipelines.

The sugarbush is deserted. Spring vacation is over for my two teacher friends, and although this is Saturday, each has morning classes. Their father, Dr. Bill, has been busy patching up end-of-the-season skiers, and no one has collected sap for several days. Half of the buckets are full and spilling over. I set out with the two 24-quart collecting pails, a funnel, and a piece of cheese cloth to filter out the moths, meadow mice and bark chips which—so say the old-timers—give maple syrup its special flavor.

Sap-collecting is hard and humbling. With a full collecting pail dangling from each hand, a man lugs some 60 pounds. The old-timers eased the strain with carrying yokes fitted across their shoulders, and two of these yokes hang on the wall of the sugarhouse.

But they are dried and split, and none of us has taken the trouble to repair them. So our shoulders ache, which is the beginning of humility. The middle and end of humility is that there is no dignified way to move around a sugarbush. Snowshoes are awkward on steep ground, do not work on rocks, and cannot be maneuvered with grace over a barbed wire fence.

Now, they cannot be used at all, because large patches of snow have melted away. What remains, however, may be three or four feet deep. The sap collector may walk daintily across this snow when his buckets are empty, but on the return trip, when they are full, he sinks to his wishbone at every third step. When this happens there is a moment when the collector thinks he can prevent his sap from sloshing, and a moment immediately afterward when he realizes that he cannot. In a very short time he is soaked with sap. It all works downward, and you can tell how long a collector has been working by measuring the level of sap in his boots.

Syrup-making, however, is not all humility. Short of piloting a steamboat down the Mississippi, I know of nothing so well calculated to improve a man's opinion of himself as taking the controls of a big maple-syrup evaporator. The thing is chest high and broad as a pool table, fired by two roaring oil burners. Cold sap is piped into the boiling pans at the operator's left. It circulates, boiling, through a maze of pans, over which a great haze of steam rises toward the open ports of the cupola roof. As it loses water, the sap gains color and density. Maple syrup must weigh exactly 11 pounds a gallon and it must boil, at sea level, at 219 degrees—7 degrees higher than water. When sap reaches this temperature it is syrup, and a sensor opens an automatic valve that squirts it into the top of a filtering tank. When the syrup soaks through a filter of paper and another of felt, it is ready to be canned.

It takes about two hours of violent boiling, at a guess, to propel a given molecule of sugar to the filtering tank. When everything works right, the journey is automatic. But the currents are treacherous. If the sap runs shallow, the thin stainless-steel pans will burn through in the time it takes an agile man to open his lunchbox. The operator must be ready to ladle sap into these shallows and also to subdue boilovers.

It is an out-of-control boiling pan that gives the gallant evaporator pilot his most splendid moment. It is a fine Sunday afternoon, and tourists have driven all the way from Massachusetts to give their children a glimpse of country life. The pilot, assuming a yankee twang and saying "a-yup" several times, obliges them with a short lecture on sap-making. One of the pans commences to boil over. The pilot pretends not to notice.

The tourists are terrified. A heaving mass of hot foam stands six inches above the pan. Just as it is about to slop over everything, the pilot takes a stick about as long as a six-iron and touches the splattering sap lightly with the end of it. Instantly and humbly the boiling subsides. The pilot goes on with his story. "Salt pork," he explains, when his awed listeners ask for an explanation, and it is true; a piece of pork fat is tied to his stick with a shoelace. A small amount of milk or fat knocks boiling sap down magically. Once, when a raccoon had stolen our last bit of salt pork, I used flecks of butter from a sandwich. It worked, although I suppose chain saw oil would have done just as well.

A day comes, toward the middle of April, when a batch of syrup comes from the filtering tank too dark to be called Fancy or Grade A. It is Grade B and it has a stronger, better maple flavor than the other kinds. But tourists don't think that anything labeled Grade B can be better than Grade A, so we finish off the last batch for our own use, and at 117 gallons call it a year. As we wash buckets and holding tanks, we boil the last bit of Grade B over a wood fire and let our children eat sugar-on-snow until they can't eat any more.

I leave, obliged to go back to work, before all 600 buckets have been washed. If I can, I will make syrup again this year; it is what you do in March. My friends will be there, of course. I think they enjoy each year being the butts of the same primordial joke. Sap is a crop that requires no planting, fertilizing or cultivating. It is there for the taking, free. My friends are New Hampshiremen, and something-for nothing fascinates them. But they do not really believe in it, and I believe they are reassured when 5,000 gallons of free sap and six weeks of donkey work produce red ink in their account books.

Or perhaps it is simpler. It may be that in that dark place, the New England soul, there is a sense of obligation. If the maple is fool enough to produce sap, the New Hampshire man must match the foolishness: He will collect it.

—*Originally appeared in* Mountain Gazette 7, *1973.*

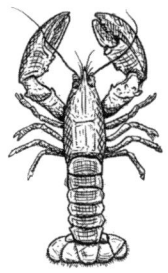

23.
Lobster Fishing in America
Written by Geoffrey Childs

Three figures appear dimly in a field at the end of the path. They are stooped over at the waist, searching for something in the wet grass with their hands.

They seem to shuffle, taking a half-step in one direction and then turning the opposite way, brushing past one another without ever touching. They are gray, sexless and ageless, through the gauze.

"He's an artist," my friend tells me a bit too breathlessly. Her mouth is very close, and her hair is backlit by the houses behind us. Moisture beads at the end of a recent Afro already turning gray at 23. "He rents the house every summer," she whispers as we move closer. "Nobody's ever gotten to know him very well. I think he's Jewish. He's from New York." Her emphasis on "New York" seems to explain everything: How he can afford to rent the house, why he is an artist, why no one has ever gotten to know him, how he came to be a Jew...

The scene comes clear as we approach—a man, a woman, a child. She is wearing a dark sweater draped loosely over her shoulders, a long skirt, a baggy peasant blouse, and she is carrying a wicker basket full of mushrooms in the crook of one arm. The boy, whose age is difficult to tell, is wearing an Allman Brothers T-shirt. He sees us first and smiles. His mother stands and nods her head in a short, European gesture.

There is no condescension in the act, only a noblesse that people were once born into. "Good evening," she says quietly with a very thick French accent. "Good evening," we both reply. Her husband is still searching for mushrooms and berries—they are what he has come here looking for, not neighbors. We grin uncomfortable goodbyes and separate. A short distance later my friend and I pass his house, a small, plain Cape with a square green lawn and painstakingly cared for garden dividing their property from the road by a long line of azaleas. There are old bottles and stones in a row across the living room window. There is no car, no driveway, no mailbox, no telephone.

As we walk, the house fades behind us into a mixture of nightfall and fog. This is the fourth day of fog on the island, the third day I have been socked in here, and the fifth of a two-day weekend I could not afford to take in the first place. I envy the artist his bought isolation, his having it when he wants it. It is what I came to the island for—a few days away from the Fourth-of-July madness in Bar Harbor—but now that I have been forced into it, it no longer has the feel of luxury. I have tried making the best of it, sitting in VanLoon's shed during the day writing or reading, but my mind seems to wander to my business and, I guess, whether or not I am missed. I envy the artist his being able to set his schedule according to his inclinations. A convenience of wealth. When we talk about it, my friend, who is not rich, shrugs her shoulders and says once you get used to it, the island is really not so bad. But she lives here and has grown used to the solitude. The artist thinks he owns it. I am the only one who would rather be elsewhere.

Everything is gone now, and we are alone on the road. I feel foolish jingling in the dark with my two six-packs of beer, but later they work to get us both mildly drunk, and I am glad about having gone to the trouble. We smoke the last of my small traveling stash in her kitchen, after her parents have gone upstairs, and driving me back to the beach she side-swipes a tree, knocking off the rear bumper. There are no inspectors on the island, no roads to speak of, so it matters little enough that we can laugh about it.

We are both too drunk and too stoned to care anyway.

We make very businesslike love in the back seat.

I stand beside the road until the headlights are gone, then turn and walk back to the shed. There are no stars, no moon, no sky. Only fog.

In my island mornings, I walk. The island is not very big—one mile by a mile-and-a-half—but there are several paths cutting through the timber lots between the wharf houses and the backside homes. I made my first trips to the island's natural wonders, but they were all hidden in fog, so most of my recent walks have been in and around the shed along the water where the men build their traps and store gear. On a clear day it could be a postcard. In fact, all summer long people stop by in their private sloops just to take pic-tures, but few ever come ashore. Usually they save their curiosity for Monhegan Island, which is south another 40 or so miles and civilized in the summer by artists, actors and fashionably rich and reclusive New Yorkers. Here, there are just lobstermen.

There is a small diner on the dock that used to serve seafood sandwiches and milkshakes at night to the local kids and would attract an occasional tourist for lunch or dinner, but its windows are broken and boarded up now with failure. Marijuana took the kids away. A few of the local boys scared off the tourists by getting drunk one night and attacking a 40-foot sailing yacht out of Portsmouth with shit-slinging catapults.

Now, the kids sit outside or in the boathouses and smoke themselves incoherent and terminally listless by 14, while their fathers sit at home or in the boathouses drinking themselves mean trying to ignore the cycle. Sometimes they will beat up their wives or their next-door neighbors, or for special occasions, go upstairs to a bedroom, lock the door, wrap their heads in towels and put shotguns in their mouths. It's happened twice in the last four years. Sullenness is the way of life here. There is no place to go except fishing, nothing to do but get sad and tired and crazy. The whiskey comes ashore bootlegged from the mainland and is sold out in 20 minutes. A man buys four bottles of Lord Calvert ("Praise the Lord" is the island motto) and holes up on it till the next shipment arrives.

The island could have legalized liquor, but its people vote it down every year. Everyone drinks, but legalization means control. It means Ezra would lose about $1,000 a year bringing in the bootleg, which means that he would probably give up the ferry-and above all, it would mean outsiders. The law means control, and this is a place with none. It is the tradition. So they get drunk on their smuggled whiskey and go up into their bedrooms.

The fishing has been good, as close as an outsider can gather. Everybody has pots down, and everybody seems to be making money. Not everyone works as hard as the next person, but a man willing to go out in a little hard weather every now and then, willing to pull his whole string twice a week, and someone who's a little bit lucky and maybe even a little bit smart about where he puts down his gear...well, a fellow like that can make himself about $30,000 a year. But people don't talk much about fishing. They are too suspicious and careful. Pots get cut off lines or pulled by someone else, locations get changed, stories spread about someone or other keeping "shorts" or putting down pots a long way from home with someone else's marking on them.

Lobsters are life on the island, and life is a game the islanders play at very hard. And that is the most striking thing about the wharf. There are only 26 full-time families on the island. Most of them are related; most of them have known one another their whole lives. Each family keeps a shed on the wharf, and each shed is padlocked and chained. It is hard to imagine who they are so afraid of. One another? I suppose that's the rationale, but it seems too far fetched—to have to lock one another out after all these years?

People whom you see every day, who have as much or as little as you? Perhaps they worry about strangers breaking in, but that, too, is unlikely. There are so few, and the ones who do come are either invited guests or tourists in sleek yawls from Rockport or Seal Harbor who are not very given to cluttering up their boats with stolen lobster traps and someone's painted buoys. There are no wild animals on the island-the deer and rabbits were hunted off and run down by dogs long ago—and yet everybody owns a shotgun. Who is it that they are afraid of, one wonders? Who is it that they hate so much?

Themselves, probably, and their lives. They are suspicious that they are wasted and atrophying, boys caught playing out a useless legend of brave men and the sea that they no longer live or believe in. So they lock their sheds, load their guns and drink too much. They grow fat on the fear of themselves.

Turns out there is another refugee like me. He has been staying on the other side of the island camping out on one of the beaches, but he has run out of food and patience.

And now he has come down to the wharf to wait. He is a small, pudgy man in his mid-thirties, very delicate and animated. He wears a small, dark-blue Basque beret and gold wire-frame glasses. He teaches Latin at a private school in Boston. He speaks with enthusiasm about his students, about their eagerness to learn and how far they seem to grow in a year towards becoming adults. I tell him that I tried teaching once and gave it up for what I am doing now: writing and climbing and writing about climbing when I can fit the two together. It is closer to a living—the way I wish to live, at any rate—than teaching. I do my usually poor job of explaining this to Phil, and he is not so stranded that he has to listen to such loose-ended apologies. He changes the subject to the island.

Coffee boils on the wood stove in the corner. The door facing the harbor is open to let out the heat, and a few darkly silhouetted masts and shoring timbers loom, just barely visible in the mist. The ocean has disappeared in gray. Boats and houses are only faintly there, occasionally defined by a voice or the sound of an engine. Few of the men have come down today. Commerce sits behind the stillness and locked doors-waiting like everything else, for a break in the weather. Phil and I turn to books. There is a growing, geometric silence. Coffee is poured without comment, wood goes on the fire when it is needed. We seem to have already exhausted our unfamiliarity to the point where further questions become prying and any more answers are unnecessary.

We are both reading when a mad boy named "100 Percent" pokes his slanted towhead through the open door. He is 10 or 11, with glasses sliding down his flat nose and a broad slash of a mouth always half-open. He was sitting on the dock trying to fly when I arrived four days ago.

"Brrrooommmm!" he says, "I just lay back, she say brrrooommmm!

I can't be givin her no other, she says, heh? Just moves her slow down a twist, say yes, yes, she say brrrooommmm..."

He turns the accelerator of his insane motorcycle, his tongue touching the bottom of his nose with concentration. Phil stands up. "100 Percent" looks oddly at him and moves back a step. He has no way of knowing that all of Gaul was once divided into three parts and that, therein, secretly is the key to maturity. I throw a scrub brush at him.

"Hey!" he squeals, just bobbing out of the way. "Don't throw that at me. Please, hey.

Okay, mister? I'm coming now. I'll fix everything, you betcha. Brrrooommmmm!" He drops down out of sight, running off over soft, bent boards and the broken trunks of dead boats, leaving the door vacant and the empty harbor open to us.

Bat Head and Littlejohn come in after breakfast and ask if I'd like to spend the morning hauling traps with them. It is warmer than it has been, and there is no place else left to go, so I agree. It is 8:30 in the morning and they are already mixing the Lord with their coffee as we pull clear of the harbor.

Bat Head is 20. He owns his boat and keeps a string of about 200 pots. That is less than most of the full-time fishermen on the island, but Bat Head is not an intensely motivated person. He has tried life on the mainland twice. The first time he spent about six months in a trade school. The second time he spent three months in a juvenile offenders' reformatory. He has not been back for more than two days in a row since. He never could quite get adjusted to so many people "ragging his ass," as he puts it. He lives with his parents now in a small prefab on the north end overlooking a wide boulder-strewn cove littered copiously with motor blocks, broken bottles, driftwood, pieces of broken boats, refrigerators, garbage, nets, storm wash and traplines. I have been told that Bat Head is the second meanest man on the island.

Littlejohn is 15 but looks less, except around the eyes. There he is 50 and crapped out. He is very drunk before we arrive at the first string. Nothing in the first two pots, three shorts in the last one.

Bat Head pulls them and tells Littlejohn to boil them down in the galley. In 15 minutes we are eating illegal lobsters and washing them down with straight shots of the Lord. Bat Head tells me that Crazy John Lasagna, who is the meanest man on the island, once ate a dead mouse. It was at a dance in the schoolhouse, and John was very drunk. He had brought down a can of dog food for VanLoon's retriever, and the dog wouldn't eat it. VanLoon, who was drunk and in a very nasty mood himself. said it was because the dog food was made of dead mice. Voices were raised, dares and threats exchanged, and finally, a bet made. A short while later John produced a dead mouse and ate it in front of everybody. VanLoon then ate the dog food, which was his part of the bet. The story has been told all up and down the coast, Bat Head tells me. In Rockland even the police know who John is and think he's crazy.

Halfway through the second string, Littlejohn, who is too high on the Lord now to even stand up, decides it is time he drove the boat while Bat Head pulls traps and stuffs the bait bags in them. The bags are small mesh nets filled with putrefied fish that attracts the lobsters. The smell of it is overpowering and Littlejohn, who has not been too accurate in his work, has the stink of it all over him. Pieces of fish dangle in his hair and on the front of his shorts. Staggering from the back of the boat, he lunges at the wheel, pushing Bat Head back against the hot exhaust pipe, and steers us directly over the trap line. None of this is a good idea. Bat Head, who is not very tolerant where his boat or being burned are concerned, strikes Littlejohn directly in the middle of the forehead with the Lord Calvert bottle, and he collapses like a card house. We pull the rest of the string and then turn back towards the harbor, which is around the other side of the island now. We have 62 keepers at $2.08 a pound. We have been working three hours, pulled approximately 80 traps, finished a bottle-and-a-half of whiskey and eaten about 15 shorts.

Bat Head throws some water in Littlejohn's face as we pull into dock and Littlejohn comes to, crying hard and holding his forehead. We leave him in the bottom of the boat sobbing about wanting to be left alone. After expenses, the take comes to about $75. BatHead gives me 10 and drops off $20 for Littlejohn with his parents. He tells them what happened and that Littlejohn ought to be up after a little while. They do not seem shocked, only vaguely alarmed and fairly respectful of Bat Head. He is, after all, the second meanest man on the island.

On an afternoon walk I cut off the main path into the woods and find a small lean-to behind a thicket of blown-down trees. The floor is sandy and dry and there is a bed made from fir boughs and a poncho. In front there is a stone fireplace with a new grill leaning in the ashes and the foil discards of many pans of instant popcorn. At the foot end of the shelter there are three crude shelves. The bottom two hold food cans mostly, and a couple of hash pipes. On the top shelf there is a small hand towel and a pack of lubricated condoms. On my way back I meet Littlejohn's father. He seems almost to materialize out of the fog on the path in front of me. He is looking for Littlejohn, who is not at the boathouse or with any of his friends. There is worry on the edge of his voice.

Bat Head, he says, gets a little carried away sometimes.

Hamburger Sam is at the shed when I get back. He is very drunk, this being Friday night and him trying to keep to some civilized schedule. Sam grew up on the island, but he is only a summer resident now. During the year he teaches literature and creative writing at a small college in the Midwest. The lobstermen usually go about their business Saturdays and Sundays just like any other day, but Sam is keeping to his mainland calendar: During the week he reads and writes, on the weekends he sinks into an alcoholic oblivion. He is building a log cabin near Land's End Point, and his hands are rough from the work. He is showing them to Phil and discussing the work when I come in.

They both advise me that the weather is supposed to be better in the morning and that Ezra will be taking the ferry in to Rockland and we will be able to catch a ride in with him if we want. Also, there is going to be a party at the schoolhouse tonight. Praise the Lord. Everyone is going to be there, and there will even be a band. Phil seems genuinely excited about the news. I am keeping my expectations low until I can look back on them from the mainland

It is dark now, and Phil has gone over to Sam's for some supper and a few beers before the dance. The room is absolutely quiet. I sit in a rocking chair VanLoon made from trap staves and look through the door out onto the black harbor. The only light comes in a zigzag from the weigh station, where Mithaud is bringing in his haul late. It is not that I can tell Mithaud's boat from any of the others, it is that Mithaud always brings his haul in late, especially if he knows everyone at the station will be pissing and complaining about not getting home in time to shower before the dance. They could close without him of course—they have before—but catch is rare in a fog like this, and they need his. If they don't weigh him in, he isn't beyond going into Stonington on radar and selling his lobsters there. There is no love lost, I am told, between Mithaud and the rest of the island. He first came here about 12 years ago, leaving a construction job in Lewiston and moving into a house he bought on the point side of the harbor. A hard worker by nature, he immediately built a dock, put up his own shed, bought a boat, a few traps, got himself a lobster license and settled down to earning a living with his new neigh-bors. But "new" is not necessarily a respected characteristic along the Maine coast, and Mithaud was wrong for the island at least three other ways, as well. First, the people here have never much liked strangers; two, they especially don't like strangers who come and put down 300 traps; and, three, God's immortal teeth forbid that this stranger should be a French-Canadian Catholic.

So, all these things taken into account, Mithaud's first years on the island were obviously lonely and antagonizing. His pot lines were continually being cut, sand was poured into his engine, his windows were broken, he could not get credit at the island store and, worse, every time he brought in a haul the weighing station would close just as he got there. If he left his catch overnight, it would be gone in the morning. If he took it into Stonington to be weighed, he burned up just about every penny he made in gas. But Mithaud was not the kind of man given to throwing in the towel so easily. In fact, just the opposite happened. He got very angry. He began playing his half of the game. When he found his lines cut, he pulled other people's traps, took their lobsters and cut the gear loose. When he had a window broken, he would break someone else's window; when he found sand in his engine, he would put sand in someone else's engine. It didn't matter whose.

Then, after this had gone on for about a year, one night he broke the picture window overlooking the harbor from the house of Crazy John Lasagna. Mithaud was at the post office on the dock the next morning when John came down. People who were witness to it say that John was never in a more evil temper. Sensing blood, a crowd followed him over from the general store and spread out in a semi-circle around the front of the post office to wait and listen while he went inside. First thing John did coming through the door was to pick up Mithaud by the lapels and hold him against the wanted posters with one hand, pulling the other one back over his hip and into an enormous fist. He was red-faced and wild with anger and about to lay Mithaud's face, once and for all, right through the wall when Mithaud told him to go ahead, hit me, you Wop son of a bitch, but goddamit you better kill me, because if you don't, soon as I get out of the fucking hospital first thing I'm going to do is to get a gun and blow the shit out between your diego eyes. Now Crazy John might well have been the meanest man on the island, but he was no fool, and it occurred to him that he was way out of his class with Mithaud, who was hanging there by his throat showing no fear at all and probably wishing for nothing other than that John would go ahead and hit him so he could sneak up behind him some night and shove a shotgun up his ass. John dropped him, made a few idle threats and walked out. Mithaud tucked in his shirt, picked up his mail and has not had a line cut since. He is still pulling other people's pots and bringing in about twice the haul of anyone else on the island, but nowadays the weigh station stays open for him even if it means being late to the big dance. People grumble about it, but grumbling is the tone of island life, and hardly anyone hears anymore. Except for Mithaud, who is probably enjoying himself.

"**Dennis,** you whore's ass, how the hell are you?"

Crazy John claps his free hand on VanLoon's shoulder and spins him halfway around until they are face to face. With his other hand he holds a bottle of gin to VanLoon's mouth. The gin splatters down the front of his shirt and over the pants of several of the men standing around holding beer cans and laughing. VanLoon gags and pushes himself free.

"John," he whines, "you motherless, pasta-sucking bastard." He coughs and pats at the wet stains on his shirt. John laughs again and takes a long drink off the bottle. The others laugh with him like a choir.

My friend is standing near the piano with her younger brother who is already drunk and looking at the floor like a man trying to find a soft place on the hard ground to lie down. I walk over to her and we try being heard above the noise of the band which is playing top volume twang on cheap guitars and fuzzy amplifiers. They are four boys in about their mid-teens, all with long hair and pale, lightly frightened faces.

"Did you hear about the weather?" my friend shouts. "I heard the fog is already breaking on Deer Isle. That means it ought to be clear here by morning."

Jubilation. A moment of silent prayer to the Lord. I take her hand and turn to watch the crowd. This is farewell, and I am suddenly feeling almost affectionate toward these people. There are about 50 of them in the room, maybe a third of them children under 18. The men and the women, except the ones dancing, seem to keep to opposite sides of the floor. The men all hold beer cans, or paper cups filled with Lord Calvert and ice.

Only a few women are drinking. They are hard-looking ladies, most of them mainlanders who met their men and followed them to the island. Nothing connects them other than their universal wish to be somewhere else. Surprisingly, there is very little infidelity on the island, my friend informs me. Everyone knows too well what is going on next door.

When the men want to get laid, they make up some excuse for going into Rockland and take care of it there.

A lot of flirting seems to go on. It is probably innocent enough, but it is very aggres-sive. The three or four women who are drinking are the drunkest in the room. One of them, a lady in her early forties, comes over and asks to be introduced. She is wearing a black pantsuit, the top of which is a very tight jersey with a deep V-neck. Her cleavage is remarkable, formed by a suspension bra whose design must be roughly the equivalent of, say, the George Washington Bridge, for serving up two melon-like breasts to just below several soft steps of chin. The woman's makeup is very heavy, and her breath smells smoky and stale. My friend mentions our names, and the woman takes my hand, coming in close until our knuckles are brushing each others' stomachs. Hers is Spandex elastic. Fascinating, she says, fascinating. She has never met a climber before. At least not a rock climber. She giggles about that, and her hand drops lower. Yes, very aggressive flirting. Later in the evening her husband will attack one of the younger men over just this sort of thing. He will have his shirt ripped in her honor and his son will get in a couple of good licks with his engineer boots before bystanders pull everyone apart.

By 10:30 or so the party has gained its full momentum. Bat Head, who it turns out plays a hot C & W guitar and has a voice like Roy Orbison, has taken over from the band with VanLoon on drums. The musicians are standing off in one corner of the room with terror in their young eyes, wondering what is ever going to happen to them and their fancy equipment and whether any of them will ever see the mainland again. Crazy John is standing with them, wearing the drummer's sunglasses and telling them about dog food. Out on the floor the fat women are up and doing the jitterbug now with wiry husbands too drunk to grab hands as they spin past one another in staggering pirou-ettes. Singularly, and sometimes as couples, they will tilt too far too fast and fall. A lot of people are beginning to make contact with furniture. Mr. Arbris, who owns the general store, misses a fast side-step in a solo dance of his own creation and falls into a row of chairs, taking most of the buffet table with him. When they bring him out he is covered with punch and chicken parts and bleeding from the nose, but his feet are still moving to the rhythm of Bat Head's borrowed Gibson. Hamburger Sam and Phil arrive about this time. Sam seems sober and composed, but Phil has the glow of the Lord upon him. Amazing grace, as they say. He is flushed, smiling dumbly and clapping his hands quietly on his buns in time to the music. My friend observes this and shakes her head.

"Sam's got another one," she laughs, but it will be some time before I pick up on the full meaning of this. I am too busy at this point doing my own odd bob and weave. On this miserable, fogbound rock, for all its unhappy souls, plundered lobsters and sad hostility, I am dancing for the first time in years. "Brrrooommmmm!" I shout, the Lord rising in my throat to touch every corner of the room. "Brrrooommmmm!"

Unfortunately, getting drunk always makes me forget that I am not much of a drinker. I have never had very much elan at picking the right time and place to vomit. In this case, I hit VanLoon with the first wave, catching him across both legs, then spreading the rest of my stolen lobster over the floor of the coat room for everyone to see.

Apparently, no one notices that they are shorts, as I feel several people patting me on the back, impressed with my work and shouting encouragement. The second wave gets most of them. Outside, staggering, I step on something soft between the porch and the ground that moans and twists wildly underneath my foot, but I am heading for the swing-set now and blind to everything else. My friend is kind enough to hold my head, but refuses to drive over me with her car. I tell her that I do not want to live like this, but she refuses to be swayed. Inside the schoolhouse there are screams and thunderous applause. John, she says, is eating a tube from one of the amplifiers.

Delirium and fringe behavior pass into unconsciousness. When I awake, I find myself sitting curled in one corner of the front seat of my friend's car. We are not mov-ing; she is talking to someone. Littlejohn's father. He is bending over, his head very near the window and the left half of his face colored by the green lights of the dashboard.

His eyes are swollen and his fingers clutch at the suspender buckles of his overalls. "I can't find my boy," he explains. He has lost his hat, and there are tears streaming down his cheeks. "I've asked everybody. No one's seen him. Not since Bat Head beat him this morning. Hell, he didn't have to go and hit him. You know Littlejohn. Shit, he ain't no harm when he's like that." His next words are lost in a gasp. He stands, turning away from the car for a moment trying to compose himself, then turns back and bends over.

"If you hear anything..." My friend cuts him off with consolation.

He's probably just wandered over somewhere to sleep it off, she tells him. You'll see. He nods and says thank you. I watch him out the back window as we pull away, standing there with one hand in his pocket, slouched over and wiping at his face with the back of his other arm.

Dust stirs around his feet and mixes with the remainder of the fog to swallow him, another lost soul on this island of misplaced persons.

The morning comes up clear. I pull on my pack, swallow some coffee and a few aspirins and spring down to the wharf. The ferry is in and loading supplies. I pay my $4, throw my pack on and crawl up some piling to snap a few photos while the other passengers straggle in. 100 Percent comes down on his mystic motorcycle, finishing the last lap of some never-never race he will always win, pulling back at his thin-air hand brakes, skidding in tennis shoes to a stop at the edge of the pier. My friend comes down with sandwiches, and we talk about seeing each other back on the mainland. Phil arrives behind the band to say goodbye. He is going to be staying with Sam for a few days. My friend grins. Behind me the dock hands push up the ramp, and I have to leap five feet for my ride home. The decks already feel like freedom. I turn and wave goodbye, and Phil and my friend wave until we are clear of the harbor.

I take a seat in the stern beside a lady in a cashmere shawl and watch the island fade behind us until it is just a lumpy, dark disk on the horizon.

"Do you live on the island?" she asks.

The question comes completely by surprise.

"No," I tell her, after a moment. "No one does."

—*Originally appeared in* Mountain Gazette *45, 1976.*

24.
Confessions of a Sauna Junkie
Written by Jack Aley

I am a self-confessed sauna junkie. Two or three (sometimes even more) times a week, I simply must fire my small cedar-lined room with the double-glazed window facing west (for natural evening light, of course) and endure the heat of hell.

If I miss just one sauna night, I get restless. If, for some (ungodly) reason, I miss two or three in a row, it's cold turkey for the kid. I get cantankerous and more obnoxious than usual. My joints begin to freeze up; my eyeballs' humour starts to congeal and my head turns to cardboard. Life ebbs out of me. I start barking at my Constant Companion and start kicking the kids and the cats, whichever get in my way. The only cure is a couple of hours in the box..undergoing that mysterious, sweat-induced metamorphosis of soma and psyche. When I emerge from the hellish rite, all squeaky clean and beatified, I'm fit to live with again. The kids and the cats can relax for a couple days until the saunatropic urges begin building in me again. The sauna is my pot, my boob tube and the monkey on my back. I wouldn't, couldn't, have it any other way.

The history of my addiction to saunas starts inauspiciously enough. The YMCA in the Illinois town where I grew up had a steam room. It was a nice place to go after a handball game. I remember how good I felt after I got out. Nothing heavy. I did discover that the longer I endured the heat, the more miserable I felt in the steam room, the better—(and dare I say it) almost newborn—I felt afterward. I stored that little experiential tidbit away somewhere.

I languished through college and graduate school without access to (or even direct knowledge of) saunas. That's probably why, applying hindsight, I have so few fond memories of college and graduate school. I think how much more bearable those hideous exams in organic chemistry and that Othello seminar would have been had I a sauna to look forward to afterward. Today, I might even be a doctor or an English professor rather than growing vegetables, cutting wood and writing confessions for a living.

Like many restless Americans of my generation, I lived in Colorado for a while after my futile schooling and took to the mountains whenever I could. It was there, in the quasi-Bavarian movie set of Vail (of all places!) where I first ventured into a sauna. It wasn't real, of course. Nothing in Vail (especially the orange Saab police cars and the mustachioed Marlboro men who went with them) seemed real. My first sauna was in one of those candy-assed jobs tucked into the frail, sheetrocked recesses of a "Texas townhouse." (I don't know where they ever got the name "Texas townhouse" except that they were somehow related to all the Dallas money and accents floating around the place. In general, names didn't make sense at Vail. Sinclair Lewis could have written a dandy Rocky Mountain Babbitt at Vail. Such a wealth of material.)

The Vail sauna was electric, the empowering box labeled Am-Finn or some such ridiculous hybrid. In my innocence, however, I accepted it as the real McCoy and rediscovered what I had learned several years back in the Illinois steam room. The more miserable I felt in the sauna, the longer I endured, the more (dare I say it again) newborn I felt afterward. (I hate to keep using newborn—it sounds so rapturous—but it was like that.)

I even took to jumping in the snow after my more miserable stints in the redwood closet. My leaps took me from a Texas townhouse balcony into snow drifts but a few steps away from the center of Vail. My behavior appeared to cause my usually tolerant hosts some embarrassment. They suggested trying a shot of five-star cognac after a bout with 210 degrees. That was very nice too. But in the long run, I've found the snow cheaper than the Martell's.

That winter, I gleaned a glimmer of understanding about the nature of the process I was learning to endure so happily in the sauna. I went so far as to reason the process had some relationship to literature. I was teaching a high school English course at the time in which I used the nature of chemical bonding as a tool for interpreting drama.

The spiel went something like this: The more energy released in a chemical reaction—that is, the more explosive it is—the firmer the resulting bond of elements; ergo, the more intense the literary experience, the more powerful and sublime the resolution of it. Sophomoric, perhaps. But the kids seemed to dig it, and I figured I had to do some-thing, someday, with a double major in pre-med and English. God, I even reduced King Lear to a case study in inorganic chemistry. See kids, Lear loses both his clothes and his sanity on the raging heath (the crucible, of course) before Shakespeare permits him a serene death. In contrast, Old Prufrock is unredeemed and unrewarded because Eliot makes of 'Do I dare disturb the universe' a rhetorical question." I understood this stuff intellectually, I think. But it was not until the initial saunas that the paradoxical curves of extreme experiences compelled me emotionally. All this suffering for redemption crap had something to it. At one sublime extreme, there was Lear on his heath. At the ridiculous other extreme, there was Aley in the sauna. Important things were becoming clear. if not particularly reassuring.

The restlessness that carried me to the Rockies (I didn't spend all my time at Vail) also swept me away... around our untidy little world. There weren't many saunas along the way. I missed them, not consciously as I remember, but enough so that when I stumbled into Istanbul, I snooped around for a Turkish bath. The one I found was located in a fetid alley somewhere near St. Sophia. I entered the dank, decaying, mausoleum place with every western hang-up firmly in place. I reluctantly divested myself of both my clothes and few valuables, sure I'd never see the latter again. The vaulted steam room was replete with the tiered marble benches I'd read about and seen in a couple of movies. Inside, it was tropical but certainly not as hot as a sauna. I was just beginning to feel the place out when one of the several, small, dark men in the room started making advances. For God's sake, he wanted to give me a rubdown. Shocked (I've always been a little naïve about these things), I retreated to a protected corner of the steam room and did my best to let the slow emissions of steam soothe and relax one very uptight initiate to Turkish baths. The result: The curve of stress and relief in a Turkish bath is nowhere near as pronounced as in a good sauna. Besides, the languid vault seemed somehow tumescent, even degenerate. There was absolutely none of that hyper-borean crispness I associated with saunas. I've never taken another Turkish bath. And, miraculously, I didn't lose my clothes, my money or my heterosexual purity.

Sweating through the summer months in Asia was very much like being trapped in a huge, overpopulated and dirty Turkish bath, one with no exit. When I finally did get out, from Kabul over the Hindu Kush to Tashkent and then Moscow, I was 30 pounds lighter and possessed of an involuntary lower intestine that had endured the bacterial wilds of Asia and could only tolerate Mexaform and boiled tea. in moderation. I resembled a tall, badly groomed prune. The bear-like (what else) visa man at the Russian embassy in Kabul laughed derisively when he saw me. It took me two weeks to get a visa.

My few days in Russia, in the stolid hands of Intourist, Russia's only and singular "tourist agency," did me little good. I even had trouble with the mineral water. But on the last day, the day I was to take the train from Moscow to Helsinki, I gambled. I traded in an Intourist chit on a plate of beef stroganoff and some red wine. It was a gamble. I lost. That night, I fouled my bed on the train between Moscow and Helsinki.

I arrived in Helsinki in about as bad shape as I left Kabul. But at least I was in Finland. Finland! At last! Pine trees, reindeer, flawless complexions, edible meats and cheeses, and, of course, saunas. I was in heaven.

My first night in Helsinki, I ferreted out a sauna, ironically an electric one located in a university dorm. The first full day in Finland's capital, I went sightseeing. My journal of those days says the picture I liked best in the gallery I visited "was of a real Finnish sauna being tended by a little girl." After two days of sauna-taking and yogurt-eating in Helsinki, I began to feel better, horny even, a sensation that had all but abandoned me in Asia.

The next two weeks in Finland were to rekindle my love affair with saunas and set the stage for my permanent addiction. I planned to hitchhike through the eastern lake district, then north across the Arctic Circle, stopping at public campgrounds along the way. Finnish campgrounds, it turned out, were not your average campgrounds. They were miniature Valhallas, and they had saunas, real ones, the ones with wood heat, warming rooms and a cold lake just outside the door. I was going, quite literally, on a sauna trip through the homeland of saunas.

I got to the lake district the first night and, as my journal recalls, the euphoria started: "I spent the first night in the veranda of an archetypal sauna, woodburning and a few sylvan feet from a clear, cold spring lake. In late evening (still light at 10 p.m...moving north now) with two Germans and three Finns (the sauna pros). I scalded and breathed utter satisfaction alternately for about an hour. One Finn just kept it steaming and once drove me out. I was sure my skin was boiling off. But the hurried dips in the lake brought that fantastic invigoration and relaxation that only saunas seem to develop." The second night, at a lovely campground in Kattka, my journal indicates what the sauna was doing to my head: "The sauna was a beauty. I was the only non-Finn, and it was still rosy at 10 p.m. after my sauna, so I took a walk in the incessant twilight looking for animals along the dirt road. It was so quiet, the light so peculiar and steady, the situation so strange and haunting. A certain timelessness and vague contented communion with things just not disturbed very much...I thought such winters here, such winters..like looking at an old man, tough and wrinkled and lying in the sun and me wondering about his winter and respecting his mere being and held a little bit in awe by it."

Christ, lyricism almost. That Illinois steam room never triggered anything like that in me. It seemed these saunas not only had the power to cleanse me and make me feel somehow virtuous, but they could also turn me on as well; me, the rational guy who always fell fast asleep at the first whiff of hashish or pot.

The climax to my sauna trip in Finland came in the Arctic Circle city of Rovaniemi, an outpost devastated by the Germans and rebuilt with the kind of severe, economic good taste often germane to northern peoples. A public sauna was included in the reconstruction (it probably was the first thing they built). Upon hitching into the city, I of course hit the sauna first thing. My journal takes dutiful note: "Bless the Finnish for their saunas. The one I had tonight at the sauna and swimming hall in Rovaniemi was fantastic... It was the biggest sauna I've ever seen. Had indoor and outdoor pool.

Swimming on the Arctic Circle! Again the sauna is creating its great effects. Rovaniemi is the highlight of the sauna circuit."

I was completely hooked after the trip through Finland. The sauna was a part of my life. I still dream about that Rovaniemi sauna and the others that helped restore my health after the exhausting tour of Asia. I was only a day or two out of Finland, transfixed by the never setting sun in the Norwegian fishing village of Tromso, when I wrote my parents a letter. I recounted my trip through Finland and vowed I would build my own sauna someday.

In the interim, I returned to the States, suffered routine (but powerful) culture shock and stumbled into a job as a wire service reporter in Maine. Those were pretty crummy years for I was discovering I could scarcely tolerate office work and, basically, was unem-ployable. To forget my troubles, I ran a lot and became a sauna whore. I started sneaking into motel saunas and college saunas and ski area saunas, and I held pass number 576 at the Portland Jewish Community Center, a pass that was good for nine saunas during the year. These were all pseudo saunas, of course, smelly and electric and sorely underheated. They were a far cry from those on the Finnish sauna circuit, those wonderfully fragrant, woodheated cedarlined rooms with windows facing west (for natural evening light of course). I suffered being a sauna whore, but I had to have the heat.

After some time in Maine (a place with uncanny similarities to

Finland, by the way), I did discover the existence of some colonies of Finns in the state. One such colony was in Kingfield, near the Sugarloaf ski area. A Finnish couple, the Pillmans, opened their wood-heated sauna to the (largely skiing) public on weekends. For two winters, I hardly ever missed. When I wasn't in the Pillman's sauna, I managed to get in a little skiing. As a sauna whore, I kept my priorities straight.

After three years of getting my fix of heat in crapola saunas, I'd had it with being a sauna whore in Maine. Enough was enough. I'd learned conclusively that Americans had done to saunas what they'd done to a lot of imported stuff...to chocolate and beer and yogurt and yoga and downhill skiing and the list goes on. We'd sexed it up, put it on a production line, marketed the hell out of it and in the process ruined it. An American sauna (actually a contradiction in terms) was a Hershey Bar.

So I did what I had to do to rehabilitate myself. I needed a worthy object of my passion for saunas. I bought some land, a fairly modest parcel in southeastern Maine with a tumbledown old Cape. Like many of the so-called "back-to-the-landers," I mouthed the platitudes about going back to basics, the owner-built house, the organic garden and the airtight wood stoves. The purists in that elite subculture could never have understood that the real reason I bought the land was so I would have a place for my sauna. I didn't give a particular shit about independence; I wanted heat and ritual. Whenever I started talking to my few Maine friends about saunas, their eyes went blank with boredom or incomprehension.

I spent the first few months on my newly purchased land trying to learn the arcane art of carpentry through rebuilding the old Cape. I wanted the hands-on experience behind me. The house itself wasn't so important. But by no means did I want to botch the building of my sauna.

I actually started getting the sauna together months before construction started.

In June, I got hold of 700 feet of white cedar logs from northern Maine and had them milled locally. I spent part of one afternoon lovingly stacking the cedar to air dry.

Also in June I found a Finn in Owls Head (a coastal town near

Rockland) who built sauna stoves in his garage. Demand at the time was low...a couple per year. I got one of them. The night I drove my old pick-up the 70-some miles to Richard Ilvennon's was auspicious... soft and clear. Ilvennon greeted me with warmth and a fish dinner. I was a stranger but I was understood. The fact that I wanted a sauna stove at all constituted a bond. Ilvennon took saunas once a week at his parents' home nearby. So he had a pretty good idea of why I'd driven an old truck so far to pick up the crude but substantial stove he'd welded together for me.

I drove carefully. I might as well have had 200 pounds of eggs in the back. Many nights during that summer, I'd go out into the shed and sit and stare at that squat source of my future ecstasy. Some nights I fondled it.

By early that fall, I'd picked up enough about carpentry to forget reconstructing the house for a while and turn to the top priority on the place... getting that sauna together.

It was with some awe and trepidation that I began to frame the 12-foot-long by eight-foot-wide by seven-foot-high spaces in the far corner of my shed. Never had I wanted something to be so perfect.

I work best under deadlines, so I gave myself one for the completion of the sauna room-October 12, a Saturday. I figured if I planned a sauna-warming party for that night, I'd have to have a sauna. I invited the poet, the proctologist and the artist down the road: everybody in Maine I knew, all 12 of them. I also invited (or rather summoned) Zee, an old ski-bumming buddy who, despite his penchant for wearing Harvard athletic department sweatshirts, knew his way around tools. Zee made the mistake of arriving from Vermont a couple of days before the party. The sauna was only about half done. I was beginning to panic, so we worked through the nights. I drove Zee unmercifully.

Two hours before party time, we were hanging the sauna door and lighting the stove at the same time. I breathed a sigh of relief, and Zee and I took off for a celebratory run. I really wanted to be primed for this one. I wanted the inauguration of my sauna to knock my socks off.

If a perfect sauna results in achieving oblivion (one of my definitions), then my first sauna in my very own sauna was perfect. I passed out just as the first guests were arriv-ing. The combination of little sleep, the long run and the sauna itself, topped by some red wine, did me in. That was okay because I really didn't feel like sharing the moment with too many people anyway.

Few, if any, of the subsequent saunas at my place have been as Dionysian as the first (I later heard everybody had a good, drunken time). In fact, sauna nights have evolved into rather quiet rites, one I and my Constant Companion have come to guard quite jealously. (She is a very physical woman who immediately came to share my raving affinity for saunas.)

We've found that the often rough passage to the calm-after-the-sauna is best made in absolute quiet. None but the two other sauna addicts we know seem to understand the importance of shutting up in the sauna. Talk blows the trance, rufflesthe concentration needed to give body and mind over to the alchemy of intense heat.

Up to a couple of years ago, we'd often have people over on sauna nights. But inevitably, in their innocence, they'd start getting social and kill it. Now, on sauna nights, we turn out the lights and don't answer the phone. We are very selfish about our saunas, we suffer no fools.

Oh, one or two people are sometimes welcome because they understand how to behave in church. Noel, a card-carrying Bohemian, craftsman and ace apple-picker who lives down the road, is one of the cognoscenti we accept from time to time. But even Noel has transgressed grievously. One night, after he'd been mainlining raw garlic for a couple of days, Noel came over for a sauna. What intense heat can do to a molecule of digested garlic being flushed through the human skin is fantastic. The result is nauseating. Poor Noel was banished from the sauna until he'd flushed his system of the offending bulb. Another time, Noel brought into a sauna a towel he'd been storing in moth-balls. Within a few seconds, the sauna smelled like the inside of a hot truck. We didn't ask him back for two months after that. Noel understands better now. He behaves well in my sauna except for the times he becomes talkative. But I've found a cure for that.

When he opens his mouth, I make sure he's on the top bench and then douse the rocks with a pail of water. The resulting wave of fiery wet heat that engulfs the room is enough to shut anybody up, and the quiet rite may resume.

Not much interferes with our sauna night. Only a phone call from more than 1,000 miles away is sufficient to get me out of the sauna and then I make the caller wait. We did, after a year or so of intense use, blow the top off of Richard Ilvennon's stove, which by that time, had settled into permanent warp. A heavy steel plate welded over the top fixed it, and we were back on line within a week. But it was a bad week for me…and for the kids and the cats. One sauna evening last summer, I noticed the sauna stove wasn't drawing very well. I went outside and discovered that the corroded chimney pipe had finally disintegrated just above the elbow. It was hot and dry outside and the fire's smoke, plus a few sparks, was being disgorged directly into the shed's cedar siding. Rather than extinguish the fire and forget the sauna, I wet down the side of the shed and (albeit a little nervously) settled in for my sweat. I guess junkies do dumb things.

While every sauna we take is subtly different, they basically seem to divide into summer and winter saunas, the difference having something to do with the metaphysics of sweat.

The nature of a winter sauna, if you are familiar with saunas at all, is what you might expect: the contrivance of extreme difference in temperature (nature contrives the cold and you contrive the heat) and commuting between extremes, the better the sauna. One winter's day a few years back, I skied (took one or two runs actually) at Sugarloaf where the wind-chilled temperature was 100 degrees below zero. That same night, I was in the Pillman's 200-degree sauna. Three hundred degrees is an extreme variance. Such winter saunas are about polarities and stretching the mind and body between them…stretching each as far as possible. Fifteen minutes in the heat, hit the snow, rest; 20 minutes in the sauna, hit the snow, the ice water, rest; permit yourself a couple swallows of beer and into the heat again.

Three times is good, four is better, but five, even for the hardened sauna taker, is to begin flirting with fainting. I've had my winter sauna as high as 255 degrees, but at that temperature the wood is almost impossible to touch and you want to touch the wood because rough-cut white cedar makes a dandy back scratcher. These days, we'll settle for 225 to 235 degrees in the winter sauna. Any lower than that and my hard-assed Constant Companion refuses to go in more than once or twice. "It's not worth it," she says with disdain. "You can't fly on 210 degrees." My god, two sauna junkies in one family and the kids are coming on strong. It's almost too much.

The summer sauna is oxymoronic. You know, cold heat, dark light and all that. As a paradox of the senses, a summer sauna is hot cold. It doesn't make sense but it doesn't have to; it is. A good one goes something like this: It is 95 degrees outside at 4 p.m. on a July afternoon. You've been cultivating potatoes or (if you're really flipped out) cutting down trees, and there is sweat-saturated earth clogging every pore of your body. Your soma is suffocating; your psyche is wilting. You are so hot you want to die. The surefire relief is not the icy tub, cold drink and shade tree; they come later. First you fire up the sauna and on a hot day it only takes 30 to 45 minutes to get the room up to 200 degrees, which is all the heat you want. (We are not now dealing with the extreme winter polarities, just the matter of 100 degrees or so.) About 5 p.m., cocktail hour for addicts of another ilk, you strip off your steaming and stinking work clothes and jump into the sauna. God, you thought it was hot outside. This is terrible... hell upon hell. But you endure a few minutes and the flow starts from your core. You didn't think you had any sweat left but you do, plenty. It erupts through your clogged pores like a million hot springs. Hang in there for five or 10 minutes, then retire (or crawl) to the shade tree and rest; it is still 90 degrees outside but they are oh-so-much-cooler degrees.

Repeat this deceptive art two or three times and, oxymoronically, you have beat the heat. It's not everybody's idea of doing it. But it makes perfect sense to a sauna junkie.

I'd feel less comfortable telling you about my addiction to the sauna were it not for the fact that it is a perfectly practical dependency. Unlike most things people cannot do without, the sauna is a big money saver. Because of the sauna, we never go out. We just go out to the sauna. We haven't been to a movie or a party or a restaurant in months.

Our sauna nights begin in late afternoon with the lighting of the fire and end in late evening with the champagne dessert to our root crop casserole (also cheap and good).

The very few times in the past couple of years we have yielded to the ever-weakening desire to go out and be social, we've spent most of the night faulting the food, the flick or the friends (sometimes all three) and fervently wishing we were home in the sauna. Since the sauna is (almost incidentally) the family bath, I long ago did away with the ancient, current gulping hot-water heater I inherited with the old house. The absence of the heater alone saves us almost $200 a year in electricity bills, which, because of our wood-heated existence, run under $10 a month anyway. We also use the sauna to dry clothes, make yogurt and heat the adjoining warming room I just finished building

Since Sauna One (the first 20 or so I recorded like Super Bowls), I calculate I've fired up my sauna 320 times. The 321st is heating up at this very moment. I've been down with a mild case of the flu and, with the help of the sauna, am going to try to blast it out of me. If it works, I'll be well. If it doesn't, I'll probably be sicker than hell and can get more sympathy and breakfast in bed. You see, you just can't lose in a sauna.

―*Originally appeared in* Mountain Gazette 70, *1978.*

25.
Gone Fishin'
Written by John Nichols

On Saturday morning, Toby woke up early because he was going fishing with Bobby Salazar. He had crashed at six a.m., setting the alarm for ten-twenty. When it started beeping the cats began skittishly prancing around, confused and disturbed. Toby cursed, swung his feet out of bed and sat on the edge of his mattress, dumbfounded, groggy, despairing, hurting all over—his neck, his hip, his right leg. Sometimes he got cramps in bed that made him yowl just as he awoke, but not this morning, thank God. His lips were so chapped and swollen they felt about to explode and drop off his face. His throat was as dry as if somebody had poured sand into it all night. The ache in his sinuses was massive, brutal, thunder-ing. The awakenings he experienced nowadays were like Olympian hangovers, earthquake survivors, the aftermath of slow and ponderous car wrecks. It was great to be sixty years old, *qué no?*

He sat there rubbing his eye sockets, too blown out to reach over and quash the alarm's irritating beep. Then he finally roused himself out of terminal lethargy, pushed the button to Off, removed the fat blue pillow from on top of his answering machine, and stared at the blinking red light, trying to make sense of its bap-a-dap-dap sequence.

Evidently it was saying, "Three messages, buttmonkey, I dare you to push me now when your brain is still in warp eight."

Later, gator. Toby shuffled into the bathroom, almost tripping over Carlos. He peed in the sink, splashed some water around, brushed his teeth. Cookie came in and started eating her Science Diet lamb and rice bits. Why was the cat dish in the bathroom?

Because when it had been in the kitchen skunks had come through the kitty door to have at it, no kidding.

From the medicine cabinet mirror, a six-hundred-year-old man, a sort of alcoholic, homeless Albert Einstein with grubby hair cartoonishly fluffed in many directions, grimaced at Toby, gap-toothed just like our hero, and said, "You look marvelous."

Toby said, "Thank you, screw you, up yours."

From the top bureau drawer he fetched his lanoxin and an aspirin, and started toward the kitchen barefoot. But there was so much grit on the eight-thousand-year-old carpet that he doubled back, grabbed a pair of socks from the pile beside his bed, sat down and tugged them on. In the kitchen he poured a glass of apple juice and drank his pills, then parted the filthy lace curtains so he could better look out at another hideously sunny day in their winter without beginning. "What's the UV count today," Toby muttered, bitterly sardonic, "eight billion, four-hundred eighty-seven million, five hundred and forty-six thousand?"

He and Bobby Salazar wouldn't need sunblock on the Río Grande today. A mud plaster over lycra Aztec ski masks was more like it. Toby still had one of those sleep-created hardons that he observed for a second rather bemusedly, wishing there was someplace pink to stick it. Carlos rubbed against one shin, so Toby bent over, scratched behind his ears, then rubbed his backbone by the tail hard for 10 seconds. He grabbed a Kleenex out of the box on the toilet tank and blew his nose, big gobs of snot.

Back on the bed, groaning as every bone in every joint in his body screeched loudly, Toby grabbed up a couple of Jobst varicose vein pressure stockings, gathered his strength for two minutes, then tugged them on, whimpering from the pain. It required a superhuman effort. If he lived three more years how would he ever have the strength to keep pulling on the stretch hose?

His heart blurped in and out of atrial fib. Toby put on a pair of filthy dungarees, an old flannel shirt, then he trudged outside to the tool shed, unlocked the door, and paused for a moment intimidated by the disarray. A bicycle, garden hoses, tool boxes, paint cans, nail bags, nuts and bolts in mayonnaise jars, a dust-clogged Casio keyboard, all of Toby's digging and chopping and hoeing tools and scads of other hardware crap cluttered the 6-by-10 space. Toby had to be careful not to straighten up in there otherwise dozens of nailpoints in the ceiling would perforate his skull. Another fabulous Toby Scott Floyd construction job. Left to his own devices with a hammer, a Skil saw, and a T-square, Toby could out-bumble the Three Stooges.

His fishing equipment lay on an old foldout table with both leaves down behind the bicycle in a mess of detritus guarded by two dozen black widow spiders flashing their Day-glo red hourglasses at him. Behind the pile of refuse that included his fishing vests and numerous busted reels stood a half-dozen rod cases in various stages of collapse.

Toby gingerly retrieved his vest, a couple of reels, and his one good aluminum rod case, and humped out of there before the black widows started spitting cobra venom in his direction. The vest he shook out spiritedly for thirty seconds, then he plunged back into the raging tool shed inferno to retrieve a burlap sack for carting his catch.

Long ago, in another century, Toby had kept up his equipment. In those days he'd been a fanatic for the Río Grande, fishing several days a week throughout the late summer and autumn, scampering up and down steep rattlesnake infested bajadas like a professional athlete, him and Bobby Salazar and Bubba Baxter, and all the women that Toby had loved: Mona Perot and Brenda the Cop, Jo Ellen and Beverly Sinclair, SherriFranzetti, even Rebecca, even Penny Sullivan a couple of times, Loretta Larson, too, and Iris Candelaria. Those girls had loved to fish or tag along. It was always the same and always wonderful. Weather warm or icy, the magnificent towering canyon walls, hot winds at gale force stinging their faces, big basalt boulders everywhere, green water roaring and splashing, redolent sagebrush on their fingertips, blossoming sulfur-yellow rabbitbrush, the canyon wrens and owls calling and bats fluttering at dark when they started out, and then languid sessions on the Dodge tailgate or in the Impala, exhausted, happy drinking beer and eating sandwiches beneath the stars and various stages of moon or cloudy, growling skies. He and the bimbos fucked in the truck, they fucked in the Impala, they fucked on pine needles among ponderosa pines on the trail down, on the trail out, they fucked in grasses beside the river, against those enormous gray boul-ders, they fucked whenever the urge or opportunity presented itself, crusty with sweat and fish stink, their moans lost in the river roar, their happiness uncompromised by earthly preoccupations.

At night, the Milky Way traveled almost exactly overhead, north and south. They made love totally wasted and then drove home thirty miles down from Big Arsenic or Bear Crossing or El Aguaje, or from Cedar Springs or Miner's Trail, or from Francisco Antonio on the west side of the gorge, completely happy and satiated, shamelessly drinking beer, tired, almost drunk, ecstatic, the heaters whirring—what a wonderful life.

Toby arranged four bottles of St. Pauli Girl in his red and white cooler, added ice and a churchkey, then made sandwiches of baloney, lettuce, Swiss cheese, and tons of mayonnaise on Potato Bread, wrapped them in tinfoil, dropped 'em in a sack. He added a couple of apples for good measure, then cranked up the D 150 and headed north on Valverde to the Salazar residence, where Bobby was waiting impatiently, frowning at his wristwatch: "What the hell took you so long, mofo?"

"Shuttup," Toby growled, "I got three hours sleep and I'm not in the mood." He was exaggerating by only ninety minutes.

"Time's double when you're goin' fishin'," Bobby grumped, by rote, for the eight millionth time, flinging his stuff in the back of the truck, then popping a Diet Pepsi after he'd swung up into the cab.

Toby hit the next speed hump so hard half the equipment almost bounced out of the bed. "Jesus Christ," Bobby wailed, "why don't you freakin' step on it?"

"Times double when you're goin' fishing," Toby said.

They were OFF, and as excited as little boys. Just because you're sixty don't mean you can't have fun. "Snow on the roof," Mona Perot always liked to say, "don't mean there ain't a fire down below."

Toby drove north on Placitas, hung a Louie on the highway, passed the blinking light four miles later, outdistanced civilization, and, for a minute before Arroya Hondo, they had mesa on both sides, wide and lavender gray, with that electric blue sky and brilliant sunshine cascading in crazy droves all around them. The Nightmare Non-Winter From Hell—but the river water was low and pretty clear, and for sure the fish would be biting.

When Bobby stuck a cigar in his mouth, Toby screamed. "Not in my truck, you asshole. Don't you dare strike a match!"

"*Toma lo suave*," Bobby said. "What do you think I am, a neanderthal? Hey, *ese*, gimme some credit, okay?"

"You light a match, I'll roll this truck over deliberately."

Bobby lit a match, saying, "Go ahead."

Toby punched his shoulder. Bobby whacked him back. Toby said, "Did you bring me any candy?" Bobby said, "Up yours and your candy, whattayou think I am, an idiot?

Buy your own candy. Plaque up your own stinkin' veins with your own money. I refuse to participate."

"OH MY GOD WE'RE FREE!" Toby hollered.

Bobby puffed on his unlit cigar. They were behind a state cop going exactly 55 so Toby had to rein it in, cursing the marrano who must've known they were headed for trout.

"Did you bring some beer?" Bobby asked.

"Does the Pope swim upstream?" Toby replied.

"You know, you oughtta grow up one of these days," Bobby said. "That childish bent is reflected in everything you write."

"I never said I was Dostoevski," Toby said.

"Dostoevski? Spare me, dweeb. In your *sueños*. Shame on you. Vonnegut's more like it. On a good day. On a lucky day."

"I'm gonna catch a 20- inch rainbow," Toby said

"Oh yeah? You and whose *ejercito*?" Bobby answered.

"Five dollars," Toby said. "Biggest fish."

"Don't bore me with your peasant gaming," Bobby scoffed. "I'm out to contemplate the natural beauty of La Naturaleza, and I wouldn't cheapen the experience by half-assed wagering for all the *oro en el mundo.*"

Toby said, "Look at the sky, look at the *sierra*, look at San Antonio Mountain over there, look at the sagebrush, look at the empty highway, ain't it great to be alive?"

"Enjoy it while you can," Bobby said. "It's a quick trip for all of us." The lads smiled in unison. Then they laughed...

But neither of them caught a single fish. Ouch. Bobby had six hits and missed them all; Toby had seven hits, same deal. Anymore, he had the reflexes of a sloth. They started climbing up from the river at dusk cursing the gods and goddesses of the goddam Río Grande. "That river beat me up again," Bobby moaned. "*Me comío los huevos*. It's like a cheap hooker from Enseñada, *tetas* the size of Vesuvius, but with her legs chained together."

"You're so gross," Toby muttered. "I'm ashamed, you chauvinist pig. Clean up your act, bro'."

"We shoulda brought dynamite," Bobby said. "*Grenadas de mano. Sulfuric acid.*"

"Stop bitching," Toby said, huffing, puffing, gasping, grunting as they climbed the steep trail leading out of Big Arsenic toward the rim two miles away. "If it was easy, we'd hate it."

"I hate it like this," Bobby complained. "I lead a hard life, I want a little positive reinforcement *en mi vida loca*. I'm 61 years, *viejito*, and I spent 61 hours this semana peering through a loup repairing a bunch of stupid digital *pedazos de mierda* I wouldn't even wipe my ass on let alone latch on my wrist. One in fifty *relojes* anymore that come across my mesa were made when craft *quería decir algo*. I spend my whole *chingada vida* fixing drek for *pendejos* who wouldn't know quality if it came in their *oreja*. I deserved a trout today, fuck you and your *estúpido gabacho locuras. Puto. Me cago en las botas de tu madre.*"

Toby sang, "*Allá en el Río Grande, allá donde vivían...Vivían truchas grande, que nuestras plumas no querían—*"

Bobby tried to punch him, miscalculated, and fell down, banging his right hand on a prickly pear cactus. Half the stars in heaven cringed when he screamed.

Neither of them had a flashlight. "Get away from me, o *seguro te mato,*" Bobby snarled, seated on a rock, fumbling to pinch out the hideous hooked needles aggravating his palm. "You made me do it, you *cabeza de basura*. A pox on your *casa*."

Toby whistled through the gap in his teeth, contemplating the miraculous clarity of the constellations. "Hey, there's Cassiopia," he said merrily.

"*Tú madre.*"

"And Ursa Major, I do believe."

"*Tú padre.*"

"And Orion's Belt—wow! *Qué cielo máravilloso!*"

"*Tú hermana, tres veces, en el culo.*"

"Ain't that big dipper glorious?" Toby exulted

"*Tú abuelita. En la boca.*"

"*La tuya,*" Toby chortled. "Man, I love this river."

"Screw this river," Bobby grouched. Getting up again, gingerly flexing his aching fingers. "Let's *lárganos* from *este infierno*. You got any water left? My bottle is empty."

"Yup. But I need it all. If I go into A-fib it's instant dehydration, I'll die, you know that."

"Gimme that *agua*," Bobby said, "or I'll slit your *gringo garanta.*"

Toby gave him the water. He watched Bobby guzzle, then took a gulp for himself and had never felt more divine in his life than right at this moment. The river, the gorge, the disasters did that to you. It was all bloody wonderful. And what a sky overhead, sparkling with flaming hydrogen, black holes, exploding nebulae. Toby could smell icy space, mingled with pine pitch, adobe dust, and sagebrush.

An hour later, they reached the truck, groaning, moaning, cursing, aching, sweating, panting, coughing. "*Hijo madre,*" Bobby said, "who taught us to suffer like this? Me I understand, I'm *chicano, lo entiendo*, it's in the *sangre, somos todos jodidos*. But you're a gringo, you're supposed to know better, it's not genetic with you, so what's the catch?" It was too cold to sit on the tailgate. Toby cranked over the engine, hit the fan but-ton, pushed the heating levers all the way to the right, and let the decrepit old Dodge idle while they ate their sandwiches and sucked pensively on the icy beer. Toby had always been a glutton for this ecstasy of exhaustion, he adored the anguish, the ache, the physical collapse so sweet as he mingled into it the sandwiches and *cerveza*, warm air blowing against his fatigue like angel breath. And there they were, two old guys, 60 and 61 respectively, side by side in the cab of an idling dinosaur with 194,866 miles on the odometer, wondering if they'd ever grow up

Sixty seemed awfully old to Toby, yet he still felt infantile, innocent, inept and childish most of the time, amazed that anybody took him seriously. How had he earned a living for 38 years, raised children, pretended to be wise? "It doesn't get any better than this," he said, staring through the windshield at darkness, at the dimly visible shapes of piñon and juniper trees.

"Tonight is kinda special," Bobby replied. "We only go around *una vez* in life."

"We've sure had some times together," Toby said.

"Ain't that *la verdad*."

Toby finished his second sandwich about the same second Bobby licked a last mayonnaised crumb off his stubby fingertip. They clinked beer bottles again: "*L'chaim*," "*La Vida*," "*Salud, amor, dinero, y mucho tiempo pa' gastarlas*." Then Toby switched on the headlights and put it in gear, popped the clutch, headed out. Between Arsenic and Cerro they saw a couple of small does and maybe the twitch of a disappearing coyote.

On such a deserted road, with the moon shining brightly, Toby could cut his headlights.

They cruised for a way in darkness, feeling awed, peaceful, happy. *Adios, Río Bravo. Hasta la próxima.*

"We're gettin' old," Bobby said. "We shoulda killed that river today."

"Shoulda, woulda, coulda," Toby laughed.

Actually, on reflection, those funky old boys had killed the river today. And they would do it again, and again, and again ... and again ... and again .... and again.

—*Originally appeared in* Mountain Gazette 80, *2001.*

26.
Coyote Song
Written by Dick Dorworth

---

*You may say that I'm not free,
But it don't worry me."*
—Keith Carradine

The highway between Wilson and Jackson crosses the Snake River about a mile outside Wilson, over a concrete-asphalt-metal bridge of uninspired, though functional, design. Past the river, the road continues for a half-mile before entering a long right turn leading to a quarter-mile straightaway and then turns left into another straightaway. That is the only section of the Wilson-Jackson highway we are concerned with here.

The road itself is not special. Just a 10 mile stretch of classic two-lane black-top connecting two western American towns. The only thing unusual and unique about this particular slice of highway is the contradictory unusualness and uniqueness common to any piece of the road we are all traveling. That is the fact observable to the patient and interested, that he who pursues the road, no matter how sporadically, will, like every gypsy who ever used unspeakable cruelty to teach a bear to dance, someday find himself once again on the same stretch of road during one or another of his swings away from his own everchanging, unvarying nature.

Wilson is little more than a road stop at the bottom of the eastern side of Teton Pass, and that's the way locals like it. Wilson is the site of the Stagecoach Bar, the one saloon in the Jackson area that is common ground for all of the diverse social elements living there-cowboys, ski bums, hippies, climbers, tourists, musicians, horny housewives, college students on vacation or leave, construction workers, restaurant workers, fat cats, lodge owners, condominium salesmen, fishing guides and anyone else in the vicinity hankerin' for a sandwich, some company, a bunch of beers, a pool game, good music, and, maybe, a lay. On Sunday afternoon the Stagecoach jumps. Jumps, hops, skips, rocks, rolls, howls, runs, back-flips and spread eagles. All good local musicians and any passing through gather there to jam. Sunday afternoon in Wilson can get pretty rau-cous; but because of the local laws, inspired by quasi religious sentiment, the bars close at 8 p.m. on Sunday. Around 7:30 there is a run on six-packs at the Stagecoach, and by 8:30 there are empty beer cans all over the parking lot, the highway and alongside every road leading out of town.

That's Wilson.

Jackson has its charms, but all in all it's about the worst tourist trap in western America. During summer, Jackson is wall to wall people, bumper to bumper traffic, asshole to eye-lid hustle, junk stores, mosquitoes and all the lost energy of displaced Americans desperately seeking their own misspent history and heritage in the noon and 5 p.m. fake gunfight held daily in the town square. The entrance to each of the four corners of the square is through an enormous arch made from the antlers of elk, a large noble animal indigenous to the area. Indeed, the elk is indispensable to the local economy, which thrives on the trade of the great white hunter in the autumn in much the same manner as it survives on the dreaded white tourist in the summer. Most conscientious wanderers pausing in Jackson overnight or a little longer will somehow drift into the Million-Dollar Cowboy Bar. At one time only the bold, the blind, the unwise or the saintly long hair would have dared venture into the then aptly named saloon. But times change, and, in one of the ironic moves of the karmic wheel, the cowboys lost their territory for a change. Not lost but came to share. And what better way to work out all the old bullshit than by sharing—both the bullshit and the bar.

That's Jackson.

The Snake River drains out of the mountains of Wyoming into Idaho and Oregon and on to Washington where it joins the mighty Columbia, which eventually flows home to the ocean. Some people speak of an ocean of love from which life comes and to which it must return. And because of all this idle talk down the years, it often crosses my mind as I cross over, bathe in, look upon and drink from the fine Snake River that, if that's how it works, then that which begins in love must, inevitably, end in love. And it is simple to make the next step of seeing the true beginnings of things in how they end That's called hindsight, but I don't hear so much about the importance of beginnings. It is the state of mind that comes before the aim that comes before the arrow is launched toward the target. The river of peace; the ocean of love; and there was even a man who is said to have walked on the water. Who knows? He may have walked on the Snake.

Concrete, asphalt and metal are materials used by the human animal to subjugate, dominate and violate the nature that gave him birth and so far continues to sustain him. The human critter can be exceedingly ungrateful.

The bridge across the Snake is a tool of convenience. From one aspect it's a piece of shit, but it serves a function by allowing people and their vehicles to shuttle back and forth across the river without getting wet. Some people and most vehicles do not take well to getting wet; though coyote shuns the bridge. In a 100 years the bridge won't be there, but the Snake will.

There may be another bridge over the same river and different men to cross it; but I cannot repress my curiosity about the state of those men's minds, a 100 years from now.

Uninspired is the state of life of the coward who would rather live with an unacceptable comfortable situation than throw it all over for a chance at joy.

Functional to an engineer or a soldier or a politician or an insurance salesman may mean something very different from what it means to, for instance, a coyote. What is functional to each person says more about the person than about function, and it is an interesting word to throw into a conversation with someone you wish to check out.

The bridge does serve a function in the material world. *Construction.* Well, shit, boys and girls, we still haven't figured out how the Pyramids were built, much less why. If modern technology can't answer that one, it puts, at the least, what man calls "construction" in a perspective that cannot help but make the honest scientific mind...pause.

Once past the bridge, the road goes straight toward a turn. Just before the turn, a small farmhouse on a hill can be observed out the left window. Right ahead is a field where the farmer grows hay, and the road bends around a field. It is, perhaps, half a mile long and a quarter mile wide; and every time I've seen the field it has been as groomed and well kept as those beautiful women in international airports who melt your heart and fry your brain, and, when you're graced, sustain your spirit during those long, alone trips around the planet...trips which find you trapped in strange cities between flights to other, even stranger, places where you know you will not tarry long, just as you know it is part of the weaving of eternal tapestry that you must visit there from time to time. And that's why there is a turn at the end of the straight section.

If you had been in the Stagecoach for 10 hours, playing pool and drinking beer without eating sandwiches or getting laid; and if you had ingested 10 reds and, possibly, snorted holes in your septum with the magic anesthetic white dust; and maybe if there were some other lethal frustration in your life...like 10 years (or 10 minutes) living with a mate no longer wanted; or a job so boring that it turns the honey of the spirit to carbolic acid, or, at the very, very minimum, a good old-fashioned scrotum-to-brain burn by the all-time honest-to-God, truer-'n-shit wonderful unbelievable down to the center of the earth higher than the cosmos perfect love of your life...then, with such a frustration or physical or psychic handicap bubbling away in your brain and being, clouding judgment with visions of devils and demons and never-ending red lights in the rear view mirror, you might miss the turn and go blazing across the good farmer's field.

If you did that, and if your vehicle and everything in it survived, which is not impossible, and you kept going with a slight lean to the left and did not hit any hay bales or coyotes or holes, you would cross the field and run through some willows on the other side from which you would emerge to crash through a hand water pump and continue up a driveway to a small cabin nestled right up against a small forest of aspens.

I once spent the better part of a summer in that cabin.

To reach the cabin by staying on the road, it is necessary to negotiate the right turn, continue up the straightaway, hang on through the left turn, continue a 100 yards, and turn back left onto a dirt road just off the highway. The hoop gate on a barbed wire fence must be opened before driving through and closed after; and there are three such gates before the cabin is reached, each to be opened and closed, both coming and going The road goes along the edge of the shimmering, murmuring aspens, mostly within the shade of the fine summer leaves; and the road must be driven with as much care as is cared for the vehicle driven. Very often hawks, ground squirrels and coyotes are seen along this road.

The one-story cabin is a beauty for people who do not mind a 100-foot walk to the pump for water, or, in the other direction, to the two-hole shitter; or cooking over a wonderful old cast iron woodburning stove; and cutting wood for that stove; and doing without electricity. It was built of wood by some less than mediocre craftsmen and has a large rock fireplace in the middle of its one room. That summer there was one wooden table and four matching chairs and a dresser and two double beds, which we never used, preferring to sleep outside under clear Wyoming skies or in the bus with all the doors open, listening to the nightly coyote serenade.

I was cruising for a time with a peroxided lady and a child who were both close and distant. On clear days I climbed the variable rock of the Tetons. Stormy days were spent writing at the cabin or in the peaceful Jackson library where there were not only free coffee and comfortable chairs and a big table to write upon, but the quiet of all the sad, lost souls seeking freedom from both sides of every page of every book of every shelf on every aisle of all the libraries man has ever built and burnt and sanctified and censored throughout a history he but dimly remembers... for if he remembered and understood he would not be condemned to the prison of repetition, and the seeking of a freedom that stands, like naked, beautiful, beckoning innocence across the ocean of love, the river of peace, the stream of understanding and the trickle of attempt.

A few days were spent in the front yard with heads full of acid, watching our neighbor tend his fields. One particular day sticks in memory. We were sitting on the ground with our friend the German woman, of fine intelligence and heart. She talked too much and pushed too hard and was never sure about living in unending sorrow over some unacceptable personal tragedy that was talked around but never about, and thus could not be plowed under to fertilize happiness; and the tears she shed inside flooded the world, drowning all not contained within the ark of her mind.

The two interweaving cross currents of our energies revolved around reading Ecclesiastes aloud to each other and watching the good farmer work his fields the entire day in the sun. The two were, of course, the whole; and holding them together in our minds was, at the same time, the most serious endeavor; the most hilarious pastime; the most arduous undertaking; the easiest frivolity; grinding work; and the most fun any of us had ever had. The high awareness that it is "all emptiness and chasing the wind" laid us out in hysterical laughter, clapping each other on the thighs and backs and repeating over and over, "all emptiness and chasing the wind." And out of that day and line we were finally able to name a route we had climbed on Mt. Mitchell in the Wind River Mountains a few weeks before. It was a hard, beautiful route on perfect rock that we started right after breakfast and which saw us return to camp at midnight. It is one of my favorite climbs. We named it Ecclesiastes, in honor of the joy of the empty chase.

The farmer worked his field in a circular manner, starting from the perimeter and advancing inward, in just the opposite direction of harvesting crops of karma. He was cutting hay that day, sitting beneath the sunshade atop his roaring machine, and a circuit of the field took about 15 minutes. He was a big man wearing a blue Levi shirt and straw hat. I never spoke with him, but for perhaps 20 seconds of each tour of the field we could hear him, above the roar of the machine, singing at the top of his lungs. There was, in the strength of persistence of his voice, a daylight counterpoint to the nighttime coyote song.

His deep baritone was filled with joy and revelry which came, we could only assume, from his work. He sang Italian opera; and, though we only picked up on his serenade for a few seconds of each cycle, it was consistent and it is fair to assume he sang the whole day long. And we were there from tea-and-capsule breakfast until sundown.

Or maybe the man was putting on a show for us...the neighbors who never, ever communicated or worked or did anything that he could see... and it is possible that he only sang during the part of his cycle which came within our realm. But that is a cynicism I recognize and cannot accept. I never felt he cared a politician's word of honor whether we watched him or not, but I was aware he knew we were watching; and in a sense that cannot be written about because I wasn't on his side of the page, he was as much a spectator as we...watching a boy and a longhair beard and a blonde and a shapely brunette sitting in front of the cabin across the way..apparently doing absolutely nothing the entire day long. He worked his fields with a thoroughness we could not envy because envy gets you hard every time; but we did not refrain from admiring and wondering about it.

While I will never know what was going on in the farmer's mind, I still would not like to live in a world without wonder; and there was no emptiness in his barn. If there is a wind to chase, the farmer made an inward circular pattern out of his pursuit.

If you witness in some province the oppression of the poor and the denial of right and justice, do not be surprised at what goes on, for every official has a higher one set over him, and the highest keeps watch over them all. The best thing for a country is a king whose own lands are well tilled.

We read those thoughtful words while watching a careful,

conscientious farmer at work upon his land; and our particular vision allowed us to see that there are many kinds of fields to till, and we were learning how much work, and fun, it is. The sun will rise and set again and the earth will abide; but whether or not human life on earth sur-vives, there's no excuse for making the living of it cruel, harsh or unreasonable.

Probably we made a mistake not to invite our industrious neighbor to join us.

But the only thing unforgivable about mistakes lies in the ones that are continued and in the song repetition blares forth about the inability or refusal of its singer to learn, for once we truly learn we move on and that's called evolution; and then the circle is not endless but only functional. Sounds in the form of words flowed from the blonde, the brunette, the bearded and the boy as easily as water in a mountain stream, though there were droughts that must have their place in nature but certainly put you through your paces and don't help at all in dealing with the lurking paranoia that must be fought at every step; and, as the killer of trust, is the most vicious of enemies, more dangerous than a shark or polar bear or cobra that can kill only your body since they carry no malice. The dry spells usually happened while the farmer was at the apogee of his orbit of contact with us, for the sound of his singing voice brought us laughter from his pleasure, faith in the feeling that someone in the neighborhood had their shit together; and then there would come the sound of our own voices talking about the farmer and ourselves and what we all might possibly be doing, should be doing, could be doing and damn well will be doing, and, actually were doing. It was fun to hear him singing.

Who is wise enough for all this? Who knows the meaning of anything? Wisdom lights up a man's face, but grim looks make a man hated. Do as the King commands you, and if you have to swear by God, do not be precipitate.

I remember the sadness, humor, terror and beauty of assurance striking home; assurance that the farmer would keep on working his fields in the pattern he had chosen beneath the sun that would continue to rise and set upon the..if you can believe Ecclesiastes... eternal earth; assurance that we would accept our destinies and take what we would from them according to how hard we enforced our own will and fought for what we wanted; assurance that the particular pattern by which each of us expressed the love within was not so important as the intensity of that love; assurance that there is not understanding without mystery; and assurance that no matter how much intelligence we use and how hard we try, there is an element outside ourselves that the irreligious call "luck" that will cover mistakes or destroy creations according to laws we don't comprehend except that finished work on one particular pattern moves us into a different standard that is only another segment of a much larger pattern seen only through the eyes of the Buddha nature in its entirety, unless we drop a stitch along the way and have to do the whole thing over again, which brings on the assurance that all is contained within the mind and that both everything and nothing is ours. It's a strange, wonderful. ah, balanced, universe, for even if it is all emptiness, there is fullness in the chase; and if that's all we got we might as well make fun out of it instead of some of the other things we might make.

I know that there is nothing good for man except to be happy and live the best life he can while he is alive. Moreover, that a man should eat and drink and enjoy himself, in return for all his labours, is a gift of God I know that whatever God does lasts forever, to add to it or subtract from it is impossible. And he had done it all in such a way that man must feel awe in his presence. Whatever is has been already, and whatever is to come has been already, and God summons each event back in its turn. Moreover I saw here under the sun that, where justice ought to be, there was wickedness, and where righteousness ought to be, there was wickedness. I said to myself, "God will judge the just man and wicked equally; every activity and every purpose has its proper time." I said to myself, "In dealing with men it is God's purpose to test them and to see what they truly are. For man is a creature of chance and the beasts are creatures of chance, and one mischance awaits them all: death comes to both alike. They all draw the same breath.

Men have no advantage over beasts; for everything is emptiness. All go to the same place: all came from the dust, and to the dust all return. Who knows whether the spirit of man goes upward or whether the spirit of the beast goes downward to the earth?" So I saw that there is nothing better than that a man should enjoy his work, since that is his lot. For who can bring him through to see what will happen next?

Accordingly, before bedding down that night under summer sky, we made ourselves a feast worthy of kings and queens and princes and laborers; and we washed it down with a couple of bottles of good wine, though not so much as we had and would again consume in the evenings of less hard-working days when unstoned heads drifted into more illusory perspectives of reality that the slight to gross wine OD makes real, or, at least, bearable.

That night and every other we ever slept at the cabin the coyotes serenaded us with their wondrous song from the center of the universe. I love coyote's song. I miss it when my life takes me away from coyote life, when coyote sings me to sleep on the bed of Mother Earth. Coyote, as every Indian and all spiritual gypsies of the cosmos know, is hunter, trickster, teacher, fool, creator, protector and wife stealer; or, as poet Barry Gifford (Coyote Tantras) writes, "Coyote drifts in and out, a searcher, a wastrel, supersen-sitive vagabond of the universe; never settled; always moving; dropping in here and there along the way. Coyote is no idealist; but he never gives up. What is most important is that he is alive; and whatever shred of nobility he wears rests in his awareness of that life. Never aimless, always grinning; forever looking, always lost; ever lonely, never making excuses; Coyote speaks for none but himself." Coyote sings for himself in the night, but he sings for us too; and in the bus or on the ground in the warm down bags that would not be zipped together too much longer past that long ago Wyoming sum-mer, we listened—carefully-to his songs of cold, lonely space travel and the distances between galaxies and the warmth and humor and wisdom of the chase, the hunt, the song itself and of the teachings you can pick up from coyote or the songs of the humpbacked whale or the flight and swoop of the hawk or the shy grace of the deer or the brute wild strength of the moose that tell you way down there in the central nerves of the solar plexus to be very, very careful of men who only understand nature through such manmade abstractions as politics, religion, war and power, and have not spent enough time in relationship to the true, eternal nature that, in functional fact, sustains and gives life to them and their abstractions and to the coyotes and trees and bears and birds and bees and elk and wolves and marmots and flowers and fish and rivers and oceans and all the other interacting forms of life on planet earth that men like that are so unconscious of.

One early morning I woke from the restless sleep that is the lot of the wanderer who has been too long in the same place, but isn't moving on just yet. We were sleeping in the bus with the back open, and the sun had just hit the farmer's field. It was early morning chilly, but a hot day was coming. Something nagged at my sleep-filled con-sciousness. And then it came again—a solitary, soulful, painful and sick coyote call from very close by. I came instantly awake, for something was deeply and terribly wrong with that call. It was not a howl of the proud loneliness and joy and interstellar communication found in the normal coyote song. It was a yell of such pathos and pain and nearness that I became both afraid and angry in the same rush of clear feeling; afraid for the animal itself and afraid, since he undoubtedly was one of the coyotes who had serenaded us in the night for several weeks and who we had seen on many occasions, for a friend. And also afraid of what a pain-crazed critter might do; and angry because I could only think of two things that could put a coyote in that sort of pain—poison and traps-both from the murderous hand of man, and, as a man, angry at that cruel, uncaring potential within myself. Motherfucker, I said to myself. Motherfuckers. Sonsabitches. Bastards Killers.

What's wrong with that poor fucker? The woman and the boy, masters of more sedentary souls than mine, were deeply asleep. I crawled out of the bag, quickly dressed, picked up the axe we used for splitting wood, and cautiously went down to the willows at the edge of the farmer's field. I hunkered down and crept through the willows until I could see the field, full, by that stage of the growing cycle, of hundreds of bales of hay waiting to be picked up. There I saw the damndest thing.

Dragging himself up the field from the south was the most pitiful, wretched coyote ever seen on planet earth. He was pulling himself along mostly with the power of his forepaws. His ass-end sort of clawed and dragged itself along behind; and the two halves of his body seemed to be disjointed, as if his back were broken or some carbolic poison and pain were wrenching the poor creature's innards in indescribable agony. He passed maybe 50 feet in front of me, too intent on his own destiny to notice me, which, of course, is the fool aspect of coyote. Every so often he would crawl upon a bale of hay, raise his muzzle to the sky, and give out that terrible, caricatured howl that had awakened me. I watched, fascinated by the scenario and by some inner resource operating in that sad beast who, I could not forget, was coyote, pre-historic animal of myth and fable and story, and, to the Indian who knows this land better than the white late-comers, creation Coyote, the trickster Coyote, Panama Red of the most ancient hipster. Just as this coyote was finishing his call of affliction from atop a bale directly in front of me, the farmer's dogs, two big hounds of indiscriminate heritage, went berserk with awareness of their cousin's plight. I could see them running in circles, jumping in the air and raising dust in the farmer's front yard. Their barks were ecstatic and out of control, but it was evident they weren't leaving their master's front yard.

Coyote flopped off the bale and continued his wearisome journey north through the field. I had decided by then it must be poison because I could see he hadn't been hurt in a trap, and his back looked intact. My curiosity wouldn't allow me to quit my seat at this show. But I was pissed. There are certain sorts of shitheads (I use that word literally) on earth who set poison out for coyote, not caring about coyote, rabbit, fox, mouse, hawk, ground squirrel, groundhog, bear, eagle, porcupine, skunk and even domestic dog who, thereby, leave this life in agony and bewilderment, wondering what evil unnatural fate has come over them. Cocksuckers. May they eat some of their own poison and see how it feels, if they got any feeling left. No! No! No! Richard, that's not the way either. You can't answer for another man's actions, intentions or karma. You got your own to take care of.

But you can, by rights and necessity and duty and fun, say what you think and express what you feel; and setting poison out for coyote and his friends is not the way and will buy the man who does it some unholy dues; but that's not the point somehow, surely not to the animal with a gut full of crippling pain and a spirit full of a cruel gift from brother man. I felt terrible about that coyote; and not hate but disgust for the pitiful excuse for a human being who had done it to him. Teacher/trickster coyote dying so ignominiously was patently unacceptable; for how could he teach or trick or find nobility in his own awareness of life with a belly full of pain?

A few yards up the field he dragged himself again atop a bale and repeated his cry of agony, muzzle to the sky. The hounds were in a frenzy. By then the farmer was out in his yard, loading gas and water and tools in his pickup, which prior observation had taught me he would next drive down to the field to begin his day's work, that day involving the loader sitting idly at the southern end of the field. Sometimes the dogs accompanied him, and my feelings were mixed about the possibilities. My attention was divided between watching coyote finish his sad song and nearly fall off the bale before continuing to drag himself up the field, and watching the farmer call his dogs into the back of his truck and drive down to the field.

Shit, the dogs are going to kill the coyote, I said to myself. I didn't like that. I also didn't like the coyote's suffering. I was stuck upon my own dislikes until, as the pickup approached the loader, I realized what I really disliked was that these dogs would never mess with a healthy coyote. All they were doing was letting out the bully that always grows from the indignity of being a domestic animal. Fucking cowards! Buzzards!

Scum! Vocabulary, as usual, falls short of feeling, but no way was I going to relinquish my spectator's seat at whatever this play was going to be; besides, I was both spectator and participant, like every man. The farmer stopped next to the loader, and I was struck by his unconcern about the two frenetic, howling hounds. The dogs leapt from the truck in a full sprint north. The farmer never even turned to watch.

I, on the contrary, swung my vision to what I was sure was going to be an ugly battle to the coyote's death; and the next few seconds seemed a couple of hours, for everything slowed down as the flow of life tends to do when attention is complete.

There is an evil that I have observed here under the sun, an error for which a ruler is responsible: the fool given high office, but the great and rich in humble posts. I have seen slaves on horseback and men of high rank going on foot like slaves. The man who digs a pit may fall into it, and he who pulls down a wall may be bitten by a snake. The man who quarries stones may strain himself, and the wood cutter runs a risk of injury. When the axe is blunt and has not first been sharpened, then one must use more force; the wise man has a better chance of success. If a snake bites before it is charmed, the snake charmer loses his fee.

As I turned my attention north, I was aware of the Grand Teton (the great tit of the great Mother Earth) overlooking all. I saw the coyote increase the rate of its struggles and thrash about between the bales as if seeking shelter among them. The hounds closed the distance as fast as they could run, howling the whole time, the thrill of the kill driving them dog crazy. Suddenly, not 50 feet from the coyote, I saw a second coyote crouched down behind a bale; and even from my perspective I could see the grin upon his face and the life within his eyes. He waited until the hounds were about 70 to 80 feet from his partner before he broke cover. At that instant the crippled coyote, like Lazarus springing from the grave, blossomed into full-stature coyote and turned on the hounds. One of the grand sights of my life was seeing a couple of full-grown mongrel hounds exchanging ass-holes for noses while involved in a full stride known only to the heat of the hunt, and get that stride headed in the opposite direction. One of them tried to back pedal, causing his rear quarters to come underneath, and he wound up skidding on his back; but he came up in a scrambling sprint with the greatest actor I have ever seen right on his ass end with coyote's own magnificent tail laid flat out behind, floating like a flag of coyote wildness in the wind of the newly directed chase. The other hound just put on the brakes. He tumbled end over end in a couple of good head-first rolls before he, too, could get back up with his powerful legs moving in the other direction, the hidden coyote of patience right on his ass. Those coyotes chased the two hounds around that field at full speed and the farmer went about his work without paying the slightest attention to the whole spectacle, as if he had seen it 1,000 times before; and I laughed aloud with the show and at my new knowledge and at the pattern of education; and I watched the coyotes chase the dogs without catching them around the field and around the field and around the field and around and around and around and around.

―*Originally appeared in* Mountain Gazette 52, *1976.*

27.
Climbing the Walls in Berkeley
Written by Karen Recknagel (Chamberlain)

The first thing was the weather. The California drought. Even a sun-worshipper realizes that each place has its own normal climate and seasonal patterns, and for me the relativity of n-dimensional coordinates, windowpane days of heavy, healthy, nonstop soaking winter rains imparted a vaguely let-down feeling. Something like buying a ticket to your first XXX-rated movie and walking into the theatre during some redeeming social continuity scene, where the only heavy breathing turns out to be your own anticipation.

On the other hand, it seems like spring's been hanging around all winter, groping about in the vacuum ordinarily filled by all that rain. Patient, puzzled sunshine. One bud, one leaf at a time. January fragrant with Japanese cherry, February sprouting plum and quince, March stiffening into magnolia, April fooling with fall's marigolds. Not that it's all so tiresome, or gives no pleasure, but simply that for a New Englander from the Rockies it requires a certain reordering of the awareness so as not to seem like some sort of Telegraph Avenue handout... What'd I go through to deserve this?) More to the point, where's the big wave? The equinox? The ritual celebration? What if somebody gave a party and it lasted all year?

In the course of this reordering, while reading physics and

molecular genetics and listening to a friend threaten me with Infinitesimals—"the ghosts of departed quantities"—I found myself thinking about the whole concept of a continuum. Beginning with Einstein's space/time and wave/particle theories and wandering off to other possible examples like Nature/History, Myth/Cliché, Trail/Freeway, City/Wilderness, to name a few arbitrary mid- or endpoints. Or spring in California...

Consider, for instance, "Myth." If the serpent that beguiled Eve is the dragon keeping Hercules from his golden apples; if Chronos is Saturn (Odin's brother?) who devours his own children; if Deucalion doubles as Noah, et cetera, then through the gathering goop we begin perhaps to see that Thoreau's "Swamp" is the paradisiacal "'Garde'" is the primeval "Woods" (for the trees...). Or for the lack of them, for that matter, Jocasta returns as Mrs. Robinson. The crystal vision of Man in the Mirror fragments into acres of TV screen reflecting millions of Captain Marvel images per minute. The medium becomes more than the message, and Salvation is safely locked up in the Gawdawful Given Moment...

Oh well. Apocalyptic tedium—yes. But I remember trying to make all the green lights on University Avenue one night and wishing, O for a little spray vial of Rocky Mountain Cloud #9, Mr. Denver's Mace, instant immunity against the notion that, jellyfishlike, we might finally be evolving into a true social organism, sections of which cannot help but oscillate at the same frequency. Cloned consciousness, to match our Jungian "collective unconscious," with a little Soma greasing the rails to ensure smooth rapid transit.

Granted the jet lag in human perspective, what remained every-day-relevant was not the relativity of n-dimensional coordinates, nor the physico-chemical implications of "myth" as a form of molecular memory, nor all those myriad particles bumbling around in one bottle with Maxwell's demon at the door. It's still scaled more to getting on and off the freeway. Or, as another friend put it, cocking one eye at a Bombay gin and the other at your deliberations on rest-mass and the speed of light: "Yeah, but you gotta watch out for the wind factor..."

And so it seemed that the first lesson in urban "survival" was to go one step further in this scaling process, consciously adopting the viewpoint evolved by generations of city-dwellers, Orientals, sailors and others who live with a minimum of stress in crowded or limited environments: a sort of miniaturizing and internalizing process whereby one allows a whole universe to occur in one's backyard. Or flower-box, even. The Emily Dickinson terrarium effect, so to speak, a kind of regressive corollary to childhood when everything was bigger than life...

Walking across campus to classes soon led to discoveries of secret little places, which, each for its own reason, held a certain charm; places that in certain moods, I could even imbue with qualities of mystery, in the way that children excite themselves with fear of the dark. The ancient enormous ginkgo tree stretching out its great branches near the Life Science Building became a favorite place to rest and read. Or again, often I would go out of my way a bit to follow the asphalt path through a small grove of flowering plum and towering young cedars, over Strawberry Creek on a stone-walled footbridge with little stone steps curving the path up the opposite bank. Breezes met here to exchange the fragrance of eucalyptus and resonated humus, the deep shadow dappled with medallions of blossom and sunlight, and almost always people passing who would say hello.

One tree, one blossom at a time ... Of course, the Women's Lib Auxiliary of Fear, Inc., caught wind of such wild places and decided to gift potential rapists with a wider perspective of the world by hacking back all the undergrowth and shrubbery. And I further miniaturized and internalized my way over to another area of the campus, figuring there'd be no disappointment from lack of supply if I learned to indulge myself in people-watching. Do we sometimes fantasize awareness itself...?

Soft, warm sunshine. Unobtrusive, insistent. Saying, look, I made it all this way, through decaying ozone, smog, noise and all that other traffic out there, in less than eight seconds, and somebody's damn well going to feel good about it... Lying on a grassy knoll outside Evans Hall, I look up from a book to watch two young bodies clinging to a 20-foot stone wall terracing a nearby building. One guy, dark-haired and strongly built, has started to climb first, body flattened, arched against its own shadow on the warm ochre sandstones. Up and sideways. He reaches the top, then leans back over the edge, apparently to coach his spidery-but-slower young friend: Outstretched fingers tighten carefully; and then, visibly, tension relaxes into balanced poise and the ascent is completed

On the terrace, a few words and demonstrative gestures are exchanged, whereupon the second climber mounts a skateboard and weaves off down the sidewalk. His dark friend nods as he passes me on the grass and is lost a moment later among the throng waiting at the Humphrey Go-Bart bus stop. Obviously, I muse, here is a man totally unconcerned with how the hell (in the name of Timothy Leary) one crystallizes oneself out of this supersaturated city cyclotron. Probably spends his weekends at Yosemite and his summers in Nepal, or Peru.

Often during this unsprung winter, I get a chance to watch while one of a couple of young climbers hang like flies underneath or between the balconies of Evans Hall, or scale that sandstone wall, or use ropes, even, to tie down the side of an apartment building. Part of me wants to say, "Hey, go pick on something Real," while the voice in the other ear whispers, "O go climb a tree-you just wish you had something you could do with a stiff vertical whenever you found one, *Parce qu'il existe...*"

Gradually one realizes that one has left nothing behind, that perhaps survival was not really the question, that perhaps, after all, There Is No Question. Still and only the immense spectrum of awareness of possibilities from which to choose (like courses from the college catalogue), leading again to the easy feeling of dining at the buffet table of the "elite." As if by that label, by such verbal backpatting, we could escape the knowledge that we still only get once to do it all (better, best, highest, fastest, with or without snakes, et cetera); that it's difficult to do nothing next, to un-do, to not-become; that freedom's just another word...

Often there is an urge to watch the sunset from the roof of my apartment building, looking toward the Bay, a watery island surrounded by city. Other people wander out on nearby rooftops, singly or in pairs, quiet. The bay haze swells thick with red, while to the south the skyline hills respire softly in stage-set grays beneath the smog, like long-anaesthetized patients. From mid-campus the campanile tower bells chime the hour, then continue with a stately melody, harmonizing with the evening's peach while at the same time creating a peculiarly poignant restlessness. (I suspect the bellringer, an excommunicated music student, I've been told, now resides in the belfry with several half-tame bats. The only evidence I have, however, is that for noontidings on St. Valentine's Day, listeners were treated to a medley that included a perfectly solemn rendition of "O Come, All Ye Faithful." I admit to a secret desire to meet him.)

Anyway, restlessness and tranquillity being not always so compatible, the tendency for cream to float makes a true virtue, not of patience so much as of the ability to concentrate on matters at hand. Not that studying is any sort of a drag; far from it. It just isn't very physical. And walks up Strawberry Canyon or down by the marina after a while take on a stop gap quality. There is the sensation of waiting. The right wave, the one that begs you to match yourself against your fantasies...

Sure enough, just as the symptoms of cabin fever rise to throat level, comes a call from Bear Valley: "Get on up here, it's a blizzard!" The Real Thing, one's own slice of the Whole Enchilada. We throw two pairs of skis and a couple of soon-to-be-neglected textbooks into the back of the jeep and head eastward under irritatingly clear starry skies.

The suspense mounts: Not until well above Angels Camp do we finally hit snow, either on the ground or falling, and in the meantime skepticism runs rampant. Lordy, maybe it's California-Dreamin' forever, and they've slid the Sierra south for a Hollywood spectacular, so the next thing we'll run into will be the on-ramp for Enchanted Interstate #201, with a Texaco totem and the Last Chance Jack-in-the-Box lighting a white-on green legend: Spokane—840 miles. Or worse yet, that somebody's figured a way to bypass the usual dam, pipeline and river diversion methods of water-stealing and has hijacked the weather directly. Using our snow to rinse the grime off the plastic palm trees...

But then suddenly snow, thicker and thicker, glistening and swirling in the head-lights, whitening the road, deeper and colder and closer, till we've passed the last plow-mark, with no tiretracks left to follow, navigating on the narrow assumption that beneath the least amount of snow lies the road. Then an interminable straight stretch where, as on the sea, time and distance collapse into one another, and the speedometer wavering around 25 mph becomes a mechanical credibility gap. Just as the conviction hits that we're not moving at all, suddenly looms up to the left a rearing wooden bear and a rustic sign—and we're there.

Two in the morning, half-smiles squinted at the sheets of cold flakes dancing in the mercury vapor lamplight as we clamber out of the jeep and poke around in a station wagon (totally camouflaged as an igloo) for snowshoes left by our friend. With these we have a chance of surfacing the distance to his house.

Winter! Better yet, *weather*! A host of city tensions softly hissed away under the tiny stinging tongues feathering our cheeks. If one snowfall is enough for winter, this is it. Lodgepole pines like sleepy sheeted Klansmen line the trail, and there is no wind, no intermittency or hesitation, just Sierra powder falling, heavily, steadily, silently, encompassing the darkness.

Fresh tracks tomorrow!—and I fall asleep dreaming a warm suit, a gossamer second skin to ski in...

"I made my song a coat
Covered with embroideries
Out of old mythologies
From heel to throat;
But the fools caught it,
Wore it in the world's eyes
As though they'd wrought it.
Song, let them take it
For there's more enterprise
In walking naked."
                    —*Yeats*

"I'd holler, but the town's too small."
                    —*Big Bill Broonzy*

"People say I'm hollerin'. Man, I feel like hollerin'."
—Charlie Mingus

"Why don't we do it in the road?"
—The Beatles

———————

—Originally appeared in Mountain Gazette 46, *1976.*

28.
The Wisdom of NEOWISE
Written by Doug Schnitzspahn

Insomnia is a bitch. I'm still up working at 3 a.m., lying on the couch, the low glow of the laptop straining my eyes, so I head out to find the comet. I've seen images of it plastered across social media by photographer friends, the long, bright tail of NEOWISE streaking like a medieval harbinger of divine intervention over night scenes of red-rock canyons and alpine lakes. The house is quiet except for the gurgling of the fish tank, and outside is even quieter. This is one benefit of sleeplessness. It's only late at night like this when you notice just how much noise surrounds us on every side, from neighbors' godforsaken leaf blowers to distant highways to the long boom of an airliner 30,000 feet above. Most days we can't hear the ringing of our own ears.

We have blinded ourselves as well. Lights everywhere at all hours means that we can't even see the night sky properly in most places. Just take a look at a light-pollution map of North America. The yellows and reds of skies that are now flooded with the fossil-fueled glow of human industry are taking over the continent like some ever-expanding blob bent on its own manifest destiny. Float the Grand

Canyon and as you finish your trip you can see the lights of Vegas far off in the night sky, slowly erasing the time when primeval stars took precedence down in the depths of the canyon. Our growing obsession with banishing the dark messes up migrating birds and throws other animals' internal clocks out of whack; it causes microorganisms to bloom in water.

On my own street there are rows of lamps, making us safer, supposedly, but I'm personally pleased most when they burn out. And at 3 a.m., the time when NEOWISE—technically comet C/2020 F3, but the nickname came from its first observers, who used the Wide-field Infrared Survey Explorer (WISE) space telescope searching for Near-Earth Objects (NEO)—should be here on the northeastern horizon, the dull glow of the closest street lamp and all the lights of Boulder and Denver give the sky a purplish cast. There are also scattered clouds, though I can make out faint but never-changing Polaris, following the pointer stars of the Big Dipper, and red Arcturus, tracing the curve of its handle. I can even make out the slight line of Draco, the dragon weaving its serpentine body between the two dippers. But most of the sky is hidden. And clouds are sitting right where the comet should be.

This comet seems apt in this age of Covid-19 and the implosion of America. After all, in 1066 Halley's comet foretold the end of Anglo-Saxon England with the coming of the Norman invaders led by William the Conqueror (who received his title only because the superior King Harold Godwinson was unlucky enough to catch an arrow in the eye and the tide of battle turned). Or the comet of 959, appearing at the death of King Edgar the Peaceful (ah, the serene scene of the 950s) and ushering in a famine. Of course, Mark Twain would arrive in 1835 with the reappearance of Halley's comet and leave this planet with it when it returned in 1910. And both astronomers and New Age conspiracy theorists have noted the coming of the first observed interstellar comet, C/2019 Q4, in late 2019, just as Covid-19 began its global scourge.

Of course, we can impart meaning to any phenomena, creating omens out of chance occurrences. We find connections when we need them. The constellations appear so obvious once you learn them—

some, like Cassiopeia and Orion, seem undeniable—but are they not just patterns we have defined in our need for stories? Science will tell you this is simply the human brain, a network of complex ganglia communicating through chemical and electric signals, arranging patterns as it does in order to function and orient itself within observational and sensory phenomena. But even armed with that knowledge, we want this comet to mean something—be it the end of times or the dawn of a new age. Nothing is more depressing than arbitrariness.

Like everyone on this planet at this time, my life is full of uncertainty. And like most 50-somethings, I feel as if I am both about to fulfill my life's purpose and that I have missed the boat. I find it hard to concentrate on a computer all day long. Once a prolific creative writer, I have become a slave of commerce, writing to pay the bills, to make sure my family has healthcare. So I fry my brain at night. When I was younger, I worked for the Forest Service, building trails and fighting fires, living out of a sleeping bag strewn out on bare ground and staring at the stars, learning the constellations every night. I know I had anxieties then, but they seem insignificant in my current spot, mired in middle age in the midst of a pandemic as everything from the health of ecosystems to the success of our democracy falls apart. Meh, it's the same for all of us; this isn't Earth's first plague.

I moved out West—again, like so many—to escape the crush of the East Coast, to shake off my demons, to find a life based around this rough natural world, skiing, climbing peaks, fishing. The first time I saw a comet was after a long season of fighting wildfires in Montana and Idaho and ski bumming in Whitefish. One of my fellow workers had told me about the wonders of Grand Gulch down in Utah, so my girlfriend and I packed up the car and drove south, camping at Dead Horse Point. We looked up that night to see Comet Hale-Bopp in all its glory and wonder what it might mean, or, better yet, to simply enjoy the show above the desert with the sky filled by stars.

Hiking down Grand Gulch the next few days, the comet—which emitted not only its long streamer of light, but also an invisible sodium tail 50 million kilometers long—felt familiar each night. By day, we walked through ruins that have since been looted of their corncobs and potsherds, sunbathed naked on the red rocks, breathed. At night, I told her stories from the constellations—Leo, recognizable by the bright glow of blue star Regulus, is the skin of the Nemean lion killed by Herakles seeking penitence for his fits of deadly rage; Orion, the hunter beloved by Artemis, met by Odysseus when he was no more than a shade in the underworld, dogged forever by the scorpion that killed him in the form of the constellation Scorpio, which always appears across the horizon from him. Those days felt as if they existed outside of time.

Did Hale-Bopp harken to something for me? For the world? Sadly, the comet is probably most famous for the 21 men and 18 women of the Heaven's Gate cult who quietly killed themselves while holed up in a swank San Diego exurb in order to catch a ride on the spaceship they believed was hiding behind it and calling to them. I soon after moved away from my beloved dark skies in Montana to go to grad school in Seattle's city lights and incessant clouds. That girlfriend and I had an ugly breakup—but grad school got me writing professionally, and she and I were not meant for the long term. And the world? Atrocities continued in Rwanda and the Balkans, but here at home Bill Clinton's definition of sexual relations and the politics of the 1990s seem bucolic compared to our current climate of nonstop anxiety fueled by social media, virus-hoax protests, and a desire to tear each other apart. (King Harold winks his one eye from Elysium.) Astronomers observe a lot of near-Earth objects; couldn't we find any sign for these events if we looked?

Staring up at a sky full of stars, the kind you see from the bottom of the Grand Canyon or out in the Sahara, should fill us with nothing more than nihilism. We are certainly insignificant in the cosmic count; even our ability to count is dwarfed by the sheer number of other worlds up there. The center of own galaxy (which even astronomers simply refer to as the Milky Way, rather than assigning it a numerical classification as, say, the romantic Andromeda is M-31 to scientists) is still a mystery to us, a hulking black hole, the gravitational mass around which our own sun—one of some 100 billion—spins like a chunk of comet dust, with an average of 10 million stars packed into every 3.3 light years all cratering into itself. We can just barely see where it is—off past Sagittarius where the visible Milky Way pools on the horizon. No wonder the ancients saw gods up there and gave that arm of the galaxy that we can see lovely names like the folksy yet delicate Milky Way, or Ngân Hà, the Silver River, in Vietnamese, or Darb Al-Tabbāna, the Hay Merchants Way, in Arabic. These metaphors let our minds find something to grab onto up in those inconceivable reaches that even today—despite the fact that we have mastered the secrets of our own planet so well that we are engaged in wiping life out on it and can analyze the line spectra of comets and distant suns to be able to tell the exact elements inside them—are impossible for us to achieve, much less comprehend.

And the Milky Way itself is just a backwater in the galactic metropolis—never mind if you subscribe to the theory of multiverses, ad infinitum, ad nauseam. We don't even exactly agree on how or if our universe is expanding, what it's expanding into, the nature of dark matter, the significance of space within space. Worst of all, we are locked in time and causality. Even the heavens are limited. Look into the night sky and, as the poet Ranier Maria Rilke, now long gone, noted, there is a star that died long ago. This should make us sick. Should fill us with a sense of meaninglessness.

Ah, but the power of the human ego, even within this infinite incomprehensibility. We are still the center of our own universes, the mass within our dark matter. All cynicism aside, the size of the universe fills me not with nausea, but hope, when I stare up at it. When I know I can't count stars, when I know there may be a multiverse where Harold's Anglo-Saxon kingdom brushed off the Normans, where my failures have a second chance, where all probability melds into one ribbon, it makes me feel at peace.

Is there any simpler human pleasure than stargazing?

I am a reader of signs. At a young age, I became fascinated by tarot cards; my grandmother, who could get deer to eat out of her hand and would tell me she was a witch when she put her finger through a candle flame, gave me my first deck. Forget fortune telling—the cards tell archetypal stories, they speak to signposts within us and through those we can tell our inner narratives, and, as any good writer knows, from there the endgame, the future, simply plays out. My favorite card, of course, has always been the Star, which symbolizes hope. It's also the card of Aquarius, my sign. I have found the constellation of Aquarius, the Babylonian river; it's very faint and difficult to make out. It was clearer in Sumerian days and is slowly disappearing as stars' shapes will do over millennia. Even the constellations are impermanent. But, yes, I feel it every time I look to the stars, the pull of a beyond, an idea that we can be something more than our human foibles. That there is nothing to fear in infinity, only in our own ego. It's like trying to reach the edge of the universe: go far enough, some physicists say, and you end up back where you began.

I am a reader of stars. There are times out in the wild when I simply let them blur, but most of the time I have found great joy and, yes, hope in interpreting them. Sea kayaking in Baja when afternoon winds made travel difficult, we launched before sunset to Mars shining red like a beacon in Scorpio as it rose up out of the Sea of Cortez. In Montana's Madison Range, building trails, I spent nights orienting myself, starting with Polaris—always easy to find, thanks to that Big Dipper—and moving on across the sky from that frame of reference, understanding how the view of the stars changes with the spin of the Earth and our planet's orbit around the sun. In Lapland, in Arctic blackness, I could see Draco's scaly body perfectly. On the Colorado River, at night in pure dark, I gazed at star reflections on still water. The stars tell me the time of night and the time of year. They comfort me.

I look up. I hope for the clouds to move on, for the bright tail of this 3-mile-wide chunk of rock and ice finally catching fire in its orbital meet-up with the inevitable heat and gravity of the sun after centuries of frozen loneliness. I know just where to look. I know I am here at the right time, alone. Nothing. So I stand there in the middle of the street, my bare feet cold on the pavement. The wind moves the leaves of the oak I planted a decade ago in my yard; they speak in a soft rustle. The pre-dawn air is crisp and clean. I am overcome by the urge to just start walking and never come back, to lose my name, to give up on a lifetime of school and career, and become a barefoot homeless hermit, a ghost, to fade.

I first really saw the stars—uncountable lights, the river of the Milky Way, the full outlines of constellations—as a child in the '70s, when I would visit my grandparents in New Jersey's northwestern Appalachian hills. My grandfather was an engineering professor at Rutgers, my grandmother, who gave me the tarot cards, a sculptress. Both performed as stage magicians. He would put her in a miniature Thai temple and then drive swords through her as she wiggled bright handkerchiefs with her hands and toes before sliding the blades back out and opening up the illusion to show her unharmed. There was danger at their house, hunters who left paper bags full of deer limbs at the end of their driveway, copperheads under the front porch, a replica of King Tut's death mask over the door of their basement, where they sent me to retrieve ginger ale from the extra fridge, full darkness at night.

Some nights, my grandmother, who had her own ghosts, would turn to me at the dinner table, after a few Johnnie Walker Blacks, and announce, "If the spaceship comes, I'm going!" It always just made me feel uncomfortable, but now, faced with the sharp realities of adulthood, I get it. And yearn, too, to move on from all that seems failed in myself and our species, to find some place that's not the mess we keep creating down here. We continue to lose even the ability to stargaze to light pollution and our obsession with our screens, and we continue to lose our need to tell stories by them. What's left when we look only inside rather than light years away?

But, of course, standing in the street, I don't start walking. I stand there longer, waiting for wisdom from NEOWISE. I am an insomniac reader of signs, looking for something of significance. If the spaceship comes, fuck yeah, take me up in some beautiful tractor beam of light. Show me how your alien species has taken advantage of great intelligence and communication and compassion in a way ours seems unable to do.

But I know I can't go, even if it were better. I am a stargazer, but of Earth. I have children and a wife and a family and friends I love, and their ability to bear their time here (we can plot it both in the revolutions of Earth and to exact detail in a map of the cosmos) depends on me. That simple love is worth everything.

There is no comet tonight. There is still beauty and places where humans have not smeared themselves all over the workings of other species. This is the hope. This is the wisdom I have gleaned from chunks of frozen gas that we see only every 4,000 years, from stars that may no longer be alive, from multiverses of possibility and the crushing size of the universe. The stars provide this respite, this moment to see not just into the past of existence and the line spectra of barren worlds, but into the silliness of trusting our own ego. That helps. Somehow. There's still a lot to stay here for. There will be more comets in future days. I head inside.

—*Originally appeared in* Mountain Gazette 194, *2020.*

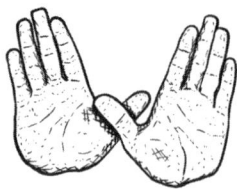

29.
Words in His Head: The Depth of Henrik Harlaut
Written by Henrik Harlaut; Intro by Gabby Dodd

If you follow freestyle skiing, you already know who he is: the dog-barking, big-smiling, early-2000s-style-influenced and hip-hop-loving Swede who is often considered the man who loves skiing more than anyone.

If those descriptors mean nothing to you, his name is Henrik Harlaut, aka E-Dollo, and you're sleeping on some seriously insane content from probably the most stoked dude on the planet. After you read this, Google "BE Inspired full movie." Dare I say you'll, uh, be inspired. Chances are you may have at least heard of him from the 2014 Sochi Olympics, when he and his pants fell midway through a slopestyle run while he also carried an uncooked, *Cool Runnings*–inspired egg in his pocket, and later gave tribute to rapper Ol' Dirty Bastard when he said, "Wu-Tang is for the children" on live television after his run.

Harlaut, 29, was born in Stockholm and has been on skis since the age of 2. After he moved to Åre, Sweden, when he was 9, Harlaut was introduced to the world of freestyle skiing and, after watching a Red

Bull big-air competition, never looked back.

By the time he was 13, Harlaut had received his first sponsorship, and he has consistently blown minds through his boundary-pushing tricks and innovative style ever since.

In 2013, at 21, he became the first person ever to land a nose-butter triple cork 1620 and received his first Winter X Games gold medal in the process. Today, Harlaut has won 12 X Games medals (the most ski podiums in the event's history), all the while putting out creative segments for major ski films and personal movie projects that feature everything from huge backcountry jump hits to stylish urban rail rides that most would not dare try.

—*Gabby Dodd*

"Wu-Tang is for the children" is a phrase I'm best known for [from the 2014 Sochi Winter Olympics]. It's just crazy, because it was not really planned out, or I hadn't thought about saying that phrase at all at that time. So everything that came after it is just crazy, and it's like, yeah, me and Phil Casabon had talked about it a few times, how much that has introduced…that basically opened our whole relationship with them, to meet any of the Wu-Tang member[s], like Raekwon right after Masta Killa, that actually made it out to our own event, be any invitational to have a live concert, to Redman and Method Man, to RZA.

Yeah, so many people have reached out, and the phrase, or that moment, somehow just connected it all. We had been for many, many years dreaming of the Wu-Tang Clan, kind of, and made video edits with their music playing to it. And I remember sending it a bunch of times to the members, and it never made it all the way to them. But it was crazy that just something that…oh, I don't know what the word is, but just came about right when I was standing there—that, that was the connection.

It's hard to know what the general public thinks of me. I think it's just pretty hard for people to fully grasp or understand me, because I am pretty unpredictable, and…definitely ha[ve] a style that's… Yeah, I think it's just hard for people to really understand who I am. I don't really know, even, the answer to who I am.

I don't know if it's myself—like, if I even created that persona. Creating a persona is hard to really take control of or understand fully. I know I don't really want to be 100 percent figured out. I don't want people to know what my move is going to be. Part of who I am is me creating it without trying to.

I got my first real, sponsored contract at 13. I think it was definitely very different back then. I went to the U.S. Freeskiing Open for my first time, which was also America for the first time, when I was 13. That same year, I got sponsored, and just the way it was at competitions was very, very different. I traveled here together with [professional skier] Jacob Wester, who was my friend, and my father. But there wasn't any structured team, or it wasn't really a team thing at all. The sport was very focused on the individual at the time.

And then, when I was old enough to travel on my own, without my parents or older brothers, then I just really chose the people who were my greatest friends, and who I could relate to the most outside and on the slopes, and that was who I traveled with to competitions, to training, to everything that was going on, literally. These days it's definitely way more country-divided. You travel with a Swedish crew, in my case, travel with a team from your home country, and it's structured and already set up to go a certain way....Before it was more you were creating your own path and going together with whoever was the closest friends.

For me, becoming a pro skier was definitely always the goal and dream. In general, always, when I grew up I knew I wanted to be professional in some sport. So I grew up playing a lot of different ones, like hockey, soccer, alpine racing. But then once I got introduced to freeskiing, and saw the culture and the lifestyle, and how it was more than just a regular sport, and really a way to express myself and do it my own way... it caught me so easy, and I was so hooked.

The fun part of it is the most important part. And that's what I try to teach as much as I can when I see young kids in the park—to not be too much in a hurry or stress too much with trying to progress to the newest, hottest trick necessarily. To just more go out and learn every basic trick and try and, as much as you can, to really not skip any steps. Many people just kind of follow trends and what is hot at the moment. But then, as soon as that trend goes away, then they just become a question mark, or really confused, not knowing really where to push it next, until they see somebody else. But if you learn all the basics and all the easy tricks, then you have all that to play with and to create your own progression instead.

I see little kids and they're like, "I learned a cork 7; I really want to do dub 10." And then I always tell them to maybe try and master that cork 7 for a week, try it with all the different types of grabs you could think of, grabbing with both left and right hands, and then try to tweak the grabs, go a little bit further back, get more inverted. And then obviously if you do bio or the rodeo, and then after that, add another 180, and just not be in a hurry, because everything will come and fall into place eventually as long as you're not stressed and just follow your own progression.

I definitely don't really feel the feeling of being burnt out, which I'm very, very happy of, because I love skiing so, so much that it's not really on the radar to get burnt out on. Basically, I don't really have even an example, but somebody that really loves food or candy or have something in life that they really, really love, that no matter what they do or eat or how much, it is always going to be a part of you. And that's how skiing is with me. There's no way I can be burnt out on it. And skiing is so big and so wide that there's so many new things to learn every time I go out, not only with my ski abilities—everything from snow conditions to mountains to different terrain. And then obviously on top of that, it's learning to master that terrain.

I am 29. It's so crazy. I really don't feel like I have aged that much, either, because I'm so in it all the time, I can never really switch off. As soon as I'm off the mountain, all my motivation and dedication is to prepare for the next time I'm skiing. I don't really have time to really think about getting older and all that. As for my body, I feel as good as

I did 10 years ago. Obviously I am aware that I am getting older, so I definitely treat my body way better than I did when I was younger.

I hope I still have a big bag of tricks when I'm in my 80s. I hope I can ski for a long time. And hopefully by the time I'm 60, [or in my] 70s, they have figured out a way to get brand-new knees and back and everything like that. I hope that the technology of healing people would be even better. I plan to ski as long as I really can. I'm probably going to be excited to try and push it some way. Just looking at even my parents—they're now 65, and they are skiing as well as they ever have in their lives.

I might not be doing triple corks or crazy butters, but I hope I can use my ski control and [that] my experience at 65 or 70, 80, will hopefully be super on point, if we're fortunate enough even to have ski resorts, snow, and the freedom of doing that. That's what I pray and hope for.

Progress in skiing is dependent on your own personality. I think anybody can just enjoy skiing and not have to progress and just stay comfortable with where they [are] at. But then obviously other people, like myself, who is pretty competitive and love to see where my limits and boundaries are, they can push it. It's cool to see because I have friends even that I grew up with, too, that are pretty satisfied, I feel like, with their level...you just can keep it at that level at all times and enjoy it so much. I have other friends that as soon as they strap in, they want to figure out some new way to ski.

If I could shoot a ski movie with six skiers in their primes, I'd choose Mickael Deschenaux and Candide Thovex. Candide would get the opener. Closer is probably Tanner Hall. I would love to be in the film, but I don't know if I'm in there if I only get six people, but for sure Phil is in there too. But then it's Corey Vanular during his Long Story Short era. I think I would put Travis Heed from Wicked in there too.

But there's so many more I'd add. Liam Downey, Tanner Rainville, Clayton Vila... directed by Henrik Harlaut. Yes, sir.

I love the way my life is right now because I love skiing so, so much. And right now, on the business side, my brother is killing it and taking care of Harlaut Apparel. He's basically just there making me look the way I want, that I dream of looking out on the slopes.

I know it will come at some point in life where I'm probably going to not go as wild on the skis, and for sure taking over the business interests me. I love designing and all this, so I definitely could see myself getting more involved with the company after as far as that goes, but I'm super happy where we are right now.

This could be the first winter in a very long time where I don't travel to the United States. I definitely think about it. I've been preparing myself for it. In a way, skiing on my own, it could be a really nice thing. It's kind of crazy to say it, but I think for my personal craft... it could be a good thing with a little bit less traveling.

I filmed and produced three two-year film projects in a row, and I have always been going back and forth competing and filming, and it's just hard to find time to really progress your skiing. I would like to have a season where I'm really just focusing on my own skiing and ability and have the time in allowing myself to work on what I'm not as good at to try and master that as well.

If it snows in the city, I'm going to film urban rails, and same with backcountry skiing... if it snows in the mountains where I'm at, I'm going to try [to] ski backcountry just because I love it. I don't want to have any pressure on myself for creating something that's so powerful and meaningful, like my previous movie projects. So I just want to focus more on my skiing. I want to lap super fast in the park and get really comfortable on my skis.

Ski movies are the most powerful art in our sport. For skiers, it's like what an album is to a musical artist. I'm still in that mode where I love albums. I buy the album and I play the full album back to back while driving, and I'm just really a fan of the full piece of art instead of just one-hitters...

And it's the same with ski movies and edits. I prefer when people just take a little bit more time to put a little bit more thought and feeling into what they are producing. For sure I think [it] is cool and nice with Instagram to see clips—you can put it out quick and have everybody notice it—but a good Instagram video usually just lasts for a few days, or, if it's really good, maybe a week, but a movie or a classic, impactful edit can last for decades.

Off the hill, I'm pretty odd, I think. I'm in my apartment in Andorra where I live; there's all these tools that are here so I can ski better. Everything from the bike next to the TV to having all these posters of skiers all over to some training equipment to the bathtub with the jets... I feel like I have so many tools that I use regularly to feel better. I'm so conscious of what I'm eating and how I'm training. I know a lot of people that fully switch off the skiing mode when they go into summer, or just when they're off the hill. I never feel the need of switch it off, because I just love it so much that I just want to spend all my energy and time into doing it better.

I definitely do enjoy a lot when I get back on my skis after a summer of training and preparing for skiing, because definitely when I'm in a skate park, I have all these ideas and dreams of wishing I could control the board like I do in my thoughts. But then when I get out in the mountains and I ski... I can basically do most of my thoughts. So it's a pretty unreal and so-cool experience—that is what really...I can do best in my life is skiing. So when I'm out there, it's what I've mastered the best. And I always, after a little break, really, really appreciate and [am] so grateful for that.

A good skier is somebody that has a nice edge control, that can do good turns, can ski through all of the conditions—slush, icy, powder—basically a master of whatever is in front of them on a pair of skis, and not be too specified into one aspect. If you are good on skis, then you're going to be good at everything—somebody who can master all aspects.

When I started street skiing, it was basically about only finding handrails or features that look like features from the park. But it's become more trying to use your imagination and fantasies out in the streets. You're experimenting with the environment, and I like to incorporate as much city feeling as I can when I'm in the city of skiing.

I think it's cool to see when people really just use their imaginations and come up with their own way to ski a city. And it has changed so much, too, with the technology of having winches and bungees as well, where you could all of a sudden go into features just from the flat instead of needing a natural speed, or a hill to get speed. That changed all the features a lot.

The best way to find inspiration is to give it a lot of time. That's mainly it—the amount of time that I'm thinking about skiing and thinking of how to do it a little bit different than I did the day before. But I thought about this not too long ago: I definitely think that I train my own brain to be more connected with skiing.

I can remember being a little bit younger, and you think about things and all of a sudden you realize that I'm thinking about all kinds of nonsense, or things that don't really matter, or I shouldn't care so much about. And I used to think in those moments, "Damn, I should just think about skiing right now instead, because that's what I care [about] and love."

It's gotten to the point after 20 years of thinking like that, skiing is naturally in my head at all time[s]. It just bounces back. If I drive through a city—even if it's in southern France, and [there] definitely will never be snow there—even if I see a rail, or some kind of an urban feature, in that city, obviously I'm always going to think about the way I would ski, or the way it would be shot or filmed... It always goes back to skiing.

—*Originally appeared in* Mountain Gazette 194, *2020.*

30.
New York is for the Birds
Written by Sadie Stein

"When I first moved here from a more rural area and people talked about Central Park birding, I rolled my eyes a little," says Tod Winston, a writer, birder, and the communications content manager at Audubon New York, Gotham's chapter of the Audubon Society. "It seemed typical of New Yorkers, who think they have the best of everything. I didn't understand how *intense* it is—because of the saturation."

We are in Central Park's "Ramble," the meandering, 36-acre bit of man-made wilderness accessed from the 79th Street transverse. Winston—a respected guide known for his skill at birding by ear—has been kind enough to let me join him on his first Central Park bird walk since the start of the pandemic. And from the get-go, that saturation is apparent: even in fall—"a strange and confusing time to bird," per Winston, due to some of the species' faint markings—there are cedar waxwings, robins, warblers, ruby-throated hummingbirds, nuthatches, sparrows, and juncos, as well as the odd red-tailed hawk, the celebrity of the Central Park birding world. (After hawks started nesting on the late Mary Tyler Moore's Fifth Avenue building, the actress came to their aid.) Winston keeps a running tally in his head to write down later; many birders log their sightings as they go, or chart them in real time on one of the many birding apps. And, naturally, there are a few rats.

As with all things bird-watching in Manhattan—like the oxymoronic term "urban nature" itself—the experience is characterized by its contrasts. By night, the Ramble has long been a byword for anonymous encounters and potential muggings, but this morning, it's picturesque, as quiet and gray as a Chris Van Allsburg painting. And although it's not early by birding standards—we meet at 7:30—the Ramble is serene, a world away from the bustle of West End Avenue. However, just as looking for birds sharpens one's senses to their presence, so, too, do you become aware of other birders, or "birdies." Quiet, of course, distanced (naturally), and masked, it's a discreet population, but like confederates, they make themselves known to each other. "Saw a goldfinch," says one young man by the Bow Bridge. "Did you hear about the woodpecker in Queens?" asks a woman in passing on a path near Belvedere Castle. (Apps like eBird mean real-time sightings are constantly updated.) Others keep to themselves. The practice can be as social or as solitary as you wish.

The famous density of birding here—that "intensity"—is due to a phenomenon known as the Central Park Effect. The park—because it's an oasis on the migratory path, a spot of green in a sea of inhospitable buildings—has an unusually high number of species in a very small space. In addition to the migratory birds, there is a large population of locals, too, making for a certain kind of bird-watching nirvana, no matter the season. "The Central Park Effect benefits humans; I'm not sure how it benefits birds," remarks Winston. In the spring, birders—in their own sort of Central Park Effect—typically converge on what amounts to a few blocks of winding path. Indeed, some observers have even suggested that the proximity to people makes native birds (and even repeat migrators) "friendlier," and easier to observe than most. This year, though, was quiet.

The problem with talking about birds is that, even at the best of times, it lends itself to too many easy metaphors. There's the fraught language of non-native species and resources; there are nests and flocks and homing instincts. There's mating songs and plumage, of course, and the dynamics of feathering nests and waiting for eggs to hatch and the early getting of worms. There's the monogamy of penguins and the gender fluidity of flamingoes. Hawks and doves, naturally. And all that is to say nothing of the putative return of the bald eagle to New York City. ("I *won't* use the term 'canary in the coal mine,'" Audubon NYC executive director Kathryn Heintz says at one point, stopping herself.)

Earlier this year, pundits had a chance to dust off their best bird metaphors for the ugliest of reasons. Because, as you may recall, on Memorial Day of this year a bird watcher named Christian Cooper encountered a woman and her dog in Central Park. Her name is Amy Cooper (as all accounts will make a point of mentioning, no relation), but you may know her as the Central Park Karen. After Mr. Cooper confronted Ms. Cooper about the fact that her cocker spaniel was unleashed, the argument escalated, and she threatened to call 911. "An African-American man is threatening my life," she said. It was the same day as George Floyd's death. Mr. Cooper's video of the incident went viral and quickly became a flashpoint in the unfolding national uproar. Well, you remember. Somehow, the very mild-mannered nature of the hobby—almost a byword to the non-birder world for unthreatening, benevolent nerdiness, where most internecine spats center on issues like the etiquette of playing recorded birdcalls—made the story, to the armchair spectator, even more shocking.

From this most fraught of places, a strange spotlight was thrown on the quiet world of urban bird-watching, and specifically Audubon New York, of which Mr. Cooper is a board member. The National Audubon Society—of which New York, at 41 years old, is a relatively young chapter—released a statement following the Cooper incident. "The outdoors—and the joy of birds—should be safe and welcoming for all people," it read in part. "That's the reality Audubon and our partners are working hard to achieve."

The public image of bird watchers, of course, is cozy: elderly, absent-minded-professor types in wacky hats disengaged from the real world, perhaps, absorbed by the minutiae of birdcalls and flight paths. Certainly that's an element, and an endearing one. But, as

Heintz indicates, birding—and certainly the Audubon Society—is inextricably tied up with the hard, pragmatic graft of urban conservation work, whether that means dealing with developers to build bird-friendly structures, agitating for safer wind turbines, or working to make the 9/11 Tribute in light less devastating to avian populations. (The twin beams of light lure migratory birds off their flight paths.) This work—like that of conservation generally—is inherently political, and, as such, the recent involvement in real-world skirmishes is perhaps less unlikely than it might seem. "We're a conservation organization, not a birding club," Heintz explains. "Birding is a point of entry to conservation. Not all birders are conservationists, but it really is the gateway."

Birding is simple, but it takes decades to master. You need only binoculars and maybe a guidebook, but those binoculars cost money. It's a pastime that calls for certain luxuries: time and, perhaps even more than this, attention. And while the hobby is open to anyone with access to a city park, it can feel clubby to the outsider: the sheer volume of vocabulary, of trivia, of things unknown. That's the appeal to many; to others, it's intimidating. After the Cooper incident, there was much written about the perceived whiteness of the pursuit; a Black man in the Ramble, as seen, will not necessarily be treated as a lovable eccentric, but as an alien threat. But if the incident drew attention to the question, perhaps it can also serve as a means of broadening that very world. Maybe, as with the joys of sourdough baking and the necessity of working from home, some people will discover that they can, in fact, bird-watch.

Of course, the same thing that makes birding an ideal quarantine activity—the fact that it's outdoors, largely solitary, and meditative—makes it hard to measure in a time when bird walks and after-school programs have been suspended. Then, too, as Christian Cooper tells me, "the birding community skews older, so that's the population most likely to avoid public spaces," especially when the city's park users have been photographed gallivanting with mask-less impunity.

Like everything right now, it's complicated. According to Audubon NYC administrators, there has been an uptick in their organization's web hits, as well as those of outdoor-focused meet-up groups like WildMetro, Latino Outdoors, and Outdoor Afro.. In response to increased interest, Audubon is re-releasing its "Birding by Subway" brochure. The Breeding Bird Atlas, a user-generated annual survey, has had unusually high participation.

Obviously, the Audubon Society wants to expose as many New Yorkers as possible to nature. "In an urban environment, the city's parks and green spaces are everyone's backyard; there are studies that show that if you're not 10 minutes from a green space, you're too far," says Heintz. "And appreciating nature, the evolution of nature, and the value of nature is so important. If you make the green spaces welcoming, so everyone can use them, you've done an enormous service to the city—and to humanity."

But much as Audubon wants residents to take advantage of, say, the Jamaica Bay wetlands, with its wealth of egrets and herons, or the state's many beaches, too much activity from city dwellers sick of their tiny apartments could be disastrous for nesting plovers. Meanwhile, dogs off their leashes could disrupt the habitats of the parks' native birds, particularly the famously rich population of Central Park. It's easy, especially when emotions are running high, to view it all as a microcosm of the dense city's tensions: between populations, between needs, between nature and urban life, between solitude and socializing. And, of course, between human beings and the planet. Bird as metaphor, again.

Coexistence is tricky. When it works, it's exhilarating. Increasingly, New York, like other cities around the country, has worked with Audubon and other conservation groups to improve conditions for birds. Fresh Kills is a grassland created from landfill, rapidly filling with birdlife. In the city's existing parks, native plants—crucial to supporting insects and birds—are the rule, with organizations like Staten Island's Greenbelt Native Plant Center encouraging seed collection and planting.

New buildings are required to be bird-friendly. "New York is a city of buildings, and that's not going to change," says Heintz. "But we want to see that, going forward, this is a city of bird-friendly buildings." New York's glass-heavy skyscrapers can prove disastrous for migrating birds, especially young ones that haven't learned to distinguish between glass and the sky it reflects. It doesn't help that what a conservationist might term "habitat-adjacent" also means "expensive park view" to residents unwilling to disrupt said views with stickers, or turn off their lights after dark during migration, as residents of Portland, Oregon. But developments like the new Museum on Liberty Island are models of avian-friendly design, while a revamp of the Javits Convention Center has cut down on bird-collision deaths by 90 percent.

But the pandemic has brought new challenges to this work. It's hard to say at this point what the lasting effects will be, on bird populations or habitat, but in the short term, dogs—or, more to the point, their owners—have become a thorn in birders' sides as a direct result of the city's lockdown. For one thing, dog runs are closed, forcing more canines onto the paths. For another, pets that are normally walked by professional dog-walkers are now being exercised by fond owners—who are more inclined to let them off-leash. At the same time, a financially strapped city means fewer rangers to enforce leash laws as more and more New Yorkers try to run along together.

Very rich people, of course, can leave the city—and have, in droves. But to those who stay, the parks are not merely a poor man's countryside. It's the very contrast between migratory birds and pigeons, squirrels and rats, and woodland and skyline—the wilderness hidden in plain sight—that makes for such a piquant experience. In a sense, of course, the experience *is* more controlled, at least from the elements, and there is a comfort in being able to take a nature bath in the certain knowledge that you can get a warm bacon, egg, and cheese on a roll within five minutes. But for New York birders, the appeal isn't just the convenience.

In any collection of passionate enthusiasts, one will find conflict. New York's birding community is no different; indeed, it's a place well-suited to eccentric know-it-alls, for whom yelling at strangers is a pleasant bonus. There are tiffs; there are disagreements; there are personality clashes and even the occasional Twitter beef. There are villains. On a recent morning walk, I observed two birders arguing over whether it was appropriate to play a recording of a chimney swift's call—regarded by many as a breach of birding etiquette in a space as saturated as Central Park. Even the practice of giving rogue unleashed dogs treats—part of what provoked Amy Cooper's ire—is a subject of hot debate. But, overall, the feeling in the early morning in the Ramble is collegial.

In the documentary *Birders: The Central Park Effect*, Christian Cooper lists the qualities that attracted him to birding when he was introduced to it as a boy on Long Island. Along with the beauties of nature and the birds themselves, the pleasures of puzzle-solving and scientific discovery, he says, there's "the joy of hunting without bloodshed."

Cooper has long been active in mentoring other bird watchers; he is in charge of his Feathered Friends After-school Bird Club initiative (naturally suspended at the moment). Most recently, Cooper has released a comic with DC Comics called *It's a Bird*, inspired by his notorious encounter in Central Park. In the book, which is available for free download, a young Black birder encounters racism while pursuing his passion—#birdingwhileblack. In the process, the text takes on larger questions of police violence, racism, and the pleasure and pain of embracing a passionate hobby. "One of the reasons why the protagonist is a young person is to connect with kids," Cooper explained over the phone. He has long worked to bring underserved communities, particularly young people, to birding—and to help create a world in which a young Black man can bird anywhere without encountering suspicion, hostility, or worse, and, in the process, can immerse himself in beauty. "Of course, there's a romance to birds, because they can fly," he has said, "and that represents the ultimate in freedom."

Birders often muse about the first bird that captured their attention, whether it was a single ruby woodpecker's plumage or maybe the sight of a vee of geese flying south, impelled by instinct. This combination—of macro and micro, inspiring and detailed, specialized knowledge and general appeal—seems crucial to birding's magic. And the courage of the migratory birds, combined with the tenacity of local populations, is an ever-shifting drama in miniature. It's the controlled chaos of a roller coaster, nature made small enough to create awe without fear. The writer Jonathan Franzen has talked about the scale of it: "just the right size."

All metaphor aside, the magic lies in the birds themselves: their beauty, their endless variety, their improbable toughness. "I'm always so struck by the incongruity—these seemingly fragile creatures that can sit on your finger, but can survive incredibly intense conditions," says Winston. "They travel from South America to the tundra and back, with just enough body fat and no margin for error. Stopping here, in Central Park. And their adaptability is remarkable."

—*Originally appeared in* Mountain Gazette 194, *2020.*

31.
Drinking With A Dead Woman
Written by M. John Fayhee

"Heaven, heaven is a place, a place where nothing, nothing ever happens."
—*The Talking Heads*

The dead woman drank an impressively steady stream of margaritas. A veritable salt-rimmed, ice-adorned River Lethe of tequila, triple sec, and lime juice. She sat two barstools to my left. I did not yet know she was dead. She looked alive enough that I struck up a superficial conversation, something I am generally not inclined to do with the dearly departed. Came to learn she had once been a trauma nurse in an emergency room somewhere in California. She was now working part-time as a motel maid in a major-league ski town populated primarily by members of the upper crust. This seemed like a big vocational drop-off, a subject with which I am well familiar. I guessed she was in her mid-50s. Pretty. Well coiffed and attired. Looked to have a full rack of dentition. No ghost-like aura. No visible signs of decomposition. No foul stench.

Though it hovered on inappropriately personal, I could not resist asking about her apparent downward career trajectory. She admitted that, yes, it might seem a bit odd to go from being a high-level healthcare professional to changing bedsheets soiled by affluent strangers. I suspected some tale of woe—like maybe getting busted stealing pills from the hospital pharmacy.

Instead, she told me that, eight years prior, she had died.

I assumed, as any of us would, that she had experienced some sort of medical emergency—a heart attack, perhaps, or a near drowning, or an overdose—and had been miraculously resuscitated, like so many stories we all have seen on TV.

No, she said, she had actually passed away. She was, at the moment we were sitting there chatting amicably in a well-polished watering hole in a beautiful Colorado mountain town on an idyllic summer's eve, dead as a fucking doornail.

As this unusual autobiographical tidbit was sinking in, my memory reflexively revisited what until that moment had been the strangest introductory bar encounter I had ever experienced. I had mistakenly wandered into a biker-gang clubhouse in Prescott, Arizona, on a very busy Friday night, thinking it was nothing more than yet another in a long line of skanky dives that have borne my boot prints over the years.

The stunningly unhygienic giant next to me did not look more frightening than any of the other patrons—most of whom sported facial scars—so I said howdy and we talked as much as we could above a raucous din dominated by the sound of pool cues being shattered over people's noggins. The stunningly unhygienic giant, who was actually affable enough, asked what had inclined me to wander into the establishment in which we were sitting, the implication being that I was essentially in the Wrong Place, my M.C. bona fides obviously being sorely lacking. After explaining my innocent disorientation and begging for my life, I, in turn, asked after his story. He angled his head in my direction and moved his face close enough to mine that I could accurately count all three of his remaining teeth and responded that he was the high priest of the biggest satanic cult in the entire state. It was only then that I noticed the bright-red goat pentagram tattooed on his, well, forehead.

I looked down at my watch and mumbled words to the effect of, "Oh, my! Look at the time! I must be off!"

The margarita-swilling dead woman trumped the three-toothed devil worshipper.

Naturally, I assumed the dead woman was bullshitting me and/or so drunk that her immediate reality was blurred, and/or batshit crazy, and/or trying to dissuade further attempts at discourse. All she did was inflame my curiosity, which, upon further reflection, may have been her intent after all, as I assume it could get a bit lonely being dead in a lively ski town.

She told me she was, of all fortuitous coincidences, in the emergency room of the hospital in which she worked when it happened: a fatal brain aneurysm. One second, she was standing there scratching her ass; the next second, she hit the deck like a monster load of elephant dung splatting down on the dusty African veldt. Almost immediately, she was under the care of a medical team consisting of her co-workers. They performed valiantly, the dead woman told me, but their efforts were in vain. She felt herself slipping away. She had always thought talk of a bright white light was poppycock concocted by the swirling brain chemistry of people with one foot in the grave who were yanked back from the mortality precipice by the miracle of modern medicine. Her opinion changed as she lay dying.

"I was greeted by my ancestors," she said, over yet another margarita. "They were standing there, intensely illuminated, waiting to help me cross over. It was lovely."

"How did you know they were your ancestors?" I asked, with the slightest hint of cerveza-enhanced skepticism creeping into my intonation.

"Among my earliest childhood memories was a great-great-aunt, who must have been in her 90s when I was a toddler," the dead woman responded. "She was there. I recognized her. She told me the other people were my ancestors."

The dead woman, though, was not yet all the way gone. Back in the emergency room, the attending physician, whom she knew well, whispered in her ear, "I am going to administer one last drug. It won't work, but I still have to try. I hope your journey to the other side goes smoothly."

(Along about here, the dead woman's narrative thread started to lose whatever minimal linear coherency it had maintained up until this point, a situation likely exacerbated by the fact that I, like her, had not exactly been practicing teetotalism during the course of our convoluted conversation.)

"As he guessed, the drug was not effective, but it was effective enough that it pulled me away from my ancestors," the dead woman said. "I was in no man's land—neither conscious nor unconscious, in somatic limbo—for three months. Back in the hospital, they called it a coma."

When she finally emerged, she was, she said, dead. And she has been dead ever since.

"Was it like an out-of-body experience, where your spirit rose and looked back down on yourself still lying comatose on the bed?"

"No," the dead woman said. "There was no disconnection. My eyes opened and I sat up, dead."

"When that happened, weren't you in the same hospital in which you suffered your brain aneurysm, and did you not then walk among the very same people who had worked to save your life in the emergency room a quarter-year prior? Did they not welcome you back to the land of the living with the same degree of enthusiasm with which your ancestors welcomed you to the land of the dead?"

"Yes," she said. "I'll admit that part was strange. It was very disorienting to suddenly be in the presence of people who did not understand that I had died."

The dead woman had previously made reference to her children, so I asked about that. How could she possibly still have interactions with her offspring if she and they dwelled on different sides of the great divide?

"I am completely different than I was when I was alive," she said. "I do not like the same things. I never used to like tequila, for instance, and now I can't seem to get enough of it. Because I am so different, my children are very different. They are not the same people they were before I died."

"You still visit them, right?"

"Yes, several times a year."

"Do you appear to them as an apparition?"

"Maybe. I don't know how I appear to them. We interact, but in a completely different way than before."

"Do they consider you dead?"

"They know I am no longer alive."

"By what means do you travel to visit them?" I asked. "Teleportation?"

"My driver's license expired shortly after I did," she said with a smile. "So I fly."

Shit, I thought, every kid's worst nightmare: being haunted by your mom after she dies. Every kid's second-worst nightmare: being visited by a mom who thinks she's dead. I mean, my mom certainly had her faults, but, in the 30-plus years she's been gone, she has never once dropped in for a posthumous visit, which I appreciate more than words can convey.

"Speaking of which," I asked, "how did you come to be in this town?"

"I was called here by forces I could not define or resist. I arrived on a Greyhound bus in the middle of the night with no money, no place to sleep, no job, no life. I did not know a soul here."

The dead woman went on to say, by way of what I assumed to be an attempt at clarification, that all of our cultural perceptions about death and the so-called hereafter are based upon notions of either/or: you are either alive or you are dead. Sure, she admitted, there are a few rare gray areas, like, I would guess, when you're lying in bed for three months in a vegetative state with all manner of tubes running up your nose, down your throat, and up your ass, and the ever-present EKG and EEG machines making those endless bleep-bleep noises—any sane person's definition of hell on Earth.

Our perceptions toward the afterlife, according to my newfound a-corporeal drinking chum, are based upon the belief that there is a partition, on the other side of which is found a world that essentially defies our understanding of rational thought and the foundational laws of physics, a confusing place occupied by spirits, angels, and characters from Tim Burton's *Nightmare Before Christmas*.

"The notion that the afterlife is totally different from the living world is complete fiction, the work of self-proclaimed visionaries looking to explain the unexplainable to people desperate enough for something to believe in that they are willing to believe in utter nonsense," the dead woman said. "There isn't a wall between life and death. If anything, it is more like a permeable membrane. Like cosmic Gore-Tex. Or cheesecloth."

But the mountain town in which this conversation was transpiring was obviously very different from the place she was during that brief time when her ancestors stood arrayed before her as the emergency-room people were trying to pull her back. Where was that place, and how does it relate to a watering hole that, I surmised, served as a sort of post-death interstate-highway rest area, a purgatory with bowls of Chex Mix thoughtfully placed before every lost soul?

"I don't know," she answered. "I'm still trying to figure that out. I go looking for them every day. I walk the streets at noon, when the day is at its brightest, hoping they will appear. I would rather be with them than sitting in this bar day after day."

I suggested she consider visiting other establishments, there being endless options in this town.

She said this was the only place that made margaritas the way she liked them.

"Have you ever thought about killing yourself?" I offered by way of a positive solution to her apparent post-mortem dilemma. "Maybe you get deeper into the afterlife the more times you die. Or maybe dying when you're already dead amounts to a mortality double negative. Maybe you would be reborn as the person you were before you died."

"I have no idea where a dead person goes when he or she dies," she said softly, staring into her glass, which was glowing in the late-afternoon sunlight. "The thought scares me. I plan to wait to see what happens. At least for a while longer."

The theological implications of the dead woman's perspectives and contentions were both well above my alcohol-numbed intellectual pay grade and unsettling on several levels, not the least of which being that, if she were indeed dead, and the place where we were imbibing our libations was some inexplicable variation on the "What's next?" theme, then wouldn't it logically follow that everyone else at that time in that bar would, likewise, have to be deceased? Including, you know, me.

"Though I do not know for sure, I would not be the least bit surprised if you were dead also," she said far more nonchalantly than I thought appropriate, given the inherent implications of the message.

"But-but-but—unlike you, I do not remember dying," I stammered.

"Maybe it happened so suddenly, the experience did not have time to imprint. Maybe you had a sudden heart attack way out in the woods and you died instantly. Or maybe you got vaporized by a falling meteor. I don't know what happened to you. That's your concern, not mine."

In the movie *The Sixth Sense*, the creepy little kid said that most dead people did not know they were dead. Could that be the case here and now?

Equally concerning in this increasingly morbid context, in that same movie, the creepy little kid was able to see dead people. That might be worse than actually being dead. But if I was cursed with being able to see dead people, then I was sure enough not the only person in this bar thus afflicted. The bartender could clearly see the dead woman, whom he addressed by name as he served her one margarita after another. Unless, of course, he, too, was dead and, like the creepy little kid, I was able to discern them both!

I was fast beginning to regret my decision to smoke a bowl of hash before entering the bar.

I have not seen, heard, or read any codified religious references to the possibility that when you die, you end up in a mountain-town bar drinking with the likes of yours truly. Such a scenario would likely not set so well with the more fundamentalist sectors of society. No lounging around on a cloud, plucking at harp strings while the dogs from your childhood frolic at your feet. No bright white light. Not even any burning in hell. Just a bar, a seemingly endless supply of adult beverages, and the occasional fellow dead person with whom you can while away the afternoon. Many would be sorely disappointed by this manifestation of the hereafter, but others, including me, would end up much relieved. Damned sight better than burning in hell. And better also than waking up and realizing that you had been reincarnated as a dung beetle or a leper in Calcutta.

We take what we can get out of life, I suppose.

(I will venture this guess: the first organized religion that promises its adherents an afterlife that includes considerable time spent drinking margaritas in a ski-town bar will see a dramatic rise in its membership. There is assuredly room for a holy man in this mythical sect, which I proclaim shall be named "Barism"—the foundational negative-reinforcement tenet of which being that all non-believers shall be stricken by a plague of perpetual hangovers.)

When I returned from a visit to the men's room, the dead woman was gone. Her glass was gone, as was the coaster upon which that glass had sat. The stool that had so recently borne her posterior was pushed up close to the bar—by whom, I do not know. The bartender who had been serving us had been replaced by his next-shift counterpart. It was as though the dead woman had never been there, which, I'll admit, seemed a bit spooky.

Many years ago, I had this buddy, long since—appropriate enough for this tale—passed away. He was one of my high school teachers. We hated each other with a passion that twice approached physical violence, which would not have turned out so well for me, as he was a weight-lifting martial artist ex-Marine. He taught physics, a subject well outside my realm of comprehension, even if I had given the slightest shit, which I did not. Though it mortifies me in retrospect, I was not just a desultory student. I was also a disruptive student, one who negatively impacted the entire vibe of a classroom otherwise populated by people actually inclined toward studiousness. I was a one-man academic wrecking crew. I do not blame the teacher for hating me.

Not surprisingly, only a single academic nugget stuck with me from that class: cold is not a thing; rather, it is a lack of a thing.

The same, I guess, can be said about death.

Once I graduated by the skin of my teeth, that teacher and I reconciled our differences (mainly because we both enjoyed ingesting illegal intoxicants) and became fast-enough compadres that we shared a house for a few months. During that time, he was dating a lady who was still in high school. These days, that would be a prosecutable offense. Even then, this affair bordered on an audacious indiscretion.

But they were in love. Eventually, teacher and student got married, and married they stayed for decades. Then, one day, with absolutely zero in the way of discernible forewarning, my friend's wife woke up a completely different person. Something had happened during the night to reshape her entire personality. Maybe a really bad dream. Maybe demonic possession. Whatever it was, when the alarm went off, she became a stranger to her husband and herself. This was not sudden-onset amnesia. She knew who she was. She knew who her spouse was. But she liked people and things she previously disliked, and vice-versa. Out went her old wardrobe. She traded in her car.

She was no longer in love with the physics teacher to whom she had long been married. Could scarcely stand the sight of him.

They visited every manner of healthcare professional, looking for a diagnosis and a treatment. To no avail. Her condition could, they were told, be a result of any one of a dozen mental disorders: schizophrenia, bipolar disorder, PTSD, et al. It could, they were told, be a result of a heart attack, stroke, or, yes, a brain aneurism. Or it could be a ruse.

The couple eventually divorced.

The physics teacher related this story on one of my infrequent visits back to the place I say I am "from." He indicated it was, to say the least, a surreal experience. "It was as though she had died and come back a different person," said the man I once detested, the man who once detested me.

Maybe this is what happened to the dead lady in the bar. She had, after all, suffered a major medical malady. Despite her insistence on labeling it as something more ethereal, she lay dormant for three solid months before regaining consciousness. If my friend's wife could rise one otherwise normal morning and be someone completely different with no apparent impetus, it is not just possible, but likely that the margarita-swilling dead woman could emerge from her vegetative cocoon likewise transformed beyond recognition.

But she was convinced it was much more than that. And who was I to disagree? If, as the margarita-swilling dead woman had speculated, I, too, no longer walked among the living, then it would have bordered on hypocritical for me to argue that she was both alive and delusional and that it was highly unlikely the hereafter, or an ill-defined component of the hereafter, was a bar in a ski town that happened to serve heavenly margaritas. And if, as I believed at the time and continue to believe, I yet live and breathe (in the traditional sense, that is), then I would have had little standing to weigh in on a subject about which I had zero in the way of applicable expertise.

Whatever the case, I did consider the possibility of having become inebriated with a dead woman to be a somewhat sobering experience.

Like every single one of us, I have no idea what happens when our time is up. It is not a subject I have spent much time pondering. It would be nice if it involved beer, bars, and beautiful summer evenings in the mountains. That would be good enough for me, even if it went on for the better part of eternity. No need for angels. No need for demons, either. But all are welcome when it's happy-hour time, so long as lyres and pitchforks are left on the other side of the gate.

I downed the last of many pints, left the bar, and ventured forth into the tilting sunlight, which was angled low enough that it dazed and disoriented my inebriated self so that consequently I came within a whisker of stumbling head first off a high curb into the grill of an oncoming Mercedes G-Class being piloted by a woman who reacted to my near interface with mortality by leaning on her horn and flipping me the bird with a well-manicured middle finger. Once I regained my composure, I floated downhill toward the sound of rushing water. There was still ample time for a stroll along the river before darkness fell.

It felt mighty good to be alive, even if maybe I was not.

—*Originally appeared in* Mountain Gazette 194, *2020.*

32.
Whichever Way the Wind Blows
Written by Amanda Monthei

Two summers ago, I was on a desert fire with the hotshot crew (a 20-person wildland firefighting team) I used to work with. It was a classic eastern Washington fire in sagebrush and grass, ripping one minute and completely cold the next, and we'd shown up when it was leaning toward the former, when nothing remained but small bits of heat and lots of blackened sagebrush.

A few days into the assignment, still on that dead fire, one of our senior firefighters gave us the morning briefing, covering weather and fire potential and telling us to keep our heads up for rattlesnakes and dehydration. We stood in a circle, shuffling from foot to foot or kicking rocks in the early morning sun, only vaguely listening because morning briefings become more or less repetitive after a week in the same place: It's hot; fire potential is high; drink some damn water; rattlesnakes exist, so don't be dumb.

"I have one more thing to add," he said. "One of my old buddies from [another hotshot crew] died by suicide last night. He was a good dude and I just want you guys to know."

He didn't cry, but he looked at the ground as we gave our sympathies from around the briefing circle. Everyone lined up to give a hug or a handshake or one of those half-hug, half-handshake things.

Others stood back, tears in their eyes—surely recalling when they were that friend who'd just heard of a fire buddy's fireline death or suicide. In wildland fire, it's not if, but when you will lose a friend.

He looked up and made eye contact around the crew. "If you guys ever need to talk, just please..." he said, pausing. "Please let me know."

Heads nodded in quiet reverence and deep understanding. A few more crewmembers worked through the line—not unlike those at weddings and funerals—to pay their hushed respects. The circle dispersed. We had acknowledged our friend's grief, and now there was work to be done.

Wildland firefighters are inordinately impacted by suicide, as well as a whole slew of other mental-health struggles. This isn't that story. This is a story of people who do this job—*love* this job—despite a myriad of reasons to hate it, even despite losing friends, relationships, and any semblance of normal life to it.

The people drawn to this job can't be shoehorned into any one stereotype, despite the fact that many of them are undoubtedly dudes with beards. I'm not saying that wildland fire wouldn't benefit from some serious diversification effort; still, I've worked alongside LGBTQ+ folks and people whose first language wasn't English. I've swung a tool next to aspiring PhD students and 19-year-old kids fresh out of high school. Tele skiers, nomads, and hippies, and, as you can imagine, quite a few straight-edge, decidedly corn-fed boys. Some of my former coworkers grew up throwing hay bales. Some grew up in Portland, Oregon. Some grew up in Mexico. Some had shrapnel in their arms, brought back from combat in Afghanistan. There are those who came to fire after struggling with addiction and alcoholism, and those who still struggled with drinking and drugs. Some were single, many had partners, some were divorced or in the process of getting divorced. Some of the people I've met in this work even fought fire while in prison, got out, and worked like hell to get a job in fire again.

Every one of my former coworkers made sacrifices to work in fire, and had untold conditions and life changes to reckon with; for one, there was smoke and dust inhalation, a near-daily exposure that you eventually just quit trying to avoid. Then there's the bizarre schedule that results in maybe eight or 10 days off from July to October. Working in the sun and extreme heat is an obvious part of the job, but it's relatively easy to acclimate to. (Hot tip: Drinking a gallon of water every day helps virtually everything that ails you.) Finally, there's the weird diet. This ranges from packaged government rations that preppers keep in their basement in the event of an apocalypse to lunches filled with sugar and "mystery meat" sandwiches, as we called them. Or sometimes just three or four Uncrustables—those little PB&J sandwiches that they'd give you in elementary school if you forgot your lunch. Dinners were often pretty good, but fueling exclusively with Snickers and gummy snacks all day certainly takes a toll by September.

The reason this is all ultimately deemed acceptable is because fire also promises experiences—helicopter rides into wilderness areas and regularly lighting things on fire, for a couple—and, perhaps most valuable above all, a deep camaraderie with crewmembers that is uncommon—nonexistent, even—in normal life.

Camaraderie is probably one of the most alluring elements of wildland firefighting; fire, for all of its other highs and lows, is a unique opportunity to develop deep relationships with the people with whom you spend nearly every waking moment from April to October. An average season on a hotshot crew can involve 110 or more days on active fires, which totals more than 300 meals together on assignments and untold others while at the station or traveling. On most fires, firefighters can be awake about 17 hours a day, and every moment but the occasional pee breaks is spent with those same 20 people. Beyond sharing a disgusting amount of time together, I had assumed that relationship development would hinge heavily on the types of experiences and conversations people have while working in the woods and doing hard things together. What I hadn't considered was the role I would need to play when a coworker's friend died, or the shoulder I would provide when someone was bummed about missing their kid's birthday. I quickly learned that trauma and grief were the foundation of these relationships—alongside momentary valor so fleeting and nonchalant I often didn't even know if I should acknowledge it.

I hesitate to toss the word "heroic" around very often, particularly so when I talk about wildland firefighting. Most of the wildland firefighters I know grimace—like, physically reel—at the idea of being called heroes. They're just doing their jobs, they'll say. Hero worship, in fact, is often counterproductive in that it makes it easier to poorly compensate the people doing said heroics. Plus, it takes a massive, coordinated effort to save homes and lives, of which hotshot crews are only a small—though important—piece of the puzzle. The heroics I witnessed and took note of were more often untold small actions that, when compounded, felt less like heroics and more like a group of people who committed, every day, to watching out for each other.

As far as I can tell, I had only one close call with serious injury or death as a firefighter, but it was a moment of this sort of nonchalant heroism that left me unscathed. It was my first fire as a hotshot and we were in the Southwest, chasing desert fires and red-flag warnings—high heat, high winds, low humidities. I'd spent most of the assignment scared shitless and feeling largely inept. I couldn't stop messing up in small ways that felt profoundly less small when considered all together—a PowerPoint of mistakes that wouldn't stop clicking through my mind. We ended up on a fire in rocky, steep terrain on the interior hillside of an ancient caldera, high enough in the alpine that our lungs burned with every hike off the line and out of the pit of an age-old volcano. Every day that I made it back to the buggy felt like an accomplishment, and a deep sense of dread defined my headspace for the first six days of the assignment. What would my next mistake be? Would I get hurt? What would our next assignment require? What fresh hell would come next? With little real-life context as to how hotshot crews worked, I made vast assumptions to answer these questions and scared myself sleepless in the process. One night, on the creek where we had spread out our sleeping bags for the night, I lay awake for hours listening to the soft flow of water over cobble, hoping and waiting for sleep but finding some small solace in the meditation of water over rocks, of hearing it all wash downstream nonetheless.

The next day, while walking off the line at the end of our shift, about half of the crew, including me, was nearly hit by a falling tree. Its roots were burnt out, but not visibly enough for us to have registered it as a threat. The only reason I didn't get hit by that tree was because a coworker—a combat veteran who'd served in Afghanistan—yelled "Run left!" as half of us ran right, which was the same path as the falling tree. We heard him, changed course, and escaped the branches by mere inches.

I hadn't considered that relationships in fire would be built like this, too.

For all the reasons we convince ourselves to fight fire, there are countless others that ultimately make us question that decision obsessively, almost every hour of every day. Any firefighter will tell you that this job is the deepest love-hate relationship they've ever experienced. Within a few months of doing fire, I realized that if I wasn't questioning my life decisions at least three times a day, I wasn't doing it right—or not doing a hard-enough assignment. Because at the end of the day, we'd have collectively accomplished something that felt difficult and important, and the satisfaction of having completed it would be enough to galvanize an even deeper love for the job.

The experiences and camaraderie and humility of digging line for 12 hours only to have the fire cross it all the same the next day—this is what we get into fire for. What we didn't expect, what ultimately ends up tipping the scales toward leaving, are mental-health issues, relationship problems, future health concerns, poor pay and lack of benefits despite increased experience and training, as well as limited opportunities for upward mobility. When I finally got out of fire in 2019, after just four years, I did it because it felt like more of a sacrifice than it was worth; I often say I wish I'd found fire when I was 22 instead of 26, so that I could have spent more of my nomadic phase chasing fires and living out of a duffel bag. But by 29 I'd learned, on a deeply intimate level, just how difficult it is to balance life with fire. I understood how important the work was—for the land and, perhaps even more so, for myself—but I couldn't kick the feeling that I'd done what I could do and it wasn't for me anymore.

I'd felt the glory and experienced a season that ended with 1,000 hours of overtime; for those in fire, this is a point of celebration and exhaustion, a simple way of saying "It was a hell of a fire season" before sleeping for two weeks straight. As I wrote in my notebook in the back of the buggy in July of that first season with the crew: "This is all important; I'm just not good at balancing it."

There's no balance in fire, just an on-and-off switch that is flipped spontaneously every day of the summer and then turned off entirely from October to April. This is what wreaks havoc on the minds of wildland firefighters—not the work itself, but the downtime, when the switch flips abruptly to "off" and there's nothing left to do but think about the moments and traumas and long, hard days that defined the previous six months.

"We've got a big wind switch, guys. Tie it in quick and RTO."

The fire, fanned by 25 mph gusts, made it difficult to hear the radio, but I could just make out "RTO." This means "reverse tool order," or, in other words, "turn your asses around and get out."

We weren't in any immediate danger, but the smoke quickly became suffocating. The wind had been favorable all night, pushing inward as we burned off a section of line along a road in Oregon, hoping to starve the coming fire by taking away its fuel. The wind switched abruptly around 9 p.m. on a day that had started at 5:30 a.m., and what had been a normal burn operation quickly became a last-ditch effort to knock down the spot fires that began crossing the line.

I was at the front of the burn, responsible for lighting the last little chunk of land between our burn and another hotshot crew's. The golden spike, as it were. My captain grabbed my arm as soon as my fire met what had already been laid.

"Get back to the buggy," he said. A guy of about 40, he had 15 years of experience on fire crews all over Oregon and regularly kicked all of our asses on crew runs.

He stayed behind to gauge just how much of a mess was about to be made as the fire crossed the road, which was not part of the plan.

I paced through the smoke to locate the rest of the crew and soon found a few crewmembers waiting for me. We collectively decided to try to knock down a few of the small fires that had started above us, a Hail Mary effort to not completely lose the burn. We clawed up the cutbank and stomped at embers before they could ignite nearby brush. Before long, our stomping grew ineffective and spot fires had developed all around us, so we bumped back down to the road, forming a line and nearly jogging back to the buggies. I attempted to crouch low enough to find fresh air, of which there wasn't any. The smoke stung my eyes and throat—the kind of smoke that makes you wake up feeling like you smoked a pack of Marlboros—while embers snuck in between my eyes and sunglasses. We made it back to the buggies, where we took refuge from the smoke and prepared to drive back to camp. While a few guys slept, the rest of us laughed about how shitty things got at the end of the burn, sharing what little remained of our lunches from the day—gummies, candy bars, peanuts.

This night undoubtedly sucked. Southern Oregon and Northern California are notoriously heinous—largely because of the poison oak, but also because of the land. "Country to be humbled in," I wrote the next day in the composition book I always kept on hand, and humbled was probably an understatement. The land was steep and brushy. I'd just spent 20 minutes inhaling only smoke. I was in the midst of yet another fire-season breakup. A few friends were on a raft trip and I was jealous. Photos of barbecues filled my Instagram feed. Was this really what I wanted? To be sucking smoke and avoiding poison oak and bees in some rural corner of Oregon while my friends drank beers and got Chaco tans?

I was talking with a fire friend recently, someone who is going into his third season on a hotshot crew. He loves his job, but simultaneously laments the time away from his girlfriend and the paradoxical nature of wildland firefighting—particularly of thinking that it's actually a sustainable or ecologically beneficial career path.

"I got into this job because I thought I could make a difference, but it seems like most of what we do in wildland just feels like a Band-

Aid," he told me.

What he means is that our deeply rooted land-management issues are far beyond what a bunch of people with hoses, saws, and Pulaskis can realistically deal with. The West's forests are suffocated by brush, irreversibly void of the type of low-intensity fire that had kept them healthy for millennia prior to the arrival of Europeans and, eventually, full-suppression firefighting. Indigenous tribes have long used fire as an ecological tool and reset—encouraging plant growth and clearing underbrush for ease of movement and hunting—but these efforts were extinguished when the homes, railways, and infrastructure of early pioneers became threatened. Fire has not had a fair chance to reintegrate with the landscape since. For just one alarming juxtaposition, data from the National Interagency Fire Center shows that in the last 10 years, the average number of acres burned in the U.S. every year has hovered around 7 million—three times the average acreage burned annually in the 1970s and '80s. Fire seasons have grown longer, more destructive, and more severe. Meanwhile, federal wildland firefighter numbers hover somewhere between 12,000 and 15,000 annually, many of whom are seasonal like me and most of the people I've worked with over the years.

Federal wildland firefighters have neither the numbers nor the job structure to do meaningful prevention and mitigation work in the off-seasons, things like prescribed burns and thinning projects that would lessen the impact of future wildfires and, ultimately, make the suppression part of wildland firefighting easier down the road. As such, wildland firefighting has developed into a last-ditch effort to save homes or critical infrastructure, efforts that often hang precipitously on acts of nature: the way the wind's blowing, the way fire interacts with a certain landscape, a couple-digit rise in temperature. And it's exceedingly easy to think that when the wind does switch and shit hits the fan, it was your fault. You should have seen that coming. You should have known the upslope winds always come at sunset here, and that the burnout operation wouldn't be completed until well after dusk. You could have reinforced the line, could have done something differently. When things go right, there's rarely a moment to celebrate, and when things go wrong, it can weigh on you for months.

As fire seasons grow longer and more intense, the weight of these decisions—and wildfires and even climate change as a whole—will continue to land squarely on the already pretty sore shoulders of wildland firefighters. These are people who just missed their kid's birthday party to dig line for 16 hours, people who haven't spoken to their spouses in days because there's no cell service at fire camp, men who have a new baby at home but have barely seen them all summer.

Wildland firefighters start out making around $12 an hour. During my last season, I made $15 an hour. Every seasonal firefighter—those who work as "1039" employees, which limits hours worked to just below the 1040-hour threshold for permanent employment—makes around $15 an hour. If you know any wildland firefighters, particularly guys in their 20s, you've probably seen them buy a new truck after fire season; this is because we do end up making decent money—by ski-bum standards, anyway—by working boatloads of overtime, of which we can get up to 1,000 or even 1,200 hours a season. In essence, wildland firefighters work the same amount in five to six months as most people do in an entire year.

They do get affordable healthcare while they're employed, but since there's little free time or flexibility in the summer, making doctor's appointments is an impossible task—but they lose health insurance in the winter, so getting those appointments done in the summer while you actually have employer-provided health insurance is sometimes the only healthcare seasonal firefighters get through the year. I either didn't have insurance or used Medicaid during my four winters off from fire.

This inevitably makes firefighters feel left behind by their employers. In response, organizations like the Grassroots Wildland Firefighters Committee, which advocates for better pay, benefits, classification, and mental-health resources for wildland firefighters (known by their employers as "forestry technicians"), have begun popping up and encouraging more widespread change through policy reform. Meanwhile, organizations like the Wildland Firefighter

Foundation help pick up the pieces when wildland firefighters suffer fireline injuries, or assist the families of wildland firefighters who died on or off the line. They help connect wildland firefighters with mental-health resources and cover lost wages. They fly fallen firefighters back to their hometowns and cover funeral expenses. The fact that organizations like this exist is evidence that the federal agencies that employ the vast majority of wildland firefighters aren't doing nearly enough to support those firefighters when things go wrong—when the wind inevitably switches and things don't go as planned.

One August night, on a fire in central Washington, our crew became technically entrapped after the fire had burned over the one road out of the area where we were working. This left us and more than 200 others stuck on the mountain overnight. We spent hours looking for a good place to set up camp, all in places that had recently burned over and were, therefore, susceptible to falling trees. We eventually found a spot somewhere along a road deep inside the fire's recent burn scar. We surveyed the area for sketchy trees and finally sat down to eat MREs—pre-prepared meals like beef chili and jalapeño beef patty, which we eat when there's no other food available. We set our sleeping bags out alongside the buggies. A few guys put theirs under the buggies to feel safer against the potential for falling trees. I found a spot next to a few crewmembers and proceeded to lie in my sleeping bag for nearly an hour, closely monitoring the burned-over tree directly above me that had been swaying in the wind, emitting a deep groan with every arc. I thought about how that tree could kill me while I slept. As I spiraled deeper into that fear, a meteor trailed across the sky, followed by another one a few seconds later; the Perseids meteor shower was peaking that night, and as the meteors fell from the sky I noticed that the fire was burning on the distant horizon, visible through the skeletons of the trees that had been recently burned over. It looked like a small enemy fire in the distance, growing in brief spurts as it burned individual trees before fizzling out again. I smiled there in my sleeping bag, below shooting stars and two dead trees that could fall at any time, and fell asleep at peace, against all odds. We woke up to find that no trees had come down that night, and we made coffee on the tailgate of the buggy while blasting funk music and dancing in the cold morning sun. It was pure beauty, a moment I'll never forget—magic amidst destruction and fear.

It's hard to explain why, amidst it all, people still choose to become wildland firefighters, whether for a few years or a few decades. What's the draw?

There are the sunsets and the helicopter rides, sure. Part of its allure is not knowing what each day will bring, but dealing with it all the same. To me, the closest parallel has come from standing on top of ski lines I've never looked at or skied, finding my way down even when it sucks or I'm scared—and coming out the bottom completely stoked nonetheless. Similarly, there's the deep, almost indescribable satisfaction of a completed day, assignment, fire season. And, above all of that, there's the people.

Most of the important things I know about myself—my resilience, my strength, my innumerable weaknesses—were learned on the fireline, taught to me by people who were tired and hungry and thirsty and frustrated, but just kept on digging anyway. People who may have just lost a friend, or people who wondered if there was a divorce on the horizon. People who hadn't seen their kids in weeks. They taught me how to find some semblance of peace in a swinging tool or in a successful burnout. But, most of all, they taught me how to put my head down and do the thing that needs done, despite everything else. They taught me the power in committing all of myself to one single thing—that motley blend of 20 people and the wild ride of a fire season—for six months a year.

Fire, in all its moods, taught me humility; the people, in all of their moods, taught me to simply love what must be done.

—*Originally appeared in* Mountain Gazette 195, *2021.*

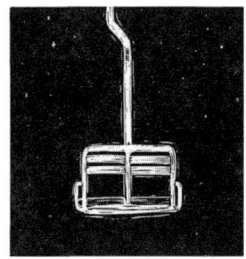

33.
Feel the Glide: How to Make a Skier
Written by Logan Imlach

My daughter's name is Stevie Jo Imlach-Carr, and she is the love of my life. From a young age, I knew that I was put on this earth to be a dad, and with her entry into the world, everything seemingly fell into place for me. Born on her great-grandfather's birthday and named after her late grandfather, she came to us as a fire-haired old soul, full of curiosity, intellectual and emotional intelligence far beyond her age, a famous temper, and somehow a sense of humor from day one.

I don't really know where to start this, where it's going, or where it will end. I can, however, tell you one truth that radiates from the deepest reaches of my soul: Being a dad is the single greatest job I've ever had, and I love my daughter with absolutely every cell in my body.

Parenthood is a fucking trip. Everything, absolutely everything, becomes magnified. Run-of-the-mill daily decisions somehow carry more weight. Every move is second-guessed and often third-guessed, and we scrutinize each decision with the ultimate desire not to fuck this up. Things have a tendency to just grow, much like writing this piece; it started as a simple idea of sharing my daughter's first full year of skiing—chronologically mapping her progress, her trials and tribulations, and showing some cute pictures of her in her miniature ski gear. Each time we got on the hill, I was hyper-focused on my actions, her mood, my role in all of this, and what it all means. There is so much more than skiing here. Like anything you do with your children or your parents, there are decades of love, anger, understanding, teaching, learning, mistakes, and successes that have led you to this moment. Telling your baby that she should take just one more run before going inside suddenly becomes loaded and analyzed. *Am I pushing too hard? Am I not pushing hard enough? Is there a need to push her to see what she can accomplish, or can she figure it out?*

The other piece of information key to this story can have its origins traced to a spiky little protein that brought our whole world to a screeching halt in early 2020. SARS-CoV-2, Covid-19, the 'rona—call it whatever you want, but it fucked up our social fabric and forced a level of isolation that I don't think many of us have ever known. Like many, this pandemic slowed my whole world down. Couple that with a pending, sudden divorce and I was primed for a tremendous amount of self-reflection and analysis as to why I am the way I am by breaking down my childhood. It was the perfect time also to discern which of these building blocks I wanted to pass to my daughter.

I was raised in Anchorage, Alaska. I'm a millennial who did great in school, excelled in sports, had a strict but loving single father and a revolving door of women in my life. I came from a fairly dysfunctional family, though we all laugh about it now. Most importantly, a majority of my teenage and adult life revolved around an obsession with skiing. I had the opportunity, which the self-deprecating side of me still doesn't understand, to film with Level 1 Productions for a number of years in my 20s. I was then able to parlay the connections I had made, some hands-on experience, and an engineering degree into a position designing skis for Armada. Even at the risk of sounding corny or dramatic, skiing has given me everything that I have in my life. I have skiing to thank for some of my greatest friendships, and for getting to see different parts of the world while slamming my body off of walls, stairs, rails, and even the odd abandoned building for the pleasure of the masses. I fucking loved every second of my time filming with Level 1. I may never have had an opening film segment or an ender, but I like to think I left my own unique mark on every movie I was in. My biggest point of pride in watching any of the movies isn't my own shots, but remembering being there to help my friends get theirs. Pole-whipping, running the winch, fixing landings between hits, taking on massive builds, pressing record on the lock-off, pulling back bungees, you name it—I was there for some of the most iconic Level 1 shots. Though the finished product is made up of individual segments, urban skiing is very much a team sport. In addition to the comradery, it teaches you a resilience that has been handed down to the mainstream through Rodney Mullen's TED Talk on skateboarding, which boils down to two words: Get up. When you ski urban, or really in any extreme sense, you are going to fall. It's a known factor in the equation. If you are pushing your limits, you're not going to land every time, and your success in that arena is measured by your ability to try again and again until you get your shot. And get another shot. And another. Until you have a segment. Getting back up is the quintessential building block to filming ski parts, and without that lesson I'm not sure if I would have gotten through the past year of my life.

Stevie's first time skiing was actually the spring prior, right when the coronavirus hit. Selfishly, I really wanted her to ski before she turned 2. I don't think she knew whether she enjoyed it or hated it, but everyone cheered her on, and when she said she was done, we scooped her up and she didn't have to go anymore. It was a win. In the middle of the summer, she saw her ski boots in the garage and asked if she could wear them. Happily, I clipped these tiny rear-entry black Nordica boots with stars on them to her feet, and we skateboarded in them. In the fall, we went to Play It Again and got her season-long rentals: 70 cm blue Elans with a DIN set at 0.75.

There are certain moments as a parent when you feel like you've been hit by a truck. They are visceral, and you don't forget them. *I have a fucking kid.* Seeing these tiny little skis and these tiny little bindings and these tiny little boots, I got emotional. *Will she like it? What if she hates it? Should I get a snowboard, too? What if she loves it and wants to be an Olympian? What if she wants to ski urban? I should buy a helmet.* We took some selfies, paid the man, and in the garage the skis sat, waiting for snow.

Being depressed is fucking hard. I know that's an understatement, but for lack of a better phrase, that's all I've got. Being depressed while you have a kid is immeasurably harder. You have this constant battle of being overcome by your emotions, but not wanting to let them see it. They provide fragments of sunshine and joy that make it through the cracks to lift you up, and it helps, even if it's just for a moment. Stevie did that for me a lot. She's an emotionally in tune 2-year-old with an attitude you wouldn't believe and a soul that draws people in. There's something different about this baby, and it's apparent how magnetic she is: Daycare teachers are always holding her and sending pictures, people are always stopping in the store and passing out smiles. She's funny and quirky and has a temper and she's everything I ever wanted a daughter to be, even though she's more difficult than any of my friends' children. I still remember a specific moment, playing on the floor with her and some toys, but just feeling completely paralyzed by my depression. She could sense it. She looked me in the eyes and said "Go to the skatepark?" with her little mousy 25-month-old voice. We packed up and went. She rolled by herself on the halfpipe for the first time, and I was so happy, I cried. Sometimes you're forced to get back up by yourself, but sometimes it's impossible without a little bit of help, and I can say with supreme confidence that this little 25-pound being saved me from darkness countless times. At a lot of those points, I truly couldn't have done it without her.

Nov. 7, 2020, was the first time it snowed enough to slide around in the driveway. It was also right around when I had moved out of our house, and the separation from Kelly, my now ex-wife, was becoming real. Not knowing what we were doing, and feeling like we were dying not seeing our daughter, Kelly and I landed on splitting every other day with her. In retrospect, this was horribly selfish of both of us, as Stevie had no idea what was happening and the instability of sleeping at a new house every night had to be hard on her. Anyone who hasn't experienced a separation from a child will likely never know the pain of finding the balance of what's best for your baby and what's best for you. That night, with a couple of inches of snow, we put our gear on in the garage in Girdwood, her little pink puffy snowsuit too tight on the ankles to fit over the ski boots that had to be four sizes too big for her. I went first, clicking into my skis, acting so overly excited that I think she could sense I was bullshitting, but she was still very curious as to what we were doing. I got her clicked into her skis, one foot at a time, her little legs unable to come close to stomping into her binding. After a quick photo op and smiling so big, I started to push her, hoping she would feel that glide, that freedom that I feel when my plastic bases melt a microlayer of snow beneath them, turning it into water and unlocking a feeling that only gravity, skis, and snow provide. Immediately, she burst into tears. Everything went into slow motion. *What do I do? Do I push her? Do I stop? Why doesn't she like it? Are the boots too tight? Maybe she'll come around if I keep them clicked in. No, you need to get her out.* Within seconds, she was unclicked and in my arms, crying. Consoling her, I found myself bummed. Then, immediately, guilt crept in about feeling bummed. The biggest source of unhappiness in a human being's life lies within the gap between your expectations and your reality. I went into this with expectations masked as hope, didn't I?

"What do you want to do, honey?"

"I want to bike," she choked out between heavy breaths and alligator tears.

"You got it, baby. Let's get these boots off."

With that, the tears subsided and her smile came back as she got on her Strider bike, but my guilt lingered. I wondered if I'd just pushed too hard, albeit only for a handful of seconds.

Parenting is 50% raising your child and 50% learning about yourself. Admittedly, I've never read a single parenting book. Maybe I should. I've found that the biggest source of learning is going back and looking at your own childhood, extracting the things you like, leaving the things you don't, and trying your best to infuse the good into your baby. But that's easier said than done. It's fucking hard. The manner in which your parents parented you is instilled in you whether you like it or not, and carrying forward those ideals is ingrained in you whether you like it or not. It takes work to leave the rest. It's much like a river, moving sediment and evolving over time to cut off an oxbow. Your channel is windy and it's difficult, weaving through good experiences and bad, and you have to move every grain of material from the cut bank and deposit it, building a new bank. The end goal is a straight channel, every negative experience cut off and separated so it doesn't carry forward, but it takes time. It takes time and it takes a lot of fucking effort. Sometimes it feels easier to just stay in the channel, even though you're weaving into a negative space, and the cognizance to stop and continue blocking that off is something that takes effort.

I've known the battle of cutting off an oxbow before, from my teens and into my late 20s battling alcoholism. I'm still battling it today. My fashion? Much like the rest of my life, being absolutely full throttle. Hitting that breakover point around six beers of shutting off any inhibitions until I am puking on the bar, getting my ass kicked, or pissing my pants. Many of the people who read this and know me well know Brogan, my alter ego, a vile human being who masks his insecurities behind being loud and "funny" (i.e., obnoxious and menacing to everyone around him). You would think that ending up in jail holding arraignment papers for allegedly stealing a hot-dog truck for a joyride would have been a wakeup call, but a handful of months later, there I was, walking around Seattle kicking over scooters after a Level 1 film premiere. There was slowing down after that point, but ultimately meeting Kelly was what saved me. I never wanted her to meet that guy. I'm proud to say that even though I'm always a work in progress, I've only Broganned out once in more than eight years—something about some triple-strength IPAs at the SIA trade show and me inappropriately touching Glen Plake's mohawk (sorry, Glen). The thing about alcoholism, however, is that the culprit is easily identified. The path to the straight channel, though incredibly difficult, is straightforward. Things like depression and parenting, things that carry so much weight and are all encompassed by air composed of words and thoughts, contain meanders that sometimes you don't even know are there. They can take years, sometimes decades, to even identify.

About a month later, enough snow had fallen to try skiing with Stevie again, this time on the road next to the house. I was so apprehensive that day, especially given the added stress of it being turned into an event with my dad (Pop), stepmom (Susan), and sister (Hailey). Would this make it better or worse? Would she feel good about it, seeing all of us skiing too, or would the pressure be too much? When my dad and sister and I are together, it's nearly always the case of too many cooks in the kitchen, with each person thinking they know the best way to do something and attempting to drive the situation. From the outside, it has to be maddening and overwhelming, and Susan is an angel for stepping back and just calmly watching us do what we do. So there Stevie was, getting geared up with the bickering that's fairly normal, each of us thinking we knew the best way to situate her boots, which method we should use to get her down the road, and if she'd be too hot or too cold. Who's carrying her up the hill? Who's filming? Should we use the racer chaser or the hooks on her tails or just hold her hands? Ultimately, due to the hierarchy, no matter what the situation, Pop usually wins these conversations. So it was me on the tail hooks with Hailey filming and Pop holding Stevie's hand. This time, unlike the previous, Stevie got to feel the glide. The look of confusion and wonder on her face almost looked like a blank stare, but knowing her, those wheels were turning. We got two laps! Then, during the third, she pulled out her kryptonite, the three words that she knows melt me every time: "Hold me, Papa." It was at that time that she found out what she loved even more than skiing: having me hold her while I ski. Admittedly, I'm a loose cannon with a heavy foot and surety in myself, even though that sometimes ends in disaster. So, immediately after picking her up, I was pointing it, jumping off of snow berms with her laughter echoing against the walls of the condos lining the road. "You shouldn't pick her up like that before you get to the bottom. She'll never learn to do it herself," came the instructions from Pop as we sped down the hill.

    Pop is my best friend. He is the hardest-working man I have ever met in my life, and though he shows a hard exterior some of the time, he is tender, goofy, and all around an incredibly loving human being. He was raised as the 14th of 15 children in an Irish-Catholic household, meaning that everyone was so focused on surviving that I'm fairly certain he never received the love, attention, and support he so desperately needed. This led to acting out as a child and young adult, causing a strained relationship with my grandpa, who had neither the time nor the patience to deal with an unruly kid. Pop was always fighting—street fighting, hockey fighting, it didn't matter. I think he was just mad and felt he had something to prove and never knew why. This led to a father who was confusing at times, switching from being very hard to very understanding, a disciplinarian to a confidant. He expected a lot of me and pushed me because he knew I was capable, but as I aged he would give me a longer leash as long as I didn't fuck up. He was always very proud of what I did, but also always telling me that I could do more or do better. I truly don't think it was malicious, and I know that I wouldn't be the man I am today without that constant pressure, but it was hard at times. I know that it just comes from a place of wanting better for your kids than what you had. But the frame of reference is shifting and the metric against which that's graded has changed. My generation's parents wanted us all to be college educated and wealthy no matter what the cost, because that's how they gauge success. Now that we're aware of the mental-health issues associated with that amount of drive, I'm hopeful that the metric we become obsessed with is happiness, whatever that means to each of us.

Stevie got her season pass to Alyeska and we attempted our first rip at the resort in mid-December. Walking up, pulling her in her little sled, I was in my head as usual. Battling my instinct to have expectations, picturing her as a teenager hitting urban, picturing her hating skiing, worrying I was starting her too young. Pop and Hailey were with me again, skiing together as a family much like we always did when we were babies, talking through strategies and beating a plan into the ground. We decided to start Stevie off on the magic carpet, with a gentle slope, low consequences, and a straight shot to the lodge for hot cocoa. Getting her clicked in, she seemed a little apprehensive—this had always ended in tears—but maybe she was just feeding off of my apprehensiveness and pensive vibe. But she did great. After figuring out that the tail hooks weren't her jam and that she preferred the traditional hand-holding while skiing between my legs, we got a couple of laps in. Stepping onto the magic carpet after the third or fourth run, she pointed upward.

"What's that, Papa?"

"That's the chairlift, honey."

"I want to go on the chairlift, Papa."

Fuck. Yeah. Without hesitation, I scooped her up and raced for the lift line, desperate to not lose this momentum. We explained to her to look back for the chair while we hoisted her on and talked about putting the bar down. Her eyes were peeled wide at this new experience. Getting to the top and off the lift went smoothly, and she was seemingly unfazed by the steeper slopes and new world in front of her. After one lap, we loaded again, and after getting off she pointed toward the beginner terrain park.

"What's that, Papa?"

"That's the terrain park, honey. There's jumps in there."

"I want to go off the jumps, Papa." Holy shit. Here we go.

Inherently, someone who is always pushing for that next level is deeply self-conscious. You're unable to look around and be happy with what you have because your focus is always on the next accomplishment that is on your horizon—looking back at what you've accomplished with disappointment because it's not as good as what you want that's in front of you. Then there's hitting stages of burnout that manifest in all forms; emotional explosions, fights, binge drinking, and self-hatred are some of the tools that I turned to when trying to cope. These cycles filled my teens and 20s. Couple those tools with being so mad that my mom wasn't around and I was nearly always a grenade with the pin barely attached. And that's how I skied. When I crashed, I crashed hard, and even when I landed, I was constantly on the edge of eating shit. Loose. Tortured and unhappy, constantly down that I couldn't ever piece together something I was truly proud of. Little did I know that no matter how well I skied, I'd never be happy, because that's how I was conditioned to perceive my body of work. It's the same reason I never watched my own skiing and instead always scrolled to the comments, searching for some kind of validation that I was unable to provide myself. Did that drive for more push me to where I was? Yeah, for sure, but at what cost? Years later, and with the help of therapy, I've identified all of these things and why I was this way. This. This is one thing I can't pass on to my daughter.

The season was going so well. Some days we would take only one run. Some days we'd take five. Every day ended with the option of hot cocoa or playing with K'NEX at the condo. Stevie had started loving being in the air. Every chance she got, she'd ask for me to take her off jumps. I started hitting rails while holding her (sketchy). Pop had been bringing her down during the week while Kelly and I were working, and at first I was anxious that he'd push too hard, but after a bunch of conversations and understanding, it seemed to be going well. One day when we were skiing, she pointed at another chairlift with her standard lead-off question.

"Papa, what chairlift is that?"

"That chair goes up the mountain, Stevie."

"I want to go up that chairlift."

Shit, here we go. The lower mountain at Alyeska is safe. Not safe for her, safe for *me*. At any point we were no farther than a couple of minutes from the sled and from home, so if she got upset or was done, the exit was fast. I was so hypersensitive about making sure that there was no inkling of me pushing her. I couldn't be that pushy parent; I just couldn't. Anxiously, I took her to the chair and got in line. So far, so good. The line wasn't too long, which had been one of our downfalls in the past, and we were able to load up. The height of the chair didn't seem to bother her at all, and we were snapping selfies and having a grand time. Life couldn't be better. At the top of this lift, which delivers you to mid-mountain, we had a very familiar conversation:

"Papa, what's that chairlift?" Stevie pointed to the high-speed quad servicing the upper mountain

"That chairlift takes you to the top of the mountain, honey."

"Papa, I want to go to the top of the mountain."

Alright, so at this point I let my excitement get the best of me and cloud my better judgement. *Fuck yeah, Stevie. Fuck yeah, we can go to the top of the mountain. You just turned 2? Who gives a shit? You got this. You're a child with a hair trigger for tantrums that send shivers down my spine? Naaaaah, we got this.* Hindsight is always 20/20, but in this situation, I should have known better. We skied to the lift line, which as usual was packed. Hundreds of people were working their way through the gates like cattle, socially distanced and with masks on. At first Stevie was enamored with the masses—so many people to see and inspect, observe. Then, after about five minutes, the tectonic plates within her brain shifted and the lava began to erupt.

"I DON'T WANT TO GO ON THE CHAIRLIFT!"

Fuck.

At this point, we were too far into the line to backtrack. The only way through this was to get on the lift. Only parents can understand the fear that was gripping me in this moment. First reaction? *Barter.* "Stevie, do you want hot chocolate? Stevie, do you want mac 'n' cheese? Stevie, do you want candy?" *Stevie, do you want a million fucking dollars? That's what I would pay to get out of this right now.* Nothing. She was full-on writhing on the ground with skis on, screaming. Holding up the line. I tried to grab her little body, but somehow it had become possessed by demons and she could suddenly dislocate every joint, so I couldn't keep ahold of her. Next reaction? *Begging.* "Please, honey, let's just get through the line and you can have whatever you want. Please don't do this." At this point people were staring, and all of a sudden I was the boogeyman. *They think I'm forcing her to go up the chairlift. Shit.* She was screaming bloody murder. As we neared the scanners, I searched for any opportunity to exit, but the horde had boxed us in. Final reaction? *Acceptance.*

"Stevie Jo, honey, listen to me."

"WHAT?!"

"We just have to go up this chairlift right now. We have to."

Which was met with the most bloodcurdling scream you have ever heard. At this point I looked abusive, and I just hoped that some of the silent bovines watching were parents who could commiserate. We made it to the chairlift, Stevie still violently convulsing her body to the point where I could only hold on to her harness to keep her on the chair. Then, like most tantrums, it ended with no rhyme or reason other than she was done. I was an emotional puddle, exhausted, and she was asking about the rocks and trees and what that big building is. Then a quick photo op at the top of the mountain, like nothing ever happened. This is parenthood.

I often wish that I could steal that ability from my daughter.

The ability to forget, move on, and focus on what's right in front of you. So much of my time is spent cycling over things from the past and stressing about what lies ahead. Two-year-olds are conduits of emotion; they have an inability to hold on to anything, and once it's out, it's gone. Are the outbursts of raw and unadulterated emotion terrifying? Fuck yeah, they are. But once they expel that energy, it's gone, it's behind them, and they are on to the next task. I'm so jealous of my daughter and her little growing brain. She has so much to learn and figure out; there's no room for baggage. Sometimes I feel like that's all I have, with absolutely no capacity to live in the here and now. So in that way I look up to Stevie, and have tried to make a habit of being more like her. Never get so caught up in your role as a parent that you forget how much your child can teach you.

I'm so fucking proud of my Pop. Learning things from your children is hard, but through all of this I've seen a tender man who is further reducing that hard exterior. Stevie softened all of us. Watching him be so patient and loving and concerned for her. Learning about all of the topics that have come into the conversation today that were not even thought about within his generation. Consent. Mental health. Feminism. Racial injustice and disparity. He is trying, and though sometimes we will argue or he doesn't understand, he is truly putting forth effort, and for that I love him so much. None of us are perfect, but as long as we keep putting the effort into listening and having tough conversations, we are on the right path.

Spring skiing came along and we were spending more and more time on the mountain. At this point Stevie was nearly always at the end of a 10-foot-long tether, refusing to snowplow because she likes to go fast. I am skiing again too, comfortable sending her off with Pop and Susan while I take some "Dad Laps." When my depression had the best of me, the only reason I would be on the hill was to take Stevie, and now I found myself back to skiing fast and jumping off of things. Probably too fast and too much jumping, but my body has always been a bit more brittle than my mind. And what's not to love about spring skiing? No gloves, sunglasses on, the sun shining. This. This is the version of skiing that Stevie has come to enjoy. On top of that, we are going off of all the tables in the terrain park, and I've gotten to where I can set her off on her own while I hit a rail, only to swoop back and grab her. Her giggle is infectious. There are fewer tears now, fewer expectations on my side, and nearly every day ends amicably and with a belly full of whipped cream because Stevie decided that's the only part she likes about hot cocoa. You do you, baby girl.

Finally, May 22, 2021, rolled around. One hundred and ninety-six days from Stevie's first day clicking into her skis. It was warm, albeit a little bit windy, but sunglasses and no gloves were the required uniform. The lower mountain was melting out, so I asked Stevie if she wanted to head to the top. "Yeah, Papa, up the chairlift." I remember watching her on the short run between the mid-mountain lift and the upper-mountain lift. Seeing her tiny little legs working so hard in the slush. Not remembering that a 6-inch slush mound was effectively half of her little leg and she didn't weigh enough for her ski to push the mass of snow and water out of the way like mine did. *She is still so fucking small. She's still my baby.* There weren't any tears, but on the lift I could tell she was tired. This might be a one-and-done day. At the top of the mountain, we got off the chairlift for the last time that year and made it a couple hundred feet, Stevie bouncing like a cork in the ocean, before she had finally had enough. "Just hold me, Papa," she said, just like she always does. "Come here, baby girl," I told her while reeling in her tether. I picked her up and we skied down together, laughing and jumping off of things. *Picking her up and carrying her is the least I can do. Because little does she know she's been picking me up and carrying me this entire year. Sometimes you can't get back up without a little help.*

—*Originally appeared in* Mountain Gazette 196, *2021.*

34.
It's All About The Bike
Written by Joe Parkin

It's complicated. Yeah, complicated is the best way I can think of to describe the connection I have with my bike. In relationship terms we celebrated our golden anniversary a couple of years ago. Which means I've been embroiled in this two-wheeled love affair for more than a half century.

It would be convenient to call it love at first sight, but it was actually more like love at first feel. That magic of gliding over the earth, almost effortlessly, grabbed hold of my entire being and has never loosened its grip.

I was just a few months shy of my fourth birthday when I ditched the oppressive training wheels and balanced on my own. My bike was small and featured a removable top tube, so that it could be set up for boys or girls. My grandma bought it for me at some kind of big box department store. It was basic and heavy, and its solid, non-pneumatic rubber tires made a lot of noise when ridden on asphalt.

In terms of both my skill and size I outgrew this first bike quickly, and my dad surprised me one sunny day with a brand-new blue Schwinn Midget Stingray. It had all the style and features of the regular Stingrays in a little-kid size—bass-boat sparkly banana seat, chopper-style handlebars and a dragster-style rear tire that laid down the most sublime skids. It was my wings, my airplane, my spaceship, my motorcycle, my bicycle, my freedom. This little blue Schwinn was the first love of my life.

But no relationship stays the same forever. As I grew taller and stronger, my bike changed with me. The little Schwinn's '60s/'70s chopper-inspired styling gave way to the chrome plating, bright gold anodization and BMX racing lines of my Mongoose.

The '70s were blending into the '80s, and the California BMX scene was blowing up. If I'd been a little older, with my own mode of transportation to the races, I would have dedicated every waking moment to BMX racing. My parents, on the other hand, saw little point in hauling a preteen all over Southern California to chase plastic trophies. But I did manage to catch a ride to a few races, and the competition bug found a perfect home inside my brain.

I earned my first money riding that Mongoose. After school each weekday and again on Sunday mornings I'd load a canvas paperboy bag with Thousand Oaks, California's News Chronicle, and deliver 70-something newspapers to people who mostly seemed angry to be getting the newspaper.

We built a lot of jumps. And we wheelied constantly. My Mongoose was the unwitting recipient of my clumsy mechanical education. It was my constant companion for five years.

And then I saw the Tour de France on TV. Until that point, skinny-tire road bikes had been for other people, not me. To me, road bikes seemed fragile and limiting, but these Tour de France riders did stuff on their bikes that gave me a different perspective. This European road-racing thing was kind of cool. So, on my 16th birthday, instead of swearing off human power for gasoline power, I bought a road bike. The childhood infatuation became a full-blown love affair.

Two years and three bikes later, I moved to Belgium with hopes of making bicycle racing my career. A year later, I signed my first professional cycling contract with a Dutch team.

If my relationship with bikes to that point had been infatuation and falling in love, becoming a pro signaled the start of a marriage of sorts. My bike and I spent all of our time together. If we weren't racing or grinding out endless training hours on the wind- and rain-swept roads of Belgium, we were tending to the mechanical needs of the bike and the physical preparedness of my body.

For the next eight years, we lapped the roads of Europe and North America, racing at least four events per week. We fought a lot. There were many days when the bike was willing but my body was weak and uncooperative. It was never my bike's fault, but we fought anyway.

When mountain bike racing became a more lucrative endeavor than road bike racing, we took our game to the dirt. The challenge of mountain biking breathed new life into our relationship. We had fun winning races, and got through the losses as best we could. But professional careers don't last forever. So, when we finally lost the flat-out speed and power it takes to be relevant on the international cycling stage, we stopped racing. And when we stopped racing, we stopped spending time together.

For the next 10 years, our relationship was cordial. I'd ride to work and back sometimes. I'd ride to the store or the bar. I'd ride around my neighborhood at night to clear my head. But mostly we were like an old married couple doing our best to avoid each other.

My bike gave me my first taste of freedom. It took me to Europe, where I learned languages and other cultures. It's why I got to rub elbows and tires with some of the most amazing athletes the world has ever seen. I wrote two books because of bikes. I became the editor of two bicycle magazines because of bikes. I met my wife because of bikes, and can thank bikes for nearly every friendship I've ever had.

A few years ago, I moved to the mountains of central Colorado, and rekindled my relationship with my bicycle. The professional power that I used to be able to put into each pedal stroke is long gone. The physical suffering, which tops the list of job requirements for a pro bike racer, isn't something I'm willing to subject myself to anymore. The word training isn't really part of our vernacular. And yet we're still pretty fast when we want to be.

It's complicated, but really not all that complicated—my bike has always been the love of my life, and always will be.

—*Originally appeared in* Mountain Gazette 197, *2022.*

35.
Into the Deep End
Written by Megan Michelson

Let's start with this honest truth: Swimming while naked feels downright glorious. The lustrous water silky against your bare skin. Nothing between you and nature's finest liquid. When you step out of the lake, or the river, or the ocean, there's no damp, constricting fabric clinging to you. It's just your flesh, drying quickly and effortlessly in the beaming sun. The whole experience feels like freedom, innocence, and beauty, wrapped into one juicy plunge.

Now that we've established the wondrous part of skinny-dipping, let's not forget the rest of it. The awkwardness. The embarrassment. The accidental flashing of body parts. I had run 14 miles on the Pacific Crest Trail with a male friend to reach the shores of Middle Velma Lake, smack in California's Desolation Wilderness along Lake Tahoe's west shore. Me: dirty, sweaty, tired. The lake: cool, refreshing, inviting. But I didn't have a swimsuit and I still had miles to run, so I didn't want to deal with a wet sports bra.

I told David I was going to find my own private spot to jump in, out of eyesight. He did the same. Except my zone wasn't very discreet from some neighboring backpackers, so I slipped out of my running clothes in a crouched position, hiding behind a too-small rock. Then I slid clumsily into a shallow wedge of the lake, keeping my body submerged in a mere foot of water to avoid striding in like Eve herself. It was not graceful. But once I was in deeper, I submerged my head, felt the water flush along my skin, and sensed a wave of stress drain from my body.

I grew up with a nature-loving, pot-smoking single mother who, much to my embarrassment, loved swimming in the nude. When I was a kid, she and I would go to the Yuba River, a stunning waterway near where I grew up in Northern California. We'd walk downstream until we were out of view, then jump into the loveliest swimming hole we could find, me in a one-piece swimsuit, her in nothing. This is a woman who didn't own a bra for decades and encouraged experimentation of all kinds. I had a blessed childhood, no doubt, but my mom's free-spirited nature somehow made me the most prude kid on the street, perennially ultra-modest and easily embarrassed by my own skin.

In my 20s and 30s, I'd go to hot springs in the Sierra with friends and be the only one in a swimsuit. I'd change under a towel in gym locker rooms. While on hut trips in the backcountry, I'd wear a swimsuit into the sauna. I was that girl. I blame my mother entirely. It's not that I was ashamed of my body; I just felt more comfortable clothed.

But now I'm a mother myself—my kids are 6 and 8—and I'm entering my 40s, the decade my mother found her most liberal nudity. Recently, I've found myself developing an uncharacteristically laissez faire approach to clothing. I'm not saying I walk around my backyard naked, but when I'm on a hike with my kids to an alpine lake and nobody else is around, it sure is nice if I don't have to haul out wet swimsuits. The question I've been asking myself lately is why have I been holding onto these garments—and this pressure to stay covered up—for so long?

So, this past summer, I challenged myself to give skinny-dipping a chance (when appropriate, of course). I wanted to see if it made a difference in my psyche or my connection to those around me or the natural world. I also decided to ask others who go in the nude why they do it and what it does for them. Maybe I'd find out that skinny-dipping is the answer to world peace and inner happiness.

Frog Lake is a precious alpine pool backed by a giant, imposing cliff. On a ridge above the lake sits a series of newly built backcountry huts, which require hiking 5 miles over a mountain pass to reach. It's a gorgeous spot, with very few people around. In mid-July, I hiked into the huts with my family, as well as three other families with young kids.

Our first day at the lake, I jumped in—wearing a swimsuit; it's weird that I have to qualify that—and swam across. On the other side, I scrambled out of the water and rested on a flat rock getting baked by the sun. The sun felt good, but I was chilled.

Day Two, I got up early with my daughter, Nora, and we went down to the water's edge. Her job was to scout my skinny-dip and make sure the coast was clear. I tossed my clothes onto a rock and hopped in, as liberated as a topless marcher at a Pride parade. The early-morning dunk woke me up better than Italian espresso, and I felt alive and recharged.

But in that split second as I was stepping out of the water, before I could reach my towel, one of my fellow hut dwellers rounded a corner, fishing rod in hand. My daughter shrieked in alarm. The fisherman looked over, concerned. Meanwhile, I was screeching and diving for the towel, like a naked Superman flying into home plate. That refreshed, alert feeling I'd had moments earlier was now replaced by total humiliation.

People have been skinny-dipping since the dawn of time. Back then, it was just called swimming. But the act has largely had a stigma of indecency for centuries. In 1449, a newspaper in Bath, England, reportedly wrote that "people were shamelessly stripping themselves of their swimming garments and revealing themselves to bystanders."

Still, it's been an underlying part of Western culture for generations. Benjamin Franklin, Huck Finn, Henry David Thoreau, and Walt Whitman swam in the nude. Artists like Thomas Eakins,

Charles Shannon, Norman Rockwell, and David Hockney painted naked swimmers. President John Quincy Adams—who's been called the founding father of skinny-dipping—used to wake up at four in the morning and swim naked in the Potomac River for exercise during his presidency in the 1820s.

The term "skinny-dipping" was coined in the 1940s, when advances in textile manufacturing made it possible to swim in a fabric that could get wet and dry quickly. From that point on, when you swam in just your skin, it was called skinny-dipping. In 1971, when now-Sen. Patrick Leahy was a state attorney in Vermont, he was challenged on the legality of skinny-dipping.

Leahy declared that in public or semi-public areas, nude bathing is not acceptable, and perpetrators should be asked to get clothed. (I think we can all agree on that.) On private land, he determined, or out of view of the public, the state has no interest in the matter, and swimmers should be left alone. And lastly, he wrote, "In secluded areas sometimes publicly used (rivers, swimming holes, etc.): If no member of the public is offended, no disorderly conduct has taken place."

Regardless of its legality, I recognize that skinny-dipping is a privileged, and perhaps self-righteous and obnoxious, activity. I am a white, size 6, able-bodied, cis-gender woman, which is to say I've had it pretty darn easy. "What is it with white people and being carefree and naked outdoors?" writes Jolie Varela, a citizen of the Tule River Yokut and Paiute Nations and founder of Indigenous Women Hike, a community of Indigenous women focused on reconnecting with their native lands. "Maybe something having to do with white bodies being the default for what belongs in the outdoors (or just everywhere) and/or their bodies are safer to be naked outdoors."

When *Outside* magazine posted an Instagram photo of two people hiking naked, Varela responded, "All white people ... Because y'all move around the world so freely that the next step is to do it naked."

I didn't want my skinny-dipping mission to step on anyone's toes. This was a matter between me and a lake far from anyone else.

A man named Fred (he asked not to have his last name included) has invited me to join him and a group of other naturists—a nice-sounding word for "nudists"—for pizza at an after-hours restaurant on Saturday night. In the nude. I cannot imagine a less appetizing food to eat naked than pizza.

Fred is a high school English teacher from Nevada and a nudist for going on 20 years. "I'd love to live in a world where clothing was the exception, but that's probably not going to happen," he says. Fred, who started a local naturists' group in his area, wrote an essay for his college English class on nudism in America. "I find it to be more relaxing swimming or sunbathing nude than with the restrictions of clothing," he wrote. "If more people would shed their clothes every once in a while, the world would become an easier place to live, less uptight and less violent." The classmate who presented after him said, "It's going to be really hard to follow the naked people."

I tell Fred I'm definitely not up for pizza in the buff, but swimming would be good. A few weeks later, he invites me to join his group at Secret Cove, a clothing-optional beach on the serene east shore of Lake Tahoe. Back in the day, Secret Cove was a quiet patch of sand where nude sunbathers were welcomed and everyone else stayed away.

But these days, the textiles—as nudists called clothed people—are moving in. Nearly half the beachgoers now are clothed. "If the textiles form enough complaints and we lose that beach, it'll be a sad day," Fred says.

Fred introduces me to a woman who's a part of his naturist group, a chatty, friendly lady named Susan. "When you remove your clothing, you also remove your judgment," Susan tells me over the phone. "It's about living an open life." Susan is 55, works for a payroll company, and has three kids. (One of them thinks her habit for nudism is very weird; the other two don't mind.)

When she says the word "clothing," she follows it with a low, guttural grunt: "Clothing...ugghh." Like the very thought of pants weighs her down. I'd called her to ask for some pointers: How do I swim in the nude without feeling so, um, awkward? "Have fun," she told me. "Surround yourself with good people. Or just pretend that nobody else is around."

In 2014, Susan's boyfriend invited her to a nudist resort in California. "That sounds different," she responded, but she agreed to check it out. When she got there, and started walking around without any clothes, she says it felt like coming home.

"I've had body-image issues my whole life. I've always been a heavyset girl, and I still don't like my body with clothes on," she told me. "Bathing-suit shopping was always the worst. I still buy T-shirts that are three times too big, just to hide my body. But take me to a nude beach and I just don't care."

Susan told me that when she's unclothed in the right settings, it feels like she's crossed into an alternate universe, one where people treat others with kindness and respect. "All the social pressures lift," she says. "Being outdoors, having the sun on your shoulders, you experience the environment as a whole. It enlightens your senses. It allows you to be the person you were meant to be."

For a minute, I consider joining Fred and Susan at Secret Cove. They seem welcoming and kind, and it would be a good crash course in skinny-dipping culture. But then I look up the Yelp and Tripadvisor reviews of the beach. "I would say 80% of the people were wearing swimsuits, also there were many families with kids on the beach," one person wrote. Another added, "Family oriented. Beach was packed." The third review, and final straw for me: "Great place for taking photos."

Yeah, no way. I thank Fred for the invite, but tell him I'm out. Fred wishes me well and offers this: "Don't expect to just dive into the deep end." Nude beaches may not be for me, but bodies of water that require a lengthy hike or run to reach and get me as far from others as possible—now we're talking.

In the 1980s, a guy named Michael Donnelly, who's now in his 70s and retired in Salem, Oregon, created a competition among his friends to see who could bag the most lakes in a summer. It was mostly a joke—a spoof on the idea of peak-bagging big summits—but they took it seriously enough that one summer, one of his friends swam in 68 different lakes to win the contest. "One year, I got 42, but normally I'd get 20-something lakes," Donnelly told me.

The rules of the contest were simple: You had to have full-body immersion, and you had to hike to reach the lake. "We count ponds as long as they're over your head," he says. Skinny-dipping is the preferred way to go—"Then you're not carrying around wet shorts," he says—as long as you're not disturbing anyone else.

He's still playing the game, by the way, counting his lakes. "We try to go to these hidden spots. To me, that's more of a pristine experience," Donnelly says. "It's incredibly peaceful and relaxing. You jump into the water and out of normal society."

I'm at Round Lake now, in late July with my mom, in a heavenly pocket of California known as the Sierra Buttes. The hike in took us a couple of miles, and there's no one else around. She doesn't flinch. Out of her clothes and seamlessly into the water. Now in her 70s, my mom is still a very strong swimmer, and still very comfortable in her own flesh. I follow her lead, cringing while disrobing, hiding body parts from the very woman who created them, then flop into the water like a gutless fish.

Maybe I put too much pressure on a silly naked swim. Honestly, how transformative could a lake plunge in your birthday suit really be?

Keon West, a professor of social psychology at Goldsmiths, University of London in England, spent more than a decade examining prejudice and discrimination. He says a lot of the research in that field was depressing and unpleasant, so he started looking for new topics that would be more fun and engaging. "Naturism seemed both under-researched and potentially interesting," West says. "I started taking part in many of the activities to facilitate that research and found them enjoyable."

West, who sunbathes naked in his backyard, according to Twitter, says both his personal experience and his scientific research found that participating in naturist activities can improve your body image, self-esteem, and overall life satisfaction. In other words, being naked more often can make you happier.

He used before-and-after studies, randomized controlled trials, and cross-sectional surveys, and found that communal nudity reduces our anxiety about how other people view our bodies and gives us more normal bodies to compare ourselves to, contrasting the unrealistic images we see in the media. I ask him if I can get the same benefits from swimming in the nude if I'm by myself, far from anyone. "I'm not sure how you'd get either of those benefits if you were always alone," he responds.

So, that's how I end up texting three close girlfriends to ask if they'd be willing to skinny dip with me. "Bring a towel, no swimsuit," I write. Shockingly, they all say yes (and respond with a lot of peach emojis). On a Monday evening after work in mid-August, we meet in a parking lot and hike to a quiet, tiny lake, belted by pine trees and granite walls.

On the hike, we swap funny stories about past skinny-dipping incidents. Like the time Kerstin went to Thanksgiving with her husband's family and all of them—uncles, aunts, cousins—jumped into the river naked. Or the time Brita took an ex-boyfriend skinny-dipping in a waterfall while on a hike, and he was very uptight. Or when Lindsay went on a fully naked camping trip with friends (except for the one guy who wore clothes the entire time) and they all jumped off a bridge naked.

At the lake, we yank off sweaty T-shirts and socks (plus everything else) and jump into the water unceremoniously, like it is no big deal. Which it isn't. These three women are supportive in just the right way, which is that nobody acts like we are naked. Just friends swimming in a scenic lake. Nothing to see here.

I float on my back in the middle of the lake, staring at the clouds overhead, and realize, *Ah, this is it.* That feeling I was looking for. I had been making such a big deal out of the antics of the swim—how self-conscious I felt, how embarrassed and unnatural—that I wasn't letting myself enjoy the experience of floating and being free, of being submersed in water in the purest, most invigorating way.

On the hike down, I ask Lindsay if she feels differently after the swim, and she shrugs and says she doesn't think so. But later, she sends me a message. "I've thought more about it," she writes. "I feel energized. I came away with a sense of thrill, even exhilaration. Still now, I feel content and happy. Just excited to be in a place, having done a thing, with people I care about. Just good energy."

Maybe that's it. We seek places in the world and communities to surround ourselves with where we can be our true selves. Spaces where we can worry less and love more. I can't tell you where to find those places or how to reach that point, exactly, but I can tell you this: Jumping into the deep end feels mighty good.

―*Originally appeared in* Mountain Gazette 198, *2022.*

36.
A Ramble in the City
Written by Miles Howard

The Mattapan Trolley is a vintage hulk of a streetcar that crawls through the woods and wetlands of Boston's southern limits like a great big orange beetle. It rumbles to a halt at Capen Street, where I disembark and find myself standing alone on a station platform surrounded by trees and sleepy homes.

It's one of those frigid, jet-black December mornings when every parked car has acquired a new glaze of frost on its windshield. The sun will start to appear in half an hour. I've got a daypack full of warm clothes, protein bars, bottled water, and Moleskin patches. My hiking boots are double-knotted, and the large Dunkin' Donuts coffee in my hand is rapidly losing its heat amid the freezing temperature. I'm ready for a long day of hiking, and the trailhead is close.

Leaving the platform behind, I click on my headlamp and turn down a short driveway to my left, striding toward a steel gate. From here, a root-festooned pathway burrows into the local woodlands and snakes past scrub and forgotten chain-link fences to a more established bike path and a colossal arched bridge over the Neponset River—Boston's southernmost waterway.

This river crossing marks the beginning of the Walking City Trail: a 25-mile hiking route that passes through more than 30 urban parks and forests to reach the Bunker Hill Monument tower at the city's north end. The trail was launched in the summer of 2022 to much intrigue from local media, city politicians, and, most of all, urban hikers, who have since explored and documented the trail.

A parka-clad figure on the other side of the bridge waves to me. It's Dan Brown, a seasoned ski photographer who's swapped the slopes for the streets of Boston. The two of us have met up on this austere winter morning because together we're going to thru-hike the Walking City Trail.

The mountains in New Hampshire and Vermont are iced up and sketchy. The holidays are straining our schedules. But goddamn it, we've been craving a rustic pilgrimage, the sort of hike that adds extra umami flavor to that ribeye at the day's end. So we've decided to test the backcountry model of epic hiking in a place where we don't usually think of hiking: a major city. And hiking the Walking City Trail in one concentrated push has been on my to-do list for a while. Because, you see, I'm the person who created it.

The trail took root during the first few months of the Covid-19 pandemic, when stay-at-home and interstate travel restrictions made it impossible for Greater Boston residents to escape to Green Mountain National Forest or the Maine Highlands for a little moss therapy. Stuck and stressed out, I took up wandering around parks and shaggier city conservation lands. When that got old, I started looking for scenically interesting ways to walk from one urban green space to another, utilizing elements like railroad overpasses, back alleys, and old staircases.

Before long, these park-to-park jaunts began to feel as immersive and tiring as going for a hike in the woods. Often they required packing the same supplies I would chuck into my car before traveling up north for a weekend of exposure in the boreal zone. But unlike backcountry hiking, an urban hike also presented unique outlets for decadence, in the form of trailside amenities like taquerías, breweries, corner stores, and—when you tire of trees and architecture—art galleries. And, best of all, when you decide to call it a day, you can hop on a train or bus. No car required!

In cities like San Francisco and Paris, residents have created trails that consist of preexisting park paths and street walks stitched together to yield a scenically immersive journey. The trails are not always physically blazed or signed. Instead, written trail directions and maps that live on a dedicated website are your navigational cornerstones.

When I read about these trails, intrigued by the idea of applying the backcountry-hiking mindset to a city environment, I realized that I wouldn't have to seek permission from city hall to create something similar. So I started scouting green spaces and "blazing" the Walking City Trail, which I named for Boston's old moniker as "America's Walking City." With a notebook and a GPS app, I spent the spring of 2021 finding the logical route for the trail—the way through Boston's parks that would take hikers through unique, visually arresting environments.

Once summer kicked off, I launched the trail website; within a month, photos with the hashtag #WalkingCityTrail were surfacing on Instagram and Twitter, and I was teaming up with city councilors to organize community hikes.

But how is an urban hike different than just taking a walk through the city? Is it the mileage? The rigor? The aesthetic qualities? These are the questions that hound urban trails. As I got busier leading 5- to 6-mile section hikes on the Walking City Trail, I would often argue that an urban hike prioritizes scenery over directness, with an intentional route and destination.

But I also wondered about the logical conclusion of that idea: What would it feel like to thru-hike the Walking City Trail? If packing for an urban hike can make it feel real—like a legitimate genre of hiking—then surely an urban thru-hike would have the same effect, but even stronger. And that's what led to meeting Dan on the Neponset River at dawn. It was time to put the Walking City Trail (and our soles) through the ultimate stress test. We were going for a ramble in the city.

We set off through a corridor of oak trees with the river chuckling by our side and refracting the inaugural rays of orange sunlight. The first leg of the Walking City Trail will take us through woolly woodlands in working-class residential neighborhoods—Mattapan and Hyde Park—before plunging us into more-sculpted green spaces like

Arnold Arboretum and Franklin Park—veritable forests in the city, where natural and man-made oddities await.

After the first 15 minutes, we're suddenly ascending over the river and out of the trees on a sloped footbridge that delivers us to Mattapan Square, where commuters are already immobilized in a river of brake lights. The clatter of skillets and the aroma of hash browns waft from the door of a nearby café as we march across the snarled road and continue down a quieter side street flanked by community gardens on one side and eye-catching murals depicting young farmers on the other.

In barely a mile, the vibe of our hike has gone from naturalistic to urban, and the pendulum is already swinging back: Straight up ahead of us, there's a denser, spookier clump of trees surrounded by a stone wall—as if the city wanted to keep some flesh-ripping beast contained.

This is the Edgewater Greenway, a pocket of conservation land that Boston will soon develop into a formalized multiuse trail. But the residents of Mattapan have already taken things into their own hands. As Dan and I pass through a crumbly opening in the wall, we find ourselves wandering down a faint yet unmistakable forest trail that visitors have broken in over the years. This is a "desire path"— the physical result of people wandering where they want, trail or no trail—and as we make our way over fallen trees and through prickly vines worthy of *Apocalypse Now*, we start glimpsing single-family homes and triple-decker apartments through the branches.

It's a striking duality. Despite its small size, crossing through the Edgewater Greenway is an immersive and gnarly green-space passage— often more of a bushwhack than a hike. And yet it's balanced with visual reminders that we're never far from other human beings. In the city, you can be out of your element and in your community at once.

This is affirmed half an hour later as Dan and I emerge from a dripping-wet railroad underpass and cross into Hyde Park. "MILES?" a voice suddenly calls out. We whip around and are greeted by the sight of Ruthzee Louijeune, a Boston city councilor. She's dressed in a bathrobe and just happened to be taking out her recycling when we sauntered by her door.

We trade introductions, giddy from the serendipity of crossing paths on such a frosty morning before most people have left for work. (It's 7:30 a.m.) Brandishing his camera, Dan suggests a photo to commemorate the moment. Ruthzee dashes back inside for a quick wardrobe change and reemerges in a sweatshirt with the names of Boston neighborhoods emblazoned in gold letters.

For the next mile, we wander past countless houses and apartments like Ruthzee's whose front yards are miniature ecosystems of their own—boasting specimens like gnomes and corn stalks. We also spot several bright-green lawn signs that read, "SAVE CRANE LEDGE WOODS." It's the perfect table setting for our next green space, which we find at the end of a hilltop residential street.

Crane Ledge Woods, a privately owned 24-acre forest, offers one of the finest views in Boston. From the top of the titular ledge, you can gaze out over rows of sleepy homes. But the future of Crane Ledge Woods looks terminal. The landowner, a local church, is on the verge of selling the property to a Texas-based developer with a plan to destroy the woods and build townhouses on the land.

While Boston needs a hell of a lot more affordable housing, giving up a substantial chunk of the city canopy feels like a regressive price to pay. (Notably, Boston's wealthier neighborhoods are not being asked to sacrifice their own green spaces for the cause.) But for now, the Crane Ledge Woods are still here.

As we stand at the entrance, sizing up the NO TRESPASSING sign, Dan looks at me and says, "Are you thinking what I'm thinking?" The implication is clear: *We're going through here.* While the official Walking City Trail route skirts around these woods, so as not to get any hikers in trouble for trespassing, I'm ready to take the blame and be the fall guy should any church administrators hassle us.

We enter the trees and crunch our way through leaves and briar branches, reaching the lookout ledge and savoring the view before continuing to the other side of the forest on a battered access road that's littered with garbage, tattered clothes, and even a few shopping carts.

There's only so much an urban landowner can do to stop people from utilizing green spaces, whether the most frequent visitors are taking a city hike, aimlessly poking around, or—in some cases—looking for a place to sleep. The harsher realities of urban life can be as much a feature of urban hiking as the trees, paths, and public artwork.

In a time of staggering wealth inequality, parks become refuges for people who are unhoused. When you pass through a green space where encampments have sprung up, your exploratory impulse is tempered by a compulsion to pass through discreetly, respecting what little privacy the occupants still have.

But sometimes the act of reaching a green space can cross the line from awkward to dangerous. Most American cities were designed for cars first and foremost, and people regularly die trying to cross the expressways where vehicles accelerate to reckless speeds. Dan and I have to sprint across one of these highly active roads to enter the Stony Brook Reservation forest.

There's no crosswalk anywhere nearby. You simply wait for a window in traffic, commit, and run as fast as you can. Our nerves are still firing as we hike along Stony Brook itself, a stream that runs through the reservation before disappearing into a pipe and continuing for almost 20 miles beneath Boston.

Turtle Pond, the source of Stony Brook, is the crown jewel of the woodland. In the summer you'll find teenagers on the docks, flirting and splashing around in the water, without a care in the world for land-use rules or snapping turtles.

It's late morning now and we've been so immersed in Boston's neighborhoods and lesser-known green spaces that when we exit the Stony Brook Reservation at the top of Bellevue Hill—the highest point in Boston, at 325 feet above sea level—the distant sight of skyscrapers downtown startles us.

It's the first of several downtown vistas along the Walking City Trail: a slow fade from landscapes that are wooded and more visually suburban to a classic cityscape. Those high-rises are our destination. Soon, we'll be hiking among them. But we still have a lot of miles left.

As we descend Bellevue Hill into Roslindale Village and switch gears to summit Peters Hill—the pinnacle of the Arnold Arboretum tree sanctuary—the mileage starts to become palpable. Unlike backcountry hiking, where bumpy and varied terrain works many muscles, walking on mostly flat surfaces activates the same muscles in your lower limbs over and over.

Aching, paces slowing, we stop at Third Cliff Bakery, a corner joint that boasts some of the crispiest and most buttery croissants in the city. I opt for chocolate; Dan goes for the Thanksgiving special, replete with turkey, caramelized shallots, fig, tamarind-rosemary sauce, and Maldon salt.

This gooey reverie fuels our passage through Franklin Park, where we climb twisting stone steps and encounter rusted bear cages from a former zoo. But as we leave the park an hour later, passing more murals and triple-deckers in Jamaica Plain—my neighborhood!—the physiological reality of hiking 14 city miles becomes unignorable. Our feet are screaming at us to stop.

And so, upon reaching the blue expanse of Jamaica Pond, where little sailboats are milling around, we call it a day and plan to rendezvous here the next morning to finish our hike.

We allow ourselves to sleep in until 7 a.m. I'm absolutely dreading the moment when my soles make contact with the hardwood floor. To my relief, no ligaments seem to have been strained. At 8 a.m., Dan texts me to let me know that he's on the commuter rail, heading for the pond.

I treat myself to a more bougie cortado this morning, then hop on the local bus; within half an hour, the two of us are back at it, hiking along the northeast shores of Jamaica Pond before crossing a parkway and descending stone stairs into the shadowy wetlands of Olmsted Park.

If there's one historic figure who did more than most to cultivate the idea of urban hiking, it's Frederick Law Olmsted—the 19th-century landscape architect who created Central Park, the U.S. Capitol Grounds, and Boston's Emerald Necklace linear park system. Unlike standalone city parks, the green spaces that comprise Olmsted's Emerald Necklace form a long green artery through multiple Boston neighborhoods—a park-to-park pathway through the heart of a city.

A former journalist and a fierce critic of Southern slavery, Olmsted was inspired by the idea of the park as a restorative space where people of all walks could be seen coming together. And so, when mapping the Walking City Trail, I knew I had to pay homage to the maestro and include some sections of Olmsted's masterwork.

Olmsted Park, which features a reed-bedecked boardwalk and a seasonal waterfall, is one of the Emerald Necklace's most enchanting charms. And unlike yesterday, Dan and I are sharing the trail with fellow travelers: joggers, dog walkers, and a lone conference caller yammering about low-fee index funds as she power-walks past us.

The scenic delights keep on coming. We climb steeplechase stairs to the top of Mission Hill, where a lone coyote darting into some bushes distracts us from the view of Boston Harbor and its islands. In the shadow of Fenway Park, we traverse rose gardens, sculpture gardens, and a briny marsh before putting our feet up at a donut shop, where I procure a frosting-stuffed cruller the size of a shake weight.

Then there's the Charles River Esplanade, a sun-splashed riverside park that serves as our gateway to the core of downtown Boston and its popular parks and shopping districts. It occurs to me as we hike through throngs of people in the Boston Public Garden and on the aromatic streets of Chinatown that we must look really weird. We're dressed like hikers. Our tights are spattered with mud and leaves. Our hair is getting progressively wild. And yet here we are, making use of the cityscape with everyone else.

Is this what it felt like to clomp into the uncharted woods centuries ago as the neighboring farmers shook their heads? Historically, we've often thought of cities as places of commerce. But the city is also a venue for exploration, discovery, and reverence. To hike a city is to discover how its natural and man-made elements transition from one to the next, in the same way you might savor the journey from deciduous woods to the alpine zone.

As Dan and I cross the Charles River on a set of walkways built atop the river locks—which are liable to start moving if a ship comes through!—the quieter and non-industrialized waters of the Neponset River feel a million miles away. Once again, our feet bear the physical burden for that distance as we push ourselves to the top of Bunker Hill, where the monument tower looms over the city.

Here, clinching mile 25 of the Walking City Trail and completing our thru-hike, we're too wasted to climb the tower's 294 stairs. We plunk down on a bench, staring up at the monument with equal parts wonder and exhaustion. Yes, we're missing the view from the top. But then our entire thru-hike has been one long view of this city.

Maybe the question of whether one can truly go hiking in a city is something that each of us has to decide in our minds and hearts. All I can say is this: After parting ways with Dan and limping home, I'm greeted with a toe blister upon peeling off my socks. The beef bulgogi that I pick up for dinner might be the most succulent I've ever tasted. And when my head meets the pillow and I begin the transition into slumber, my mind is briefly wandering through the prickly vines of the Edgewater Greenway again.

It's a memory *and* an unspoken promise to return there one day. If that's not the outcome of a hike, then I've been doing it wrong.

—*Originally appeared in* Mountain Gazette 199, *2023.*

37.
Palm Springs Shralpinism
Written by Jeremy Jones

The plan is loose and nimble, an "It would be so cool to ride that someday" mission. We are making our way toward the highest peak in Death Valley. From there, we will keep the trend south toward Palm Springs and beyond. Strict agendas are dangerous in the mountains. Weather and new information gained will keep our plans agile and fluid. It was in this line of thinking that our plan and crew came together fewer than 12 hours ago.

The atmospheric river in the sky that started flowing in December and hardly subsided has finally started to slow down. We are almost into April, and our itch for stretching our legs on some bigger vert in the bigger mountains south needs to be scratched. However, a more complicated snowpack than any one of us cares to tinker with has our compass set to the obscure. We are chasing snow on a wing and a prayer.

It is no surprise that I am crammed into a truck with Jeff Dostie, Brennan Lagasse, and Ming Poon next to me—three Sierra lifers who all could write their own version of *The Art of Shralpinism*. You can find Jeff breaking trail every morning at 5:30 a.m. and getting in 4,000 to 6,000 vertical feet of skiing before work at 9:30 a.m. Brennan is a college professor who will ski 200 days this year and is on year five of skiing every month of the year. Ming is a photographer with whom I frequently "work," but most of the time the camera stays in the bag and we just ride. All are devout members of the Church of the Seventh-Day Recreationalist. They are lovers of pow, of course, but are equally okay with those "love of sports" outings that lead to Class V bushwhacking and scratching down "less than optimal" surfaces. More than a mission crew, these are my friends.

An avalanche that took out our main road south has us driving farther east into Nevada. The mind surfing is incredible, enhanced by large, puffy, broken clouds. Hour after hour the wonderful problems (too many mountains) of varying size and shape pass by our windows. The empty vistas are broken up by an occasional one bar, one gas station town that time has forgotten.

Ernie's Desert Oasis is our last stop for supplies before dropping down into Death Valley. Walking the sand dunes 152 feet below sea level in my bare feet, surrounded by vast valleys and grand peaks, I feel as if I am in the Mad Max version of an Alaska Range void of ice and snow. This lack of snow on the peaks is concerning to anyone out of the land of white for the first time in months. I see new vistas glowing in the evening light, so stark and different in color, fauna, and rock; they leave me satisfied regardless of snow quality.

Taking in the scale of these mountains, I am confident we will get in some much-needed large-vertical days to whip me into High Sierra Strong shape. The question is, will it be an "uphill both ways" scenario where we are making only a few turns, then forced to walk downhill?

Death Valley Surf Club

"Every once in a while, a squirrel gets a nut."

We roll the dice and get boxcars (double sixes). Of the 7,500 feet of climbing and riding, close to 7,000 of it is desert powder. However, it is the bristlecone pines that steal the show. To be among the oldest living organisms on the planet from sunup to sundown is otherworldly. Judging from the horizontal rime ice coating on the leeward side of the trees, it is clear this place sees some serious weather in line with that of the Arctic regions. We feel none of that today and take a prolonged picnic on the peak while marveling at the countless other incredible lines to the south. We seriously consider hitting pause on the rest of our loose agenda, but we simply cannot work out the logistics of getting to those areas without a camp. This is just example No. 2,364 of the wonderful problem: Scratch one line off the list only to add five more. This one carries particular weight knowing how rare the formula for getting these exact conditions is. I take one last look before turning my back on the sea of possibilities. It feels like I am saying goodbye to a loved one I will never see again.

Once strapped in, all past thoughts vanish instantly. My focus turns to the incredible opportunity that lies ahead. Rolling off the top of the peak 11,000 feet off the valley floor and floating on powder through perfectly spaced living dinosaurs for thousands of feet is an experience I will never forget. We end the run with a long surf gully. I lead a party wave with the plan of "stop when the snow turns for the worse," but that never seems to come. So I drain it another 1,000 feet toward a closeout gully. There is plenty of fruit left on the vine, but we are on the opposite side of the mountain from our truck. Jeff sets the skin track toward the beer. We top out in the evening light, run into a lone snowshoer from Connecticut, fill his empty water bottle, give him a few bars, and continue the bristlecone powder party. We eventually hit the snow-covered road and glide on 6 inches of snow all the way back to the truck, which sits perfectly at the edge of the snow line. Driving through Death Valley, we see our peak in the twilight. Is it a mirage? Did it really happen? It looks like there is just a dab of snow on the summit—hardly worth the effort—but this is due to the massive vertical relief: That little dab is three or four thousand feet of winter.

Our southern trend continues toward Palm Springs, where our next line awaits, home to the biggest vertical drop in the lower 48. Specifically, we aim to ride the north-facing couloir that starts in the high alpine and pierces the mountain in one continuous, direct chute to the desert 11,000 feet below. Without seeing a picture of this line, I am skeptical. Is Palm Springs really the home of the biggest line in the country? How far can the snow really go down? Our plan is to take the Palm Springs Aerial Tramway, the world's largest rotating tram car, 6,000 feet up and hike the rest of the way. There is still debate over if we take it to the valley floor or ride the line until the snow turns for the worse and hike back up the chute. Reports of a Class V desert thrash, mega avalanche debris, and heavily policed private land have us leaning toward hiking back up and out, but we will bring our shoes and leave the option open. Ultimately the decision will come down to which we deem safest. There has been record snowfall, so we do not want to linger in the funnel of the mountain any longer than necessary.

It's all a crapshoot at this point. After today's score, we are playing with house money. Sleep when you're dead; send while you can!

Palm Springs Shralpinism

"Where am I?" Dusty and groggy, I wake in the vacant lot we stumbled into a few hours ago. The hint of a new day is in the eastern sky. The wind is cranking and I hide behind a small wind block I'd made by the rear tire with bags to hide from the blowing dust. The first thing I see is windmills, lots of them. At the end of my sleeping bag is one of the biggest mountains I have ever seen, with a never-ending white snake that pierces the center of it. It seems so out of place; my mind struggles with the scale and reality.

The fact that we are taking the tram to start our day allows us to sit down for our first real meal in two days. We are in a strip mall on the edge of Palm Springs and surrounded by yogis and power-walking retirees. We look like dirty aliens in our snow gear, but two college kids on their way to an all-day pool party recognize us.

"What are you doing here?"

"Snowboarding."

"Where?"

"Up there."

"It's rideable?"

"See that big chute covered in snow? Look up there this afternoon and you can watch us ride it."

Coffee kicks in, we kit up and walk the steps to the tram, excited for our day of Palm Springs Shralpinism.

"The backcountry is closed," says the security guard at the entrance. "It's too dangerous."

We are told this three more times before entering the tram. We nod our heads in agreement each time and keep moving toward the tram, summoning our best "These aren't the droids you're looking for" faces.

The tram is not only the longest tram in North America, but also seems to be the steepest. We ascend through a multitude of ecosystems ranging from low-lying desert to proper high alpine akin to the High Sierra. Think Baja into Joshua Tree, the Coast Mountains into the Sierra foothills, and finally high alpine. It is not just the vegetation and geology, but the animals. The change and diversity is crazy!

Getting off the tram, we run into two snowboarders dejected after getting turned around by a ranger. They point out the direction of the ranger station. We put our heads down and follow a snow-covered hiking loop in the other direction from our objective before dipping off the trail behind a massive old-growth pine to get into our touring gear. Any anxiety about a bust fades away and we settle into the landscape—spectacular, towering old growth, granite boulders, and these beautiful snow-covered fields of pow, chutes, wind lips, and cliffs. We stumble into a fresh skin track that appears to be on our same covert operation and follow it to the peak.

On the summit plateau, thick, weathered pines are covered in fresh rime ice. I stumble among them in disbelief; again, it feels like I am in the Arctic. We must be on the heels of a recent weather event. But the ice is so thick; is this a season's worth of weather? Does it not get warm enough to melt?

Topping out, we run into our phantom skinner. Her name is Andy. She has a plan to meet her boyfriend, Mike, who has been hiking from the desert floor since 2:30 a.m., then ski the line back down to the desert where he started. But her plan is broken. He got caught up in a labyrinth of gullies, Class V bushwhacking, and never-ending avy debris. He has been moving for nine hours but still has 4,000 feet of climbing to reach us on top.

This confirms our concerns about taking the line to the desert. Andy wants to wait up top, but we convince her to join us. The top of the line is wind-spanked, steep, airy, and technical. After some monkeying around, we can see the guts of the line, and it is pool-table smooth. Drop a basketball here and it will be in the desert 11,000 feet below in minutes. Think two Jackson Holes and a KT-22 stacked on top of each other, or three Snowbirds and some change.

Andy drops in first and makes smooth work of the big-mountain conditions. Brennan and Jeff follow, doing the same until they are ants and out of my view.

I opt for an alternate entry to a different chute that will meet back up to the main one a few thousand feet below. The top is spined and technical. The first turn is about as real as it gets. I ask Ming if I can borrow his ax. He is doing a lower entry and will not need it. Ming is surprised, because I have grown accustomed to using my pole except for the extreme scenarios. This is one of those scenarios.

Dropping in, I am happy I have it. I am in a no-fall zone and there is rime ice hidden under the 6 inches of chalky windbuff powder. This is a scenario I have never encountered. And it freaks me out. I am forced to stay on my toe edge and "ride my ax"—a rare move I do not think I have had to do since riding Shangri-La in the Himalayas, and Denali before that. Himalayas, Denali, Palm Springs! After gingerly picking my way down the first hundred feet, I commit to my first heel-side turn.

The slough erupts around me and I am in a free-fall—not out of control, but I certainly can't stop. The slough subsides a little, and a rock fin pops out several inches where a second before it had been all snow. I am forced to boardslide it and grind it lightly with my hip and edge, but thankfully I keep from cartwheeling. Regaining control, I am now in the upper chute and no longer fighting gravity. My turns grow and I am mowing vertical on the smooth, edge-able chalk. This is shralpinism at its finest—a stark contrast to the glitz, flamingos, and partiers below us grooving to a poolside DJ with exotic drinks in their hand.

We regroup and descend the endless ramp, stopping only when our legs say, "No more." Good islands of safety are in order, considering the lower we get, the bigger the gun barrel we are at the end of. If any rock or snow above us dislodges, it will be going 100 mph down the gut of this line that we will be calling home for the next five hours.

We finally come across Mike. His spirits are high and he seems unfazed by the morning epic. We start getting ready to climb with him, but he insists we ride the next 1,000 vertical feet because it is so smooth and perfect.

The chute tightens and corkscrews and the warm chalk provides some of the best turns of the day. Coming out of a choke, we see the debris Mike mentioned. It fills the tight valley with earth-shaping amounts of debris that is only a few days old. To keep descending seems ominous and brutal. We happily put our crampons on and start the long climb back out. Once again, the scale is deceiving, and it feels like we are hardly moving even though the footing is decent. We try to catch Mike and Andy to help with breaking trail, but, impressively, they never stop. Our effort pales in comparison to Mike's, but we are all worked from 4,200 feet of front-pointing and cross-stepping in our crampons. Flamingos and fruit drinks, please!

Topping out, we regroup in a grove of trees, trying to hide from the biting wind. It is double-puffy cold. Mike's effort is extraordinary.

"How you feeling?" I ask him.

"Stupid," he says with a smile and a twinkle in his eyes. "And ready for a beer and a bed."

We celebrate the effort with a perfect refrozen-corn run for 2,000 feet with our new friends in the waning twilight, finally gliding to a stop at the pathway that leads to the tram. There are kids sledding, grandmas watching, and a couple kissing. It is a bit of a hard landing getting into the tram line filled with tourists, like we fell through a portal into the line for Walley World.

The ride down, however, is one I will never forget. It is now nighttime, and as we descend into the dark on the spinning tram, the operator stokes the crowd while slipping in facts about how unique the land is and the animals that live there: "Sixty-three avian species—hawks, eagles, and owls. Fourteen different mammals, including mountain lions, lynx, and bears."

Soon we are cheering at every tower swing and singing and laughing our way to the base. It is the liveliest tram I have ever been on and it makes me wonder why we take ourselves too seriously. Peacocking in our fancy suits, flexing on the day's agenda—why are these sightseers so jovial and us mountain riders so stoic?

Walking out of the building where we'd passed the security guard 12 hours earlier, Ming declares, "The backcountry is now open."

LA Extreme

It starts to take shape as you ascend a winding two-lane road upward through a canyon lined with big, steep flanks that ascend thousands of vertical feet to high-alpine mountain peaks. Old ski cabins with hand-carved signs tucked among older pines line the road until we pull into the parking lot. Lars—who is wearing a sparkling sports coat, a button-down shirt, and a tie, with slick-backed hair, sunglasses, and ski boots—guides us into a parking spot. "No need to park close to that car," he says. "We've got plenty of room. Space it out."

I compliment his outfit. "I always dress nice on Sundays," Lars says. "It's the day we pray to the Church of Mount Baldy."

"Your church, it sure is beautiful," I respond.

"It's paradise," he adds. "On the good days, we surf, ski, *and* play golf. Bobby is expecting you. Sara has your tickets."

Bobby is his brother, Sara his cousin. Everyone is related. Baldy is a family business and minimalistic: one bathroom, a gift shop, a ticket office, an admin building, three lifts, and a mountaintop restaurant/bar.

It's a loose lift line made up of a wide array of ethnicities, skill levels, outfits, and equipment, and the queue slowly deforms into one big hangout as we wait for opening. Everyone talks to everyone. It is now 9:30 a.m. and we have been waiting for a half hour.

"When does it open?"

"It's Baldy. We never really know, but usually by 10."

No one complains. There is no sense of the entitlement or posturing that is often found at the mega resorts. One person, Snow Dawg, becomes a quick friend. He is an older Black snowboarder who drives mega dump trucks and has been riding for 30 years. His kit is a throwback to the '90s, but tight and polished. His board, a 20-year-old Forum, is in mint condition; he recently haggled a guy down from $300 to $150. He is a wealth of wisdom and wit and keeps us all entertained and cracking up.

The lift opens and we meander onto it. It is a double chair that is 50 years old. The chairs are so close together that it is easy to hold a conversation with the people on the chairs in front of and behind you. Snow Dawg keeps the knowledge flowing from the chair behind me. "It's a small town, big mountain," he says. "The chair goes slow for a reason: so you can look around."

Twenty minutes later, we get off the lift and can now see our surroundings: huge peaks on either side of us, stretched far and wide. One more slow double and we are above tree line. We immediately spot a rock-laden peak laced with steep chutes a layer back.

We slide off the groomer and into the backcountry toward the untracked peak. The snow is the best powder of the trip. We enjoy some turns before traversing to the saddle, switch to crampons, and hike our way to the peak. Chucking snowballs and small rocks onto the face, it is clear the wind has blown the snow off the top, leaving some proper ice. Jeff is our test monkey and eases his way onto the face, making sure his edges will hold. Not sure if Jeff has felt ice all winter, but it doesn't show. His edges hold, and he makes a few controlled turns that quickly stretch into GS turns. Brennan and Ming follow a similar dance, and, judging from Ming's screams of joy, it is quite good!

I opt for an alternate route with a tight chute. The texture tells me the top is firm, so I skittle a few direction changes aimed at what I surmise is a texture change to pow. My assumption is right and I gently release the governor pin for the first time of the trip. The shackles come off. I let gravity take me. I am flying. Uncontrolled screams of joy break the silence as I glide to a stop.

What the fuck was that? Am I outside of Los Angeles right now?

A short skin track placed purposely near a few junipers by Brennan and we are back at the saddle and changing over on the side of the groomer. Two older women in ancient gear ski up to us: "Was that you guys? That was fun to watch." This starts a conversation and we learn that they have skied every Sunday together for 40 years. They are so kind and happy, and they ski away making beautiful turns on old skinny skis and rear-entry boots.

Looking across to the other side of the resort, we spot a 2,000-foot chute and it quickly becomes our next objective. We take the lone groomer of the resort over to the other slow double. Crampons go back on and we are hiking a corniced ridge that gives us more new vistas. The topography is starting to make sense. The setup could not be more perfect for sidecountry hiking. We need more time! Halfway up the ridge, we get a good view of a serious face that drops off the back side. It is complex, steep, and large, far bigger than any face in our home Tahoe area and as impressive as anything I have seen in the Sierra. Is this the face I once saw in *Powder* magazine in the '80s? It was so beautiful in the magazine then that it still has a steady hold on my memory 40 years later.

Our next line is exposed, steep, and serious by anyone's standards. More rocks and snow are thrown onto the slope and bounce instead of stick. The top section is a no-fall zone and I still have some mental scar tissue from yesterday's unexpected ice, so I carefully down-climb in my crampons to feel the first 5 feet of the slope.

Strapping in, I feel the nervous energy running through my veins and focus on my breath to ease the tension. These are feelings rarely experienced in the Sierra, let alone outside LA! I quell my nerves with some deep breathing, keep one pole for an ax, and ease over the ridge onto the steep face with my eyes burning a hole in the exit choke. It is critical to beat my slough to the choke so I can get off the exposure. The slough is minimal, the snow is perfect for this type of terrain, and on and on I go before pulling up under some rocks halfway down the line.

"Snow's super edge-able and smooth," I call up. "Send it!"

One by one, Jeff, Brennan, and Ming make good work of the upper face. We regroup under a rock and take a moment to celebrate where we are: "Can you believe this?" We are still in serious terrain, so the pause is short. We ride the bottom half together into a gully, hoping it will put us back to the parking lot. The corn is soft and we hoot and holler, bouncing and slashing our way through the natural halfpipe.

Toward the bottom, we link into a cat road and I pull up behind a 12-year-old skier and follow him down. He is flying off the side hits and making nice turns. The cat track takes us perfectly to the parking lot and I start talking to the kid. Baldy is all he knows. He loves to ski. He is a ripper, but doesn't know it. I tell him he is really good and I urge him to check out the junior freeride comps.

Back at the truck, we pull out the chairs, dry our gear, and enjoy a beer with the locals. I am in shock. Who would have known the soul of riding and the home of the best sidecountry in the U.S. lies on the outskirts of LA? It feels like we've gone on an exotic journey to the Andes or Bolivia, but seven hours later we pull into home sunburned and malnourished, with heavy legs and lightened minds.

We gave the mountains every last step and they returned the favor with memories that will last a lifetime. Our minds are expanded along with our hit list. New vistas open new opportunities, perspectives, and friendships. You don't know if you don't go! Why did it take me so long to scratch that itch?

—*Originally appeared in* Mountain Gazette 200, *2023.*

38.
The Last Hike to King Lake
Written by Jason Harmon

I was afraid to open the package when it arrived. An ominous star image was emblazoned on the front, with the words "Sheriff's Dept., Grand County, Colorado." The return-address label read, "Rodney P. Johnson, Sheriff."

Slowly, I slid it open. Inside, I found my blue Guatemalan-made fanny pack along with my Arkansas driver's license. I'd lost them the previous week while hiking and fly-fishing in Colorado.

I thought the pack and license forever gone and was surprised to see them again, but that shock was nothing compared to the accompanying letter.

"Dear Mr. Harmon: Enclosed is the denim belt pack which you reported lost. It was brought to the Sheriff's Office by an unknown party....The items included are all that were retrieved with the belt pack. Less than 1 ounce of marijuana, the possession of which is illegal in the state of Colorado, was in the pack and was removed and destroyed. We have no way of knowing whether this belonged to you. Very yours truly, Patricia A. Agnew, Investigations."

By the time I finished reading the letter, I was trembling a little but grateful that I'd narrowly escaped legal troubles and retrieved my license. What luck!

Even though I lost a little Mexican marijuana—along with $75 cash that wasn't mentioned, but I assume was my "get out of jail" fee—I've never misplaced the memory of that Colorado adventure. I kept those recollections, along with the sheriff's now-faded letter and a handful of photos, because I never want to forget the last hike to King Lake with my friend Jeff Gann.

Long and Winding Road

The road to King Lake is rough and rocky, and only the best four-wheel-drive vehicles should attempt the trek. I wish I'd known that before I drove my 1978 Volkswagen van many miles to the trailhead, located at the top of a dangerous switchback track that winds uphill toward the treeless, towering Continental Divide.

No tow truck can reach your stranded vehicle there in the Indian Peaks Wilderness Area. No flat tires can be changed on that steep mountain slope, and there are no turnarounds for a dozen miles. Once you start driving uphill, you can't stop until you reach the top, and the road is so narrow that you cannot even pass an oncoming vehicle.

The treacherous road didn't scare us; ignorant of its dangers, we were young, foolhardy, and determined to reach King Lake no matter the effort required. My friend Jeff Gann, my longtime girlfriend Caelin, and my yellow Labrador dog Cassidy all traveled nearly 20 hours from our Arkansas home to reach the Rocky Mountains. I don't know why or how I selected King Lake and the 76,000-acre wilderness around it for our destination. I'd never been there or known anyone who had made the trek. There were no feature stories in fly-fishing magazines, no glossy photos of fish taken from the lake's alpine waters. The only motivation I had was to ensure my friend Jeff enjoyed life as fully as possible, because, at just 25 years old, his days were already numbered.

The year before, in 1993, I got the sad call no one wants to receive. Jeff reached out from his home in Kansas City, Missouri, where he was studying at the Kansas City Art Institute. He didn't sound happy, and his voice quivered as he oddly explained—in third person—that "a friend had contracted HIV" while exploring that city's promiscuous homosexual culture. I asked Jeff directly if he had HIV, and he gingerly admitted it was true.

Bad news burns moments in time onto our memories like branding irons—deep scorch marks that linger and last. Nearly 30 years later, I still recall placing the phone receiver back into its cradle and wishing that life wasn't as terrible and unforgiving. I remember the phone's color (1970s yellowish plastic) and the wood paneling that covered the walls of the room where I stood, unwilling to believe the bad news despite the undeniable phone confession.

That day, I determined to do what I could to help Jeff live the best life possible with his remaining years, because HIV/AIDS was a near-certain death sentence in 1993. I invited Jeff to move in with my girlfriend and me in our Fayetteville, Arkansas, rental house. There, Jeff could live rent-free and focus on being healthy and happy, and I could spend time with my old friend before he died.

When I'd been a teenage runaway during the summer of 1986, Jeff's mother allowed me to live in their home. She fed me and ensured I was safe and no longer sleeping alone in a tent in the woods up the hill from their house. I wanted to show Jeff the same kindness his mother had offered me. He agreed and moved to Arkansas.

Jeff and I became close friends the moment we met in homeroom class on the first day of school in 1985. Earlier that same year, my parents had moved our family from Springfield, Missouri, to Evansville, Indiana, and I was a stranger in a strange land. After growing up in the same town with the same friends my entire life, I suddenly lived in another state where I had no friends. Such drastic changes are never good for a 16-year-old trying to navigate high school and teenage struggles.

Jeff and I grew close because we were mutual misfits adrift in the modern world. We were both born during the Vietnam War, with Cold War threats of Russian missiles raining nuclear hell on America any day. Add to that the movies we watched—*Blade Runner* and Pink Floyd's The Wall , among other dystopian depictions—and the books we read—Orwell's *1984* was set the year before Jeff and I met)—and it's clear the mid-1980s was a scary place for everyone, especially two lower-middle-class Midwestern teenagers. We clung to each other for camaraderie, but also as allies against a terrifying world.

That day in homeroom class, I knew immediately Jeff was different than the other kids. He was winter-sky pale and beanpole thin, with long, dark bangs that he combed downward over his eyes. He also wore a gray trench coat festooned with both Eurythmics and U2 pins on the lapel. Jeff's hairstyle and clothes were not socially acceptable in the mid-'80s, even if such symbols seem hardly radical in today's American culture, where people are mostly free to express their identities. As an aspiring punk rocker, I dressed differently too. I wore black Army boots and ripped jeans that I'd written on with pen and marker, and a sloppy T-shirt with a long-sleeved flannel shirt wrapped around my waist, like a flag declaring that I was "alternative."

That was the code word of the day, "alternative," an umbrella term that incorporated a variety of social misfits from goths to punk rockers and anyone in between. If it didn't fit the socially acceptable norms of the early '80s, it could be called alternative, even if there was a vast chasm between the ideas. For example, when buying music in the '80s, a person who wanted selections beyond Top 40 bands perused the small offerings marked simply "alternative." Those included music as disparate as Bauhaus (English art-rock that Jeff adored) and the hardcore, fast-driving guitar and drums of punk bands that I enjoyed. There wasn't much alternative music that even made it to the record-store shelf, and all genres were crammed together regardless of the musicians or musical style. We took what we could get in isolated Evansville and were happy for the music, even if options were few.

Much like alternative music, alternative sexual expression also was repressed in the 1980s, especially among teenagers who were forced into conformity by intolerant peers. Deviation from the one socially acceptable orientation—heterosexuality, for both men and women—was well hidden underground. Our alternative clique recognized three: straight, gay, and bisexual. As individuals, we often wondered aloud which of those categories reflected ourselves, and we openly discussed the benefits and drawbacks of each sexuality. There was never discussion about gender, although boys sometimes wore makeup and girls wore tank tops and spiked bracelets and presented as "butch." None of us truly cared who the others fucked or loved, but that didn't free us from the social stigma of publicly declaring our sexuality. There was a commitment that came with claiming a sexual identity that went deeper than clothing style and friend group. Coming out as gay or straight or bisexual meant that was your identity from that moment onward, not a mere sexual experiment. Stone writing was a big commitment for teenagers who can change beliefs and personas daily.

Jeff's homosexuality was not a belief or an experiment, but he didn't openly adopt it as his public identity until he was in college and 22 years old. Until then, Jeff had had a well-crafted public heterosexual identity (although largely sexless) that found him falling for tall, thin women with powerful personalities and fine fashion sense. Ultimately, those were the women Jeff wanted to emulate rather than date. He wasn't a transexual in a homosexual body—Jeff was all gay male—but he admired the elegance some women carry and craved those qualities even before he could express those desires publicly.

I was not sexually attracted to Jeff, although I believe we shared what Walt Whitman famously called "the manly love of men." Some mistake that poetic phrase for Walt's own homosexual expression of male friendship, but I always understood it to mean that males can love each other with or without sexual attraction. My bond with Jeff was manly love for him, not love for men. I do not know if Jeff was sexually or emotionally attracted to me, but he never expressed it openly to me or others. However, a friend once remarked that "Jeff thinks you hung the moon, Jason." I had similar respect for Jeff as a fellow human being and friend, but we never shared romance.

Naturally, all of Jeff's friends suspected he was gay before he came out, but we never pressured him to make a public commitment. We all loved him and wanted his expression to be organic rather than forced, so we didn't ask questions and he didn't offer details. At a gathering in 1990, a random partygoer casually declared Jeff to be gay in front of dozens of people, and although none of them cared about his homosexuality, Jeff aggressively refuted the observation. "But you're wearing makeup," the partygoer insisted as proof. An embarrassed Jeff quickly left the room to avoid further public exposure. That was only five years before AIDS killed Jeff, and it reveals that he was uncomfortable embracing his sexuality even as the 1990s brought more social acceptance and therefore freedom for Jeff and other homosexuals.

Jeff's refusal to admit his sexuality came to a head one night when I took him to a strip club, shortly before he came out. A mutual friend was a dancer there, and she invited us to have free drinks. Jeff was reluctant to go, even with free alcohol offered, but he agreed on one condition: He would wear a ball cap to blend into the crowd.

Jeff never wore hats because they ruined his perfectly styled hair, and choosing to don a cap to blend into the redneck strip-bar crowd was a huge personal sacrifice. With the hat, Jeff felt he could hide his true sexuality like some gay men use marriage and child-rearing with women. Lucky for Jeff, there were no lap dances offered, but lots of free booze, and the night's masquerade was successful. I suspect the charade forced Jeff's hand, and when he finally came out in person a year later, my response was the same as everyone else's: "Finally!" His family and friends all loved Jeff, and none rejected his unsurprising declaration.

As Jeff and I grew older, and our musical and cultural influences diverged, we grew closer rather than distant. Each person influenced the other musically and in lifestyles. Jeff migrated to dark-growling, grungy bands like Skinny Puppy and Jane's Addiction, while I discovered the Grateful Dead. (My sister once asked me as a teen what old punk rockers become. I instantly replied, "Hippies!") By the early 1990s, Jeff had expanded his musical taste to include the Dead, and he and I saw at least half a dozen shows with Jerry Garcia playing guitar before Jeff died.

After Jeff graduated with an art degree, he enrolled in the Kansas City Art Institute to pursue his dream of attending a well-known art school. Meanwhile, I attended the University of Arkansas and enjoyed life in the Ozark Mountains, where I learned to fly-fish. In 1991, I traveled to Colorado to backpack in Rocky Mountain National Park and sample alpine lake fly-fishing. I was stunned by the experience and determined to return as often as possible to explore Colorado, and a few years later I took Jeff on his first—and last—hike to King Lake.

High-Mountain Hike

Located in the Arapaho & Roosevelt National Forests, the trailhead to King Lake begins where the rocky road ends. My Volkswagen's engine smelled like hot oil after climbing thousands of feet in elevation up toward the Continental Divide. Although inanimate, the van was likely as glad to be parked and done with the uphill journey as I was to be done with that dangerous, white-knuckle drive. Sheer stone cliffs rose on the left, while equally steep walls dropped off into oblivion to the right, all without guardrails to prevent vehicles from plummeting to certain doom below.

That rough road was just the beginning of the journey. Next, we needed to hike more than 5 miles to reach our campsite at King Lake, where I hoped we'd find fishing and fun for three days. We packed our bags, grabbed our gear, and headed uphill with Cassidy-dog leading the way, white-tipped tail ever wagging. The trail follows the track of a now-forgotten narrow-gauge railroad bed up the mountain and across the Continental Divide. Past the tree line, at nearly 11,000 feet above sea level, there is no shade among the rocks. And the same death-bringing drop-offs that shadowed our drive up the mountain followed us all the way to King Lake. At one point, the trail crossed decrepit train trestles that shook and shimmied with each step, and we took turns carefully crossing the chasm below on those antiquated pine timbers.

Halfway up the mountain, we could see the high ridge of the Continental Divide ahead. That humbling sight didn't make up for the strenuous hike at high altitude with scarce oxygen for weary hikers. I turned to see Jeff sweating and huffing, looking down at the ground as he struggled to traverse the trail. "How's it going?" I asked jokingly, knowing that he was neither built for such strain nor a happy hiker.

"Fuck you," Jeff declared as he angrily met my gaze with sweat running into his eyes. I still laugh to this day about his crass reply. Far from insulting, it was a funny and appropriate response there in the hot sun, hiking high above the green valley below. Unfazed by the outburst, I grinned, and we hiked onward to King Lake.

King Lake Camping

We learned two important facts about King Lake when we arrived: First, it was exactly as lovely as I'd imagined. Nestled in a glacial cirque at 11,431 feet above sea level, the lake was cradled by granite-boulder slopes and year-round snowpack on two sides. An adventurous skier even slid down the slope while we watched, amazed that someone would travel all that distance to reach the summit only to ski for about 30 seconds on the tiny section of snow that remained. *Skiing must be as important to that person as fly-fishing is to me*, I thought. The lake's other shore offered easy access to the water, which looked like a flat, silver disc set into a field of gray rock and white snow patches, like a strange obsidian mirror gleaming at the sun.

Besides the lake's beauty, we also learned far too late that a road offered easy access to King Lake, with a parking lot perched just above on the nearby mountain ridge. When Jeff and my girlfriend realized the lake could've been reached without a grueling uphill hike, my companions weren't too happy with my adventure plan. Their dissatisfaction vanished after we'd set up camp, and I explained that we could reach the nearby roadway access only by driving a full day around the mountains. Lucky for me, the alpine meadow's beauty replaced their frustration.

Below the lake, a meadow full of wildflowers and soft grasses rose between the boulders and offered a perfect place to set up tents. The lake's outflow meandered through the meadow, creating small falls and plunge pools as it flowed downhill to become the headwaters of the South Fork of Middle Boulder Creek. Well after sunset, perched high atop the rugged spine of North America, we could see the lights of Boulder shining eastward onto the Front Range. Mortality didn't matter there under the stars, and Jeff's illness didn't seem to affect his health or spirits that night on the mountainside. Those might have been the last truly healthy days of his short life, although we didn't know then that Jeff would be dead the next year.

The next two days, I learned how to fish King Lake while Jeff and my girlfriend hiked and explored the area with Cassidy-dog. She loved the water, like all Labradors, and could always be found running in the stream or lying in a soothing cold-water pool. Jeff always wanted a dog, but never had one as a kid. Cassidy was his adopted friend; she slept on his bed at night and loved retrieving tennis balls endlessly for him. As an angler, I was happy they distracted Cassidy from jumping in the lake and spooking the fish, a skill matched only by her ball playing.

By the second day at King Lake, I still hadn't caught a fish. The hike to our campsite had consumed my efforts the previous day, and I didn't even wet a line. However, I witnessed a hopeful sight as I walked to the water's edge, fly rod in hand: I saw more trout rising than I thought possible. In fact, the entire lake was covered with concentric circles, each formed by a cutthroat trout as it sipped insects from the surface. Stunned by the thousands of circles dotting the entire lake, my awe was echoed when I heard another angler shout from across the water, "I've never seen anything like it!"

The cutthroat trout in King Lake are not native fish. The only native Colorado trout is the greenback cutthroat, which was rare and threatened with extinction until recently. Luckily, the efforts of fisheries biologists and supportive anglers have increased greenback trout numbers and restored them to much of their original Colorado habitat. The King Lake cutthroats are not native, but still wonderful to see and catch in that high-altitude habitat, where they are stocked by dropping them from the sky with fixed-wing aircraft. The fish in King Lake are not large. That's because the lake's altitude keeps the water frozen much of the year, and the sluggish fish don't eat much or grow quickly. That lack of food most of the year is why the cutthroat feed nearly nonstop when ice is off the lake's surface. Still, heavy feeding didn't make fishing easy. It would take me another full day to learn how to catch a fish from King Lake.

The bright sun and clear water worked against my trout-catching efforts, and the flies I'd brought were not appealing to the fish. I tried dry flies, including bright attractors that I thought no fish could resist, especially given the thousands of surface-feeding trout I'd seen the day before. No luck. Then I tried streamers, which always caught even the most selective trout. Again, no luck. Finally, I tied on a yellow-bodied, pheasant-feathered soft-hackle fly.

The fish liked a little color in their food. They didn't want to feed on top of the water, but just below the lake's surface. The thousands of rippling rings I'd seen the day before were caused by sub-surface feeding on emerging insects, not eating bugs floating on top. I had to present the correct fly and simultaneously place it in the proper part of the lake to lure fish into biting. King Lake taught me many lessons about fishing that trip that I carried home and to other waters.

Our final night at King Lake, Jeff and I hiked together as high above the lake as possible before daylight faded. There we perched atop a granite boulder to smoke a special treat: opium! I produced a small foil package I'd secreted away in my fanny pack and carefully peeled back the edge to expose a gooey ball of stinky black "opium." Little did we know it wasn't opium we were about to smoke, but a terrible fake product concocted from perfume and incense, then sold to unsuspecting young hippies like us as opium. We didn't know the difference, and we eagerly spread the tar-like stinkiness on a bowl of bad, brown Mexican weed. We puffed and passed and coughed and talked about how high we were. In reality, we were probably more intoxicated from oxygen deprivation at 11,000 feet than from the bogus opium we'd inhaled.

After we finished the bowl, we talked about anything but the future. It seemed taboo to break the moment's spell, so we focused on sunset's last light rippling across lake water rather than where we would be next week, let alone next year. Despite our small-talk approach to enjoying the moment, I knew that our adventure to King Lake could be our last, but I kept morbid thoughts to myself. The truth was undeniable that our trip was Jeff's "Make-a-Wish" journey, but we both ignored the facts that night under the stars. Instead, we laughed and enjoyed our "opium" high before heading down the mountain back toward camp.

By the third day camping at King Lake, I'd caught about a dozen cutthroat trout. Our food ran short, so we packed up and hiked downhill to the waiting Volkswagen van. The entire hike was difficult and we were exhausted, but the journey was worth the exertion.

We stayed in Colorado a few more days and explored Rocky Mountain National Park and the upper Colorado River. Our last day in the state, we stopped along the river, and I fished while Jeff and my girlfriend ate lunch. That's where I lost my fanny pack, which contained my driver's license, the last $75 to my name, and our tiny weed stash. When I discovered the bag missing, we were nearly an hour down the road at a gas station.

We backtracked and spent hours retracing my steps along the river and beating willow thickets surrounding beaver ponds, without luck. Desperate to retrieve my money and license, I reported the loss to the sheriff's office before giving up and heading home. We'd spent a little time on the mountain, as the song says, and, bummed to be broke and budless, we drove back to Arkansas.

Jeff's Final Journey

The backpacking adventure to King Lake was Jeff's final hike. It also was the last meaningful journey he and I ever enjoyed together. Although we'd been to Dead shows and the 1992 Rainbow Gathering, and had hiked, camped, and explored a half-dozen states—and turned high school friendship into a lifelong bond—we struggled to remain close as Jeff's illness closed in and his difficulties increased.

One night about 3 a.m., I woke up to police pounding the door. Jeff was in jail, arrested for "cruising the town park for sex buddies." I went to bail my friend out of jail and got good and harassed by a cop whose real name was Officer Slaughter. The bail-bond company asked for my Volkswagen van's title to cover Jeff's bail, and I balked. The bond fellow called the cops over and said, "He's being difficult." Next thing I know, Officer Slaughter is forcing me like a drill sergeant to stand at attention and asking why my eyes are so red.

"It's 4 a.m. and I woke from a dead sleep to get my friend out of jail," I replied. I didn't want to share a cell with Jeff, and I complied with all stupid commands, feeling humiliated.

After I was sufficiently demeaned by the officer, he grew bored of the mental torture and we arranged a bond agreement without my VW title involved. Jeff appeared disheveled, cussing and angry at his misfortune, but apologetic that I'd been roused to his rescue. That afternoon, I'd been scheduled to take the GRE test for graduate-school admissions. With only three hours of sleep, I did poorly and blamed Jeff directly and bitterly. That wasn't the last time we argued as roommates and friends. I'd offered Jeff free rent to ease his economic burden a bit while he tried to stay healthy and fight the AIDS virus, but he still needed extra cash. My girlfriend was a waitress at The Grill restaurant in Fayetteville. She was able to get Jeff hired as a waiter. Jeff worked as his health allowed, but still borrowed money from my girlfriend to drink and have fun at the gay bar. By the spring of 1995, he'd borrowed hundreds of dollars without repaying a penny. My girlfriend complained privately about lending Jeff money he didn't repay, and I confronted him angrily. That was a mistake I regret to this day, because Jeff soon moved back to Indiana. Sadly, we never had time to repair the rift, because his mind and body failed shortly thereafter.

Years later, I wrote to Jeff's mother about my money-talk regret and explained that I wished I'd never concerned myself with a few hundred dollars in the face of losing my friendship just before Jeff lost his life. She wrote back simply, "Thanks for trying to teach Jeff to be responsible with money." I appreciated her exoneration, but still carry the guilt. Today, I would laugh at such a small debt and focus on enjoying our friendship, but that lesson came only from years of reflection and regret about the loss.

Fayetteville had a progressive approach to treating HIV and AIDS. Jeff found a good doctor at the local clinic to monitor his health and give advice on living longer with the disease. No smoking. No bad diet. No unsafe sex, to keep others from contracting the virus. Jeff followed only the final rule, and he suffered physically from cigarettes and junk food. His body didn't receive the care necessary to fight the illness, and he felt worse with each passing day. Shortly after we'd argued about money, I found him packing his belongings into his Ford Festiva. "I need to go home and be with my mother," Jeff said through tears. I cried too and hugged my old friend, and we said goodbye. I considered Jeff to be the brother I never had, but our friendship could not heal him and save his life.

Later that same year, I visited Jeff at his mother's house in Evansville, but the man I met that day was not the same person I'd hugged as he left Fayetteville months before. Rather than engaging and talkative, Jeff was stoic and distant as he walked slowly to the front porch and sat beside me on the metal swing. The medicines he took for AIDS complications had fogged his brain, and Jeff's slow movements matched his brain capacity and slurred speech. Strange warts had grown on his face, symptomatic of his body's failing immune system. The man who was once vain to a fault—who cared more about how hiking boots looked than how they functioned on the trail—would've hated the sad sight of his mirror image by August 1995.

The Volkswagen van we'd driven to King Lake was parked on the street, and Cassidy-dog roamed nearby. Jeff always loved that dog, and tirelessly spent endless hours throwing the spit-covered tennis ball for her to retrieve. That day at his mother's house, Jeff barely noticed Cassidy as she nudged his hand with her wet nose for a pet. He was too sick and unable to enjoy life; even the simple act of petting his old friend Cassidy-dog was too much mental and physical exertion. Despite his distance, I told Jeff about visiting the East Coast, seeing the sunrise over the ocean at Acadia National Park in Maine. How we ate steamed clams at Singing Beach in Massachusetts and swam the clearwater pools of New Hampshire's Kancamagus River. No amount of coaxing generated interaction from Jeff, however. His brain seemed incapable of even casual conversation. After a half-hour visit, it was clear that the Jeff who'd hiked to the top of the world with me the previous year was gone, even though his body remained. I embraced him one last time, loaded up the dog, and drove away through tears, knowing that my old friend would never return.

Jeff didn't live to see the New Year. By December, he was in a hospital bed surrounded by friends and family. Jeff was never a healthy man, always a little too skinny, and he had few reserves to fight AIDS. He'd also contracted toxoplasmosis, and his brain and body couldn't compete. Today, most people with AIDS do not die, thanks to a potent combination of lifesaving drugs. Good for those people and the people who love them. Unfortunately, Jeff missed those treatments by about six months. His mother appealed for early access before FDA approval for widespread use of the drug cocktail, but her desperate plea was refused and Jeff died.

Jeff's father was chief of police in Evansville, and distraught by his son's illness. Before Jeff died, a steady line of uniformed officers filed through his hospital room to honor their boss's son. Even FBI agents arrived to show their respects to their colleague's ailing child. I don't know if Jeff was aware of the colorful cop parade, but he would've been honored and thought it was funny that a pot-loving freak like him would get such attention and respect from uniformed police officers.

When I got the news that Jeff was dead, I was at The Grill, where my girlfriend had worked with him just the previous year. Standing in the busy restaurant with the phone pressed tight to my ear, I listened with tears forming as our friend Sarah Wolf explained that Jeff had died the previous night and that the funeral was upcoming. Even though I wanted to attend, I had no money to travel. Worse yet, the VW van broke down and I had no transportation. If it weren't midwinter, I would have hitchhiked to Indiana. With so much distance and no resources, I could not make the journey to Jeff's funeral, a necessary choice that I regret to this day.

He's Gone. Nothin's Gonna Bring Him Back

At just 27 years old, Jeff was in good company as a young dead artist. That dangerous age is known for taking many lives, including those of Janis Joplin, Jim Morrison, Jimi Hendrix and even Pigpen, a keyboard player for the Grateful Dead. Jeff was not always a happy human, and he shared depression and disillusionment with those famed artists too.

I've now lived nearly three decades longer than Jeff, which is three times as long as our original friendship from 1985 to 1995. I often wonder how he would view the modern world if he'd survived, because my own perspective is dismal after circling the sun nearly 30 more times. I know Jeff didn't enjoy living every day, but the artist and adventurer within him craved the experience of existence and the search for beauty and meaning in life. If reality was science fiction, and I had a machine that could exchange my life for Jeff's, I would gladly give every remaining day I have on this planet to allow Jeff to enjoy a life he never lived.

Yet, like most time travelers, Jeff might find himself in an unfamiliar and unpleasant world. Jeff missed the entire social media and internet revolution because he died at its inception, which is a mixed blessing. Jeff never used a cell phone, sent a text, or even had an email address. He never owned an iPod, never streamed music or bootlegged a movie file. Perhaps a resurrected Jeff would adapt quickly, however. Always social even before social media, Jeff loved to gossip and titter, especially on the telephone. He loved fashion, wore makeup, and fussed endlessly about his hair (which he called his "coif"). And Jeff was enamored with certain Hollywood celebrities and political Democrats. (His hatred for Trump would be immeasurable.) Those interests would've been fostered by Twitter and Instagram, but the apps would've fed both Jeff's narcissism and his insecurities. If alive today, Jeff might discover the modern world is a difficult struggle to navigate and remain unhappy, even with technological wizardry and greater social connections.

I like to picture Jeff happily married to a man, we'll call him "Phillip," who works in academia while Jeff paints pictures of their three rescue dogs. Maybe we'd talk on the phone when birthday times came around each year. He'd tell me about his latest painting or their newest puppy. I'd describe my garden flowers and cats and I'd smile, knowing that Jeff is living his best life. Those fantasies are best left to science fiction, although it's nice to imagine our possible pasts as years pass by.

Today, loneliness makes me think about Jeff more than ever. I'm now twice as old as Jeff was when he died, and no happier than when he left this world. As life progresses, it's difficult to make better friends than those we made as teenagers. Most people have fewer friends with every passing year. My life is no different. Although I've endured many tragic losses since Jeff died—even Cassidy-dog has been in the ground more than 20 years—and no loss was easy, no death altered my life more than Jeff's, in part because he was a unique human whose life entwined with mine at a vulnerable and formative time in our youth. Only rarely do people replace those losses. After almost 30 years, I'm still waiting. Jeff's grave is difficult to find in the crowded Evansville cemetery where he was buried, but Sarah showed me the headstone in 2004. She and I were headed to see the remnants of the Grateful Dead perform the next day, and we stopped by the graveyard to say hello. Silently, we stood for a few minutes as we stared down at the simple stone, depicting a female in flowing robes. "He should be at the show with us, goddamn it," I said through slow-falling tears. That night at the concert, we danced extra hard for Jeff because he couldn't dance with us.

In 2013, I again spent time at Jeff's grave, while visiting his mother and other old Indiana friends. Alone and armed with a guitar that day, I sat on the cold winter ground and leaned against his gravestone. Endless tears flowed as I struggled to sing and play for three hours. I smoked a fat joint and told a story or two about good times together, but I know that only the passing birds heard my words. Jeff is gone and "nothin's gonna bring him back," as the song says. And, like our last hike to King Lake, today only wonderful memories remain of that friendship we once shared among rocky ridges, high above the world, along Colorado's unforgettable Continental Divide.

—*Originally appeared in* Mountain Gazette 200, *2023.*

39.
Kitzbuehel
Written by Peter Kray

In Denmark scientists used carbon dating on a ski discovered in Greenland in 1997 to reveal that the single board was at least 1,000 years old. They said the 85-centimeter plank, made from larch, was a common tool for winter travel used by the Norsemen who in 980 A.D. somehow first crossed the cold open ocean. Older skis have been found in Mongolia, Norway, Finland and Sweden. There are Chinese cave paintings of hunters on skis thought to be more than 2,000 years old. The ski predates Christ, and in some regions, even the wheel.

But the modern birthplace of the sport is Kitzbuehel, where the Hahnenkamm, alpine skiing's most famous roller coaster, is run every year. Begun in 1931, the race down the steep white throat of the Streifhas only ever been interrupted by drought or war. The entire World Cup was built around the drama of the Mausefalle, and the shudder when you first drop down that face like a man falling by the window.

When the Frenchman asked me to watch "The Race" with him, I felt as if there were offerings I should bring or old clothes I should wear. As if he were inviting me to Mecca. We had talked about starting a magazine together, and had become friends in the little pleasures we took in the particulars of travel—a glass of wine with lunch in Italy, or the quality of German beer. I remember how his face lit up when they gave us the Mercedes Kompressor at the rental desk in Munich because they didn't have the car we had reserved. On the Autobahn he kept pushing it faster whenever the speed limit signs above the road were clear.

"*Ahh*," he smiled. "*I have a mee-stress now.*"

He had the face of a sunburned badger, like one of those retired athletes on the sideline watching the score. He had a big strong nose, a shaggy head of pepper hair and sleepy blue eyes that lit up when it was his turn to lead the conversation, which he adored.

He said, "*T-e long-eng is too Ameri-can,*" when I told him about the story I wanted to tell. "*You pee-pull all-ways talk about what isnt t'ere.*"

The adrenaline of gravity was still on our faces like coffee with Schnapps from skiing all afternoon. We drank yellow glasses of cold Pilsener at the hotel outside of Oberndorf and decided we would make a movie about the World Cup season.

"*We weel call it t-e Alpine Cir-cus,*" Jean-Marc said with boozy authority. "*It wheel show what we fee-yul.*"

The highlight would be of the Hahnenkamm: behind the scenes with the coaches pacing in long parkas and foreshadowing shots of the slope like an icy slide straight to oblivion; the Austrian soldiers grooming the course with crampons on so they don't fall off the edge of the earth. And the orange fencing down the Streif like a luge to the first gate covered with the "yellow line" from the piss of fear.

By the time the racers reach the first gate they are going 70 miles per hour. The name of each winner, the flag of his country and the year he won is painted on the gondolas. Buddy Werner, 1959, was the only American for more than 40 years. So when we thought we would follow three racers for our movie, I insisted one be an American—Daron Rahlves or Bode Miller. Jean-Marc wanted one to be French, and of course, an Austrian, like Maier.

"But the French are no good."

His thick face flushed. He looked around the room.

"*Swiss?*"

"They're fading. It would be better if we could find an Italian."

"*Italian?!*" Jean-Marc exclaimed, and looked at his big dark hands. He had given up smoking only weeks before. "*Merde.*"

The crowds filled the streets. The bars are open all night, and more than 100,000 people took the bright red trains up from the cities, from the farms with their gray, tall uber-Abner bumpkin hats, red and white painted faces and cases of Zipfer biere. Most of them didn't even bother to get a room, staying warm on the beer and the gluhwein as whole families, mom, dad and the kids all got drunk together.

But they were good drunks, so we hardly saw any fighting. We would film that too, how skiing was their national pastime and their birthright in the cold speed, the crosses on the peaks and the endless road of snow. We would film the finish lines and high speed crashes where the racers are into the nets like splaying, unfortunate fish. And in the starting house where it's the cold and the nerves at the same time and there is always the idea of an ocean somewhere far below.

We would make gods out of wind and wine and the history of candy-coated towns with blue walls and warm windows, a beautiful eternity forever lost in the perfect faces of passing women, and that sound of our heels clicking on the cobblestone.

"Austria is t-e heart t-at's all-ways beat-ing!" the Frenchman said, and pounded his fist against his chest. *"Eet is a love song now."*

The next day we stopped at the top of the gondola where there is a small museum with posters and photos and a restaurant with big glass windows that looked toward the valley where the racers were all sitting by the fire. It was the first day of training and there were half-eaten plates of sausage and bread, half-empty bowls of cereal, little espressos that went untouched and songs that kept starting and stopping. From a few tables away we could smell their fear.

"I would say 'good luck,'" the Frenchman said. *"But t-ey would not hear."*

"The training's even harder," Prince Hubertus von Hohenlohe told us when we went looking for former racers to interview. "Because you still have to ski the course and there's nothing to win, or lose."

Von Hohenlohe was a Mexican-Austrian prince and part-time rock star. He had thick black sunglasses and a Mexican flag on the back of the black parka he wore. His beautiful blonde girlfriend was as fine as fresh snow. Each turn of her head revealed another discovery of her white smooth-skin, and she held a cigarette as if it were breathing on its own.

"Can I light that for you?"

Von Hohenlohe said the organizers might as well canvas the mental hospitals to try and find skiers to forerun the course—to "set the line" down the frozen groomed face for the racers to follow. He told us about being on the World Cup and the last time he raced at Kitzbuehel. The two skiers he was traveling with were a Swiss who had skied for eight campaigns and was thinking of retiring, and an African from Senegal.

"What do you think is cheaper?" the Swiss racer asked Hubertus. "The hotel in Wengen, or the hospital in Kitzbuehel?"

"But the downhiller from Senegal did come," Hubertus smiled. It was a flashbulb smile. "He didn't know enough to be scared."

He said they were like pirates off the train, with their bags, their bright coats and the bottle of wine they shared. They stopped at every bar. It took them seven hours to make it to the hotel. But that couldn't stop the morning, and on the gondola they hardly spoke a word. Hubertus said he was curious to notice how his friend was getting so pale. "It was a transformation, really. He did not look well."

They stood against the fence to watch the training runs, catching their breath as the first racers came by, dropping away like marbles. And as the Senegalese kept getting paler he suddenly turned to von Hohenlohe and demanded, "Do you believe in God?"

"Of course," von Hohenlohe replied. "I am a Christian."

Then the next racer came, with the battered fabric and desperate scratch of skis as he disappeared down the Streif, on his way to the stark sudden drop of the Mausefalle, where he would have to fight with all his body to resist the forces of gravity and velocity trying to pull him sideways off the hill.

He flew like they all do, like an awkward reluctant bird toward the steep face of the Steilhang. Into some certain disaster or glory waiting far below.

The Senegalese was white as a ghost. He asked von Hohenlohe, "But does God believe in you?"

—*Originally appeared in* Mountain Gazette 182, *2011.*

40.
The Driving Lesson
Written by Adam Howard

When we left Gunnison, Colorado, on June 10, 1997, there were some knowns and some unknowns about our several-week trek to Anchorage, Alaska. We knew the mode of transportation: a 1971 VW Campmobile named Victoria (after the soaring 1969 Kinks song: "From the West to the East/ From the rich to the poor"). I knew, but my passengers (3-year-old border collie named Coors and master Pat) did not know that the radial weave on the rear tires was starting to show through. But I had two spares just in case the Cassiar Highway did its worst. I was nominally aware that the right tail light was mostly but not entirely on the fritz, the locks didn't work, and, given the vacuum-advance braking system, that when the motor cut out, we were reduced to about 30% stopping power. But we all knew we wouldn't be going very fast to begin with.

We knew we had three joints—enough to get us to the Canadian border and no more—$1,000 cash, a Marlin 30-30, two mountain bikes with no suspension, tons of fishing gear, a wooden sea kayak, and various other possessions stuffed into a 40-horsepower vehicle. We had a maintenance journal and an oil-soiled spiral-bound copy of John Muir's *How to Keep Your Volkswagen Alive: A Manual of Step-by-Step Procedures for the Compleat Idiot*. I knew we'd need that in 5 miles or 5,000. We had a loose timeline, no credit cards, and no cell phones, and our only commitment was to get to Talkeetna, Alaska, to catch a

411

bush plane to Papa Bear Lake, where we'd survey a 10-acre plot that our outdoorsman landlord had picked up sight unseen. He'd paid us $1,000 cash to locate its corners.

What we didn't know was that one of our good friends, Randy, had put what would be a fourth joint in the ashtray, which he certainly thought we'd be thrilled to find. It's about four hours to Vernal, Utah, from this part of Colorado. And it was in Vernal that a police officer knew that I hadn't signaled properly at the stoplight at the corner of routes 40 and 191. This officer also knew we were dumb kids.

"Mind if we do a routine search of your vehicle?" he asked, leaning fully on Vicky, both elbows on the door. "No, I guess not," I responded, thinking those three joints were well hidden in the denim pocket of the jean upholstery my fiancée had sewn special for the trip.

We got out, he got in, he opened the ashtray, and we were kneeling in handcuffs beside Highway 191 in less than a minute, more officers and dogs swarming, Coors barking. Good girl. "You'd better show us where the rest of the drugs are, boys." Pat conceded the location of said joints, which I didn't know had moved to his sock. "What's this cash all about? This gun?"

Somehow the conversation turned to fishing and hunting and camping and travel, and while Officer Routine Search didn't exactly let us off, he did actually let us go. "You need to call the judge on Friday and explain this ticket."

I remember an unsettled sleep that night in Flaming Gorge before driving the following day without incident to Jackson, Wyoming, then on to Missoula, Montana, where we'd type up guilty pleas in the library at the U before heading north to Glacier National Park and driving Going-to-the-Sun Road.

In the end, I remember remarking that after that whole trip, from Gunnison to Anchorage to San Clemente, California, where I'd intern at Powder magazine, back to Gunnison and then finally to Vermont, we'd gotten searched more times than we'd paid for camping. That ratio was a bit of a coming-of-age epiphany, which I committed to memory then.

More than a quarter century later, that coming of age sometimes feels more like getting old, depending on my mindset. There are those old-man powder days for me, and for Vicky the mornings when the air density is just right it's like EPO in the old Solex 30 PICT 2 carburetor and she runs like a rally car and I can still drive her that way. Both are getting rarer year to year. These fleeting moments are just that, but, more than the feeling of exhilaration, there's something almost gentle about our relationship. I still have her and she still has me.

Vicky came into my life as part of a no-cash deal in the autumn of 1995. She'd belonged to a friend of a friend and was left for dead in Powderhorn, Colorado, at the top of Nine Mile Hill on the way out to Lake City. I traded an operational 1986 Volkswagen Golf and got this van and a Husqvarna 51 chainsaw. No drugs changed hands. I towed Vicky (not her official name yet) back to town behind my 1969 F-100 firewood truck, driven by a drifter called Canadian Jim who could cut Douglas fir like a son of a bitch.

Fortunately, there was a fantastic VW shop behind the junkyard east of town on Route 50, called Mountain Metric. Tony Cooper had a nice little spread there on Tomichi Creek, and it was a liberal redneck's dream. Old air-cooled VWs everywhere, willows for shade, and Tenderfoot Mountain keeping watch over it all. Tony was always willing to trade grunt labor, and he helped me get Vicky going in return for general carpentry, a cord of wood, and a few bucks here and there.

That summer, my girlfriend and I drove it to Vermont with our two dogs and a giant by the name of Big. By Nebraska, Big was learning Victoria's secrets and how to behave among the driving public. The secret wave among air-cooled-Volkswagen drivers is simply the peace sign. Wave only at Volksies with round headlights: Beetles, Buses, Fastbacks, and the like. Do not wave at Vanagons unless they wave first. Yes, I see the irony of this logic now.

Also, at that time people would chat you up at the gas station: "I used to have one of these." Or they'd relate some epic adventure they once went on, or the Dead shows they'd seen, and on and on. One common refrain was something to the effect of "I wish I'd never sold it." "Couldn't tell you what I did with the money, but it wasn't worth it." Even at 22 years old, I resigned myself to growing old with Vicky. I never wanted to wonder where she'd be or how long ago those adventures were. And so I didn't. But, in keeping her alive, I've had to accept a few things about our aging.

I suppose the first thing is that growing old can suck. It's also expensive. I can't keep her up the way I like. The paint job my childhood friend put on Vicky over 10 days that summer of '96, while we were in Vermont for a quick visit before our senior year at Western State College, has long since faded. Sap buckets have been riveted over body parts so Vicky can pass Vermont's onerous inspection law. 2021, Vicky's 50th birthday, was always going to be the year that I totally restored her for a second time, only to come to the reality that I had kids who liked to ski and that I was a writer and there was no extra scratch for that.

The lovely motor I built in the spring of 1997 blew in 2006 in western New York thanks to a 10-millimeter bolt on the oil pan that fell out and with it everything viscous. It seized, I cried, and my dad rented a flatbed to come get my young family home. Vicky would sit silent for a year as I saved up for a new powerplant. This "new" aftermarket "Mexican" runs well enough still today, but has always had a taste for Castrol GTX.

My teenage daughters love the idea of driving Vicky, but they don't know how to drive stick, and frankly, as any Bus owner knows, it's an art form. Feather the gas going down the driveway, so you don't lose power. Use the speedometer as a tachometer: 10 mph means shift to second; 20 to third; the shifter isn't a shifter, it's a swizzle stick; you have to loose-wrist it into third. Thirty-five to 40 is for fourth. Keep it below 80 always. The speedometer is off by 10 mph at 80 anyway, so you're only doing 70. Downshifting is especially hard for kids, I've learned. Brake, clutch, dab of gas. Mind the road; she lists a bit. And, honestly, no one younger than a Gen Xer should drive a Bus anyway, because it's "dangerous." Kids today don't understand the meaning of that word.

There's something magical about driving a vehicle you know will not get you to your intended destination on time and likely won't get you there at all on the first attempt—usually. Those tires did actually blow, both of them, on the freshly graded Cassiar Highway somewhere north of Prince George, British Columbia. That trip back with Big, my then-fiancée, and my two dogs? We didn't have a starter.

Pop-started it the whole way across the country. "I can't believe you kids are still driving these," a cop said, peering intently into our living quarters at a Nebraska rest stop as he and Big pushed to get us going.

"Blew out a spark plug and spent the night in Illinois at a truck stop with no hassles," I wrote in Vicky's journal a day later. The next morning, we reinstalled the plug with some J-B Weld and rolled gently over the highway in search of a real fix. Not a few miles down the road, in the middle of farm country, we came upon what appeared to be a mothballed VW shop. Clunkers all around. I walked to the door and an old man answered. Said he'd been retired for years and he was just there to keep out of his wife's hair. "For $20 he put in a new spark plug with a heli-coil, a new [distributor] cap, checked our timing with a light, and said it was good," I wrote. "'I don't know how long it will last,' he said. 'God bless you,' Big said. He's Catholic and he meant it."

I think often of that trip. A new love and an old car and a large friend and God watching out for us all. There is something very humbling about moving through the world like this and not needing to be on schedule and giving the rest to a higher power. Good vibes come to you when you're vulnerable. And with Vicky I'm always so. Now, too, I think about my daughters in the age of locking doors and air conditioning, Google Maps and a billion songs on their phones. Will they ever really want Vicky? Will Vicky really want them?

There are countless stories Vicky and I and our family, friends, and strangers might recall. Vanagon drivers, now that they're old too, actually wave, and I flash the peace sign without irony. Cops don't profile me anymore because most of them were born after the Reagan administration. And even though it's mostly legal now, I leave the weed home. Or at least the weed I know about.

—*Originally appeared in* Mountain Gazette 200, *2023.*

41.
The Pathfinder
Written by Rachel Sturtz

After six years of drought in North Dakota, the first wet springs were a torrent. In 2013, the waterlogged desert prairie of the Little Missouri National Grassland and the Little Missouri Badlands gave new life to an incorrigible mix of sagebrush, switchgrass, and sedges that grew like beanstalks and strangled its famous Maah Daah Hey Trail. The vegetation that once scraped ankles now scraped knuckles, forcing cyclists like Nick Ybarra to shoulder his bike and bushwhack buttes to find the next four-by-six trail marker.

Ybarra, now 40, is an optimist to a fault. He patiently waited for the North Dakota Forest Service to mow it. Weeks passed; the grass grew, and the trail became faint. Ybarra bided his time, aware that the Forest Service had lost its funding and 14-person trail-maintenance crew a few years earlier, but still hopeful that they might make a dent. He watched sections of the backcountry path disappear. His bike rides became impossible.

Ybarra had more to lose than a trail: The year before, he'd started the Maah Daah Hey 100, a point-to-point mountain bike race, partly to further his pro-mountain-biker ambitions and partly to introduce people to the Badlands, his favorite place on Earth. It also happened to be the place where the former youth pastor felt closest to God. Losing the Maah Daah Hey would mean losing himself.

As the yellow clover topped 4 feet, Ybarra realized the trail's very existence hinged on whether or not he borrowed a mower and got to work. He didn't yet know that the trail was too narrow, too uncompromising, and too gnarly for a riding mower. His best option—his only option—would be a brush mower that averaged 2 miles per hour, wide enough to mow only one side at a time.

To save the Maah Daah Hey—the longest contiguous single-track mountain-bike trail in the U.S., then 107 miles from end to end—Ybarra would have to mow it twice.

"**One of my favorite books by John Aldridge** describes the stages of masculinity that boys go through to become men," says Ybarra. "He calls one of those stages 'The Cowboy.' Every boy has that question inside: 'Do I have what it takes?' That's when we all begin testing ourselves in short, controlled trips."

When Ybarra was a pastor, he was at his best during Badlands camping trips. He cheered as kids who'd never canoe paddled 40 miles down the Little Missouri River, as those who'd never slept outside spent the night in an igloo, and as nice Christian boys who'd never tussled started a fistfight while on the water. His charges always returned home profoundly changed—black eyes notwithstanding.

Perhaps Ybarra was the perfect Cowboy-stage guide because he's never left it. That youthful magnetism is why so many people are drawn to him.

"Nick is a dynamic force," says Jennifer Morlock, former owner of Dakota Cyclery and a Badlands cycling guide with her husband, Loren. The Morlocks have known Ybarra for years. "He has the charisma, personality, enthusiasm, and passion to jump into just about anything."

To see if he could work like his father, a large-equipment mechanic, Nick served in the North Dakota Air National Guard as a jet-engine mechanic for F-16s. In 2006, he earned Airman of the Year and got to ride in one of the F-16s pulling 8.8 G's. When it came to flying, Ybarra did not have what it takes. He threw up four times in the jet and a fifth time back on the ground.

To see if he could work like an oil-field roughneck, Ybarra endured

12-hour shifts—two weeks on, two weeks off—as a derrickman, drilling the honeycomb of the Bakken Formation. In -40 F windchill that made Popsicles out of his 5-Hour Energy, Ybarra pulled out 20,000 feet of drill pipe 90 feet at a time, standing on what was essentially 120-foot-high scaffolding. He was unfazed but unmoved.

It turns out he wasn't meant to be a youth pastor, either.

"I resigned from that position after two and a half years," says Ybarra. "I'd barely made it through college with undiagnosed ADHD, and I couldn't handle the paperwork." But he knew he wasn't the first to feel this way.

"When I look at Jesus Christ, I see someone who had an undeniable impact on our world," says Ybarra. "I also see someone who often retreated into the wilderness to be alone. I mean, Moses had to climb a mountain in the middle of nowhere in order to talk to God. That's my pull too. Some people are drawn to mountains, some people to beaches ... others to the prairie. The terrain of my heart is the North Dakota Badlands. That's where my heart is happy, my soul [is] refreshed, and my spirit feels closest to God's. To quote Teddy Roosevelt, the Badlands is 'where the romance of my life began.'"

Embodying cowboys and Jesus is crucial if you're going to mow terrain apocryphally described by Brigadier General Alfred Sully as "hell with the fires out...grand, dismal, majestic." The job would overwhelm an experienced trail crew. When he started this project, the closest Ybarra had ever gotten to trail maintenance was riding past volunteers when he lived in Minnesota.

"My college friends and I figured out that every Wednesday morning, about a dozen volunteers would be working on the trail," he says. "It never crossed my mind to help. We just stopped riding on Wednesdays because we thought it was annoying."

In a way, it was a miracle the Maah Daah Hey ever existed in the first place. A rancher named Morris Tarnavsky dreamt it up because his horseback rides with friends were so popular that he figured a trail would make it easier to show off the Badlands. He convinced the Forest Service that a trail that went from park to park was a good idea.

Posts went in, and as the Forest Service mowed the path, marker by marker, wild game followed along, wearing it in further.

Gerard Baker, a full-blood member of the Mandan-Hidatsa Tribe and a longtime National Park Service ranger, named the trail Maah-Daah-Hey, meaning "grandfather" in the Mandan language. The trail corridor was long used by the Mandan Tribe for hunting parties, war parties, and travel. Baker wrote about the naming, "'Grandfather' is one whom you learn from, like the trail you could go to it and walk and listen. If you listen with all your spirit you not only hear but you learn."

Before 2013, the Forest Service mowed certain sections, but only as far as budget and staff allowed. Even without the resources to keep it up themselves, they were hesitant when Ybarra approached them about mowing it himself. Ybarra had to ask permission to do so; after all, it was national grassland. Then, the bigger ask: to use one of the USFS mowers. The gas would be on Ybarra. How to use the mower? Well, he'd figure it out.

"It was like they'd rather have the trail go away than risk having a volunteer get hurt out there," says Ybarra. Eventually, they agreed to let him mow.

Ybarra gathered three friends from Bismarck: Brian Fried, Chad Bergen, and Ian Easton. Fried brought his mountain-bike club's Billy Goat brush cutter, Berman brought a DR brush mower from Harmon Lake trails and two string trimmers. The goal: Mow 10 miles point to point, using two trucks with a gas drop halfway. It wasn't a hard sell.

"Nick's a very spiritual person, and the Maah Daah Hey has a lot of spiritual character to it," says Bergen. "We all connect out there—well, now I'm getting choked up—and I see him work hard every day. And pray. And meditate. It's a way to live. He's a special person, and there aren't many like him."

But problems mounted. Mowing worked only if the trail held up. As they went, sections got rutted and edges collapsed. They found themselves mowing and shoveling to sculpt and build back parts of the trail. As they got scratched up by branches, they realized they'd overlooked trimming.

To make matters worse, Ybarra was a perfectionist. ("I was trying to burn that trail bed back to the ground," he admits sheepishly.) His attention to detail was so complete that the guys with the 2-miles-an-hour mower were moving too quickly and had to wait for Ybarra to catch up.

It took an entire day to cover 10 miles. As the other three headed home, Fried let Nick keep the Billy Goat to tackle the next 90 miles.

The thing about North Dakotans is that they don't complain. And that unique, quiet, proud suffering is like a siren call.

When Phil Helfrich heard that Ybarra was mowing the whole damn trail by himself (though Ybarra's friends had pitched in), he says, he got competitive. He spent all of his spare time hunting and hiking and, back when things were wild and woolly, riding his motorcycle in the grasslands and Badlands. Known to everyone as Uncle Phil, he remembers the day when he was out hunting and spotted a single four-by-six post where no rancher would build a fence. It was one of the first Maah Daah Hey markers. His hunting buddy was horrified at the idea of bringing more people into the Badlands. Helfrich was excited that he'd have more trail to hunt.

Helfrich decided he would start mowing from the south end, near Medora, and see if he could beat Ybarra to the middle. By day, he drove all over eastern Montana, North Dakota, and Minnesota as a traveling pharmaceutical rep. By night, he scrounged up a truck and a trailer from one friend and picked up the Harmon Lake mower from another. He'd mow until 3 a.m. (despite his fear of the dark), return everything in reverse order, and then grab a few hours of sleep before going to work and doing it all over again. When a mower broke, he learned to fix it on the fly. When he and his mower fell down a washout, he borrowed a ratchet strap and rope from a nearby farmer to winch it out. He once woke up driving across the Montana state line.

Helfrich didn't know Ybarra yet, but he'd seen him at some races.

Ybarra didn't know Helfrich yet, but he'd seen him once on the trail, riding his horse with a machete in his hand, lopping off the tree limbs that threatened to knock off his cowboy hat.

If the Maah Daah Hey was overgrown in 2013, it was a jungle in 2014.

In fact, Ybarra's worst day of trail maintenance was the final one, and it began when he lent Big Bertha, the Forest Service's most unwieldy brush mower, to a group of overeager first-time volunteers from Dickinson.

If his head had been on straight—if he weren't elbow-deep into fixing a smaller mower or near-catatonic from almost 100 miles of mowing in triple-digit heat—he never would have dreamt of handing over Big Bertha, which jerked newbies around like a bison. But he did, with the explicit direction that she stay off of the Wannagan switchbacks.

The Wannagan switchbacks climb at an 18% grade, bringing mountain bikers to a near-standstill, and teeter over a sharp drop whose distance to impact would hurt you as much as the terrain shearing off chunks and strips from your body on the way down. As a perk, you climb it in front of a campsite lot full of gawkers.

For pride alone, you take stock of how to tackle that climb before you start. For life alone, you don't take up a 400-pound mower.

But that's what a volunteer did, of course. And Ybarra knew it the moment he pulled into the Wannagan campground. Most of the crew were kicking rocks when they should have been a few miles down the trail. Ybarra and Easton got out of the truck with the fixed mower and followed the men's gaze up, up, up. Ybarra heard someone shout for help, and then he heard Big Bertha—not mowing, as she should have been, but tumbling ass over teakettle, shedding bolts and springs and bending blades as she cartwheeled down the switchbacks and landed in a mechanical heap. She was as done with her job as Ybarra wanted to be with his.

Sometimes, it's just like that. Twelve years of trail maintenance and Ybarra's learned that no matter what you do, you're fighting something. Erosion. Saplings. Heat. Gravel. Cattle. Exhaustion. Inexperience. Mowers.

Ybarra handed off the smaller mower and ordered the Dickinson crew to mow to mile marker 22. He and Easton got to fixing Big Bertha, which, amazingly, still ran.

Just before sunset, Ybarra and Easton finished their portion of the trail and decided to clean up the final few miles. Big Bertha, banged up and down a muffler, roared along the path with a flame shooting out of the exhaust manifold.

"We hit section after section of eroded, nasty, rutted trail, and we couldn't get the mower through," says Ybarra. It was stop, shovel, stop, shovel. Then the shovel's wooden handle broke. Finding no sign of mowing at mile marker 22, Ybarra and Easton kept going. Then, during a midnight break, Ybarra heard a noise across the valley.

He'd been a hunter long enough to know that small animals make big noises in the wild. Loud rustling in a bush signals a chickadee. But these noises weren't big. Mule deer are stealthy, but you'll hear a soft huff when they're spooked, and then they'll bound away. The thing in the bush wasn't spooked.

"Only animals used to being hunted get spooked," says Ybarra. The last time he'd noticed similar noises was when he was coyote hunting and found fresh mountain lion tracks around his decoy. Ybarra heard a clump of dirt tumble down a butte. Then, nothing.

He handed his .38 Special handgun and the trimmer's battery pack flashlight to Easton. Ybarra mowed; Easton aimed and tried to sight an approaching cougar. But, with Big Bertha flaming and dust swirling, there wasn't much to see. So Ybarra pressed on, hoping a big cat wouldn't leap through the haze.

One mile from the truck, Big Bertha's nose dropped into the barren Crooked Creek. Ybarra's hands were grip-locked around the handles, and he couldn't let go. The wheels lost contact with the trail, and Big Bertha's four-wheel drive yanked Ybarra's upper body down with it, pulling his back out. He used the self-propelled mower to pull himself out of the creek bed and hobbled the final mile to his truck. He took some Advil, swallowed down a couple of PBRs, and lay on his tailgate with his gun across his chest.

Mowing looks a lot different these days. Instead of cutting the entire length one way and then the reverse, crews meet at a trailhead and split: One group mows south and back, the other north and back. Instead of starting in June (which led to complete regrowth by the

August mountain-bike races), they begin the week after the Fourth of July and do it all in a 10-day "big push."

Every morning, volunteers—anywhere from two to 12, depending on the day—gather at a designated campsite at dawn and work all day. During a North Dakota summer, it's a very long day, from first light around 5 a.m. until last light around 11 p.m. The rule is that the crew needs to do as much as it can at 2 miles per hour. Though you never know how far you'll make it on any given day.

There is a pecking order. You work your way up as a washout digger first, mending and sculpting the trail enough to let Big Bertha through. This happens at least once a mile. Next, you become a pruner, cutting away the branches ahead of the machine.

Then on to tail gunning, manning one of two string trimmers that flank the mower to clean up and cut down sagebrush, saplings, and whatever else needs a haircut while rocks pepper your shins for hours. You are head down all day, constantly trying to hold your trimmer at the right angle, feathering the throttle to conserve fuel. The less fuel you use, the less you need to carry.

If you can handle those jobs—and you must—only then may you handle the mower. Mowing is the one job that allows your eyes to drift upward and actually take in the splendor of the Badlands. There are now five, soon to be six, mowers in Ybarra's fleet, including Big Bertha, Dr. Evil, Pepe, and Doc Holiday, plus two named after friends the crew has lost, Kyle Brierley and Brad Bosch.

"It's a dance," says Ybarra. "You learn to move with the mower, or it will throw you around and tire you out." The crew has figured out how to strap supplies to the mower and build racks for hand tools. Volunteers average a half-marathon every day. Most importantly, Ybarra and his wife, Lindsay, have learned how to fundraise.

"For the first four or five years, we spent our own money out of our own pockets, borrowed or used our own vehicles and equipment, bought our own gas," says Helfrich. One year, a group was trying to get a section of the Forest Service property and trail near the CCC Campground designated as "suitable for wilderness." The Forest Service trail manager at the time thought mowers would be prohibited from those areas.

"**That was the day Nick went to the store** and bought a scythe and sharpened it up," says Helfrich. "He didn't know I was thinking the same thing; I'd bought one too. I got in 10 feet before mine broke. He got in 12 feet. We had both figured, If we can't do it by mower, let's do it by hand."

At first, Ybarra requested money from the Maah Daah Hey Trail Association (MDHTA), which began in 1999 when the trail was created. While the state awards Recreational Trails Program (RTP) grants for trail-improvement projects, trail maintenance isn't eligible. The MDHTA applies for RTP funding to add much-needed amenities like benches, bridges, and restrooms at campgrounds, but when Ybarra, then a board member, asked if they could donate money for a mower, they denied his request. So the Ybarras began fundraising, eventually starting a 501(c)(3) nonprofit in 2016 called Save the Maah Daah Hey to drum up money for their work.

To give an idea of scope: MDHTA volunteers dedicate one day a year to trail maintenance. In 2023, Ybarra and his crew mowed 154 miles in 10 days. It was the first time they mowed the entirety of the trail expansion that added 47 miles in 2014.

"What Nick does is astronomical by comparison," says Jennifer Morlock. "Words can hardly describe. What they do in 10 days is a miracle."

In close second is the success of the Maah Daah Hey 100. In 2012, 67 mountain bikers showed up for the first race. In 2024, the Ybarras estimate, there will be 400 riders. And now their trail-running series has dwarfed the bike races. When the Medora Foundation asked the couple to take over their trail run and special-use permit for the Maah Daah Hey, the Ybarras created the Badlands Race Series, which includes the Badlands Gravel Battle, Maah Daah Hey Trailrun Series, Bold St. Nick's winter fat-bike race, and MDH Buck-Fifty Ultra Race for runners, cyclists, and equestrians. This year's Maah Daah Hey 100 trail run alone has 1,100 registered runners.

Ybarra's dream of introducing people to North Dakota's Badlands has come true. In an era when every city boasts purpose-built bike trails, he's delivered a true single-track trail race.

It's hard to find a race more brutal and rewarding. Like the Leadville 100, the Maah Daah Hey 100 has a 50% dropout rate and requires more than 12,000 feet of climbing. Unlike Leadville, it's point-to-point, finishing three counties away in a different time zone. This explains why Leadville's course record is under six hours and the Maah Daah Hey's top times are just over eight.

Single-track is a different beast. There's no peloton to draft behind. There are rivers to cross and cattle gates to raise and exposure to battle.

Which is why most first-timers are in over their heads. Everyone knows North Dakota is cold in the winter, but most don't know that it also can be an oven. Some years, the races see 110 degrees in the valleys, with no wind. Other years, it's 110 degrees with 40 mile-per-hour winds, and it feels like racing toward a hair dryer.

The race series' success has come with its own set of problems. Ranchers and the county sheriffs have their hackles up about the traffic; EMTs rankle over resources they need to dedicate to the race. Then there's the fluid nature of the management within the Forest Service: New humans show up and have different ideas of what they'd like to see.

Others even gossip about how much money Ybarra and Lindsay must be making off of the natural resources. That last one makes the Ybarras laugh.

A life in service to a trail takes its toll on a marriage. The Badlands may be the terrain of Ybarra's heart, but his wife loves the beach.

"I can go overboard," admits Ybarra. "Anyone who is married knows that one spouse cannot make a sacrifice that doesn't affect the other spouse. We never anticipated trail maintenance when we began a race. All of the time and resources we used to save the Maah Daah Hey we could have used to go to school or launch another business venture."

When the Ybarras moved back to North Dakota after college in 2008, they settled in Lindsay's hometown of Watford City. Six months later, the oil boom hit. The town's population erupted from 1,200 to 12,000 in metropolis-sized man camps. Lindsay, fresh from school with a business degree, faced the daunting task of taking over two of her parents' three motels in town at the time, which were overstuffed with roughnecks and too understaffed to wrangle them.

While Ybarra was mowing the Maah Daah Hey and planning races, Lindsay was watching the front desk, cleaning rooms, and dealing with rowdy guests. They also had two very young daughters. Lindsay was the breadwinner, and the pair lost money on the trail and race for six or seven years.

"Nick is passionate, and he knows what he wants. He lives with heart and dreams," says Lindsay. "A lot fell on me because of [that]."

When Ybarra first pitched the idea of the Maah Daah Hey 100, Lindsay admits, she and their families weren't exactly supportive.

"Nick's dad said, 'No. People will die,'" she says. "Then we told him, 'No one will come, because we're in the middle of nowhere.'"

Even when more than five dozen people showed up to the first race, nearly everyone said, "That was horrible. We're never doing that again." Everyone got lost. Racers were mad.

But then pro mountain biker Kelly Magelky met the pair in 2012 and said he thought he could ride the Maah Daah Hey in under nine hours, which seemed unfathomable at the time. It was enough to get Lindsay on board for one more year. But she had conditions: They needed a website, and they needed to charge people. She now runs everything in the background, from the race series' online presence to merchandise and volunteers.

"I don't even like the outdoors that much," Lindsay admits. "I was surprised that we managed to turn this into a business. We have two employees. I'm really proud of that."

Both Ybarra and Lindsay are trying to find a balance between the motels and their race series, but both credit what has made their life special to the support of their friends, families, and volunteers.

"Uncle Phil and his wife, Beth, have been a huge part of our journey," says Lindsay. "I always ask them, 'Why? Why do you help us?'" Their answers echo the sentiments of the rest of the Maah Daah Hey community.

Beth says, "Because we love you. Phil says, "Because you need it."

"I've matured a lot since 2014," says Ybarra. "If you would have asked me who I was then, I would have said I was a mountain biker. That was my identity. I mowed the Maah Daah Hey because I otherwise wouldn't have had a trail to ride. There were a lot of selfish, immature reasons."

"Then I discovered it wasn't going to be in the cards for me to be a pro mountain biker," he continues. "But I found that volunteering to save the Maah Daah Hey, sharing the trail with others, and hosting races kept me in the Badlands. That's exactly what I wanted."

The last few years, the MDHTA has begun using RTP grants to surface sections of the trail. They're hoping to make it more amenable to hikers and riders, but the loose gravel has led to a host of problems for cyclists. Last summer, Ybarra leaned into a left turn in a gravel section, slid out like he'd hit ball bearings, and broke his collarbone.

The gravel eventually combines with the clay like concrete. And Save the Maah Daah Hey volunteers can no longer fix trail ruts with hand tools. They can't mow over gravel for fear of setting off sparks.

It's another new worry on a long list for the Ybarras. Trail maintenance can feel like a meditation on futility, but Ybarra has come around to this new version of life because the sacrifices—at least for now—are worth it.

"There's a feel-good feeling you only get from turning around after a sunup, sundown day mowing, and you see that shining ribbon of single-track running through the Badlands," says Ybarra. "You think, I just did that. I made a small part of the world better."

—*Originally appeared in* Mountain Gazette 201, *2024.*

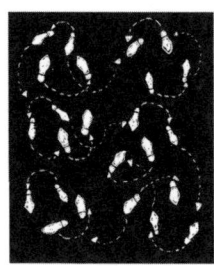

42.
Learning to Dance
Written by George Sibley

This is a story about doing ridiculous things in an effort to get truly serious about life and its living. A story about trying to learn how to dance.

That probably sounds ridiculous—even to me, with my still mostly Western-civilized ear. And that quest to learn to dance is what struck even me as a ridiculous beginning for the most serious thing I've probably ever done in my life. It began with going absent from the U.S. Army without official leave, planning never to return. And it was moved by a movie.

Well, a movie and other things—like an escalating American "defensive action" halfway around the world. And a growing realization that the ways for an individual to initiate and exercise democratic alternatives were diminishing toward nothing. And an Army class the previous week, where I'd taken exception to the standard "if it looks like a duck, walks like a duck, and quacks like a duck, it must be a Communist" drill and been quashed not just by the ranking instructor but by most of my colleagues in the class. Socialism = communism = bad because everyone said so. And there seemed to be nothing constructive to do about any of it in 1965. Especially on active duty in the military-industrial complex.

So I went to the movies—Zorba the Greek. At the movie's end, after Zorba has depleted the protagonist's inheritance on a wild idea that didn't work, the protagonist implores him, "Teach me to dance." And that happens, in a beautiful, wild, sentimental scene, and it was the straw that broke me. I went back to my post quarters, loaded my few personal belongings into my 1956 Nash Rambler, and headed West. To learn to dance, whatever that meant. A ridiculous serious move.

I was then on temporary duty in Fort Somethingorother near Chicago. My home base was Fort Carson, Colorado, but I wasn't going back there. In a headlong adrenaline rush into the dank Midwestern dark, I formulated a plan to go to some Wyoming-like place of the spirit to figure out how to create a new identity as a cowhand or coal miner or whatever—and somehow learn to dance.

Why dancing? I'd never enjoyed dancing, all the way through high school and college. I had been carefully trained to march to the beat through years of convergent learning while sitting in straight rows of bolted-down desks. And in church—a flash memory of marching around a room, clutching little American flags while singing "Onward, Christian Soldiers," pepping for Christian nationalism 80 years ago with a mainstream Methodist congregation. Dancing in high school (pre–Chuck Berry, pre-Elvis) was just another kind of marching, toward love and marriage, horse and carriage. And now I was throwing away 20-some years of marching to the drumbeat of how to succeed in imperial America, land of the great military-industrial complex.

But I didn't go to Wyoming. Instead, after a few days in Denver with a college friend, I chickened out and returned to Fort Carson to face the music. It could have been a lot worse; doing something really ridiculous has the advantage of not having much coverage in the books that armies and other corporations march to. I spent some time with some very polite military intelligence guys, seeing if I walked, talked, or looked like a Communist. I spent a couple of days with two Army shrinks who passed me back and forth in a bad cop, good cop process until one afternoon, in a session with the bad cop, I suddenly realized something: They no longer had me. The Army did not have me. And I laughed out loud.

I had just remembered a story/joke I'd heard or read somewhere but not understood, about an Indigenous man. He'd committed some defined felony on the reservation, and in the usual plea bargain, he was told he would go to jail if he didn't cooperate. He answered everything with his people's version of "whatever"—but then added, "I'll show you your jail." He rounded up four chairs, put them in a square, then sat down in the middle of it. "What kind of a jail is that?" the prosecutor asked. "You tell me," he said. "You're the ones in it."

Finally understanding, I laughed out loud, surprising the doc who'd thought he had me over a barrel but no longer had me at all. The Army could put me in jail, but it no longer had me. The psychiatrists declared me a little mad (masochistic) yet harmless, but there were some dark months of house arrest waiting before the Army finally agreed.

Finally, one November day, a "general discharge" verdict came down with instructions to immediately process me out. Five years later, at the height of the more organized Vietnam protests, I probably would have gone to jail. But in 1965 I was just a nuisance, though possibly infectious, so they decided, "Get him out quietly."

Nevertheless, I had that blot on my record: an ambiguous military discharge. I'd been told all my life that meant I could never have a good career in the imperial nation that America was becoming. In 1965, that sounded to me more like a promise than a threat. I decided, however, that if I was consigned to shitwork for the rest of my life, I'd rather do it in the mountains than in some neo-biblical Pittsburgh Gomorrah.

So I came to the mountains in what I believed was a retreat from the imperial-industrial juggernaut, working ski resort jobs in the winter and construction jobs in the summer. It was the work I could get to support myself, and it made me realize that I wasn't fleeing the empire; I was just in the front ranks, advancing the empire. (No one has ever asked about my military record.)

I lucked into work in a small mountain town; however, that was in a real sweet spot in its history. It had been a coal-mining town until the 1950s and still had a modest hard-rock mine operating on one of the mountains overlooking the town; on another, there was a small ski resort with big dreams just coming out of bankruptcy proceedings the year I arrived. But the town was really between old and new economies, with the illusion that the American imperium had maybe forgotten it. The future felt open—a sweet time to be there.

The population was still mostly first- and second-generation Central European immigrants who had not left when the coal mines closed and knew how to get along. There were retired miners and business owners who couldn't afford to leave. The town also had a small but growing population of post-urban, post-industrial immigrants from the urban-industrial imperium like me. The old-timers cautiously welcomed us newcomers, wanting their town to survive.

And … they danced, the old-timers—something they'd brought with their pre-industrial European heritage. There were a couple of local accordion bands, and it seemed like every week there would be a dance in one bar or another. Two or three beers into one of those evenings, watching a roomful of people swirling around to the honk and wail of the accordion, a woman I knew came over and asked me to dance. I told her I didn't know how.

"Can you walk and count to two at the same time?" she asked.

I thought so.

"Follow me," she said, and I did, achieving a kind of beer-fueled galumphing polka that cleared a big defensive space around us.

Once I started, I got into it so much that, later that same evening, the proprietor told me she either had to teach me to dance right or kick me out. "Teach me to dance, then," I said. And she did. It involved a lot of little things, like how to move your partner around rather than throw her around, how taking smaller steps enabled quicker moves, et cetera.

But the main thing she told me was to remember that when you're dancing, you are dancing with the whole room. That was 50-some years ago, and it took probably half of that interval for the full cultural weight of her words to sink in. You're not dancing unless you're dancing with the whole roomful of everyone else who is dancing. And, by implication, since no one is in charge of the dance, guiding you into some arrangement, everyone is responsible for everyone else's experience.

Beyond that, I don't want to beat the obvious analogies to death, except to say that dancing isn't marching, where someone puts you in formation and calls the cadence. What's good about that is when you're just in the ranks, you don't have to think about anything but staying in step, whether the cadence-caller is worth following or not. No responsibility for anything you march over.

I was involved in launching a number of things in my years in that town, some of which we would call serious—attempts to make the inevitable renewed march on the valley of urban-industrial civilization as culturally non-destructive as possible. We were not always successful.

But I was also present at the creation of an end-of-winter festival, an unapologetically joyful, goofy weekend whose main event is a ball with an accordion band, keeping alive the old-timers' roomful of dancers. After more than half a century, those who gave us the dance are all gone, but we still dedicate the festival to them, making it a celebration rather than just another party. But mostly it's an occasion to dance, and we dance we do. And we are a serious bunch, some of us, who've followed ridiculous routes to get there, but we're all learning to dance.

—*Originally appeared in* Mountain Gazette 202, *2024.*

43.
To Live is to Fly
Written by Charlie Warzel

If I'm being honest, I already had the first line of this story written in my head before I spoke to a single soul. It went: *All the people I wanted to talk to for this story are dead.* It was glib, perhaps appropriately ominous, and, at the beginning at least, true enough.

How do you talk about BASE jumping without talking about death? Judging by most everything I've read, it seems impossible. Death haunts pretty much every description of the activity. *The Great Book of BASE*, the sport's unofficial Bible, begins thusly: "BASE jumping is extremely dangerous. It is so dangerous that we seriously encourage you to not do it. In fact, we honestly think it's a bad idea." It's an admirable warning, if not a little bit ineffectual. If you are the type of person who might be inclined to hike up to a precipice, don a suit that turns you into a nylon bird, take in the panorama and the sheer verticality of the situation, breathe in, engage in the dozens of physical and metaphysical calculations and self-negotiations that come with life-and-death activities, breathe out, wait for the appropriate moment, say *yes*, and hurl yourself into the rarefied air...well, then you might also be the type of person who would take "It's a bad idea" as an enticement—a challenge, even.

When I came up with my snarky little opening, I knew so little about BASE jumping that I was not even aware the word wasn't even a word, really—that it was an acronym (a pretty rad one) for "building, antenna, span, and earth." I knew only what so many normies know: It was dangerous. It was the sort of thing that a 37-year-old magazine writer with a healthy fear of heights could not earnestly comprehend. It's not only that I lack the fortitude, disposition, focus, and fitness of these athletes, but also that the fabric of my being appears to be woven out of an entirely different cloth. If you're reading this, there's a good chance you possess a more adventurous spirit than the one that lingers in me, which induces vertigo near cliff faces. This is a long, tortured way of me telling you that I did not have a dog in this fight.

But make no mistake: There *is* a fight. There are, across the world, an unknown number of BASE jumpers. (There's no official count, but figures from 2017 suggest around 3,000 people participate in the sport.) These athletes are almost always trained skydivers. They often wear elegantly constructed ripstop-nylon wingsuits with parachutes that catch the air currents and ingeniously convert what would be a vertical free fall into glorious horizontal flight. These jumpers—who soar and glide through canyons and down cliff faces like Red Bull–sponsored birds of prey—love to jump off tall walls of rock with riverbanks or wooded valleys below. Unfortunately, a great many of the best walls of rock with the best, most unspoiled climbs, vistas, faces, and landing areas—in the United States, at least—happen to be inside America's national parks. Even more unfortunately, the National Park Service (NPS) has, for all intents and purposes, banned the activity.

Jumpers who free-fall in the parks are subject to fines and jail time. In Yosemite, the national park with many of the sport's most coveted jump spots, enforcement is especially intense; rangers have chased, interrogated, searched, arrested, and tased suspected and attempted jumpers in the park. The whole affair has gotten pretty acrimonious over the last three decades. The jumpers want to jump, believe they have the right to do so in recreation spaces funded, in small part, by their tax dollars, and are pushing for access. The NPS, for its part, has not budged.

"I've racked my brain as to why BASE is looked at as a crime in national parks," Jeff Shapiro, a climber, paraglider, and wingsuit BASE jumper, told me recently. "And I think confusion is the foundation. It all stems from this idea that a lot of people in the government or in other walks of life don't pursue fulfillment through activities that involve risk and consequence. They don't understand it, and it clouds their notion of why people would want to do this."

This is classic David versus Goliath stuff—a passionate subculture versus a sprawling bureaucracy. What seems clear-cut is actually frustratingly complicated. BASE jumping in national parks isn't actually illegal, it seems. Instead, it is governed by a federal regulation—36 CFR 2.17(a)(3), for those following along at home—passed in the 1960s. The regulation prohibits "delivering or retrieving a person or object by parachute, helicopter, or other airborne means," except in an emergency. "This regulation applies to BASE jumping," an unnamed National Park Service spokesperson told me in a terse email. To a layperson, this would appear to be a pretty broad, ticky-tacky interpretation of the regulation. But here's the catch: Theoretically, you can obtain a permit to get around it. "Park managers must undergo a planning process (Section 8.2.2.7 of NPS Management Policies) to determine if BASE jumping is an appropriate activity in the park," the NPS said in response to my request for comment. "The planning process is critical to understanding the potential impacts to park resources and visitors from this activity and must be completed before superintendents can consider a permit application authorizing it to occur."

The problem for jumpers is that the NPS doesn't appear willing to issue permits to BASE jumpers who've requested them.

Brendan Weinstein is one such jumper. He's the board president of BASE Access, a nonprofit initiative petitioning the NPS for access to responsible jumping inside the parks. In 2023, Weinstein and BASE Access drafted 10 proposals for permits in Yosemite and other parks, like Big Bend, Glacier, and Zion; all of them were denied in 2024. Weinstein told me that BASE Access is stuck in a bureaucratic doom loop with the NPS. "In official responses to our permit applications, the parks emphasize that before they can grant permits, BASE jumping needs to go through a park planning process. This has been their standard response since at least 2004. Since then, each time jumpers have contacted the NPS about how to kick-start such a process, they've stonewalled us, as well as have ignored public comment during formal rulemaking and management policy drafting requesting that BASE be considered an appropriate activity"

On paper at least, what Weinstein is asking for sounds pretty reasonable. The Yosemite application includes, among other stipulations, "No jumping except from sunrise to 10 a.m.," "No jumping from El Cap during May–June and September–October to help alleviate congestion," "No jumping from Glacier Point," at least a 20-second parachute canopy ride, and provisions not to jump anywhere peregrine falcons might be nesting. Weinstein's proposal even offers that permittees would call a number before they jump, to ensure safety for others in the surrounding area. But Weinstein told me that, despite some extensive efforts, he's had minimal conversations with NPS officials explaining their rationale.

Other BASE jumpers I spoke with seemed so eager to hear anything from the department that a few of them excitedly wondered if I would be able to crack the cone of silence and get some intel. For the record, I was not. For this story, I reached out to three current and former rangers and park officials, as well as the NPS media office. In all cases, I asked to better understand the park service's rationale for enforcing the regulation and for more context about their interpretations of BASE Access's applications. None of the individuals responded to my requests. After two weeks, I received a response from the National Park Service media team that consisted solely of four copy/pasted paragraphs of park service rules—government speak for "We do not wish to have a discussion."

Official channels seem to yield a maddening death-by-paperwork vibe for jumpers. David's out there filling out forms, playing nice, and trying to get the attention of Goliath, while Goliath has on noise-cancelling headphones.

This, of course, is where I must remind you that, historically,

David has an unflattering track record. Remember all the dying? That's real. In 2016, 31 people died during the sport's deadliest year, which coincided with one jumper unintentionally livestreaming their death on YouTube. The fatality stats are a little murky, and, in my experience, discussions that try to put a number on just how safe BASE jumping is tend to quickly veer into a gross, inhumane bit of back-of-the-envelope math. To its great credit, it seems the sport has gotten a lot safer since 2016. In 2023, there were no BASE jumping fatalities in the United States. One jumper told me in our conversations that USA BASE jumping has a fatality rate of two deaths per 1,000 participants. Another noted that since Chamonix re-permitted wingsuit flying in France, circa 2019, there have been zero wingsuit fatalities there. (Chamonix still has a ban on the two gondola-accessed jumps in the city, but every jump that requires hiking is allowed.) This is real progress, ushered in by people who take the sport and safety seriously.

But the NPS and its rangers have plenty of evidence to cite if they want to shut down a conversation about allowing BASE jumping. This past August, there was a fatality at the Grand Canyon (though multiple jumpers, who did not wish to comment publicly, said that evidence suggests the person was perhaps reckless and not well trained). Speaking to the *Washington Post* last August, a ranger brought up BASE jumping fatalities and suggested that rescue missions to retrieve jumpers could also be dangerous and/or resource-intensive. This is understandable, though jumpers I've spoken with ably countered most every point I brought up. In terms of rescue, they argued that they ought to be required to purchase helicopter-rescue insurance, that most wingsuit jumping doesn't require cliff-strike rescue, and that the community self-regulates and pledges to work with search-and-rescue teams to make sure not to jump in places where SAR teams are overwhelmed.

BASE jumpers argue, not incorrectly, that people die doing mundane things in national parks. According to National Park Service data, there were 205 fatal falls across the entire park system from 2014 to

2019 (seven of those from BASE jumping). One jumper suggested that in the next decade there would be hundreds of fatal falls unrelated to BASE jumping, resulting from legal activities. BASE jumping is dangerous, they argue, but so is free-soloing massive rock walls, an activity that is not banned.

And yet, of the BASE jumpers I spoke with, none try to sugarcoat the risk involved. Even in a sport that's getting safer, you need only listen to its participants talk to understand the degree of loss involved. Everyone has a story, a friend, a name referenced in the past tense in a solemn voice. To say that this acquaintance with loss is a point of pride for the BASE jumping community would be crass and incorrect. But they talk about death a lot and so openly that it can sound, depending on your persuasion, either enlightened or overly casual.

BASE jumpers are portrayed as adrenaline junkies, daredevils, and, perhaps most uncharitably, aerial party-pirates with a death wish. The gnarly, slickly produced YouTube videos probably don't help here, nor does the fact that, like any community, the loudest, most obnoxious, and most flagrantly reckless members tend to make the headlines for doing stupid stuff. BASE jumping fatalities get written up; a quiet hike and soaring wingsuit ride to a field below usually doesn't make the paper. Stereotypes abound, especially in a sport that's small, insular, and allows you to rip through the air at 140 miles an hour. But the BASE jumpers I met, to a person, seemed to defy the stereotype entirely. The more we spoke, the more it seemed to me as if the birdmen and women were occupying a different plane of existence, vibrating at a higher frequency of sorts.

As Jeff Shapiro hikes up toward an exit point, his mind is on fire. He's scanning constantly. He's nervy, but the world around him is alive with data. The clouds tell a story about air mass, as do the birds flying in the air. The leaves, shimmering on the trees along the ridgelines, are clues; so is the river below him. Each piece of information moves Shapiro that much closer to the question he's here to answer: *Should I jump?* It's an emotional experience, he says, "and then you get up there and you have to shut it off."

That's when the logic part of the brain kicks in. Shapiro cycles through everything with a cold calculus: *Do I feel up to it? Yes. Is the gear ready and working? Yes. Does the jump really fit my skill set? Yes. Are conditions safe up here? Yes. How are conditions at the landing zone?* "If everything points to yes, and I decide to jump, I can feel secure in it," he told me. What comes next is something pure. The emotions flood back in the second the chute is opened. He is flying. His mind, at last, is quiet.

"When you jump off a cliff headfirst, wearing a wingsuit, the part of your brain that generates memories doesn't work, and time is no longer relevant," Shapiro says. "You're living a lifetime every single second." What Shapiro describes is a "level of presence so profound that you're completely unable to have bandwidth for anything else."

Here's how he explains it: "The world ceases to exist. Time slows in a cliché but very real way. You experience this incredible moment of pure action and spontaneity." Shapiro is not, it should be clear, spontaneous with the planning, calculation, and training. "You do as much as you can to ensure safety," he says. "But at the same time, when you choose to live life this way, you have to be okay with every potential outcome."

Shapiro is saying that you have to be okay with dying. If that sounds insane to a deskbound, terra-firma-loving normie, well, maybe it shouldn't. Shapiro argues that confronting mortality through the sport isn't about a death wish; it's about introspection and a search for true gratitude for being alive.

"Risk with real consequence can be a gift," he tells me. "It allows me to view my own mortality and existence as a very lucky thing. I don't feel entitled to life; I feel lucky to be alive. And that reflection, for me, comes from doing something like flying the wingsuit in the mountains and the incredible immersion in nature." That feeling, for Shapiro, isn't just grounding. It's a kind of nirvana.

What you learn when listening to jumpers talk about what they do is that many of them describe the sport—which reads to outsiders as brash, loud, and violent—as meditative. "When I am in free fall, I feel a sense of freedom, rhythm, and flow that I have never managed to match anywhere else," Amber Forte, a wingsuiter, tells me. "It gives me dreams and goals to work toward and therefore brings focus and balance into my life. It pushes me to explore and expand my comfort zones. For me, it's not about the risk, or [the] thrill of doing something dangerous. It's quite the opposite. I want to be safe and careful and enjoy the sport in a calm and gentle manner."

"Ultimately, it just made me happier than anything else," Jacob Whittaker, a longtime Yosemite climber and former BASE jumper, tells me. Whittaker used to think BASE jumpers were out of their minds, but the more he learned, the more he saw that they were jumping for the same reasons he was climbing. "Our mental approach to it is almost identical to climbing," he adds. "Pay attention to everything, learn as much as we can, and do it in such a way that we can be as safe as possible." But ultimately, for him, it's about joy.

He shares a text message he sent to a friend after a jump, which captures the sentiment: "Just thinking back gives me a trickle of ecstatic neurotransmitters, not specifically for the flying even, but for that entire period of my life. It was my peak, maximum connection to the valley, the people, the planet, the universe, and I was just so present and happy."

You may remember that, earlier, I said I had no dog in this fight. Perhaps it is because the park service declined to engage me, or maybe it is because the BASE jumpers know how to appeal to my writerly instincts by eloquently describing their pursuit in utterly human terms. But the BASE jumpers have won me over. Over text, Whittaker sends me photos snapped just after dawn. In one, he supposedly captured a fellow wingsuiter soaring over a valley in a park I won't name. To my untrained eye, there is no evidence of a human—proof, Whittaker might argue, of the sport's minimal impact. The second photo was taken by him mid-flight. The sun has risen just enough that half the valley is bathed in golden light, while the other half is shrouded in gentle shadows. It's an old, grainy cell-phone picture, and yet somehow it captures the stillness and awe of the moment.

I spoke, often at length, with six experienced wingsuiters, listened to hours of BASE jumping podcasts, watched countless YouTube videos and a documentary, and read legal statutes as well as sworn affidavits from court cases, all to try to better understand the contours of the BASE jumping/NPS issue. I understand the bureaucracy, the supposed complexity of permitting. I believe I understand the reasons why wingsuiters want to take on this risk, and, frankly, I very much understand why the government might not want to engage with any of that—why it is easier to say no to any potential liability, to stonewall requests and hope that it might all go away.

But it's not going to go away. The jumpers are going to jump. This is clear when you listen to them talk about why they do it and what it means to them. Jumping is a choice, a product of careful training, risk assessment, and skill. Many also describe it as a bone-deep need. Not quite a compulsion, but the pursuit of something deep and essential. They will keep jumping. Which poses the question: Why not offer a non-clandestine pathway that could potentially make it safer by bringing wingsuiters out of the shadows?

It's possible that one answer is that national parks are not ready for wingsuiters—or, rather, that the people in charge of such decisions view the sport as a crass, technologically enabled activity that undermines a very specific, aesthetic idea of what the parks should be: a frontier-style offering of unspoiled nature for humankind to pursue in a specific, unmodernized manner. Hiking, riding on horseback, shoving your fingers into the cracks of a rock wall—the stuff of the Wilderness Act. It's possible that people who feel this way see expensive wingsuits and parachute deployments as a violation of all of this spirit—Teddy Roosevelt rolling over in his grave upon seeing a Red Bull–sponsored human hurling themselves into the ether.

This is, perhaps, understandable. But jumpers see it differently. "We are engaging the wild human," Whittaker told me. "Those words aren't written in the Wilderness Act, but it is in the spirit of it."

And so I can't help but feel that there is a disconnect—a chasm of communication that if bridged might allow the people who preserve the wild areas of our country to understand BASE jumping as a communion with wilderness. How else could one interpret Shapiro saying this: "When I land after a BASE jump, there is so much clarity. I very acutely recognize that the natural world would be unchanged whether I were alive or dead. The birds would still be chirping, the wind would still blow, and the river would be flowing exactly how it is whether I'm there or not."

You cannot talk about BASE jumping without talking about death. But the more I started listening to BASE jumpers, the more I realized it's impossible to talk about the sport without talking about the glory and privilege of being alive.

—*Originally appeared in* Mountain Gazette 203, *2025.*

44.
Raising Bull Riders
Written by Ari Schneider

For 16 days in January each year, the National Western Stock Show comes to Denver, Colorado, during which more than 20 professional rodeos take place. There, the world's best compete in bareback and saddle-bronc riding, bull riding, steer wrestling, team roping, tie-down roping, and women's barrel racing. But this year I was less interested in these world-class contests than in a kindersport called mutton busting (literary: bustin'). It's the T-ball of rodeo, the first step for young children who desire to one day be bull riders or horseback performers. Kids as young as 3 and as old as 7 bestride sheep, grab handfuls of wool, and try to hold on as the ungulates sprint around dirt-floored arenas.

A tall and chatty photographer named Chip was assigned to help me document this phenomenon. The two of us were not the obvious journalists for the task. Chip is a vegetarian and comes from a family of animal-rights defenders. Rodeo is controversial among his set, and mutton bustin' is especially so. The ASPCA has accused mutton bustin' organizers and participants of promoting inhumane care of animals, and a fruitless petition by activists to ban mutton bustin' at National Western received more than 100,000 signatures in 2017. Chip was a little uncomfortable with our forthcoming rodeo immersion, though he endeavored to have an open mind.

I'm not much of a rodeo guy either. I grew up in Vermont, where I gained some familiarity with agriculture but never witnessed a competitive rodeo. While I was fortunate as a kid to try many different sports, bull riding was never suggested. I was curious what it would have been like, for me and my parents, if it was something I had ever wished to do.

National Western is one of the biggest rodeos in the country. Likewise, it's one of the biggest stages a young mutton buster can perform on, with some contests taking place as brief interludes during pro events in the Denver Coliseum and others as dedicated one-hour nonstop child-versus-sheep entertainment in the Stadium Arena next door. I was expecting some dazzling exhibitions, as the Stock Show website had informed me that Frontier Airlines Mutton Bustin' is "one of the National Western's most popular events."

The most important consideration for any large event is, of course, parking. I could not find a spot. Media folks were instructed to park in lot K, but Chip arrived moments before me and took the last space. I was directed to try lot G, or maybe it was J, but I was a bit flustered by this whole ordeal and I pulled into lot I. The most frustrating part of finding parking at an agriculture event is navigating all the dual-rear-wheel trucks. Given that I had never been to one of these things (nor anything like it), I had not experienced the irritation of searching for a spot in a lot filled with duallies. The reason for my vexation was this: When you see two duallies backed into their spots side by side, it appears from the front that there is an open space between them. It's an illusion. In fact, the four wheels at the rear of one of those trucks jut out so far as to nearly touch the heavy-duties beside it. After driving in circles (I lost count of how many), a space finally opened in K, the media lot, where it seemed most everyone came in a crossover.

I tracked down Chip, who had been wandering for a while, and we proceeded to wander together in search of the media lounge. Nobody we asked knew its whereabouts, and we got a few suspicious up-and-down glances. Nevertheless, we found it up some stairs and hidden in a nook from which I feared I would not be able to retrace my steps. We walked through the doors to a room that smelled of newly fabricated low-cost furniture, and it occurred to us that the media lounge was a veritable showroom for American Furniture Warehouse. Tags with prices were prominent on the laminated furniture, faux plants, and kitsch decor for newspeople's use and amusement. SUCCULENTS IN SQR GREY VASE, $14.99. CNT HT BRSTL [counter height barstool], COMPARE AT: $189/ALWAYS THE LOWEST PRICE ANYWHERE/$98. (Get the matching table for $288.) TALL CACTUS, $28, attracted Chip's attention.

Chip and I introduced ourselves to the director of PR, Karen Woods, while one of her colleagues fished our purple credential tags and matching purple lanyards out of a filing cabinet. Woods frowned when Chip said we were there for mutton bustin'. She wanted to know if we planned to mic up any of the kids during their rides. Apparently there have been some PR issues with the audio of trampled children yelling things like "I think I broke my arm!"

Woods was delighted to hear that we weren't recording a podcast. She started rattling off statistics and history about National Western, and I could hardly keep up, but the one number that shocked me was that mutton bustin' was in such high demand that National Western received more than 1,000 entries in a lottery for only 200 available spots. Keep in mind that the only busters eligible to enter at National Western are children ages 5 to 7 and weighing less than 55 pounds.

The Denver Coliseum was packed for the first rodeo Chip and I attended on the morning of Jan. 7. Eight thousand dollars was up for the winners of the day's professional contests, and a belt buckle for the winner of mutton bustin'. It smelled like farm. The lights went out and a voice boomed across the venue: "DENVER, COLORADO, IT'S TIME! ARE YOU READY FOR DAY NUMBER ONE OF THE NATIONAL WESTERN?" I settled into a small concrete moat below the front-row seats and next to the bucking chutes. There were strobes and lasers and techno music as the announcer introduced the star athletes. Flames burst up from the dirt floor with a temperature so intense that from roughly 10 yards away it felt like my face was in front of an open oven.

Behind me, I noticed a sign taped to the wall:

ATTENTION
Everyone in this area
Must wear Western Apparel,
except Photographers
(Cowboy Hat, Collared Shirt, and Boots)
And have proper credentials on them
Or they will be asked to leave.

I was without a cowboy hat, and my nylon-and-rubber boots were of a French brand and certainly did not qualify. I hoped the exception to the dress code would be honored for all media and not just photographers, but I wondered if I ought to run upstairs to the vendors and buy a cowboy hat. I couldn't imagine myself in such a uniform, though. A Jewish boy from New England wearing a cowboy hat? I'll admit I was a little uncomfortable with the thought of assimilating. I was there as an observer and recorder, but I didn't think rodeo was for me. My family survived on agriculture a century ago. Before war upended their lives, my great-great-grandparents raised cows and hens and grew crops in a small village that is now a part of Poland. But they did not wear cowboy hats. Ranching in the style of the American West was something foreign to them. Likewise, foreign to me is the Christian subculture entwined in the rodeo sports born from the day-to-day activities of Mexican and American cowboys. Several vendors outside were selling bedazzled crosses, but no bedazzled Stars of David. After the light show concluded, and before the national anthem, a steer wrestler delivered through the microphone a prayer in Jesus' name. I found nothing offensive about this display of faith; I only felt like I didn't belong there. I started to doubt I'd be able to write this story. How could I, such an outsider, understand what brings more than 700,000 fans to the Stock Show and what captures the imaginations of the children who long to perform in the rodeos there?

Those thoughts fled when the chute opened for the first time.

Cole Hollen, a 21-year-old bareback rider from Texas, stood on top of the chute with his legs spanned over a horse named Stump the

Rump. Hollen lowered into a squat and carefully centered himself on Stump. The riders and horses are matched at random, and, according to the announcer, Stump the Rump had a 50% buck-off rate. "In other words, one of every two cowboys that tries to ride this horse can't," the announcer said. These aren't just any horses. They're masters at bucking and worth hundreds of thousands of dollars, specially bred and fed and exercised for the job.

The procedure of rough-stock contests is thus: The rider, holding on with only one hand, must stay on the horse or bull for eight seconds to complete the ride and receive a score. He is evaluated only for those eight seconds; there is no bonus for staying on longer. Half of the judged score (up to 50 points) is awarded for the animal's performance (how difficult the horse or bull is to ride). The other half is based on the rider's performance. The most graceful ride on the most vicious creature would theoretically earn a perfect score of 100.

Hollen nodded to signal that he was ready, and a man whose attire was caked in dirt swung open the gate between the chute and the arena. Stump leaped toward the middle of the Coliseum while Hollen whipped back and forth, looking about as rigid as rope. Two seconds in, Hollen's cowboy hat flew far above his head. One second more and he was tossed to the ground, face first. I had never witnessed a spectacle so exhilarating.

I partake in ski mountaineering, big-wall climbing, and motorcycle riding. I was once a competitive freeskier. Extreme sports are something I'm very comfortable with, and after watching this rodeo I do not doubt that professional rough-stock riders are among the toughest of extreme athletes.

The rides were always gripping and unpredictable, like when an 18-year-old Californian named Jacek Frost, the youngest bareback rider of the day and ranked fifth in the world, took his turn on top of a horse named Fatherly Love. The gate opened and it appeared Fatherly had a case of stage fright. A long, awkward hush befell the Coliseum as Fatherly stood like stone and Frost held on, waiting for something to happen. Then, Fatherly turned his head and, looking like he had been startled awake from a nap, sped off. Frost's head slapped back into Fatherly's rear, then shot forward again. The boy squeezed his legs above the horse's shoulders, desperate to stay on. A buzzer sounded, marking eight seconds, and Frost lunged off the horse. Seventy-six points. I was high on adrenaline from standing close. I almost lost the time until Chip tapped me on the shoulder to tell me the mutton busters were suiting up in the back.

A minimum of 10 volunteers were needed to get 10 little children into padded vests and hockey helmets and then lined up to ride. Essential to this operation were the rodeo queens, winners of state and regional rodeo pageants (think beauty pageants with Western flair and competitions on horseback). There was Miss Rodeo Colorado 2022, 26-year-old Ashley Baller, dressed in a maroon shirt (bedazzled), a maroon hat, and maroon lipstick; she wore a sash embroidered with her royal title. The queens doted on the children, providing motivation for and distraction from their upcoming engagements with beasts three times their size, and their inevitable collisions with the ground. The children mostly stared, smitten and mesmerized by the sparkly crowns atop the queens' cowboy hats.

We were now in a big room below the Coliseum seats. It felt removed from the commotion in the arena, even though it was just through a doorway. There I met Anna, whose 7-year-old daughter, Lena, was trying mutton bustin' for the first time. Anna explained that Lena had practiced with a big stuffed sheep. She called it her "stuffie." I was skeptical. Real sheep move. Stuffed animals do not.

Anna couldn't resist approaching the line of competitors to wish her daughter a good time. Mom curtsied and skipped away on muted feet, aware her interference was loosely prohibited. The queens endeavored to keep parents distanced from their children. The prevalent attitude of the mutton bustin' organizers, spoken in whispers I oft overheard, is that parents get in the way; they might fiddle with the helmet straps, which the volunteer equipment managers have ostensibly adjusted to regulation tightness, or, officials worry, a particularly nervous parent may send forth energy inciting a squall. If one child starts crying before the show even starts, the worst-case scenario is a chain reaction of tears, and the queens must then comfort 10 crying kids who are no longer willing to mount their sheep. Thus, the queens also assume the role of bouncers, keeping moms and dads sectioned off from their offspring.

Anna told me Lena had been worrying about her outfit for days. The stress of picking out the perfect earrings drove mother and daughter mad.

Lena was wearing purple plaid. I couldn't see her earrings under her helmet.

The parents were soon ushered to a viewing area near the chutes, and Anna told me on her way out that I was welcome to interview Lena. It was a daunting suggestion, as I'd just remembered that I had no clue how to talk to children. I don't have kids, and wanting them has never crossed my mind. None of my close friends or family have little kids. I could not recall, before reporting this story, the last time I'd tried to have a conversation with anyone younger than 12. It was a somewhat foreseen but foolishly ignored flaw in my plan. I was about to learn, on the job, that children are the most difficult interview subjects to crack.

Lena had her mouth hanging open. She appeared unamused by the spectacle around her.

"Are you excited?"

[Unamused] "No."

"NO?"

[Twiddling her fingers] "I don't know."

"Do you think you're going to win?"

[More excited now] "Yes!"

"What's your favorite animal?"

[Unsure again] "I don't know."

"How about sheep?"

[Defensive now] "NO!"

I went to find Anna.

She was finding her space where the parents were cordoned off into a small area overlooking the chutes. When the mutton bustin' began, the parents started swinging elbows, pushing to the front to see their kids go, and waving their iPhones with the cameras recording.

A man in a dusty blazer scooped up the first kid and placed him on a sheep's back while another man held its head. As soon as the sheep was released, the rider flopped off. I worried I'd vastly overestimated the thrill of this sport. But then I started seeing one kid after another on wild rides, their little bodies latched on top of high-speed sheep. It was cartoonish, the crashes especially. (There is no chance I would have done such a thing at 5. I was far too cautious, far too much of a crier at that age.) One 6-year-old girl held on to her sheep's wool with such a grip that, as her body rolled off, she overturned the animal too, and the sheep landed belly up on top of the girl. (She ended up winning.) During the longest rides and the biggest tumbles, the Coliseum erupted with spectators screaming so loud I could hardly hear the music blasting through the stadium speakers. Miss Rodeo Colorado 2022 quickly ran over to the children after their rides. She pulled their arms up into a victory pose, then rushed them off to the side. (More deafening cheers from the audience.)

I turned to one dad with a wiry and sweaty beard, whom I had heard rooting for his 5-year-old son, whom I had watched get trampled.

I said, "How do you think he did?"

"Oh, he did fine. He was really scared," Dad said.

"Was he?"

"Oh, yeah. He's good now. He realizes he's all right... You gotta make them do things that scare them a little bit. It's good to be scared."

It was Lena's turn. Lena's turn was over about one second later.

Announcer: "LENA GOT LAWN DARTED!"

I looked over at Anna, and Anna grinned at me. Anna said, "That was pretty funny. She got right off!"

When it was over, all the kids were handed 4-foot-tall trophies, which they carried over their shoulders.

Afterward, I found Anna and Lena back in the big room. Now Lena was animate. She said, "The sheep was really fuzzy!"

I asked if it was anything like riding her stuffie.

"Yeah! But I make my stuffie bounce more."

She added, unprompted, "I have dirt in my underpants!"

Another round of mutton bustin' was scheduled for the afternoon performance. Chip and I were beginning to grasp the workings of this whole rodeo affair, and we now felt a lot less like bumbling donkeys who'd somehow wandered into a stallion convention. While Chip went over to the chutes to shoot the action, I wandered to the back of the big room to inspect the piles of protective gear for the mutton busters. I wondered whether a sheep hoof could fit through one of the square holes in the steel helmet cages. (I never got a sure answer, but I think not.) I was about to search the internet for hoof diameters when a woman came over with a few mutton busters and started stuffing them into the equipment. She wore a name tag that said "Debbie Mills" and "Volunteer," and I gathered she was in charge of the mutton bustin' operation.

She turned to me and said, "[REDACTED]."

"Oh, really? Why'd you do that?"

"[REDACTED]."

"So you can make sure everything is on right?"

"Yeah, [REDACTED]."

"Yeah."

Mills returned to what she was doing, which included a lot of hurrying back and forth. I waited for all the kids to line up in front of the queens leading pregame stretches.

I'd begun mingling with some parents when Mills, who was about to walk past me, stopped and turned. She looked at my credential hanging on the purple lanyard around my neck. Mills asked, "Are you with Stock Show media? Or are you—"

"*Mountain Gazette*," I said.

Mills said, "Oh! Okay. I was talking to you like you were..." Her voice dropped. "What I said earlier about the parents... You're not going to put that in there, right?"

I shook my head, not wanting to lose access on my first day at National Western.

Mills smiled and continued on her way.

I started chatting with a mom named Kate, whose 6-year-old son Maxwell looked to be the smallest one there.

"Has he ever done this before?" I asked.

She shook her head. "Nope."

"Was it his idea to sign up?"

"Kind of." She explained that he'd seen it at the show last year and seemed into it then. "He's nervous. I can tell."

"Are you nervous?"

[Very blunt] "Yes."

"For what?"

[Much less blunt] "Uhhh..."

Kate paused.

"I don't want him to get hurt. I think that's it. He'll have fun."

"Has he been talking about this a lot the past few days?"

"Oh, yeah. He has a classmate who's doing it too. He's just been really excited. He goes between saying, 'It's going to be fun, and the point is to have fun' and saying, 'I hope I win.'"

"Did he do anything to prepare?"

"We did a little bit on Dad's back this morning."

"Do you think he will want to do grown-up rodeo someday?"

"I don't know. This could make or break it."

I looked over at Maxwell. Maxwell was picking his nose.

The parents were rounded up and escorted to their viewing area. Mills, now aware that I was a journalist and not a PR person (the credentials are both purple), came over again to make sure I was briefed on the requirements that riders wear long-sleeved shirts and closed-toed shoes for safety.

I asked if there were many injuries.

"No," she said, "because they're pretty low to the ground, and the kids kind of automatically tuck and roll."

Mills told me she loves seeing children bonding with animals through mutton bustin'. She persuaded me to ask the kids what names they'd given their sheep. Apparently, Mills and the queens encourage the kids to name the sheep they are about to ride. (The kids I later asked told me they did not name their sheep, but I'm half convinced they did and did not want to tell me.)

We stood there for a minute longer, waiting for the cue to bring the mutton busters into the arena.

Mills leaned in and said, "I'm sure you've heard it—I probably shouldn't say this—but they always say this is the only legalized form of child abuse."

I faked a laugh.

The event was now beginning, and I went to watch with the parents. When it was Maxwell's turn to go, he walked right up to his sheep and fearlessly tried to throw a leg over it as if mounting a bicycle. He made a good effort, hopping on one foot, but the sheep's back came up to about Maxwell's shoulder level. A cowboy scooped him up and plopped him on top of the sheep. The sheep took off, and Maxwell held on. Then, the sheep took an unexpected turn and ran straight toward one of the volunteers. Maxwell's head, sticking out slightly, clipped the back of the volunteer's legs, and Maxwell went cartwheeling. He got up from the dirt and waved to the crowd. I saw Kate. I said, "How do you think that went?" She said, "Better than I was thinking it would!"

I've noticed the sheep have poor aim. Besides occasionally running into people, they'll sometimes run straight into walls. One girl got slammed into a fence twice.

As the kids were collecting their oversized trophies, one dad looked at me, beaming, and said of his son, "He got on. That was a win. I was worried he was gonna say, 'Ehhhhh, I don't know if I want to get up there.'"

"Which one is he?"

"Van, the one on the end there. He's real quiet, shy, nervous all the time."

"How old is he?"

"Six. He saw the trophies last year. He said, 'I want one of those. Mom, sign me up!' But he's been a little nervous."

Dad introduced himself as Ryan.

"Do you think he'll want to stick with rodeo when he's older?" I asked.

"Yeah. He loves to ride. He's talked about maybe doing trick riding. We have horses."

I haven't had a chance to talk about trick riding yet. There were brief trick-riding performances between contests at National Western. I can best describe them as circus acts on horseback in which riders clad in assorted neon and glitter did all sorts of splits and upside-down maneuvers, dangling from their saddles while they rode around the arena.

Back to Ryan: "How do you feel now?"

"I feel proud. I'm proud that he got on there."

The parents and children soon filtered out, and I was left standing in the big room next to Ashley Baller and the newly crowned Miss Rodeo Colorado 2023, Randilyn Madison. I chatted with them for a bit about mutton bustin', for which they expressed much affection, though Baller bemoaned "the long-distance running at a very high pace" required of her to retrieve fallen children across the arena. What seemed to get them most excited was the opportunity to introduce kids to livestock and to share something beloved with the next generation.

Some of the biggest rodeo stars and enthusiasts came through mutton bustin'. A 29-year-old bull rider named Tyler Bingham, from Utah, who was performing that day at National Western, began riding sheep-back at age 7. Now he's a three-time National Rodeo finalist, has won more than $580,000 in contest earnings in the Pro Rodeo circuit (not including endorsement deals), and was ranked fourth in the world in 2019. But there are hard realities faced by the parents of any child who wants to follow in Bingham's footsteps. Bull riding is deadly, as is bronc riding, but bulls take it up a notch. Broncs tend to buck straight up and down, while bulls spin, lurch, and twist. After a horse bucks off its rider, it will usually trot away. After a bull bucks off its rider, it's likely to charge him. Also, bulls have horns. The first bull rider I watched at National Western made it to eight seconds before falling off, but as he stood up to walk away, the bull butted him, catching a horn under one of his legs and sending him flying.

Bulls—and broncs, for that matter—are only getting more difficult and dangerous to ride as the DNA of the hardest-kicking rough stock is harnessed to breed even rowdier successors. (Semen samples of top-scoring bulls are worth thousands a pop.) The cliché is that they're "bred to buck." I read in The New York Times that in 1995, eight-second rides were completed 46% of the time, but now that rate is down to about 29%. This isn't a concern in mutton bustin'. The sheep are just run-of-the-mill sheep. But as future bull riders progress to riding calves, then small bulls, then the legends of the herd, the stakes get more and more severe.

In 2020, Bingham had a near-death accident at the National

Finals in Texas. He'd matched with an infamous bull named Spotted Demon (86% buck-off rate, career average score of 44). The bull was 12 years old and scheduled to retire after that ride. Spotted Demon quickly threw Bingham to the dirt; in the process, the bull's shoulder caught the side of Bingham's helmet, knocking it off and Bingham unconscious. (Helmets are not required in bull riding.) Spotted Demon then spun around and stomped a hoof down in the center of Bingham's chest. (He was, fortunately, wearing a protective vest.) Bingham suffered nine broken ribs, a broken sternum, a broken clavicle, bruised lungs, a bruised heart, and a concussion. While he recovered in the hospital, Spotted Demon was sent for his retirement to a California cow pasture to sire bucking babies with the progeny of one of the greatest bucking bulls of all, Bushwacker (97% buck-off rate, career average score of 46). I shiver at the thought of one of the mutton busters I'd met one day trying to ride a bull of both Bushwacker and Spotted Demon lineage.

Bingham got bucked off in about six seconds at National Western that afternoon. I watched his legs swing above his head before he smacked down on his side. He managed to scurry away from the bull's stamping hind legs this time.

I tracked down Bingham in the big room after he'd gotten out of his gear. I told him about the story I was working on and asked if he remembered his first rodeo, at age 7.

"I was so scared," he said. Everything happened so fast when the sheep took off; the ride was a blur to him now. But he recalled how captivated he was by the whole event. "Your first couple youth rodeos," he said, "you feel like you're at the NFR." (That's the National Finals Rodeo.) Bingham went all in, and by the time he turned 8 he was riding calves, steers, and mini bulls.

I asked him what made him fall in love with it so quickly.

"The adrenaline rush," he said. "Me and my brother, when we were little, we used to do a lot of wild things. We had dirt bikes; we even had a motocross track at one point in our backyard, and that was pretty fun until my brother broke his leg on it. And then, right after that, we got rid of the motocross track and we got mini bulls, and we rode them all the time, and we'd take them over to our friends' houses."

"When did you get on your first real bull?" I asked.

"I got on my first big bull when I was 10," he said. "He was perfect for a kid. He was friendly. I probably started riding decent bucking bulls when I was 12."

I asked if he would recommend starting so young.

"Oh, absolutely," he said. "The earlier you can get into it, the better off you are."

I returned to National Western the following day, hoping to find a buster with bull-riding dreams. As it so happened, the first parent I spoke to was the father of one such boy.

The dad, Chris, wore a blue cap backward, a blue collared shirt, and blue jeans. His 7-year-old son, Callan, was a veteran mutton buster; this was his eighth contest. "They call him 'Boots' at school because all he wears is cowboy boots," said Chris. "He wants to be a bull rider when he's older. He's been talking about that since he was 4 years old."

Chris told me he'd ridden steers himself until he was about 13. Then, when it was time to move up, he took one look at the bulls and said, "Nope."

I asked if he was worried about Callan riding bulls eventually.

"Oh, yeah—100%," said Chris. "At the same time, you know, there's this whole dream factor. If that's what he wants to do, I'm just making sure I'm being transparent about the risk. He's potentially entering a sport that is life-threatening. But, you know, at school, none of the other kids really do this type of thing, and so he feels unique, and it's like this whole confidence booster for him. I'm not going to crush that. I'm not going to be the one to say, 'You can't do this.'"

I asked about Callan's goals for the day.

"He wants to stay on for eight seconds."

"How close has he gotten?"

"He's done seven, but that's also Dad counting."

"Oh, okay—so, like, 6:49?"

"Yeah, exactly."

Callan did not make it to eight seconds. Not even close. The sheep took a few steps and Callan fell to the dirt. He stood right up, dusted himself off, and gave a queen a two-handed overhead high-five. Chris was laughing.

I said, "He looked like he had fun."

"He tried."

"He didn't quite make eight seconds, but…"

"Honestly, he walked away from it, so I feel real good. Come tomorrow at school, this will be the talk."

Callan came over to his dad and me in the big room after an obligatory group photo with the big trophies.

I asked Callan, "How'd that go?"

"Super good."

"You've ridden a few times before, right? What's your favorite part of it?"

"Umm, probably getting onto the sheep because it's so furry."

I asked Callan what he planned on doing later to celebrate. He said playing cowboys and robots with his friends. I had never played this game before. I asked him how it worked. He explained that everyone dies. I'm sure it's a fun time.

Before going home for the evening, I went to ask a question of a queen named Amanda Cook, also known as Miss Evergreen Rodeo 2023. She had long, dark, braided hair and wore a black shirt with sleek purple trim. She told me mutton bustin' got her "into this whole mess." After sheep, she did trick riding from ages 11 to 19, and now at 22 years old she reigns as Evergreen, Colorado, rodeo royalty. I noticed she was good with the children, and I felt like I was still having trouble connecting with them. My attempts to interview the kids produced few answers other than "I don't know." I asked Cook if she had any advice.

She insisted it was easy. At least, she said, "it's easy wearing what I am, because they say, 'Your crown is so shiny.' They're like, 'Oooh, I want to touch it. It's so pretty!'"

I took down the note: Be shinier. (I decided I'd rather not.)

Chip and I came back to the Stock Show a few days later, but instead of going to the Coliseum, we went across the street to a smaller venue called the Stadium Arena for a special 50-competitor mutton bustin' extravaganza. We set our bags down in a staging area near a pen of a dozen or so sheep and two red sheep-sized chutes. Chip had opened his bag and started assembling his camera equipment when a short, bespectacled woman with short gray hair came toward us waving a finger. She had volunteer credentials (blue lanyard). She paused and said, "Oh, I didn't see your purple lanyards." I realized she thought we were random people shuffling through someone else's camera bag. "If it wasn't yours, I was going to..."

She stopped mid-sentence, pulled out a pocketknife, and unfolded it in front of us.

Chip conveyed his appreciation for her careful eye. It was reassuring to have someone watching over our stuff. Though not much later I saw her leaning back in a chair, half asleep.

Chip went to calibrate his equipment, or whatever photographers do, and I stood around the sheep pen. Then something remarkable happened: The sheep next to me defecated. I don't know why it did not previously occur to me that the animals eject feces into the same dirt the riders fall into, but I was suddenly struck by this obvious fact, which I found repulsive. I am a little bit of a germaphobe. At least, I would rather not play in a sheep's litter box.

I looked for a distraction.

I noticed a young woman with intern credentials (yellow lanyard) pointing her iPhone camera at a giant screen cycling through commercials for Chevrolet, John Deere (0% APR financing available on tractors and round balers), and sundry other sponsors. I asked what she was doing, and she told me she was taking pictures to show company reps that their ads were indeed being served. Countless logos adorned the arena walls, which she had to photograph too. Cinch Jeans, U.S. Army, U.S. Bank, Centura, Steel Structures America, Mountain Dew, King Soopers, 9 News... This much brand promotion is not unusual for a major American sporting production, though I was astounded that not even an amateur sport for 5-year-olds was immune to such excessive commercialization.

The kids felt far away when they were competing in the vast Coliseum, but I had a much closer vantage point on the floor of the Stadium Arena. I was able to see many more red, snotty, tear-streaked faces. Some kids cried as they approached the sheep and reality set in.

Others cried after falling off and taking a hoof to the belly. It seemed the medical team was mostly in the business of cheering kids up. I saw one EMT tending to a crying child for a while, and I asked what was wrong. It was a case of some dirt in the eye. More often than not, the kids returned ecstatic, yelling something about how fast the sheep went.

At the rodeo, parents were cordoned off by the queens, but at the Stadium Arena mutton bustin' extravaganza, the parents were confined like cattle within a 10-by-10-foot chain barrier. Nearby, I noticed one particularly confident boy: Wyatt, 7 years old. He had blond hockey flow coming out the back of his helmet. Right before his ride, he turned to his mom, who was standing in the chained area, showed off a big smile, and gave her a wave.

Mom yelled, "Hold on, baby!" She had her phone out and was snapping photos at random without looking at the screen.

Mom noticed I'd taken notice. She told me Wyatt wants to ride bulls.

"How do you feel about that?" I inquired.

"Great!"

"Really?"

"Yeah! I'd try it too."

I was surprised. She was the first parent I'd spoken to who expressed no concern for the risks of bull riding. I also found it relieving. So much brooding can be a bit exhausting.

"He likes anything that goes fast," she said. She told me he rides dirt bikes and does martial arts, too. There was much excitement to try mutton bustin'. "He asked me to play victory music on the way here."

"What is victory music?"

"Queen."

I hoped not "We Are the Champions." That would have been cliché. I thought "Keep Yourself Alive" would have been a suitable choice. I refrained from suggesting judgment for any one song—instead, an album. I said, "I listened to Queen on my way over here, actually. A Night at the Opera."

She said, "That's my favorite."

Rodeo is indeed operatic.

A couple of months prior to the Stock Show, I consulted a single mother named Axie, whom I found on social media. I'm not sure if rodeo has the equivalent of a soccer mom; if so, it would be her. (Instead of a minivan, she drives a Ram 1500 with a bull bar.) She was kind enough to invite me to her friend's ranch in the Colorado prairie, where her sons take horse-riding lessons, to teach me what I'd need to know about rodeo before embarking on this story.

Her 3-year-old, BeauJangles, and 5-year-old, Braydan, want to ride bulls and broncs, respectively. Axie and her two sisters pitch in, taking the boys to twice-weekly riding lessons and weekend mutton bustin' contests hours away.

BeauJangles was too young to compete at National Western. I had hoped to watch Braydan there, but he was one of the more than 800 kids who did not draw a spot. Nevertheless, Axie and BeauJangles share a birthday, Jan. 17, and their celebration was an evening at the National Western rodeo. I bought a seat next to Axie's, at her invitation, in a middle row above the chutes.

The boys always dress in matching outfits. At the rodeo, they wore brown quarter-zips, big belt buckles, and cowboy hats that swallowed their small heads. BeauJangles had brought with him his new Buzz Lightyear action figure, which he waved in my face upon my arrival. He didn't have much to say. BeauJangles is a quiet boy.

When bareback riding started, Axie turned to Braydan and said, "That's what you want to do, right?"

Braydan was standing up from his seat, nervous. He looked at me with a sort of grimacing-emoji face. "No! Scary!"

"Now it's scary?" Axie said. She feigned surprise, but I think she was relieved by Braydan's reaction. Axie wants her boys to pursue their dreams, whatever they are, but she had told me at the ranch that she hopes they pivot from rough-stock riding to team roping, in which two cowboys on horseback work together to lasso a steer. "It's less dangerous," she'd said.

I looked away for a moment, but when I returned my attention to Braydan, he was back in his seat, mirroring the riders' motions with one hand swinging in the air. He had not abandoned bronc riding yet.

When I first met Axie, I had wanted to understand what mutton bustin' is really about, in a sense deeper than mere play. Themes of courage, confidence, education, culture, and camaraderie came up. But what seemed most impactful were the dreams it inspired.

I did not see Braydan ride, but I don't think that matters. I realized, while I was watching the show with him, that it's not about the ride. It's about the dream. The dream is what I saw. Braydan started jumping up and down, pointing at the riders. He shouted, "That's me! That's me!" He had a vision of himself out there, something in his imagination that he can cherish, and that alone is worthy, regardless of whether he actually becomes a bronc rider.

—*Originally appeared in* Mountain Gazette 199, *2023.*

45.
A Woman's Place Is at the Top
Written by Ingrid Backstrom

The first time Arlene Blum climbed a mountain, she tore the skin completely off her butt. After reaching its high point, her group started their descent; her partners said they would need to slide down in order to get off the mountain before dark, and they gave her a quick demonstration on how to glissade. Then the guys, more-experienced climbers whom she barely knew, sped off out of sight down the bumpy, icy slope of Mount Adams on their buns, protected by the leather on the seats of their special mountaineering pants. Blum gamely began to slide also, on the seat of her wool dress slacks, not realizing that her companions had a protective advantage.

As she rested below snowline in the dark, exhausted and exhilarated from the climb and the glissading, she discovered with horror that she had shredded her pants and the ice-numb flesh of her backside. Mortified and soaked in blood, she put an extra pair of shorts over her pants and said nothing to her partners. After getting lost in the dark forest with no batteries for their flashlights, they finally found the car at 3 a.m. and drove back to their respective dorms at Reed College.

The following day, a doctor picked small rocks out of Blum's backside and instructed her to sit on a medical donut for several weeks. Blum sheepishly toted the embarrassing seat with her to classes while she healed. She tried to focus on school and hoped the "real" climbers on campus weren't laughing at her. But all she could think about was getting back up high on a mountain. She wrote home to her family that her day on Mount Adams had been the best of her life.

That was 1964. Once her buns healed, Blum climbed every chance she could—rocks, mountains, whatever was available—throughout college. She graduated in 1966 and chose to get her doctorate in chemistry at Harvard, but was told that the prestigious Harvard Mountaineering Club wouldn't allow women. So she chose MIT, only to be told by a professor upon arriving that no woman at MIT would be allowed to get a doctorate in physical chemistry. So, after putting in a year studying surface chemistry in Boston, Blum transferred to Berkeley. Closer to good climbing in the Sierra, and with a supportive and encouraging advisor (a climber, no less!), she was able to advance her personal climbing goals while also advancing science.

Over the next 15 years, Blum created a series of scientific and mountaineering breakthroughs despite sexism and antisemitism on the rock and in the outdoor community as well as devastating losses of friends and climbing partners in the mountains.

During her first year at Berkeley, inspired by the necklace of a fellow climber on a school climbing outing, she formed beads into an H-like structure to show her hypothesis of what a three-dimensional representation of a tRNA molecule might look like. Her model seemed incredibly promising toward helping understand how proteins in a cell are made, but her advisor encouraged her to go back to the drawing board and do the painstaking research experiments that would provide concrete proof. Meanwhile, she searched for a climbing expedition to join; she had saved up some money and was ready for a challenge.

Inquiring about a trekking trip to Nepal, Blum was told she couldn't join because there wouldn't be another woman on the trip with whom she could share a tent. Applying for a trip to Afghanistan to climb a 21,000-foot peak for which she was well qualified, she was later informed that she hadn't been accepted because having a woman on the trip might create issues for "excretory situations high on the open ice." Her friend, a male climber who'd never been higher than 14,000 feet and was thus much less qualified than she, had been invited along. When asked about an expedition in Denali, the guiding outfit said women could come to base camp, but no higher, as they were neither strong enough to carry loads nor emotionally stable enough to handle the high altitude. When she expressed further interest in Denali at an American Alpine Club meeting, a man in the room said, "No way dames could make it up that bitch."

That was 1967. Between her research and studies at Berkeley, Blum climbed in Peru, managing to ascend about 20,000 feet despite a debilitating, undiagnosed case of hepatitis. She also summited Mount Waddington in British Columbia with a guided group, and then by 1970 had assembled a team of six women to attempt Denali. If successful, they would be the first women ever to summit the mountain. Spoiler alert: The dames made it up that bitch.

Bolstered by her success leading the trip to Denali, she organized an Endless Winter trip, where she and a rotating cast of partners made their way around the globe for months, climbing and trekking in Afghanistan, the Rwenzori Mountains in Uganda, Iran, and Kashmir, among many other places, completing three first ascents and reaching more than 23,000 feet at their highest point.

On a dramatic and chaotic trip to Peak Lenin organized by the Russian government in 1974, Blum had a lightbulb moment contemplating drops of ice melting off of the glacier. She realized that by rapidly freezing the protein ribonuclease, she could perhaps get a nuclear magnetic resonance image of the folded protein. The prevailing wisdom at the time said capturing a protein mid-fold wasn't possible. In fact, one of her professors, Robert "Buzz" Baldwin, flat out told her it wouldn't work, and still she didn't listen. As Baldwin said in 2017, "She was a very persistent person. She still is." Sure enough, after many tries in the lab, her idea finally worked. Baldwin later said that her pioneering efforts had been "groundbreaking and resulted in a whole new field." Studying proteins and their folding remains critically important to understanding and seeking cures for many common conditions, including Parkinson's, Alzheimer's, and some forms of diabetes, among other illnesses.

Her experiment a success, Blum hopped on a plane to India to climb the Trisul massif. During their summit bid, her dear friend and former partner Bruce Carson, a young, talented, environmentally minded climber, fell through a cornice to his death. Distraught, Blum vowed to dedicate her career to Carson, who had always striven to leave the world, every base camp, and every place he went better than when he arrived. She shifted her focus toward studying the chemistry of the products that people put into their bodies and the environment.

She began by assessing early forms of birth control for cancer risks, then studied the chemical tris(hydroxymethyl)aminomethane, also known as tris, a flame retardant that at the time was put in children's pajamas (and that is still in wide use in furniture and children's car seats, among other products). She, along with Bruce Ames, determined not only that tris is cancerous, but also that it was being absorbed into the bodies of the children who wore the pajamas, and Blum lobbied effectively to get it banned.

In 1976, Blum reached 24,500 feet on Everest—at the time, an altitude record for an American woman—on a trip that she helped organize and produce. Weakened from a bad case of giardia, and victim to macho decision-making—the men on the team later admitted to feeling threatened by her competence as well as competitive toward her for the coveted summit spots—she felt discouraged by the trip, and was still mourning the loss of Carson. While two members summited—the second-ever Americans to do so, which was considered a massive success—the expedition left Blum feeling empty, ready for a more purposeful adventure and perhaps a bit more altitude.

In 1978, after much planning, training, work, and fundraising, including selling 15,000 T-shirts that read "Annapurna ... A Woman's Place Is on Top," Blum led the first all-women's trip to an 8,000-meter peak, purposely hiring a smaller fraction of (male) porters than standard all-men expeditions of the era typically enlisted to help carry gear on the mountain. The trip was both a triumph and a tragedy. Two members successfully summited, while two others perished after attempting the summit despite Blum and the other women pleading with them to turn around. Blum's book on the trip, *Annapurna: A Woman's Place*, was a bestseller.

That book was my own first introduction to Blum. As a teen

obsessed with adventure and mountaineering books, Blum's—alongside *Miles From Nowhere* by Barbara Savage—stood out glaringly to me amid the hordes of tales by men, and I devoured them. Her honest storytelling read simultaneously matter-of-fact yet warm and personal, and I felt validated as a young woman who had objectives and goals in which the established norms might sometimes interfere. In a gesture of teenage female solidarity, I petitioned my high school to allow women into the all-male Knights of the Cutlass club, members of which were entitled to prestigious high school honors like performing skits for school assemblies and getting special patches for their letterman's jacket. Since Blum made inroads into male-dominated spaces, then I would also.

Throughout my own life and ski career, I have been fortunate to have Blum's and many other women's examples in my mind at all times. We take it for granted that women belong in the mountains. When I was invited on a trip to Denali in 2010, no one was worried about my "excretory situations high on a glacier"—except me, because have you ever tried to change a tampon on the side of a mountain in a snowstorm when it's blowing 60 miles an hour?

I've celebrated the joys and bemoaned the challenges of ski road trips—to ski areas, mind you—while Blum thought nothing of trekking across the Alps with her partner and their baby in a backpack for several months in the 1980s.

After having children myself, I began to learn about the constant health risks lurking all around us in the form of toxic chemicals. They're in the personal hygiene products we use, the pans we cook in, the clothing we wear, and countless other everyday items as varied as paint remover and countertops. While reading an article one day about toxic chemicals in kids' toys, my heroine's name appeared. *Wait, I thought, could it possibly be the same Arlene Blum, mountain-climbing pioneer? How could one woman be a massive success and a complete trailblazer in two very important and seemingly very different aspects of my life?*

When her daughter was born, Blum left academia, leading trips around the world and teaching courses in leadership. Her memoir, Breaking Trail, was released in 2005, to critical acclaim. In 2006, after her daughter went to college, Blum decided she wanted to return to industrial chemistry after 26 years. She discovered that while tris had been banned, other chemicals had been substituted in its place, a game of whack-a-mole where once one substance was proven to be dangerous (a years-long process with little to no regulation or oversight, all hinging on individual scientists and their funding to do the work), another substance in the same class of chemicals would simply be subbed in, posing a new suite of unknown health risks.

"The best thing people can do is spend some time to get educated about these classes of chemicals," Blum told me when I had the honor of talking to her—on her landline. This recent work led her to start the Green Science Policy Institute, "to mobilize scientists, industry, governments, nonprofits, and consumers to reduce the use of toxic chemicals."

Since its founding, Blum's been working tirelessly on behalf of the institute and her "Six Classes" approach to chemicals, which holds that if we eliminate an entire class of toxic chemicals rather than each of the hundreds of individual chemicals within it, industries can no longer perpetuate the creation of new, unsafe products. She writes two regular newsletters, available at arleneblum.com and sixclasses.org, dedicated to educating people about the ongoing efforts of chemists like her to research and lobby on behalf of our planet and our health.

When not working—whenever that could be—Blum hikes every day in the Berkeley Hills. "But only for two to three hours," she says, "to save my knees." Cross-country skiing, however? She can go all day.

—*Originally appeared in* Mountain Gazette 200, *2023.*

46.
Follow the Footprints
Written by Kade Krichko

I was in third grade when I realized my mom was a big deal. It was early February in Ridgefield, Connecticut, and she'd come to speak to Mrs. Galdo's class. Parents did that from time to time, explaining what they did and how they'd gotten there, urging 9-year-olds to start thinking about five-year plans, Roth IRAs, and other things that went in one ear and out the other.

Her talk was different, though. Instead of a PowerPoint and bar graphs, she showed up with race bibs and medals. She brought long ski poles and a jacket with "USA" embroidered across the back, throwing around words like "World Cup," "World Championships," and "Olympics." The latter earned a collective gasp from the kids in my class. *Was Kade's mom really…?*

None of it—aside from a few of the medals—was earth-shattering to me. I knew my mom had Nordic skied in the Olympic Games, that she'd had a long career in a sport most people didn't really understand anything about. I even knew she'd been a national champion and Maine's first female Olympian. But mostly she was my mom—the woman who made me go to bed at 9 p.m., didn't let me or my younger sisters eat sugary cereal, and worked out more than anyone else "her age." I knew she had achieved some pretty cool things, yet I needed that classroom reaction for it to truly hit home. I left class that day proud, but also a little embarrassed I'd never asked for the whole story.

Honestly, it would be years unti if l I got that story, and even today she'll sneak in a new anecdote at the unlikeliest of moments. I think a big piece of that was by design; my mom never wanted her accomplishments to shape our paths or overshadow our modest victories. Even as her heart ached for the mountains of Maine, she was good at carving joy from sports-practice shuttles and suburban Girl Scout Cookies deliveries—so good, in fact, that we never knew what she was missing, or how much of her we carried with us along the way.

Nordic ski racing is built for masochists. It's an aerobic sprint that claws at your lungs and pumps battery acid through your arteries. World-class athletes often melt before finish lines—bonking, seizing, crashing despite months of intensive training. It's a sport that knows your limits, yet routinely asks you for more.

"I like it because it makes you hurt all over," my mom once told me, laughing. "I think I love it because it is so tough." How she could give her heart to such a thing was always beyond me. She had us on skis as soon as we could walk and made us agree to a reluctant truce that for every day we got to ride chairlifts, a Nordic day would follow. Still, my relationship with the sport more or less ended there.

I put up with Nordic skiing, but Leslie Bancroft fell for it—hard. My mom had grown up downhill skiing and running, but didn't combine the two until her freshman year of high school, when the football coach asked her to help round out his new Nordic team. By the next year, she was a Maine state champion. More-experienced skiers didn't understand how the lanky teen who ran her skis uphill and tucked down could race, much less win, but she kept doing it. And winning felt good. By junior year she'd earned a junior national championship in Deadwood, South Dakota, skiing on gear cobbled together from friends' equipment stashes back home. It was only her second time on a plane, and when a Fischer rep approached her about a ski sponsorship, she boasted that she didn't need any skis: Her dad had gotten her a new pair for Christmas. (After a lengthy explanation from her mom, she would eventually ski with the brand for the rest of her career.)

When the U.S. Ski Team came knocking a year later, in the spring of 1977, she nearly turned them down too, but that ticket proved harder to pass up. Head coach Marty Hall was incubating a group of young skiers for the 1984 Olympics—and he wanted Leslie to be a part of it. Four years ahead of schedule, in Lake Placid, New York, she proved him right.

Ask my mom about the 1980 Olympics and she'll talk about how she and teammate Betsy Haines tried to sneak next to Beth Heiden (the sister of five-time speed-skating gold medalist Eric Heiden) to get on TV during the opening ceremony, or how she spread Team USA swag on the floor of her Olympic Village dorm, counting out each piece like Halloween candy. She'll remember how she spent her 21st birthday at the Miracle on Ice (yes, *that* Miracle on Ice) and still has Al Michaels' famous call etched into her memory bank: "Do you believe in miracles?!" (After that night, she did.)

Press her a little further, though, and you'll uncover a deeper flame. Her eyes will light up talking about the three events she skied, and she'll still get a little salty over tiny mistakes on the 4x5 kilometer relay—a young team that still somehow took seventh against the best skiers in the world (and enough doped blood to float a balloon).

My sisters and I always joked about these outbursts, how my mom had "no chill" when it came to the things she was passionate about. I mean, in our defense, there were stories to back it up. Like in 1981, as the anchor of the 4x5 kilometer relay for the University of Vermont, when she rallied from 39 seconds behind to win her team a collegiate national championship. After making the pass, she dragged the suddenly second-place racer with her, knowing that the skier needed to stay in second to assure UVM the overall team championship. "I bribed her with two cases of beer," my mom would say after the fact. "I knew she liked to party."

But that kind of passion wasn't just a competitive streak. It was, and always has been, a road map. With Title IX in its infancy and mainstream popularization of women's sports still decades off, my mom and her teammates navigated daily minefields to even set a single ski on course. Dwindling support systems led to overtraining, eroded mental health, and created toxic team cultures, while distorted power dynamics and a general disconnect between female athletes and male coaches created scars that haunted athletes their entire careers. Long before Larry Nassar and Alberto Salazar faced their very public reckonings, hundreds of top-level athletes in the '70s and '80s endured varying levels of abuse for years—alone.

"It was a different time, but I wish they'd given us a voice as women athletes," Mom tells me. "We just weren't listened to, and not just by coaches, doctors—all of it."

My mom still feels like she walked away at the top of her game. Injured just a few months after the 1982 World Championships, she was left to navigate treatment by herself. After a doctor misdiagnosed her pain for weeks ("He said that couldn't be what I was feeling because that was for old ladies who wore heels," she remembers), she was forced to diagnose her own Morton's neuroma. When an exploratory surgery (at the time an incision from the top of the foot all the way around to the bottom) proved her correct, she rehabbed on her own, isolated on an island away from the team and the life she'd lived for the past half-decade. She'll admit that the pressure of a return got to her, but says it was the lack of support—not even a phone call—from the people she'd come to trust that ate her alive. She felt exposed, discarded. For the first time, her heart pointed away from the snow. Just a few months shy of the 1984 Games, her Games, she left the U.S. Ski Team, and competitive skiing, in the rearview.

That history never sat right with me. Little Kade wanted to call somebody, or send an angry letter. It didn't seem fair. It wasn't. But my mom saw something else. She went back to school for nutrition and then exercise science, her chance to correct what her fellow female athletes battled in the shadows. She spent more time with my dad and made friends away from skiing. She unfurled her map a little farther and started building the life she wanted.

Still, the story could never fully leave the mountains. Leslie would still find time to roller-ski around the streets of her new home in Portland, Oregon, and she picked up a few shifts at an outdoor gear shop. She fell in love with getting people on skis. One fall day in 1985, her store manager pulled her aside—she thought she was getting fired—and said something she didn't realize she needed to hear. "You need to get back to ski racing," she remembers him saying. "Do you want to be 35 wondering why you didn't try one more time?"

Two years after retiring from racing, she skied to fifth at the 1985 National Championships in Bend, Oregon. It was enough for national coaches to come calling again, but she told them the timing wasn't right. This go-around, she'd come back on her terms.

After racing ski marathons for a year, she returned to Nationals in '86 and won the whole dang thing. The extra time gave her a chance to reconnect with the sport again, and the U.S. Team had little excuse not to bring her back full-time.

The comeback alone would have been poetry enough, but my mom had other plans. She raced the World Championships in 1987 blazoned in red, white, and blue, and, despite suffering another foot injury a few months later, battled back to qualify for the '88 Olympics in Calgary. At 28, she was the oldest returning member of the U.S. squad—and the only one growing a baby, me, on her uterine wall.

Leslie skied her three events in Calgary one month pregnant with me (her only indication at the time being a strong aversion to the food in the Olympic Village). She crossed the finish line to family and friends from around the world, celebrating her 29th birthday with a cake decorated with an array of mismatched candles. At the closing ceremony a couple of days later, she let gratitude trickle down her cheeks.

In those days, the U.S. Ski Team included a pre-written retirement letter in its athlete information packet—a neat and tidy option to bid farewell to international competition. My mom never signed hers, but a few weeks after the '88 Games she delivered a typed-up resignation. She'd wanted to write her own.

I've spent my life placing the pieces of my mom's story, but it wasn't until I started looking at my own puzzle that I understood how hers came together. I never became a ski racer, but that passion thing is real. My mom recognized it, and instead of tightening a vice grip on my world, she let it run, even when it led farther away than she ever imagined. I chased words and stories to the West, and then overseas. I've learned about success, lived failure, dreamed and wandered a path far from the comfortable. It's gratifying and sometimes lonely, even when I'm not alone. I think about my mom a lot in those moments—how scared she might have been, how brave she had to be. It's a silent reassurance that somebody has come and done this, in her own way, before me, and that she found joy in the process.

She's a coach now, helping a younger generation avoid the traps that nearly snarled her career.

"I've learned a lot from mistakes that were made," she said recently. "Now I have a chance to make sure my skiers never have to."

There's a sense of duty there, but also a new path to channel that fire. I can hear it in her voice over the phone; it's the same excitement she brought to the start line as a metal-mouthed teenager on borrowed race skis.

An extra Nordic setup is always waiting in my mom's garage. When I came home last winter, I knew it was just a matter of time before she'd pull them out and tell me to jump in the car. Skinny skiing has become my homecoming ritual, something I'll fake-complain about, but secretly look forward to. My mom is still faster than me, but the distance between us is shorter. On a cold, sunny day in February, she attacked the uphills and I found meditation in the glide of a skate ski. Talking trailed off, the soundtrack of soft winds and forest birds taking over. We bobbed our way around winding corduroy, our skis sliding together, apart, together again, gaining speed around the bend.

—*Originally appeared in* Mountain Gazette 200, *2023.*

47.
Good Work

Written by Will Grant

It's just a job. People will say that it's a lifestyle, a calling, that it chooses you, but the reality is you can quit anytime the going gets too rough or the solitude wears on you or you want more out of life than calluses and fresh air. It's good work, though. The walls of your office will be blue mountains as far as the eye can see. Wind and sky will be your constant companions. And your horse. You'll want to look after that horse because, let me tell you, the territory gets a lot bigger when you're afoot.

The nature of the job is the nature of the North American savanna. You'll see an elemental side of the country. Birth and death and fire and ice, and when the first blades of tender grass pierce the frozen prairie, you'll know it. It's a job not so much at the mercy of the environment as in lockstep with it. The sagebrush flats and the shortgrass prairie and the pine-clad ridges of the American outback—glimpses of what it all looked like a thousand years ago.

You landed the job because the last guy split for greener pastures. Now you're in the tax bracket of one of the lowest-paid agricultural workers in the U.S., and the boss is waiting for you to get that first month under your belt so you'll quit tripping over your own feet. It'll take longer than a month, but you can't sweat the learning curve because there's not a cowboy alive who didn't go through the same.

The work doesn't get easier, but you'll get less awkward and more efficient, finally catch your breath once winter rolls around and the rhythm slows. That's when you can tell the folks back home: The romance is real. There's growth to be had in those hills.

Cowboy life holds many secrets. Sitting in a saddle all day will give you boils on the insides of your thighs. High-heeled, narrow-toe riding boots will disfigure your feet. You'll get to know every square inch of a mother cow. It's animal husbandry on a landscape scale: pastures measured in square miles; a summer range up high, a winter range in the valley, and a two-day ride between; a simple camp far enough away from the ranch headquarters that it's easier to leave you out there with a few good horses and a dog and send a resupply truck with news and provisions once a week than to have you driving back and forth every day.

The magic is in the partnership with the horse. A thousand pounds of flesh and bone working in your favor is a tremendous sensation. The whole becomes greater than the sum of its individual parts. It's like walking on water. When you ride an animal, nonverbal communication takes over, and, in accomplishing your job as a cowboy, the horse can do a lot more than meet you halfway. The trick is to never lose your cool and to leave your ego out of the equation. That's the best advice I ever received regarding a horse.

No other job in the world can hold a candle to what no one will be there to see, but eventually you might decide that looking at the back end of a cow all day isn't the future you had envisioned for yourself. Then you can do what everyone else does. Go to work at a laptop. Check email rather than newborn calves. Dreams of the purple sage won't help you sleep at night, but your loved ones can rest assured that you didn't go crazy out here. You did the right thing. You went home, left the bleeding on the mountain to someone else, and it's probably just as well. The beauty of the landscape is in its dearth of people, and the cowboy line of work isn't going anywhere.

The future of the cowboy, though, is more secure than you might think. His greatest threat of extinction is that he breaks his neck while galloping off into the sunset because his horse stepped in a badger hole. All that rhetoric about us being a dying breed, that the cowboy's days are numbered, that nowadays people herd cattle with drones and you can hang up your spurs, old man—that narrative sells for public consumption, works for what a lot of people want to think about the 21st-century West. Let them think it. But on the millions of acres of patented land out here where remotely grazing livestock remains the only feasible economic carrying capacity, the cowboy will find work. It's not a trend or a fad. It's a job.

—Originally appeared in Mountain Gazette 204, *2025.*

48.
What the Girls Know
By Emily Leibert

Patterson is a place where the lawns are inoffensive. Manicured, but not so much that they jut out from the rest of the scenery or set off warning signs of stomach-curling wealth. Like a teenager's messy bun, they are coiffed and tousled just enough to convince you all forces here are working as intended without toppling the natural order of things—or, in this case, without sacrificing the tangles of flora and fauna against which the yards are transposed. It's the Americana, mostly rows of bunting flags on the porches, that give up the jig. Really, it's the red. Red not as in anemones or azaleas, but as in synthetic dye extracted from petroleum distillate and coal-tar sludge. It's an otherwise convincing diorama of tranquility and simplicity, but the red knows better.

From the back of a taxi—the old-school species from the pre-Uber fleet that you have to dial up and hail—that blur of bunting flags is a welcome distraction from the winding drive up to Camp Kaufmann. The camp sits one town over from Patterson in Holmes, New York. A two-and-a-half-hour train ride from Grand Central, it's a 425-acre plot of land (more than half the size of Central Park, according to camp director Kristen Glass) that once belonged to the critters and now belongs to the 25,000 girls who make up the Girl Scouts of Greater New York (GSGNY). Last year, the organization, which serves only New York City, spent millions renovating the camp's Great Hall, now called Girl HQ, the funds raised in a hellfire by GSGNY CEO

Meridith Maskara and her disciples to beef up the facilities available to the girls they serve. ("Serve": They always phrase it like that. Dutiful, almost militant, sometimes ecclesiastic, as though the girls are God.)

The campgrounds are sprawling. You need golf carts and Subarus to make the trek between cabins and trails, ponds, and a butterfly sanctuary. But the refashioned Girl HQ is the star, architectural feat that it is: Think *The Parent Trap*, but with towering beams and reinforced floor-to-ceiling paned-glass windows. It's a church just for the Scouts, only the sound of hymns has been replaced by shrill giggles and shrieks marked by that lilting pitch belonging only to 8-year-olds. An 83-year-old woman known to the campers as Mama Ribbet, dressed head to toe in tie-dye and wearing a Girl Scout–green bucket hat, guards the entrance, gargoyle-esque, addressing each visitor with a knowing nod. I make a mental note not to piss her off.

As the camp staff are eager to point out, they've taken care to rescue some of the 1960s wood that formed the bedrock of the last iteration of Girl HQ. The 100 or so Scouts and counselors staying for the weekend touch the old slabs throughout the day, paying their respects to the structure that once staved off the elements and protected their forebears. In nearly every room, including the bathrooms, 8.5-by-11-inch sheets of paper taped to the walls galvanize the girls: "Remember, a Girl Scout leaves a place BETTER than she found it!" This doesn't really sound like a suggestion.

Before I introduce you to this particular group of girls—before I allow them to run away with your hearts, as they have with mine—we must first address the sensationalism of the cookies. All 200 million boxes a year. Because, as the Scouts will begrudgingly tell you, the question that follows "Are you a Girl Scout?" is almost always "Do you like selling cookies?" It's a call-and-response that mimics the cadence of a Marco Polo game, the answer to the former halfway out of the Scout's mouth before the inquirer begins the latter. As NPR writer Bill Chappell observed earlier this year, the Scouts' cookie sales, after all, have all the markings of war. The father of two daughters recalled his experience joining the "Girl Scouts Army," driving in a "convoy" of minivans and SUVs to a D.C. parking lot (the "Thin Mint trenches") where parents of various privilege loaded their cars with sustenance: Caramel deLites, Do-si-dos, Peanut Butter Patties, the works. "It reminds me of large-scale relief efforts I've visited for NPR, where the sole objective is to distribute massive quantities of food," he noted of the 170,000 cookie boxes on site.

Divisive among parents (building entrepreneurship skills, or exploiting kids and their parents for free labor?), even more so among eco-conscious warriors (the organization has come under attack for trying to justify the use of environmentally nefarious palm oil in its cookies), there's certainly a story to be told about the Girl Scouts' cookie-industrial complex—a training ground for baby capitalists, or, as the organization has sorted and labeled them based on their efforts, cookie bosses, cookie networkers, cookie innovators, cookie market researchers, and cookie influencers. And while it's certainly one worth telling, I find that story to be a bottom-shelf rendition of the Girl Scouts' legacy. It does nothing by way of explaining why, when faced with an increasingly bleak future as well as an ungendered one, today's girls continue to stake their girlhood in this fertile ground. This ground reaped by Girl Scouts, of all things.

"Everyone always wants to talk about the cookies. We're more than cookies! I want to shout it from the rooftops!" camp director Glass says through laughter. "I hate to say 'capitalism,' but yeah, we're a brand-driven world, and I think it reduces us. It does."

With that said, she adds, the Thin Mint is still the second-favorite cookie in America. Just after the Oreo.

The Girl Scout brand is one that's hard to shake, having crept into the public consciousness like an apocalyptic fungus. If not on a street corner, where your neighborhood's most tenacious 9-year-olds are developing early business savvy and public-speaking skills, that unmistakable clover leaf can be seen lining the shelves of the hygiene section at your local CVS, or stacked on a plate at IHOP in the form of chartreuse pancakes, or working its way onto your eyelashes from a tube of cookie-inspired mascara. "Ubiquitous" is a strong word, but it's one I'll use confidently here: In just 48 hours, twice I stumble into accidental mentions of the Girl Scouts. First, in the 2015 smut hit *Fifty Shades of Grey*: At the hardware store where she works, a doe-eyed Anastasia Steele pulls rope for Christian Grey with precision, and he, with raised eyebrows, ponders aloud that she must have been a Girl Scout. (I'll add that this reference makes considerably more sense when taken with the fact that Girl Scouts have also received the sexy-Halloween-costume treatment, à la Leg Avenue). The following day, book open on my lap, there they are again, in Sigrid Nunez's pandemic novel, *The Vulnerables*. The National Book Award winner recalls her Brownie troop visiting a nursing home to deliver Valentine's Day gifts in the late 1950s: "Not a duty we looked forward to. We did not want to go to that place. Those people—holy moly, what had happened to them? What calamity had bleached and bent and shriveled them?" I can't say she had a nice time, but it was, nonetheless, a memory she carried with her well into her 70s.

Forty-odd years later, a little girl from Moorpark, California, who loved porcelain dolls and ballerinas became, like Nunez, a Brownie. As a 9-year-old who didn't yet know the horrors of puberty or of suburbia's high school cliques, being part of a Girl Scout troop wasn't really something I opted into; it was instead an assumed social exchange. My troop visited Disneyland together to brave Space Mountain; I cried the whole way through, but still, it was an achievement we celebrated. We learned how to descend a hiking trail: feet planted sideways, socks rolled atop cargo capris to ward off ticks. We made friendship bracelets with glitter beads and received patches for everything we did, hanging them on our vests with pride and sometimes arrogance. When I recount these memories to Lyssa Aruda, a 31-year-old former Girl Scout who participated through her senior year of high school and completed her Gold Award—the highest distinction in Girl Scouting—she laughs as she connects the dots. "I was a crazy perfectionist, so I wanted all of the badges, and there was a big sense of pride in that you earned all of this recognition," she remembers. "It really created a lot of high-achieving people pleasers, I'm sure."

Save for the cookies (and oh, what glorious cookies they are), perhaps the laziest path to go down when tasked with making sense of the Girl Scouts' place in the modern landscape is one of bygone compulsive domesticity. To women decades removed from their own Scouting days, those pint-sized brown vests can feel like an emblem of tradwifery—of the historically feminine duties of sewing, cooking, and modeling a particular breed of martyrdom that swallows the self whole. While Aruda points out that today's badge activities have corrected for the gender gap in math and science—Scouts can now earn badges pertaining to roller coasters, model-car engineering, robotics, and cybersecurity basics—she remembers clearly all the "home-ec-related" badges her troop chased: "the baking badge and cookie badge and the sewing badge and the knitting badge and the crochet badge." Take that, plus an unquestioning view of authority and patriotism (remember "On my honor, I will try to serve God and my country?") that mirrors the modern-day subservience of some red-pilled women, and you've got yourself one unsavory image of the Girl Scouts of America, however uninformed.

"I am constantly fighting the stereotype [that this organization is made up of] wealthy white girls in suburban USA," Maskara, who has helmed the New York sect of the organization for eight years, tells me from an office back at Camp Kaufmann. "You know, Norman Rockwell types...conservative values as opposed to equitable values, as if this [organization] is for those who *have*."

The informed, like Maskara and Mama Ribbett and all of the girls flooding Camp Kauffman that June, tell a different narrative—one they seem to have tattooed on their hearts. They prefer the version of things in which the Girl Scouts, at the beginning as well as presently, is radical in its mission. The story goes like this: In the late 1800s, Southern debutante Juliette Gordon Low is living in Savannah, Georgia, where she sews the clothes of those poorer than she and saves stray animals. A good kid. At 26, she marries a cotton merchant who, legend has it, cheats on her, kicks her out of their home so he can live with his mistress, then dies and leaves the entirety of his estate to the other woman. Low sues him, gets the house back, moves to Scotland, and happens to meet a lord, as one does. But this particular lord is Lord Robert Baden-Powell, founder of the Boy Scouts in the U.K. The seed is planted, and on March 12, 1912, Low pieces together the very first troop of the American Girl Scouts. So it goes.

From a humble troop of 18, the Scouts boom into a brigade of 7,000 by 1916, armed with domestic knowledge, outdoor smarts, and a sense of civic responsibility. The Girl Scouts get involved in the First World War, sewing uniforms and growing gardens for sustenance. They allowed girls of all races to join from the jump, later becoming one of the first groups to desegregate in the wake of Brown v. Board of Education. Dr. Martin Luther King Jr. later praises them as a "force of desegregation," thanks primarily to Black Scouts and troop leaders who spearhead the effort. This is also why Maskara isn't at all surprised that today's Scouts are consciously tackling food deserts, racism, and the migrant crisis, and, in some states, advocating for trans girls. This streak of activism is baked into the organization's core, she insists, and because the idea of femininity was far more aggressively prescribed in the early 1900s, Maskara sees that very same activism in Low: "Because it was such a binary world, the marginalized gender at that time was girls."

As I'm shown around the campus, I realize I'm nervous to meet the Scouts. At least from afar, I find teenage girls utterly horrifying. Those dead-eyed grins. The power with which they scan your face, body, and clothing and show you, with one condescending look, that they find you entirely uncouth—that the particular lens through which you process the world is not only wrong but embarrassing. They can always sniff out your fear. They can also sniff out your envy.

We make our way first through some of the cabins. One troop leader, who has three daughters in Girl Scouts, is relaying a story about the camp's signature night hikes when a 15-year-old runs by, smacking the woman's rear. "Don't worry, it's not weird!" the girl calls behind as she jets about. "She's my mom!" There's an easy relational being to it all, a spatial comfort as the younger girls torpedo around corners, warping their bodies in S shapes to avoid crashing into their troop leaders and counselors, while the older girls dance around the kitchen, trying not to char their mac-and-cheese to ashes for the second time.

After a quick car ride back to Girl HQ and an introductory spiel from Glass, I'm escorted to a small office just off the corridor leading to the Great Hall. I swivel three office chairs in front of me and park myself up against one of the desks, like I imagine someone with authority might. In they come, one, two, three counselors in training, or CITs, as the Scouts call them. They're usually juniors and seniors in high school, occupying a middle ground between children and adults. While still Girl Scouts, they're readying themselves to assume more responsibilities. There are a few nervous giggles and pleasantries exchanged, and then we get down to business.

Sixteen-year-old K'mehia is first. Their camp name is "Nerdy."

"Did you pick that out?" I ask.

"It was kind of given to me, and I just accepted it."

"Who gave it to you?"

"Bookworm."

"Who's Bookworm?!"

Nerdy laughs, explaining that she got her name because she brought all of her homework and three different-color highlighters, with which she color-coded her annotations, to their first training session. She's next to Amy, 17, also known as Sunny, because she's "bright and always smiling." And then there's Maria, 17, who's been dubbed "Flora" by her fellow CITs. "She shines bright like a flower, you know?" Amy says. "There's always something new. She blossoms." I like the way their eyes shift amongst each other, searching for little pushes of motivation. It's not unlike looking to a maternal figure for permission to proceed.

When I ask what Girl Scouts has taught them, Maria volunteers an anecdote that she rattles through with confidence. A little girl came up to her during field games yesterday, crying that no one would play with her. "I felt so sad," Maria says. "I'm like, 'Come here. You're okay. I'll find someone to play with you.'" She asks the girl, "What do you want to do? That's most important. Do you want to play soccer? You want to play jump rope? You want to play Hula-Hoop?" First the girl said soccer, but she wasn't able to kick the ball well. Then she wanted to play catch, but she wanted the ball the other girls were playing with. So Maria walked her over to the big girls, asked if they wouldn't mind playing with her, then watched over as they integrated the younger girl. "And now she's fine!" Maria says proudly. "It's definitely a sisterhood. There's always bonding moments. There's good, and there's bad, but that's okay! That's life, and that's what we bond over."

"Yeah," Amy agrees. "And you can't always get an adult. You have to *be* the adult."

It's when I ask about TikToks and Sephora that something blooms among them. Soft, supple, an ecstatic energy that, if there before, was caught like a butterfly in hands, contained. Wings flapping now, they ramble at the speed of little girls who can't quite finish one word before chomping onto the next—sentences without breaths in between, hands cupped over mouths to conceal their laughter. "We got the Hourglass concealer here, the Too Faced blush, the Milk blush, Anastasia brow gel, Fenty Beauty lip gloss," Amy rattles off, detailing the contents of her makeup bag. "And Rare Beauty!" Maria adds. "Looove Rare Beauty." When I confess that I still get zits well into my 30s, Amy gives me a reassuring coo. "Girl…you look, like, 22 at most," she says. "MOST."

When we hear "Cotton Eye Joe" blasting from the main hall, I release them back into the wilderness, though K'mehia/Nerdy sighs this time away has been a *much* welcome break. The dance party resumes, and it's then, kaleidoscopically, that girlhood bursts into view. Here, they can join in the universal adolescent act of stuffing balloons up their shirts, hoping to understand what it feels like to have breasts, to be a woman, to inherit a wisdom that will long evade them. I remember that feeling. An unrelenting want to know what secrets awaited us in womanhood, in motherhood. It sat on the edge of fear, I think. I want to tell them that I don't have the answer yet. That I, like them, am still waving my hands around in the dark. I want to tell them the night hikes don't end at age 9 or 16 or 31, or here, in upstate New York.

The purity of camp: It's the kind of place I imagine the constellations, unblinking, might whisper the secrets of the universe to the girls. A download of celestial knowledge to which only they are granted access. I've always liked the idea that we're all made from the same ancient stardust anyhow, that we might've hung in the indigo sky side by side, unaware that we'd know each other in the next life, and the life after that. The girls, though, are stars: pure, blue, and burning. Not yet turned to dust or made of it, but on fire with the hope and desperation we've flung at them. It burns in their bellies. They don't yet know we expect them to save us. And Girl Scouts, perhaps subconsciously, is training them to fight.

"I fell in love with the idea that [Girl Scouts] is more relevant now than ever. I wish we could become obsolete in what we need to do, but it's crazy that, even in the landscape that we're in now, so many of these girls have less rights than I had growing up, politically," Maskara says. "Bodily autonomy, the right to identify the way you want to…it's still an incredibly unsafe world for marginalized genders."

At Camp Kaufmann, at least, the girls can relax into the safety net of the outdoors, where Girl Scouts started and where it trudges onward more than a century later. That the Scouts are surrounded by all that forestland—green as in four-leaf clovers and Lucky Charms, as in crisp dollar bills folded and handed off to those who will care for these children—is by design. Here, the leadership team stresses the importance of conservation efforts and of delivering the calm of nature back to their homes in urban centers. Also, the outdoors experience is intended to provide a grassy knoll on which the girls can tumble and flail and throw themselves at obstacles without any real stakes. "Kids are supposed to fall and then learn how to get back up, learn grit and resilience," Glass says. They can do that here in the woods, far removed from whatever their home situation may be.

"Being in a cabin in the woods is not a horror movie—all of those stereotypes that city girls think of when they think of camp," Maskara says. "So to build this and have them walk into that Welcome Center, and every girl knows that she deserves to walk into a place that looks like a ski lodge in Vail that only the elite can go to? They deserve this. They deserve to have this."

Of course, some of the Scouts have also worked for this fresh air. Two of the graduating seniors on hand are receiving special honors at camp for completing their Gold Award, the Eagle Scout–adjacent honor that requires hundreds of hours of service work and sometimes years of organizing on a topic of their choosing. (For what it's worth, Aruda remembers the Boy Scouts of her time getting high praise for building park benches and repaving hiking trails, while the girls in her troop were planning multipronged city-wide events requiring months of planning and coordination.)

Eighteen-year-old Jayleen chose to raise awareness for Moebius syndrome, the rare neurological disorder her brother suffers from. Fellow high school senior Kathryn developed a reading program for 2- to 10-year-olds to encourage them to get off their iPads. But perhaps one of the more prescient examples of a living and breathing Gold Award is that of incoming college freshman Kate Lindley of Hanover County, Virginia, who fought her school district's book ban by creating a "Banned Book Nook." Girl Scouts as a national organization likes to pretend it is apolitical—it has no nationwide stance on abortion, for example—more of a greener pasture for girls to grow in than a boot camp for future congresswomen, despite the fact that 75% of sitting female senators are former Girl Scouts. I ask Lindley about the politics of her project.

"I appreciate that Girl Scouts isn't necessarily political one way or another, because there are different people in different situations, and taking a broad-stroke political view across the nation doesn't really make sense," she says. "But it is certainly, in my opinion, at least a feminist organization, and the entire point is to empower young girls to discover opinions about the world and to be able to make choices and make a difference in what's happening around them. That doesn't necessarily have to be something that's outright political. A bunch of projects aren't going up against the local government or going up against specific policies. A really powerful Gold Award that someone else in my troop did was about fentanyl awareness, and that is certainly important, and perhaps more important, even, than censorship, in its own way."

Girlhood, as I remember it: 13, riding the bus to Zuma Beach, Tower 7. Sweaty palms covering the puss-filled molehills growing on our cheeks, our foreheads, our chins, where little pools of oil collected. We laid our lanky bodies, ribs poking out, on towels printed with hibiscus flowers, Minnie Mouse, or, if we felt brave enough to behave as young as we were, the Powerpuff Girls. We roasted our bodies in the sun because we could not see a future where such things would matter, where something as boring as skin would be a consideration; "consequence" was just a big word with too many syllables. Rumors of sun spots and wrinkles were just that: ghost stories, Greek myths. Fun was Boogie Boarding and cartwheeling and molding our sandy friends into mermaids with corset-narrow waists that wouldn't take up residence on our own bodies for years, if at all. Trouble was as simple as drawing sunscreen obscenities and stick-figure genitals on the backs of our sleeping prey. And then we joined them, letting the red of the California sun light up the insides of our eyelids, counting the veins. We slept and slept, little pride of lion cubs, because we could and because someone older would wake us when it was time to go. Our future, like the flocks of seagulls loitering above, yawned out across the shoreline, infinite. We wouldn't see mortality coming until it had already dug its fingernails into the crepes around our eyes. Crow's feet, age spots. Cancerous moles.

For Girl Scouts, this and more. Glitter. Crafts. But also conflict resolution. STEM. Community building. Anti-racism training. All things they are confident in tackling because the organization has reminded them of such. I wish someone had told me what the counselors and volunteers and troop leaders are telling these girls every day, which is that, actually, they possess the sort of power, influence, and strength of thought that scares most adults. And while everyone else is losing their self-esteem in a slow-drip IV throughout adolescence, these girls are growing theirs. They're becoming unshakeable and putting down roots. What would it have been like not to have been uprooted by the world as a teenage girl?

What we don't like to admit is that heartbreak and the passage of time render our experience of girlhood moot. Not quite matrecense, but something like it. A sudden shift occurs, and the feelings once alive and beating take on the dull slate crackle of VHS footage. They turn to memories, which are as good as dust in relating to the young. We've lost the texture of it, the memory of the pain a shadow of the real thing. We become untethered. Like trying to imagine the ferocity of a winter storm through a fogged window. Insulated, warmed, we know nothing of what rages outside—of blackened and frostbitten fingertips—save for a vague impression of "how dreadful" it looks. One uncolored remark usually does the job, giving us the self-satisfaction of having pretended that we understood. But we don't actually remember the experience of the dread. Our bodies save us from the electrified feeling of it. We keep photos and videos to recall it, but we cannot relive it, all exercises in empathy futile in the realm of the girl. That as much as a certain breed of mid-20s woman might prefer the emotional weightlessness of naïveté, you can't just crawl back under a rock, save for the most talented dissociative minds of our times. What happened out from under the rock will haunt us ceaselessly and without mercy.

When called upon to give impromptu summaries of their Gold Award projects, the young women arrive on a raised platform as if at a podium, addressing constituents. Suddenly, the vision of these 18-year-old girls in slate-gray pencil skirts and Gucci suit jackets with shoulder pads feels within reach. They resemble pint-size politicians who accidentally left their readers on their desk or in the pocket of a devoted aide. Their stature changes: shoulders back, measured pace, even tone. A blink turns the child into a woman. The ease and speed with which this transition happens is frightening. I think briefly that should I run for public office today, I must call up a Girl Scout to coordinate my campaign. The Daisies and Brownies listen, rapt. One of the Daisies realizes I'm filming. She pauses her wiggling, studying me. Then she squares her shoulders straight to the camera, plops her hands on her hips, and yells louder.

    This place is an oasis, combining forces of girlhood and nature, each magnifying the other in their presence. The girls, somehow younger than they've ever been, more playful than they've ever been, as they fish perch and sunfish from the murky waters of a man-made lake. Still, here is this ongoing narrative that hangs around the camp, that nature has something to teach us. That we've lost our connection to what some call the universe, and that we've tried to doctor a reality that better suits our collective goals, which someone in a boardroom decided were technological advancement and the conquering of other nation-states. But it is absurd to look to our children, mostly our girls, to carry on the communal mothering and nurturing that our state has neglected. Girls were never supposed to care for all of us, but that became the reality, and so we continued training them.

With an hour left before bedtime, the girls are dancing to Miley Cyrus' "Party in the USA." It reminds me of what we might look like should we allow the beckoning of drummers on the subway to do their jobs, like snake charmers. You know what I mean. Sitting, sensing the twitching of the other riders, flicks of eyelids here and there checking to see, "Are you going to dance?" Who will be the first brave soul to allow themselves shriek in delight and let the music lasso itself around their body? Who will be the first to admit, screaming, that there is no regret more crushing than yearning to have danced? The girls don't yearn. The girls don't practice restraint. These regrets don't harden in their guts like stones. Back in the city, not a single toe taps on the linoleum floor. I wonder if, put in our place, the girls would dance. Probably, they would.

The train window opens up on a lake, and my breath catches. When did I last see a body of water in this state? A lake, in general? My eyes water, hand searching for my phone. I catch a few usable seconds of footage before the lake zaps from view. I post it to Instagram, then continue watching TikToks the rest of the way home. Only later, when I watch the video from bed, do I see the six swans. Preferred literary metaphors of Eve Babitz and Truman Capote. Ethereal beings, those that float along glassy waters, not a single bubble betraying what's going on beneath the surface. All that kicking and treading. Who does all that pretending serve? I hope our girls kick and scream and bare their teeth. I hope they know, as I do, how fragile they are not. How brutal they can be.

—*Originally appeared in* Mountain Gazette 202, *2024.*

49.
Politics & The "F-word"
Written by Hunter S. Thompson

"You had all do well to learn politics ... or I'll lay your souls to waste."

Mick Jagger said that, about midway in the Rolling Stones' classic "Sympathy for the Devil." And now, in the long shadow of that recent election, it seems like a fitting epitaph for the sad, elegant, raucous, mis-managed, frightening and finally failed campaign, which almost everybody except the people inside it called the "Freak Power" thing.

Which was true, in a sense—but we were never quite able to explain that sense. And there is not much doubt, looking back, that those two very heavy, very mean, very sharp little words were in fact the twin millstones that sunk us.

They were also what launched the campaign in the first place; like the powerful first-stage rocket that launches a satellite into orbit, and then drops away. But ours stayed attached, a dead weight we could never get rid of. The term "freak power" was too active, too menacing—and in the end, just a little too real.

Finally, 10 days before the election, we took a full-page hand-lettered ad in The Aspen Times, in a final attempt to say what we actually meant. The ad was composed and put together under extreme pressure, in an atmosphere that had suddenly turned ugly with death threats, bomb warnings and fear. But the ad didn't show that, somehow, and in retrospect, it reads pretty well:

"THE EARTH BELONGS TO THE LIVING
... NOT TO THE DEAD"
—Thomas Jefferson: June 24, 1813

"Gentlemen, nature works in a mysterious way. When a new truth comes upon the earth, or a great idea necessary for mankind is born, where does it come from? Not from the police force or the prosecuting attorneys or the judges or the lawyers or the doctors. Not there. It comes from the despised and the out-casts; it comes perhaps from jails and prisons; it comes from men who have dared to be rebels and think their thoughts and their fate has been the fate of rebels. This generation gives them the graves while another builds them monuments; and there is no exception to it. It has been true since the world began, and it will be true no doubt forever."
—Clarence Darrow, 1920

The ad included a photo taken at a debate between the two leading Sheriff candidates, with a cryptic one-line caption that said: "Thompson Contemplates the Bust of Whitmire." That was our last attempt at public humor during the campaign, and it fell very flat—for reasons we didn't fully understand until much later. All we were sure of, at the time, was that our collective sense of humor was bombing badly. Not even our friends understood it.

And the others... well, they were far beyond humor at that point; a lot fur-ther, in fact, than we knew. There were already rumors of collections being taken up—by Guido, by Bidwell, by the Ski Corp., the local contractor's association—to bring in hired "hit men" from Nevada, professional killers, who would "lower the boom on these freaks who were trying to take over the town."

"Freak Power" was no longer a joke—not to anybody. It had mushroomed into genuine Bogeyman status...

Like the "Yellow Peril" of the 1940s, the "Red Menace" of the

50s .. and "Black Power," a phrase tossed off by Stokely Carmichael during an angry speech one hot afternoon in Mississippi in 1966. The awesome reaction to that one staggered even Carmichael, and all along Madison Avenue, men wept with envy. Pure genius, they said. New York is füll of advertising copywriters who would gladly trade a lung and a kidney for the ability to conceive a two-word marketing concept. as effective as "Black Power." It terrified a hundred million Honkies within 24 hours. Fantastic ... Especially when you consider that a mouthful of watery garbage like "Ford Has a Better Idea" was worth at least a half-million dollars to the man who wrote it. But compared to "Black Power," it sucks.

Language can be a strange weapon. Unlike a sword or a bullet, its power is unpredictable. There are millions of otherwise intelligent men in this country who will go all to pieces and start swinging hysterically on any stranger who calls them a "sonofabitch." Others can't stand the word "fuck." It rips up their nerves and scrambles their brains; within milliseconds after hearing that word, their knuckles turn white, their earlobes are gorged with wild blood and their lymph nodes start vibrating in the manner of laboratory rats on a raw electronic grid.

This kind of reaction is endlessly fascinating to people in the word business. You look down at your typewriter and you see that row of steel keys with the letters all scrambled and you know it's just another goddamn machine, just a tool like any other... but you also know that by moving your fingers around that silly-looking keyboard in just the right order, you can put those 26 little letters together in simple combinations that will drive millions of people completely wild: Send them screeching off their rails into seizures of lust, violence, greed, hatred ... and occasionally even something right, but not often.

And the weirdest thing of all about the power sitting idle in a typewriter is that even a chimpanzee-can make the thing work pretty well, and sometimes better than most humans. Even raccoons have learned to type. And a rat named Bob will learn to spell "Bob" on a typewriter almost as soon as he makes the connection between the machine and his next meal. In 1936, a huge water rat named "Keno" won the Democratic nomination for mayor of Ely, Nevada on the basis of his ability to solve basic survival/logic problems with a typewriter.

Which is neither here nor there, actually. This kind of random gibberish serves a very useful purpose in journalism, by preventing the writer from indulging his worst instincts. The idea is to say less than you know, very smartly, without seeming to be either crazy or ignorant or both. As a standard tech-nique, it is used almost constantly by syndicated columnists, music critics, editorial writers and politicians who understand, but can't prove, that whatever bad stomping came down on them in the last disastrous election was in truth the result of lies, frauds and treacheries so gross that they can only be hinted at— and even then, with a keen regard for the libel laws.

Fortunately, this is not the style of the Wallposter. From the very beginning, our editorial policy had been to run full bore and straight at the enemy's strength, and libel laws be damned. We have a stable of ruthless attorneys to handle that sort of thing, and besides that, we have no money. (Our editorial staff, more-over, is keenly aware of the drastic possibilities made manifest by the landmark U.S. Supreme Court ruling in the case of *The New York Times* vs. Sullivan.) None of which matters a hell of a lot in this instance, because any detailed account of the mind-boggling skullduggery that went on behind the scenes during Aspen's last election campaign would blitz "libel" right from the start, by lashing the whole argument almost instantly onto the Criminal Fraud and Felony Conspiracy level.

———

—*Originally appeared in* Mountain Gazette *79, 2001.*

JADED LOCAL
A Flower Grows Through The Pavement: The Resurrection of *Mountain Gazette*

Written by Hans Ludwig

You can't really tell the story of the rebirth of this magazine without talking about the utter destruction of contemporary media from which it rose like a fiery phoenix from an ash heap. Because if that hadn't happened, Mike Rogge and I would still probably be happily working for a ski magazine and *Mountain Gazette* would remain in hypersleep, just an archive in a dusty file cabinet somewhere.

Instead, what happened was that corporations gradually, and then rapidly, took over independent publication companies. This was not necessarily a bad thing at first. For a magazine like *Powder*, where Rogge and I used to frolic among the expense accounts and bar tabs, it meant bigger budgets and a sense of stability amid economic fluctuations, meant that if we (and the ad sales department) did a good job moving newsstand sales and ad pages there would be more budget the next year, more opportunities to do cool stuff and share cool stories, more bar tabs and lift tickets.

But then came The Internet, and Facebook, taking a blowtorch to a 150 year-old business model. Everyone knew it was the future of media, but nobody figured out how to actually make money with online content. Who was going to pay to read a website? Who was going to click on the ads? Nobody. Then the fine, fine people at Facebook, using fake ad numbers, convinced the corpo boys that web video was the answer and the layoffs began as every big media outlet did the "pivot to video," laying off editors and kickstarting the inevitable decline in quality. Which drives away readers, which reduces budgets, which leads to more decline, which drives away more readers...

Soon the big media companies (like the succession of them that bought and sold *Powder* and its stable mates at Surfer Publications) were in serious trouble. Which leads us to where we are now, where the corporations falter and private equity investors step in. In a tech-economy world where investors are hunting for massive Silicon Valley-style growth, the big money boys looked at something like *Powder*—an established and profitable enterprise (albeit one that would never generate massive returns)—like they would something stuck to their shoe. Predictably, they threw money at dumb plans to target a market that didn't exist instead of their loyal readers, and then fired everyone and put the lowest-paid, youngest people in charge of content-farming worthless clickbait on the websites of once-proud print publications.

Which is where Rogge and I stepped aside—he to do snappy short documentaries and marketing videos, and I to bang nails into ski town condos and securely hold down a barstool. The assholes had won, print was dead, and it was time to move on, maybe gradually spiral into the alcoholism that is every writer's last refuge. When Rogge purchased the rights to *MG* over a beer, I was more than skeptical. Former editor-in-chief at *Powder*, Derek Taylor—now enjoying his new career as a stay-at-home dad—was too. He suggested that Rogge should have bought a boat instead, so at least he could have some fun while losing money.

But the money (all of about $5,000) didn't evaporate. It turned out that previously-occupied top-tier professional photographers and writers were sitting on hard drives full of great stuff that no longer had an outlet. And that readers were desperate to put down their phones, to avoid the mental pollution of recycled corporate marketing and empty clickbait that dominates the electronic ecosystem. And that it doesn't take a lot of those readers to cover the overhead when you're not paying for a big office and a big staff, and most importantly–not paying a huge cut to useless non-writing, non-photographing MBAs in a C-suite on the other side of the country.

And so, thanks to Rogge's vision, the contributor's work, and your support, *Mountain Gazette* doesn't just exist, it *thrives* in a world where print is supposed to be dead. There's no magic formula—just the same one that *Powder* was built on: Make a beautiful magazine that people can't read in one sitting, and can't bear to throw away. And because *MG* has a history, we don't have to look further than the archives for direction. Previous generations of editors and extraordinary writers like Edward Abbey, Hunter S. Thompson, and George Sibley already blazed the first part of the trail. We just have to see where it goes now.

As I said, I was skeptical. When Rogge offered me the back page to continue the Jaded Local column that I had written for a decade at *Powder*, I demurred. And then he published the first issue, and the second, and the work was immediately weirder and more interesting than anything coming out of big media; the contributors were getting paid right away, and the subscription list steadily grew. No big ads, no investors to pull the rug out when they got bored, no MBAs, no glowing blowjob profiles of corporate-sponsored athletes, no reviews of shiny, expensive, and soon-to-be landfill gear that you don't need. No Biggest, Best, and Most. Just beautiful photos, eclectic writing, even handmade art. Stories about kayaking in downtown Chicago, wildland firefighters, poems about the Appalachian Trail, Alaskan bears fishing for salmon, obscure music festivals, an investigation into a golf course at a private ski area for millionaires that's polluting a pristine river, dirtbag eccentrics, hippies, scientists, trailbuilders, surfing Lake Tahoe, a cartoon from Steve Martin and Harry Bliss(!), teaching kids to ski in Afghanistan…

So I told Rogge I was in. *Powder* is running articles about The Best Resorts For Families (kill it with fire), *Outside* is trying to sell you cryptocurrency with a subscription (nuke it from orbit), but the *Gazette* offers this jaded, mountain-town local a weird, diverse, ecstatic, and sometimes surly place to call home, where the only instruction from the publisher is to "write whatever the fuck you want." I'll be sticking around, and I hope you do too. We've done enough issues now where the arc should be clear: It's just going to get bigger, weirder, more colorful, more ecstatic and eclectic. Kinda makes it a little harder to stay jaded, but I'm doing my best.